PEACE MAKER

ピースメーカー

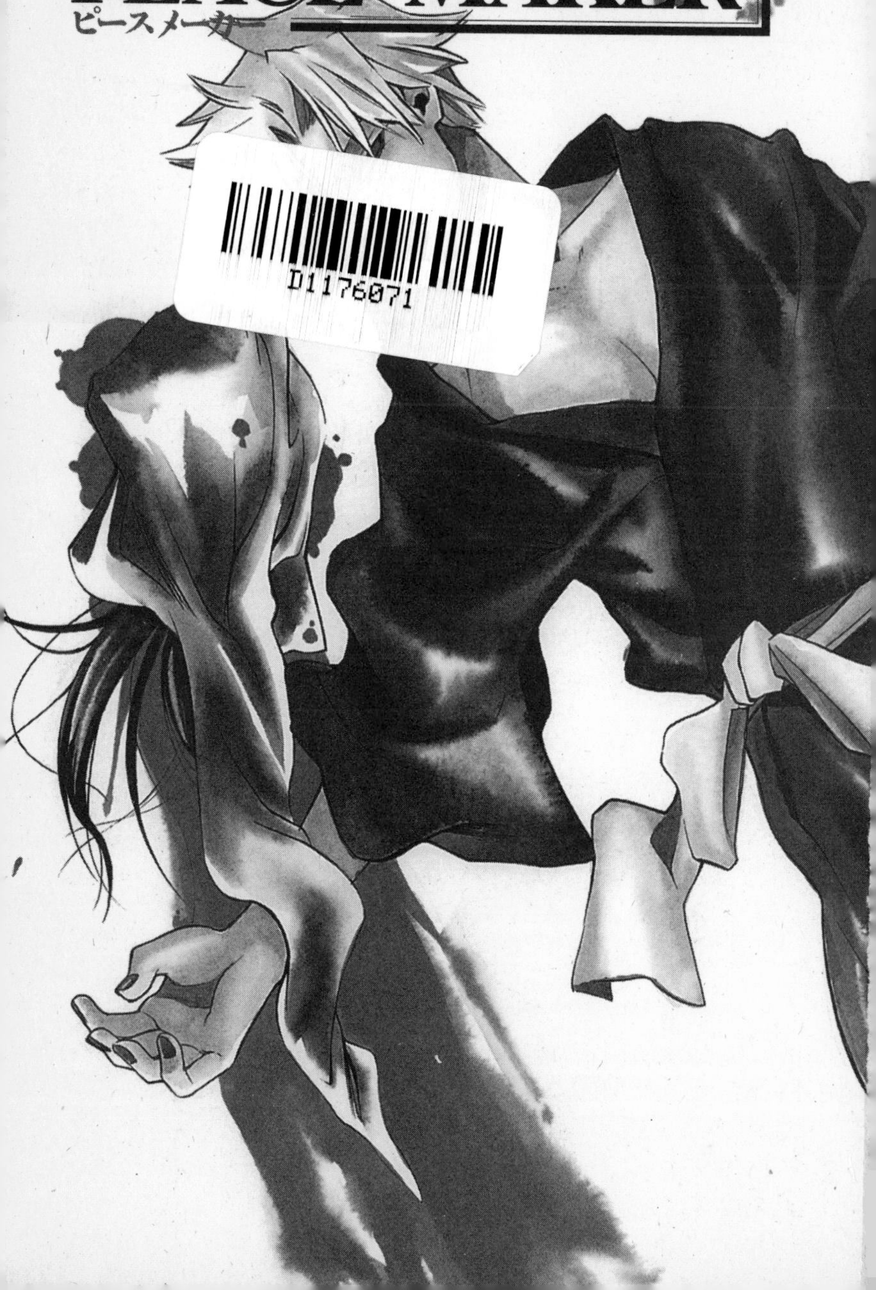

Peace Maker Volume 5
Created by NANAE CHRONO

Translation - Ryan Flake
English Adaptation - Christine Boylan
Retouch and Lettering - Star Print Brokers
Production Artist - Lucas Rivera
Graphic Designer - Chelsea Windlinger

Editor - Hyun Joo Kim
Pre-Production Supervisor - Vicente Rivera, Jr.
Print-Production Specialist - Lucas Rivera
Managing Editor - Vy Nguyen
Senior Designer - Louis Csontos
Senior Designer - James Lee
Senior Editor - Bryce P. Coleman
Senior Editor - Jenna Winterberg
Associate Publisher - Marco F. Pavia
President and C.O.O. - John Parker
C.E.O. and Chief Creative Officer - Stu Levy

A  Manga

TOKYOPOP Inc.
5900 Wilshire Blvd. Suite 2000
Los Angeles, CA 90036

E-mail: info@TOKYOPOP.com
Come visit us online at www.TOKYOPOP.com

ISBN: 978-1-4278-0079-4

First TOKYOPOP printing: November 2008
10 9 8 7 6 5 4 3 2 1
Printed in the USA

HAMBURG // LONDON // LOS ANGELES // TOKYO

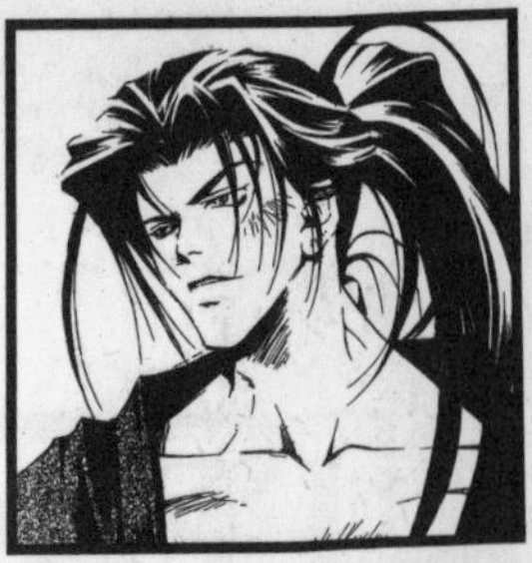

HIJIKATA TOSHIZOU

VICE COMMANDER

BECAUSE OF HIS COLD DEMEANOR AND BRUTALITY, HE IS KNOWN AS THE "DEMON VICE COMMANDER."

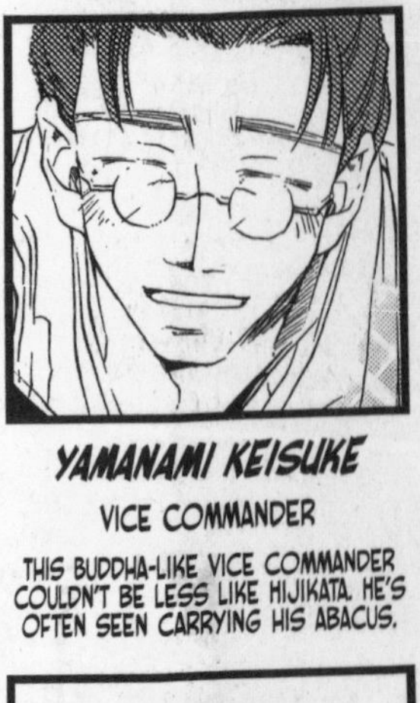

YAMANAMI KEISUKE

VICE COMMANDER

THIS BUDDHA-LIKE VICE COMMANDER COULDN'T BE LESS LIKE HIJIKATA. HE'S OFTEN SEEN CARRYING HIS ABACUS.

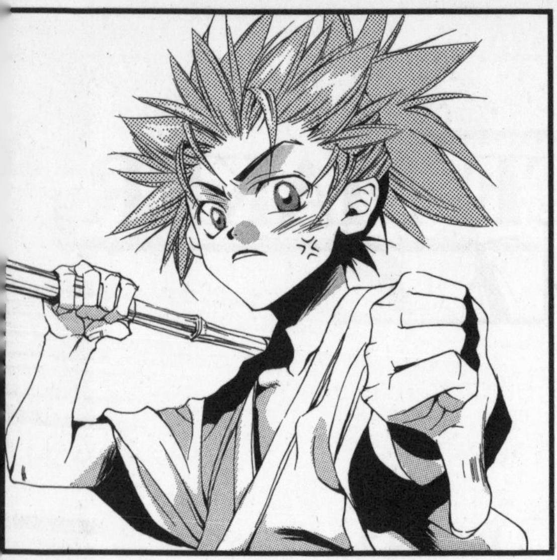

ICHIMURA TETSUNOSUKE

HIJIKATA'S PAGE

BRASH TETSU HAS JOINED THE SHINSENGUMI TO LEARN TO BECOME STRONG. HE WANTS TO GET REVENGE ON HIS PARENTS' MURDERERS, CHOUSHUU REBELS. ALTHOUGH HE JOINED THE SHINSENGUMI WITH ASPIRATIONS OF BECOMING A SWORDSMAN, HE'S BEEN ASSIGNED THE THANKLESS DUTY OF HIJIKATA'S PAGE.

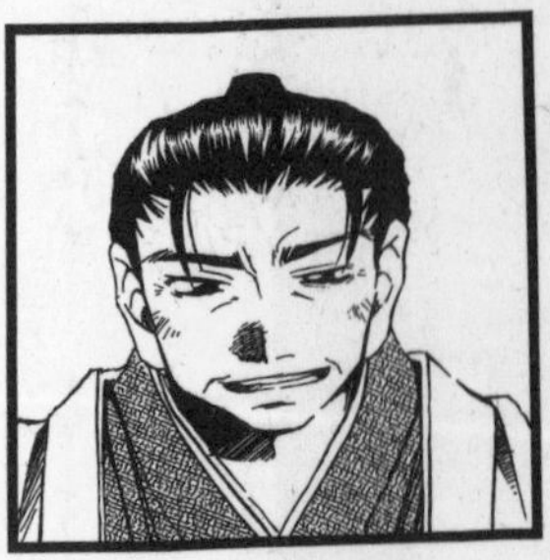

KONDOU ISAMI

DIRECTOR

A FOUNDING MEMBER OF THE SHINSENGUMI AND ALSO A MASTER AT THE SHIEIKAN DOJO IN EDO, THE MAIN DOJO OF THE TENNEN RISHIN STYLE.

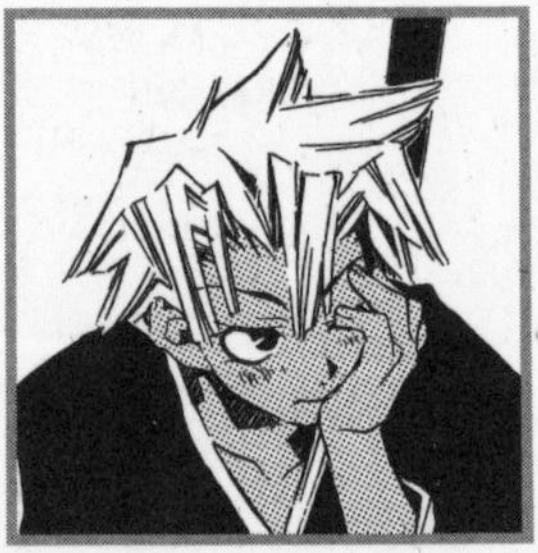

KITAMURA SUZU

A BOY WITH SILVER HAIR. HE HAS NO FAMILY AND LIVES WITH HIS MASTER, YOSHIDA TOSHIMARO. HE AND HIS MASTER OPPOSE THE SHINSENGUMI.

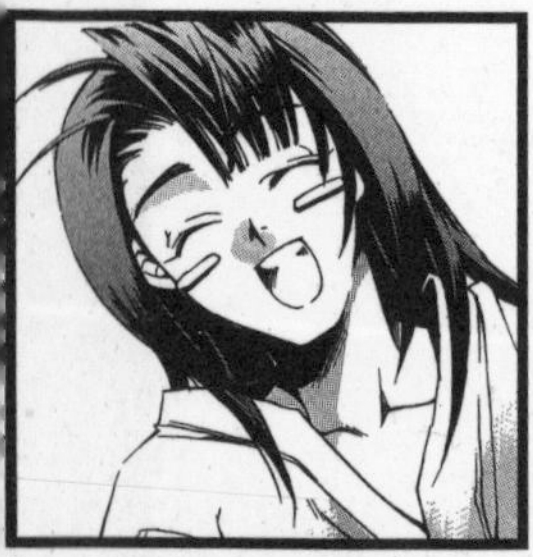

OKITA SOUJI

CAPTAIN OF THE FIRST SQUAD

THE BEST SWORDSMAN IN THE SHINSENGUMI. HE'S GENERALLY CALM AND FRIENDLY, BUT WIELDING A BLADE CAN TRANSFORM HIM INTO A HEARTLESS KILLER.

MAIN CHARACTERS

NAGAKURA SHINPACHI

CAPTAIN OF THE SECOND SQUAD

SMALL BUT STRONG. A SWORDSMAN LIKE OKITA. HE FIGHTS IN THE SHINTO-MUNEN SCHOOL STYLE.

TOUDOU HEISUKE

CAPTAIN OF THE EIGHTH SQUAD

ONE OF THE THREE STOOGES OF THE SHINSENGUMI. HE LIKES CUTE THINGS, INCLUDING TETSU.

HARADA SANOSUKE

CAPTAIN OF THE TENTH SQUAD

A GIANT AMONG MEN, HE'S A MASTER OF THE SPEAR IN THE HOZOIN SCHOOL STYLE. HE'S GOOD FRIENDS WITH SHINPACHI.

ICHIMURA TATSUNOSUKE

TETSU'S OLDER BOTHER AND GUARDIAN. HE'S ALWAYS WORRYING ABOUT TETSU. TATSU WANTS NOTHING TO DO WITH SWORDFIGHTING, AND IS A BOOKKEEPER FOR THE SHINSENGUMI.

YAMAZAKI SUSUMU

SHINSENGUMI NINJA

A SPY FOR THE SHINSENGUMI, HE REPORTS TO HIJIKATA. TACITURN AND COLD, HE HOLDS MANY SECRETS.

SAYA

TETSU SAVED HER FROM SOME RUFFIANS, AND NOW THE TWO ARE FRIENDS. SAYA CANNOT SPEAK, BUT COMMUNICATES THROUGH HAND GESTURES AND WRITING.

☐ SHINSENGUMI MEMBERS

☐ PERSONS OUTSIDE THE SHINSENGUMI

THE STORY OF PEACE MAKER

IN THE FIRST YEAR OF GENJI, 1864, JAPAN WAS IN GREAT TURMOIL. MILITANT AND XENOPHOBIC FORCES, WHICH HAD LONG OPPOSED THE TOKUGAWA SHOGUNATE, ADVOCATED EXPELLING WESTERN INFLUENCE AND RESTORING THE EMPEROR IN KYOTO TO POWER. TO PROTECT THE SHOGUNATE'S INTEREST IN KYOTO, A LEGENDARY PEACEKEEPING FORCE WAS FORMED FROM TWO HUNDRED-SOME RONIN. THEY WERE THE SHINSENGUMI. THIS IS THE STORY OF ICHIMURA TETSUNOSUKE, WHO SOUGHT TO JOIN THEM.

CONTENTS

Act.24
A Hard Day's Night (Scene 1)

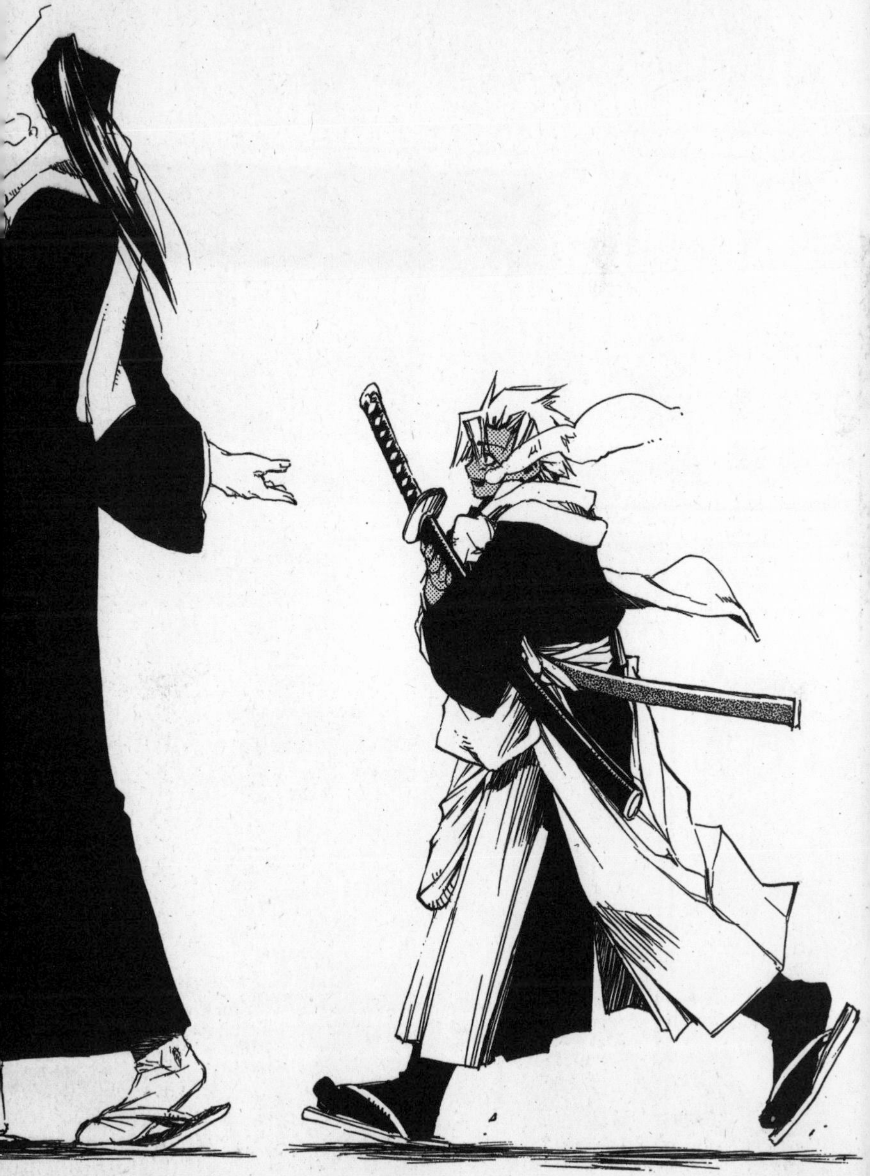

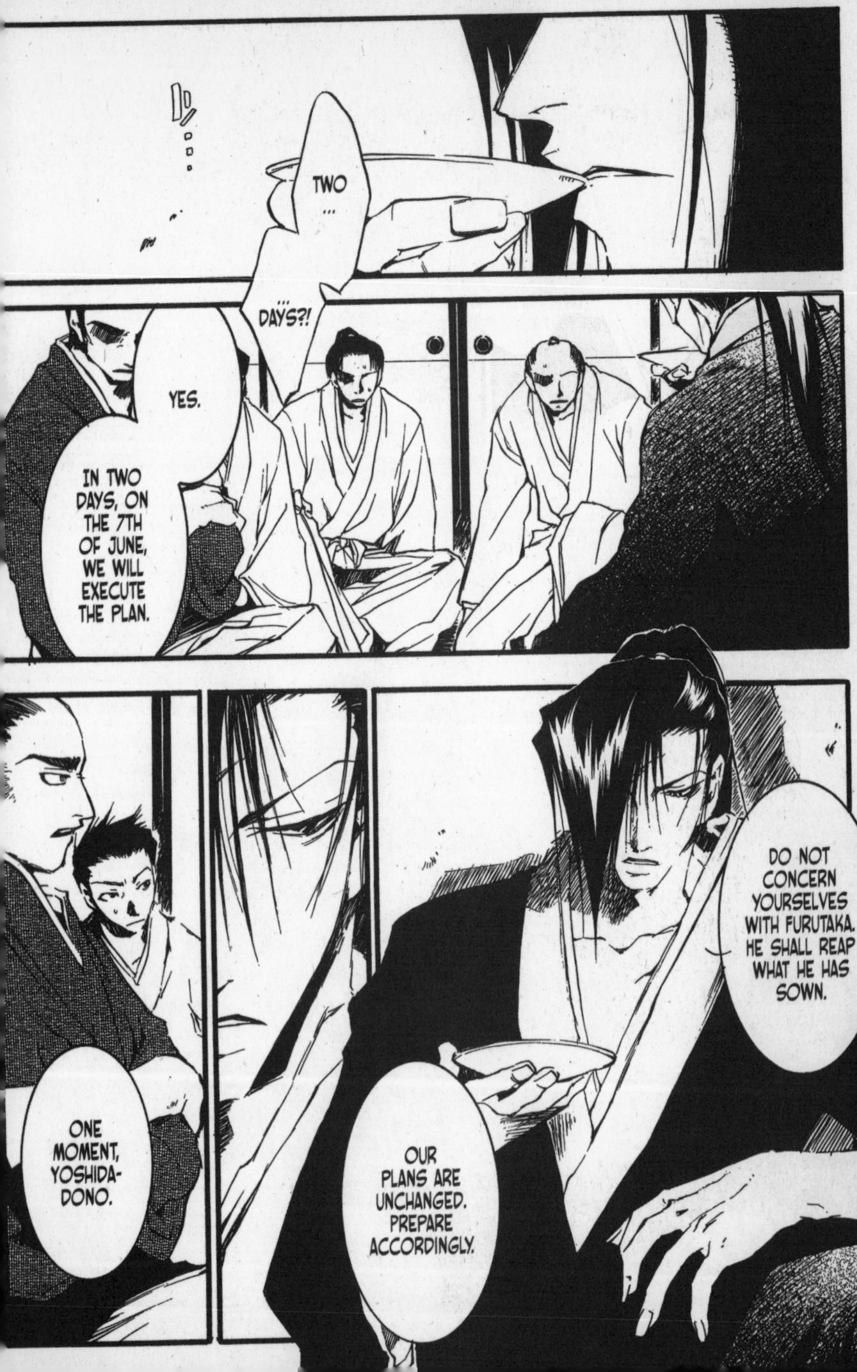
TWO ...
... DAYS?!
YES.
IN TWO DAYS, ON THE 7TH OF JUNE, WE WILL EXECUTE THE PLAN.
DO NOT CONCERN YOURSELVES WITH FURUTAKA. HE SHALL REAP WHAT HE HAS SOWN.
OUR PLANS ARE UNCHANGED. PREPARE ACCORDINGLY.
ONE MOMENT, YOSHIDA-DONO.

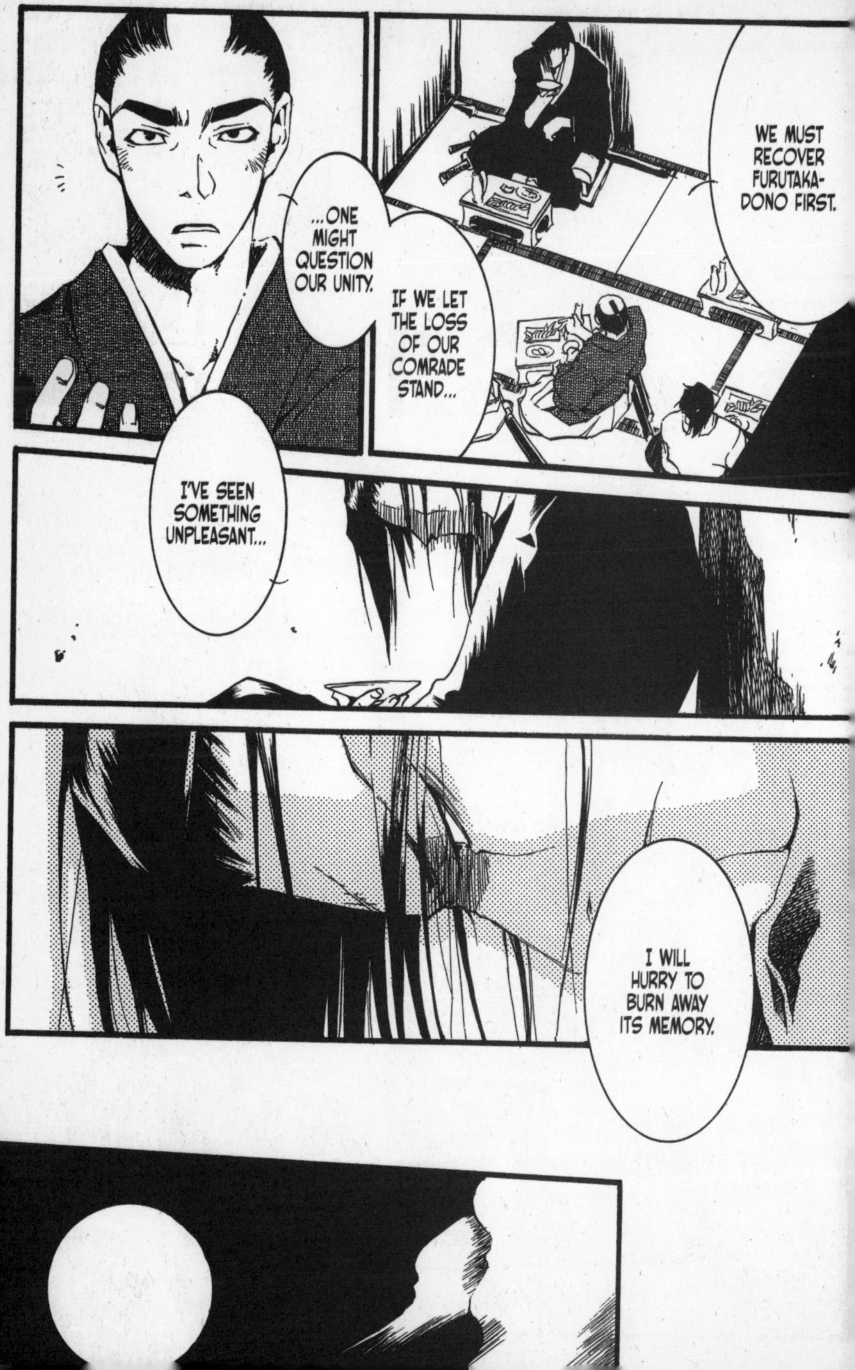
WE MUST RECOVER FURUTAKA-DONO FIRST.
IF WE LET THE LOSS OF OUR COMRADE STAND...
...ONE MIGHT QUESTION OUR UNITY.
I'VE SEEN SOMETHING UNPLEASANT...
I WILL HURRY TO BURN AWAY ITS MEMORY.

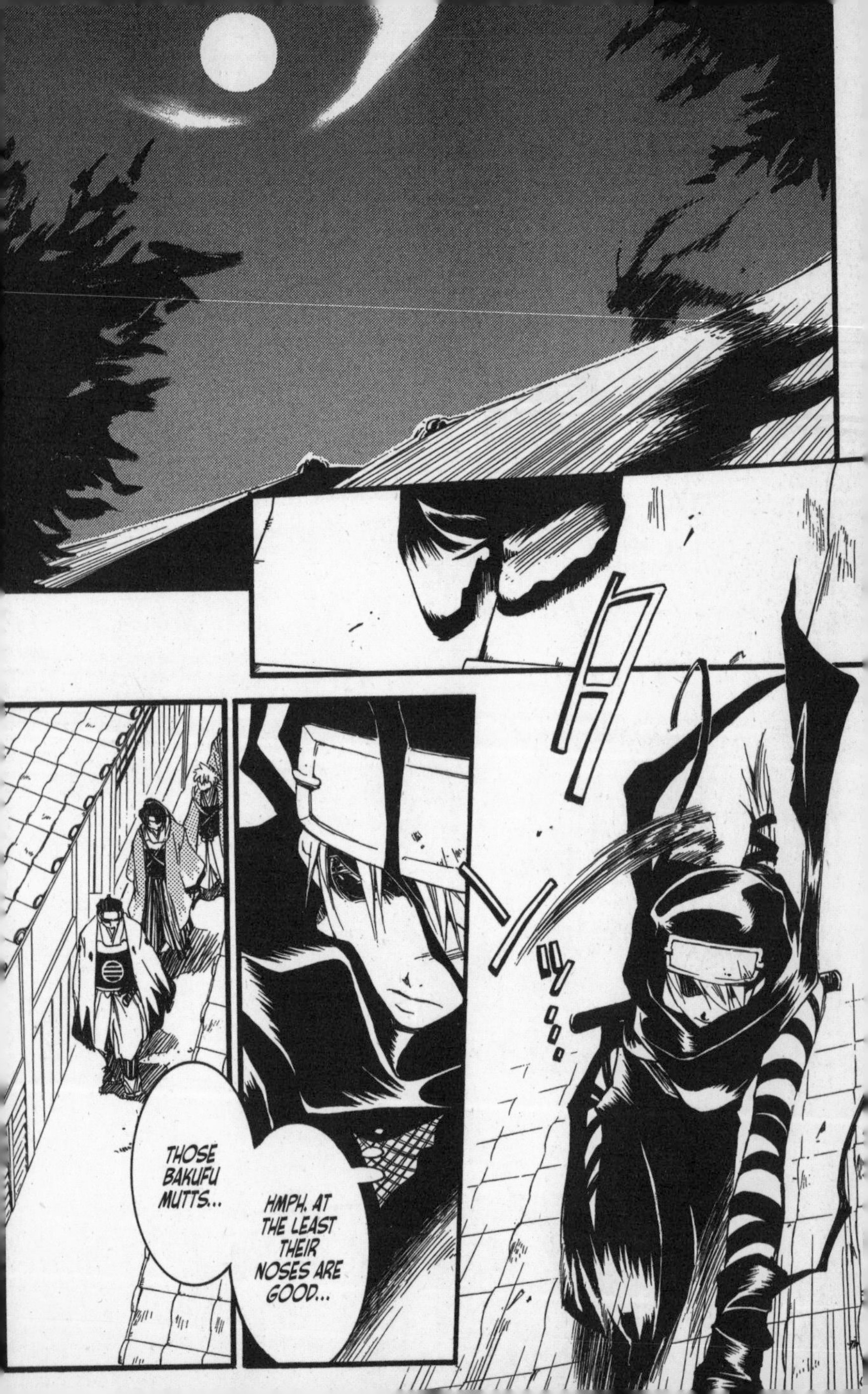
HMPH. AT THE LEAST THEIR NOSES ARE GOOD...
THOSE BAKUFU MUTTS...

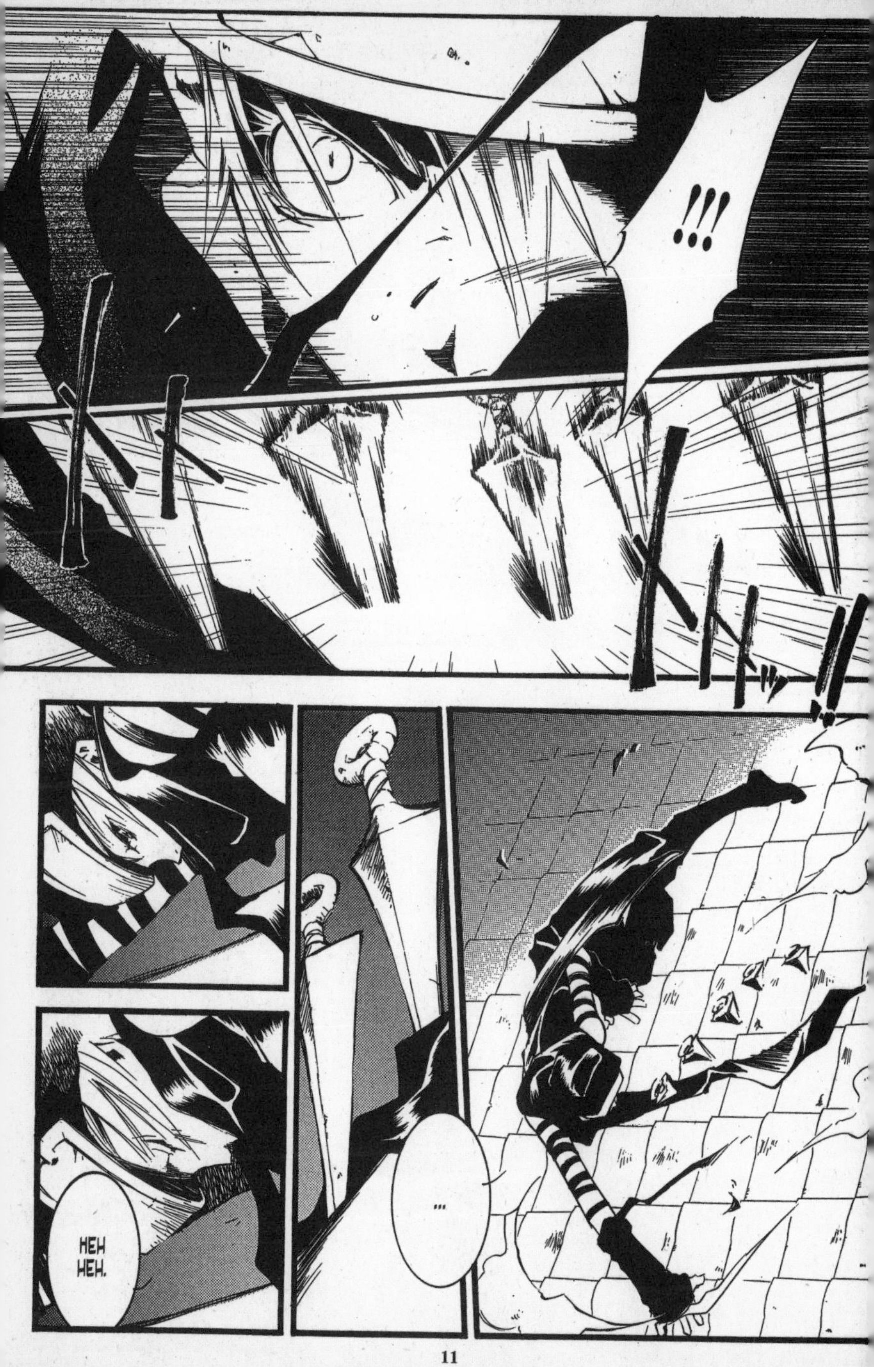
!!!
!!
...
HEH HEH.

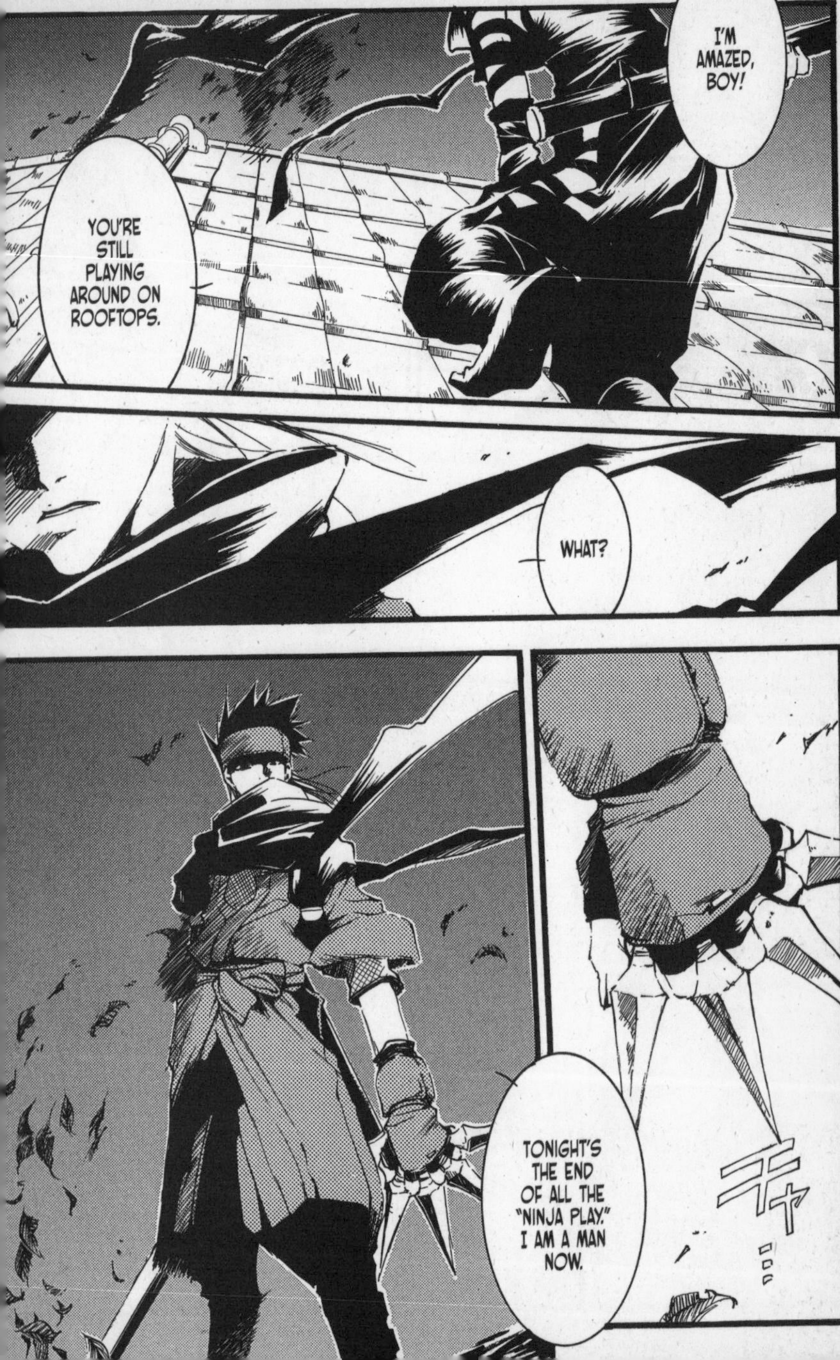
I'M AMAZED, BOY!
YOU'RE STILL PLAYING AROUND ON ROOFTOPS.
WHAT?
TONIGHT'S THE END OF ALL THE "NINJA PLAY." I AM A MAN NOW.

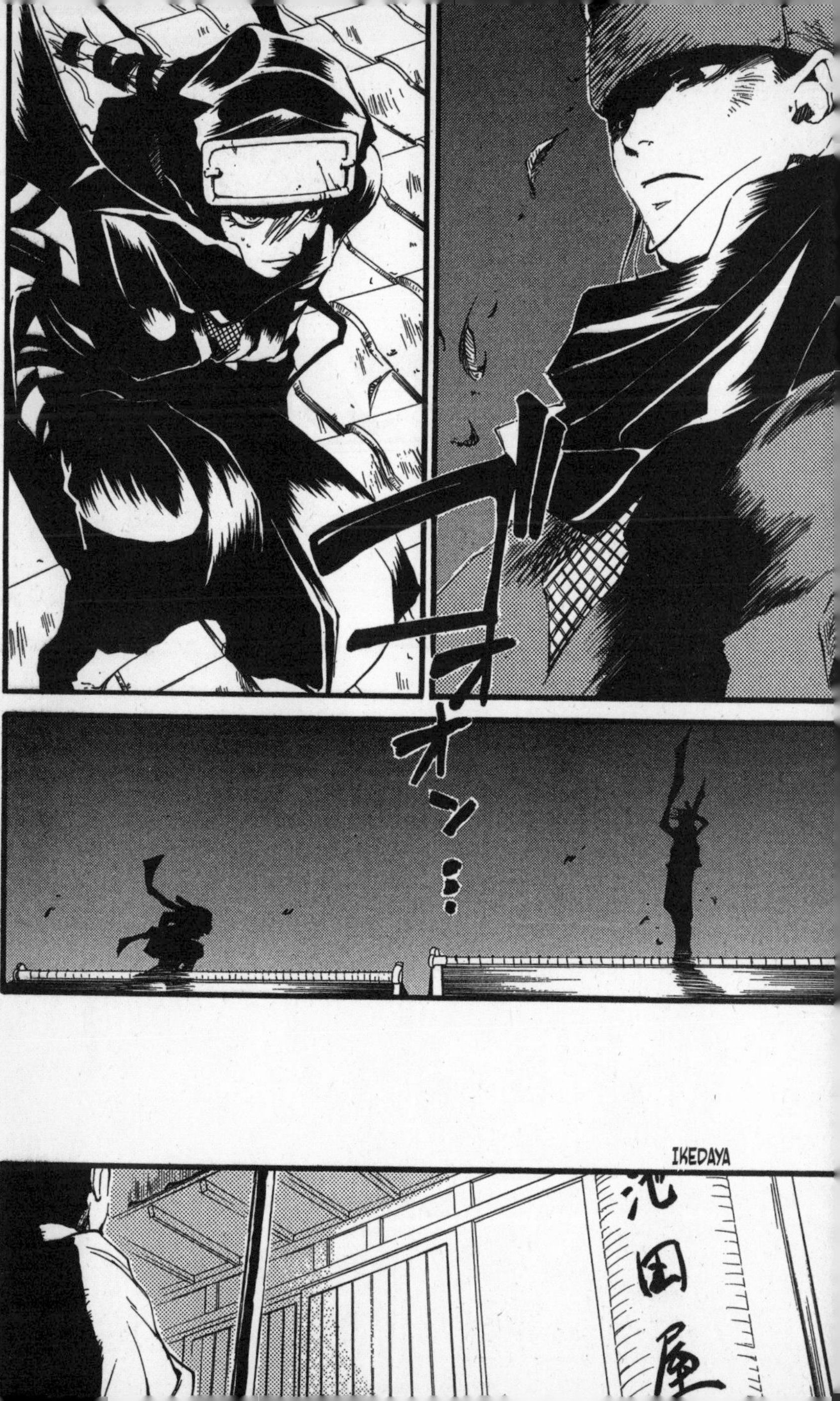
ゴオオッ…
IKEDAYA
池田屋

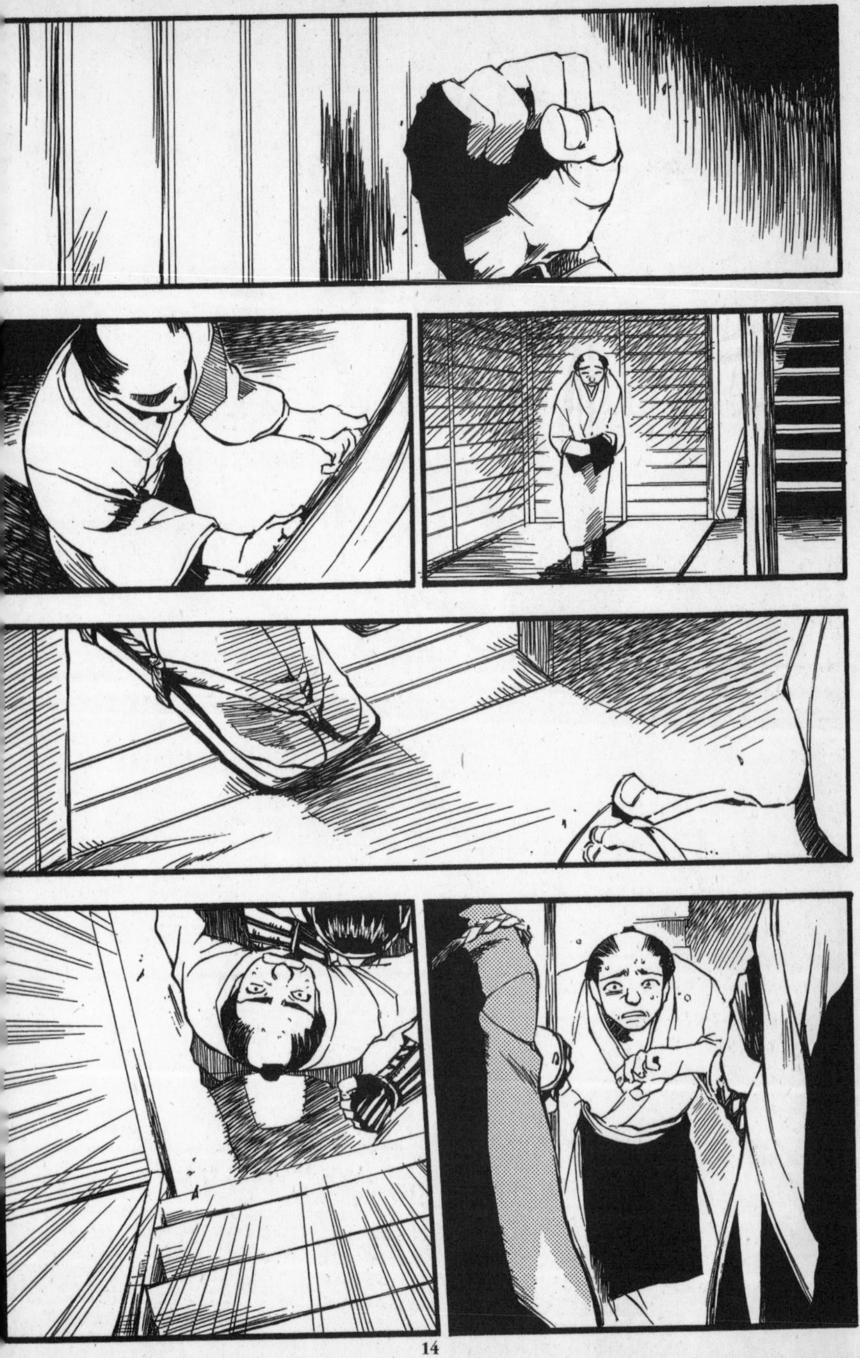

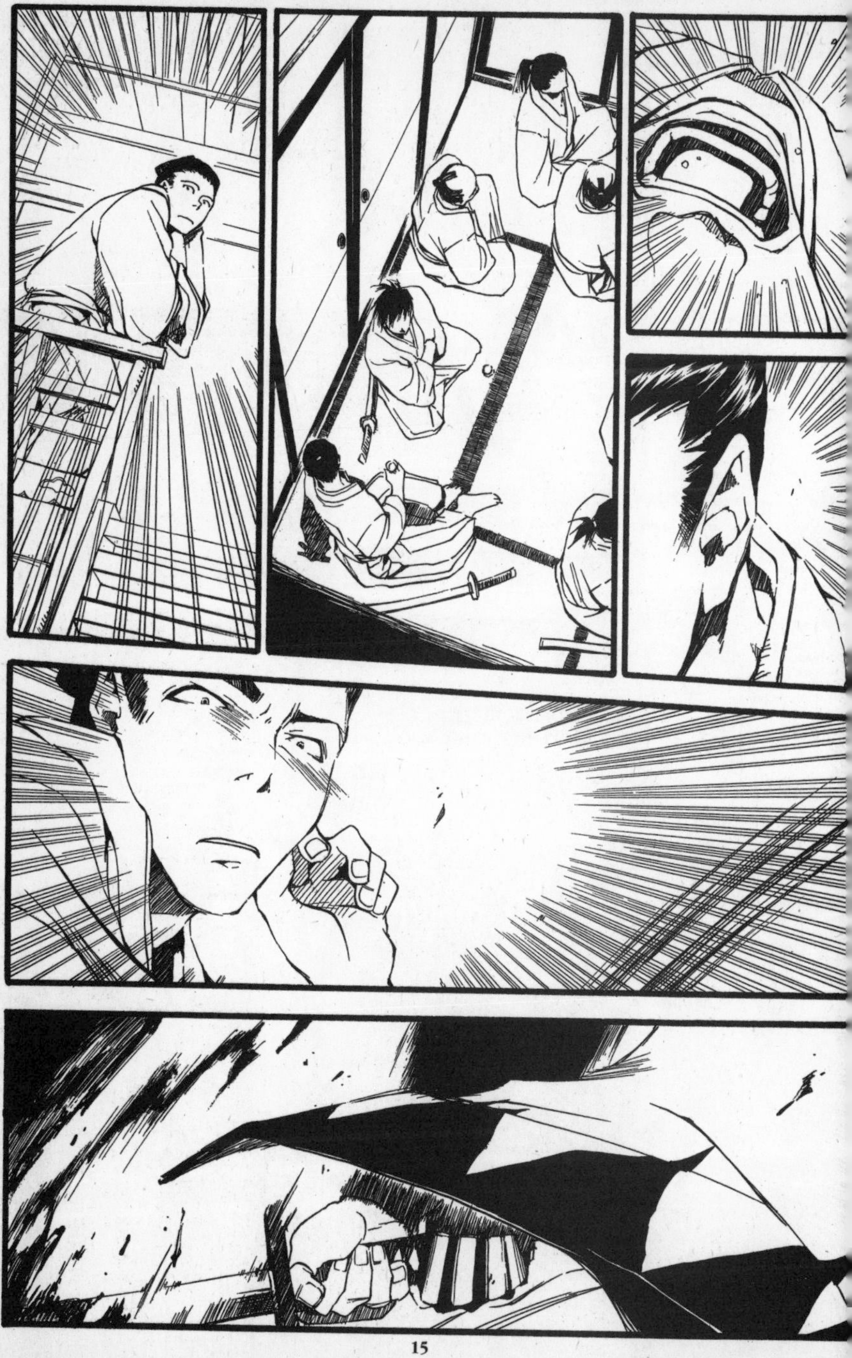

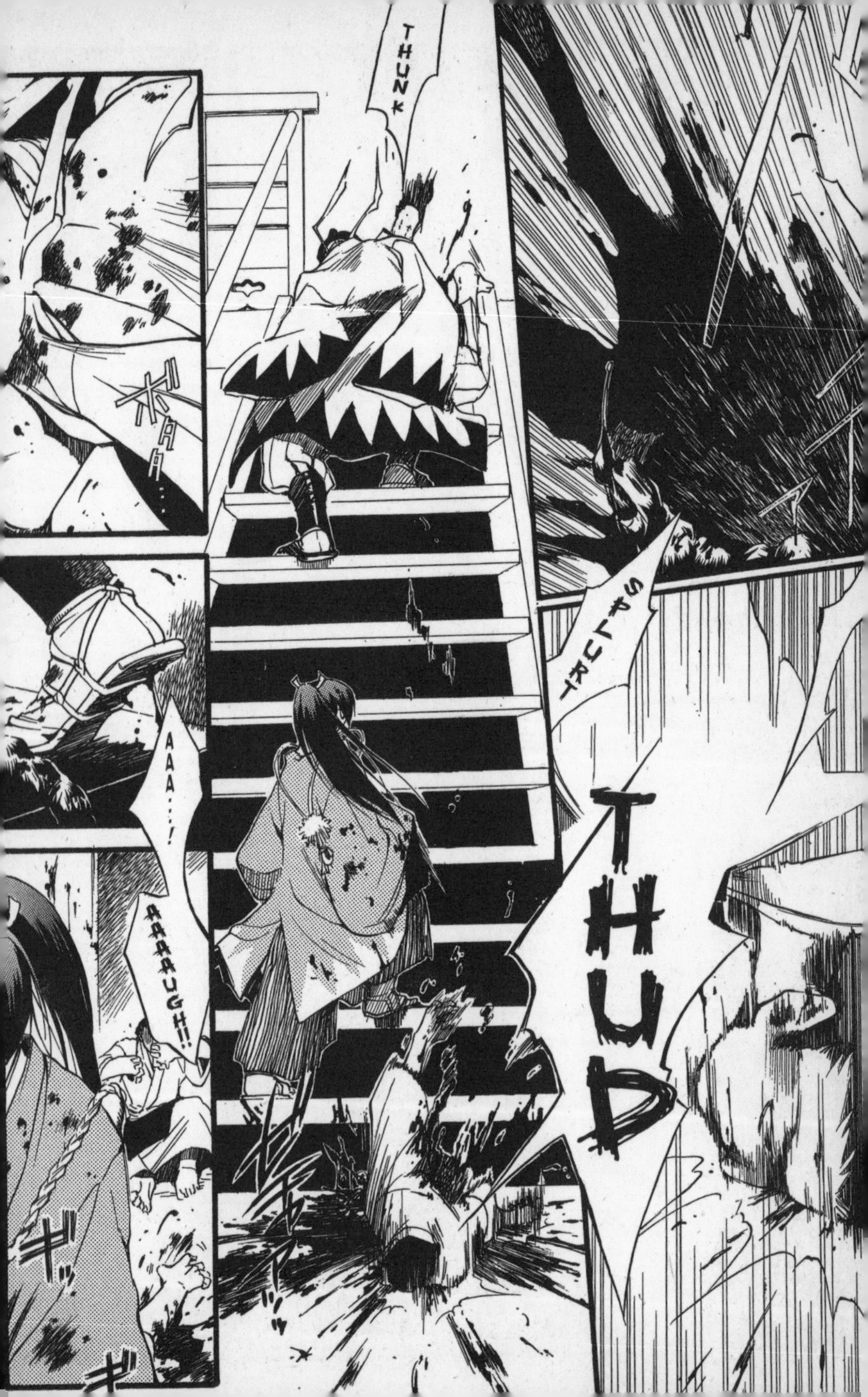
SPLURT
THUD
THUNK
ボAA...
AAA...!
AAAAUGH!!

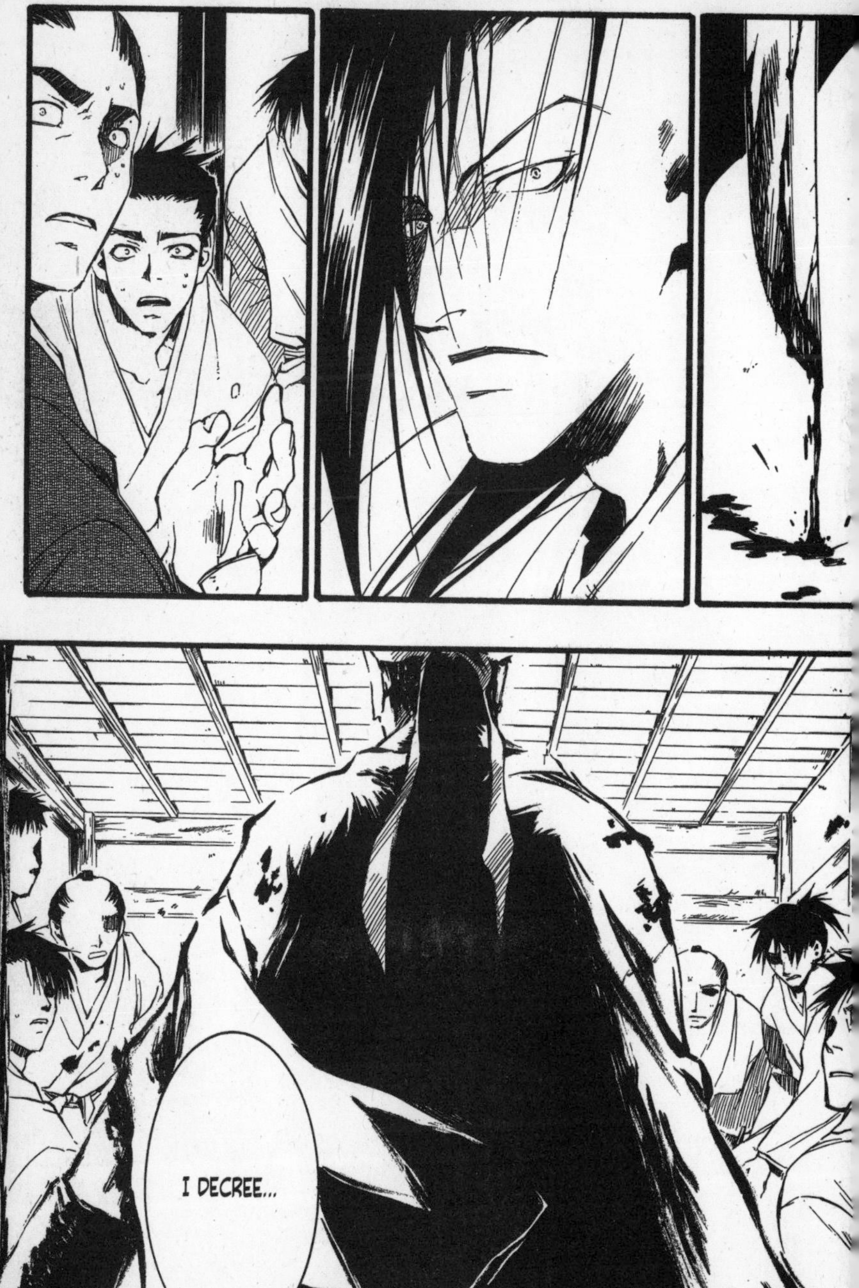
I DECREE...

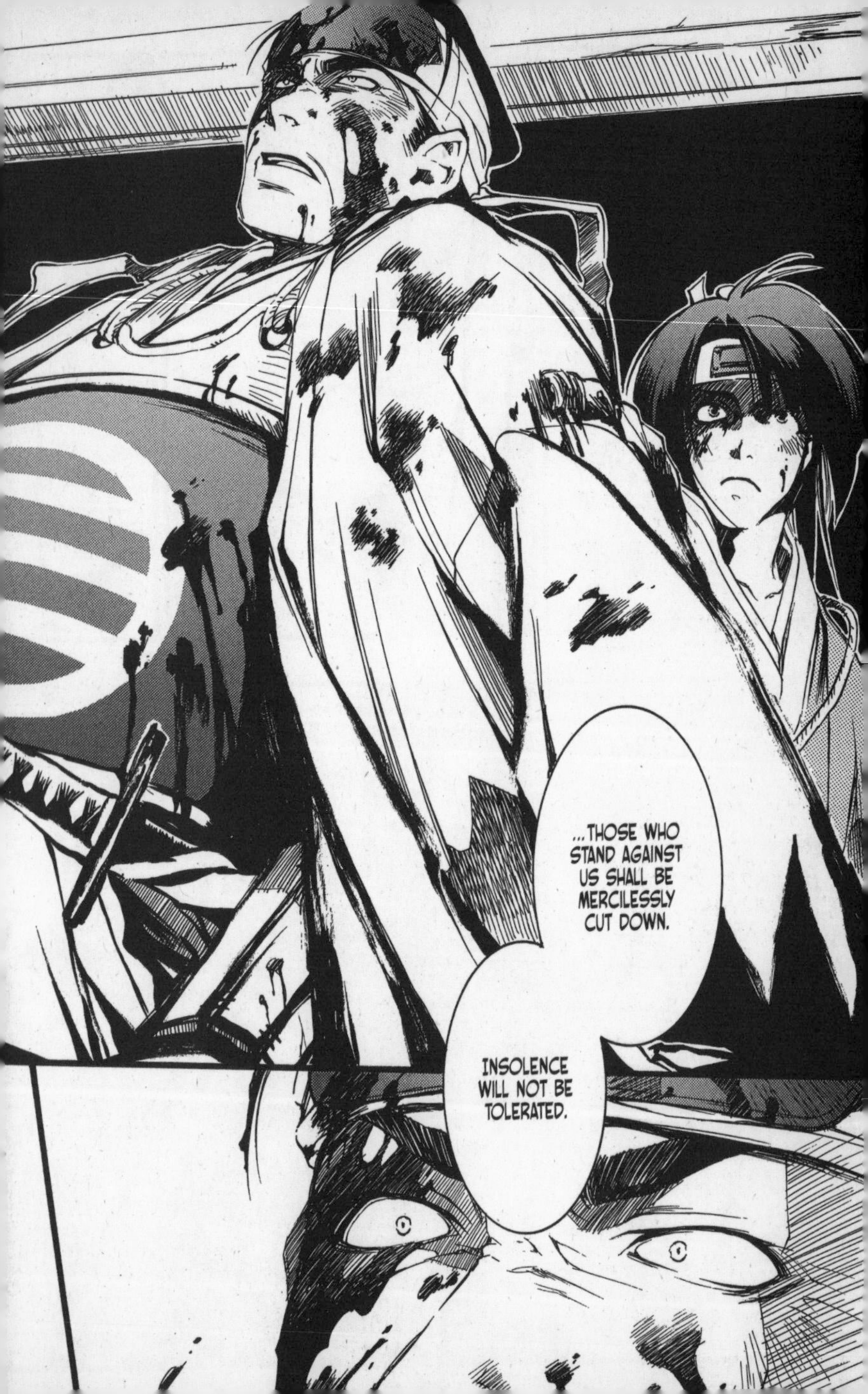
...THOSE WHO STAND AGAINST US SHALL BE MERCILESSLY CUT DOWN.
INSOLENCE WILL NOT BE TOLERATED.

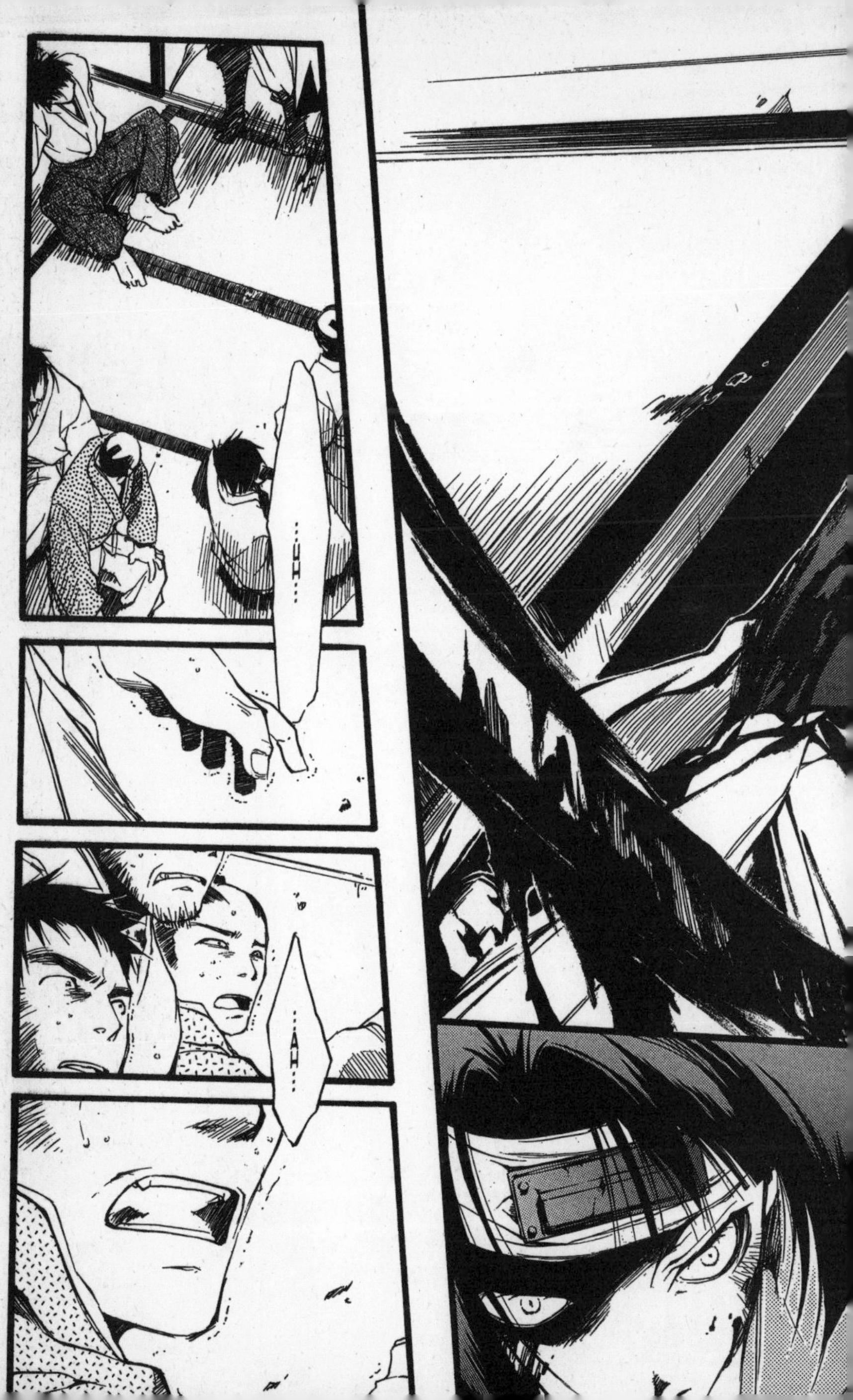
...UH...
...AH...

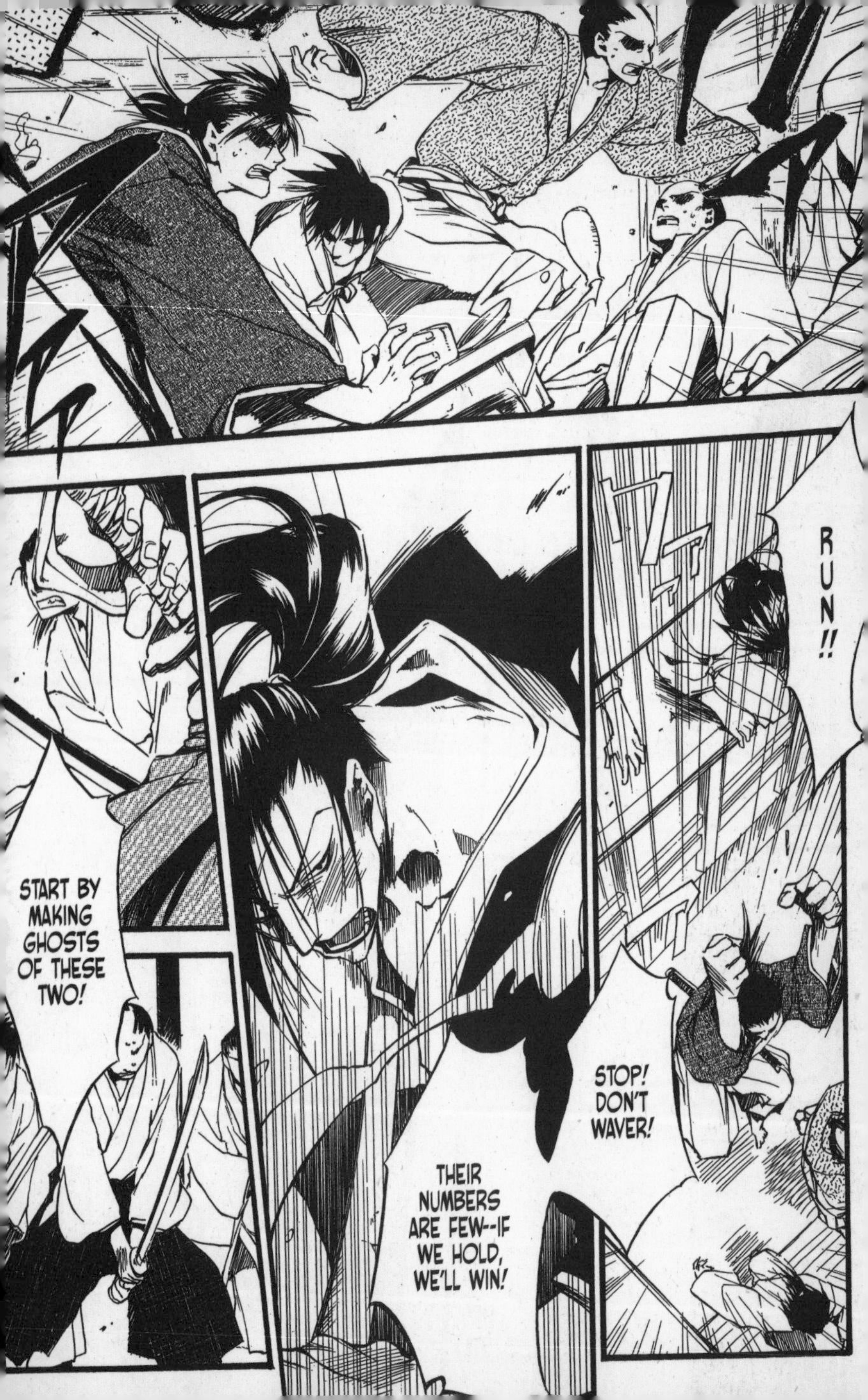
RUN!!
STOP! DON'T WAVER!
THEIR NUMBERS ARE FEW--IF WE HOLD, WE'LL WIN!
START BY MAKING GHOSTS OF THESE TWO!

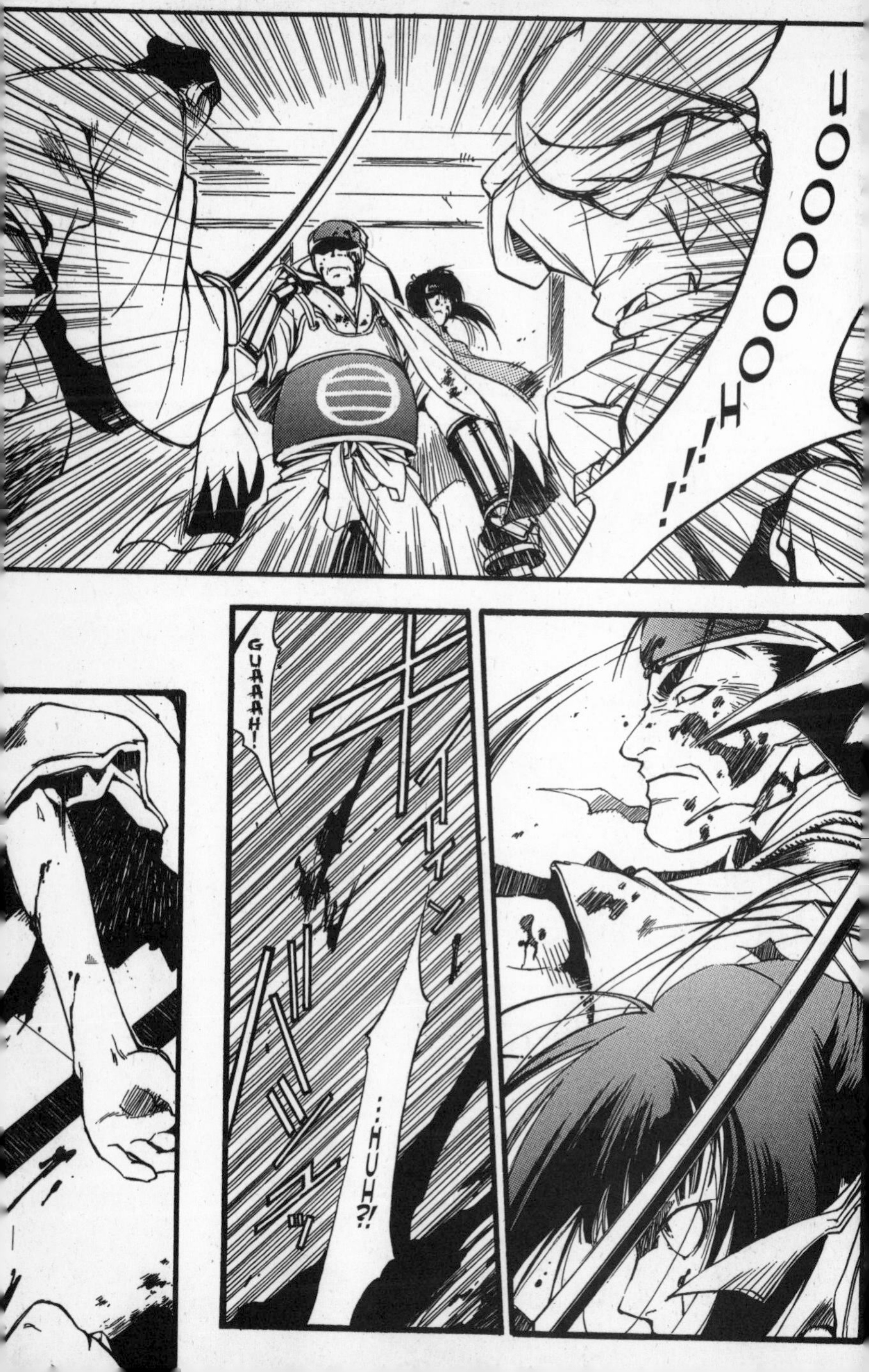
UOOOOOH!!!
GUAAAAH!
...HUH?!

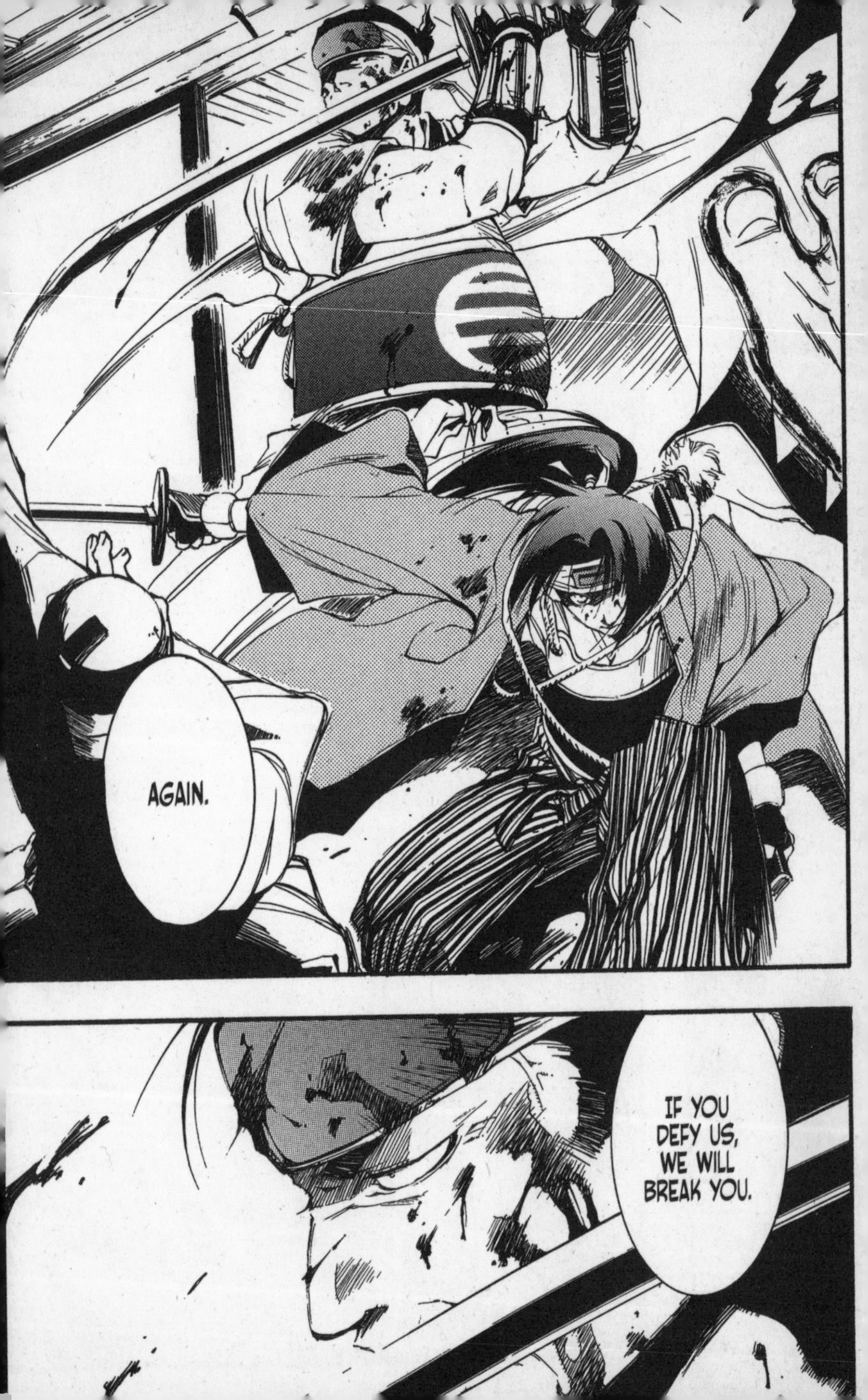
AGAIN.
IF YOU DEFY US, WE WILL BREAK YOU.

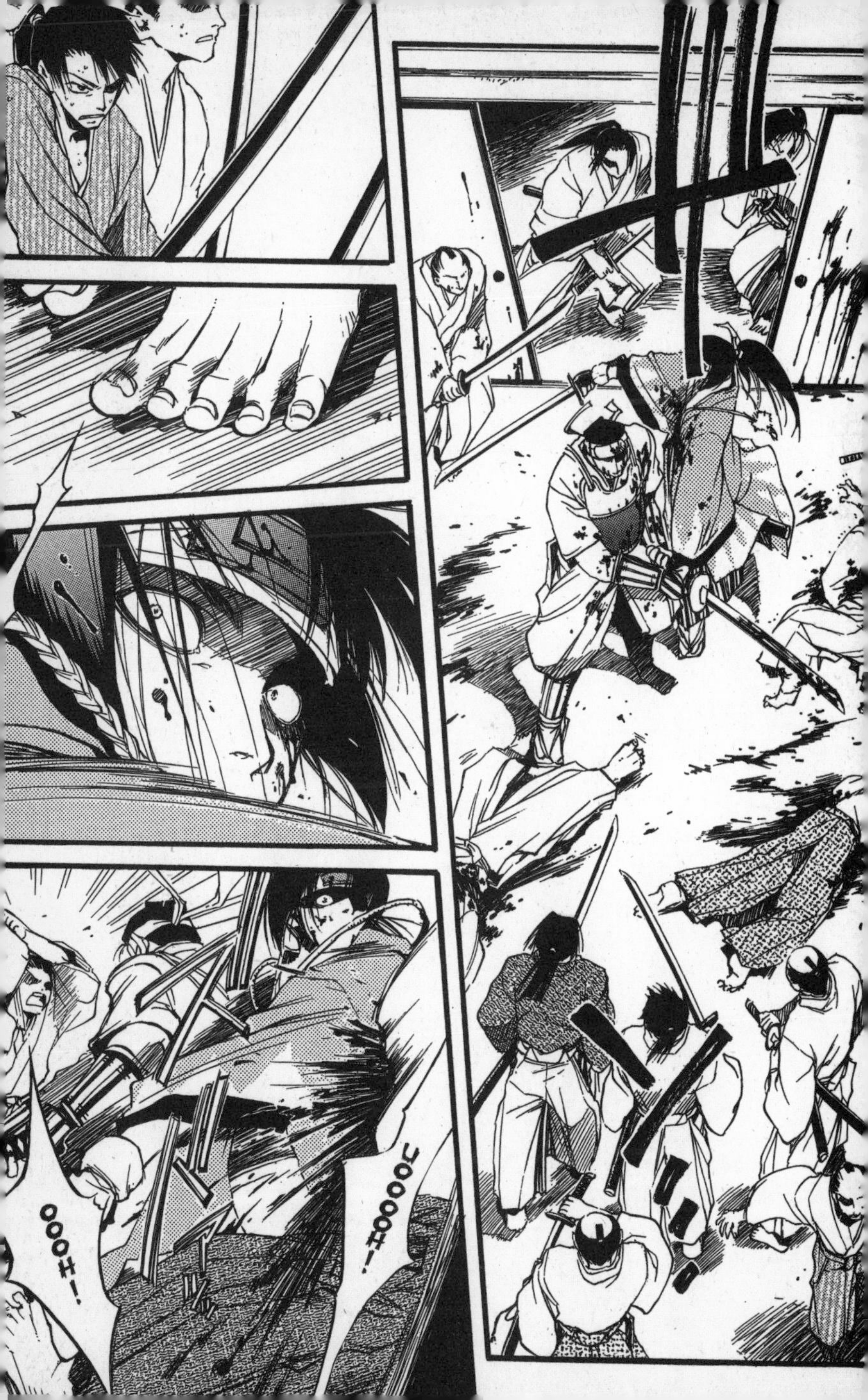
UOOOOOH!!
OOOH!!

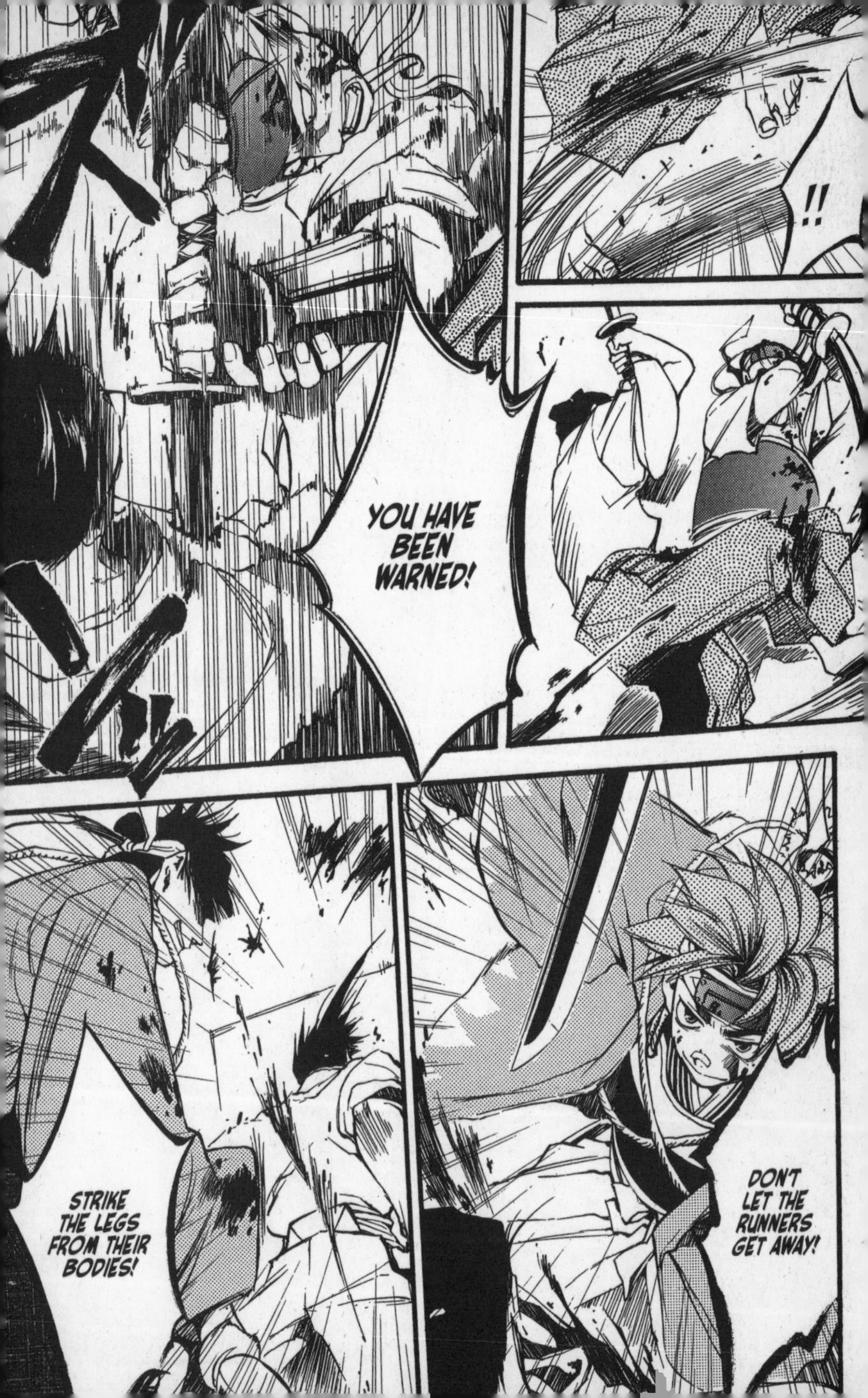
!!
YOU HAVE BEEN WARNED!
DON'T LET THE RUNNERS GET AWAY!
STRIKE THE LEGS FROM THEIR BODIES!

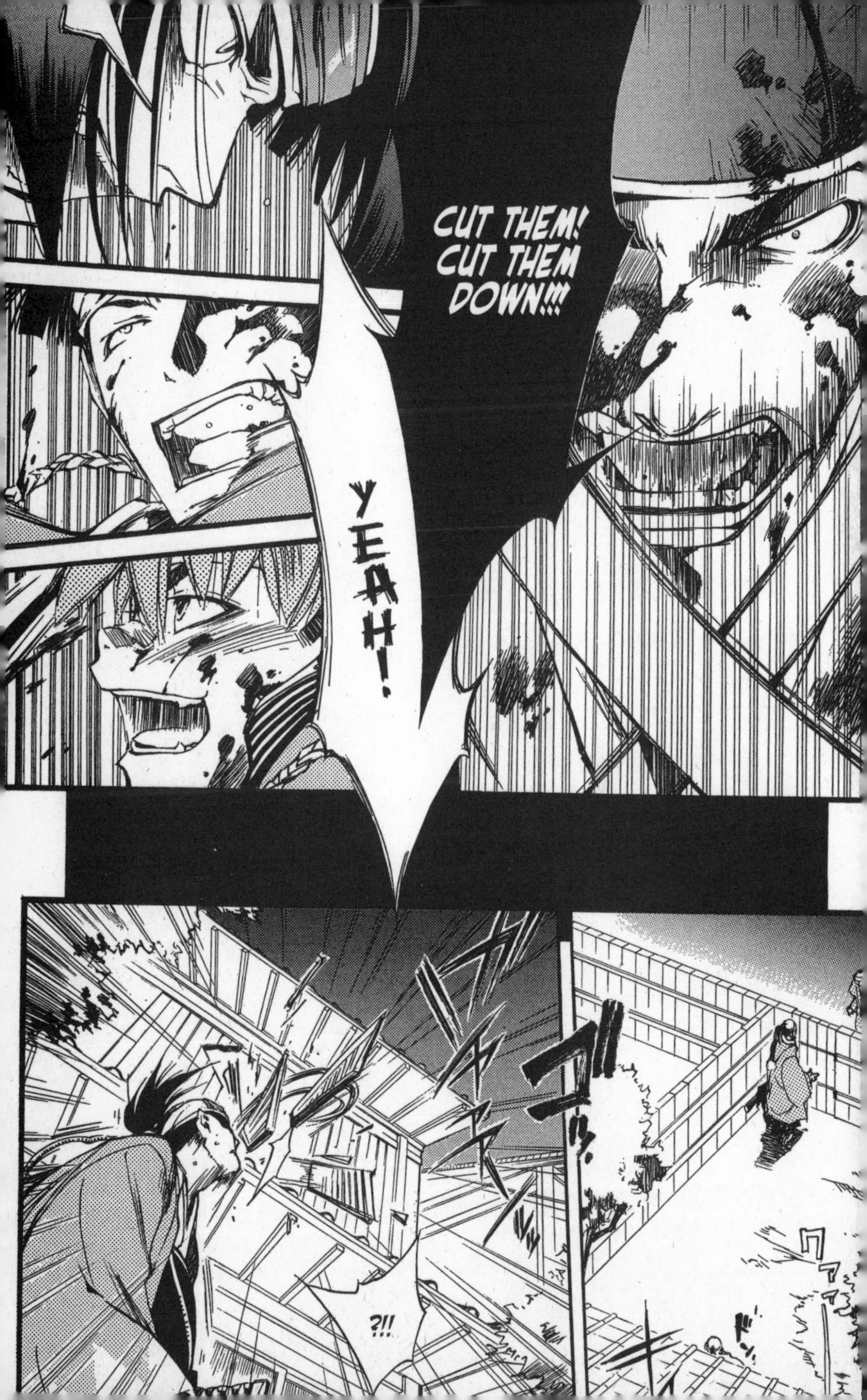
CUT THEM! CUT THEM DOWN!!!
YEAH!
?!!

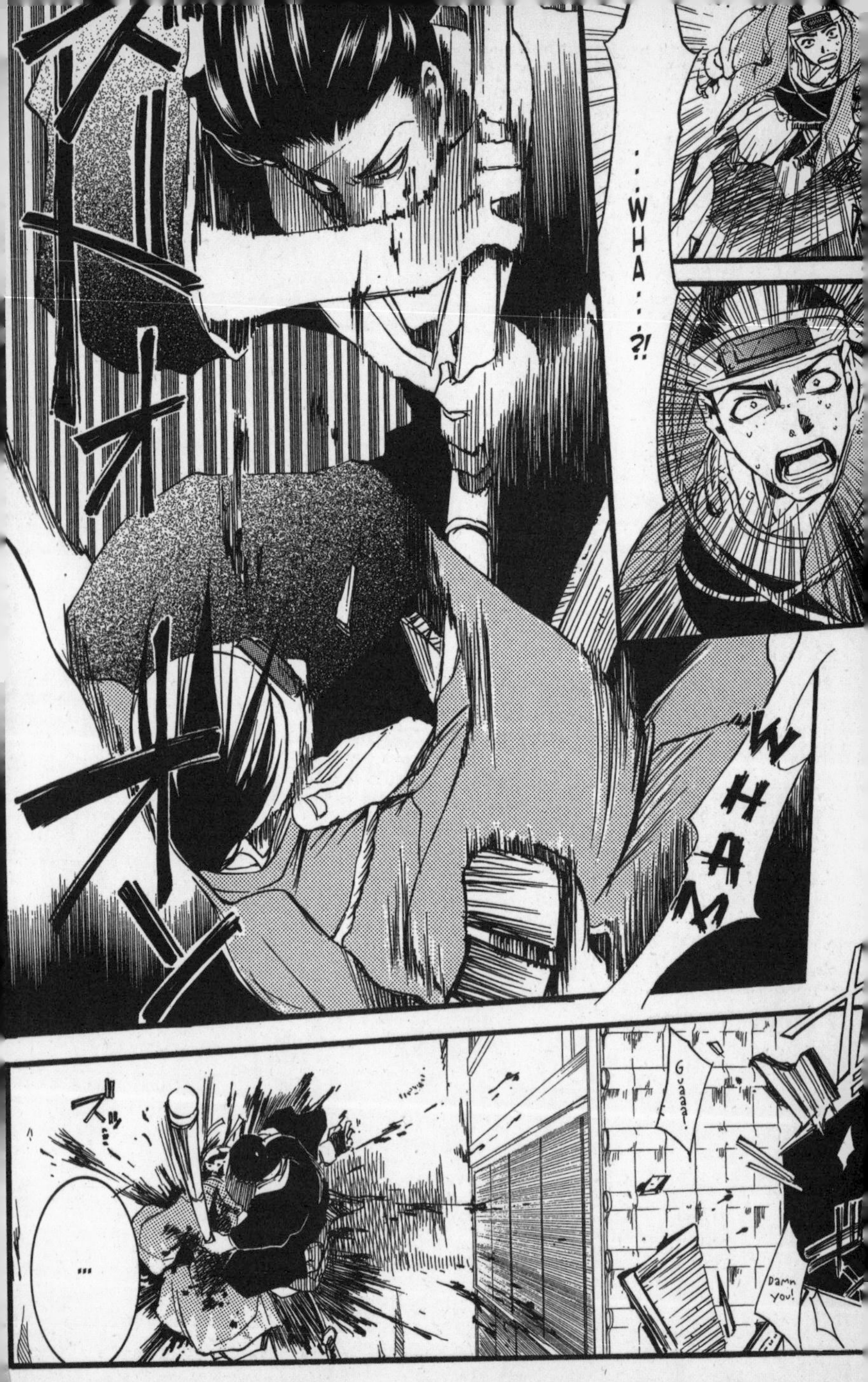
...WHA...?!
WHAM
Guaaa!
Damn you!
...

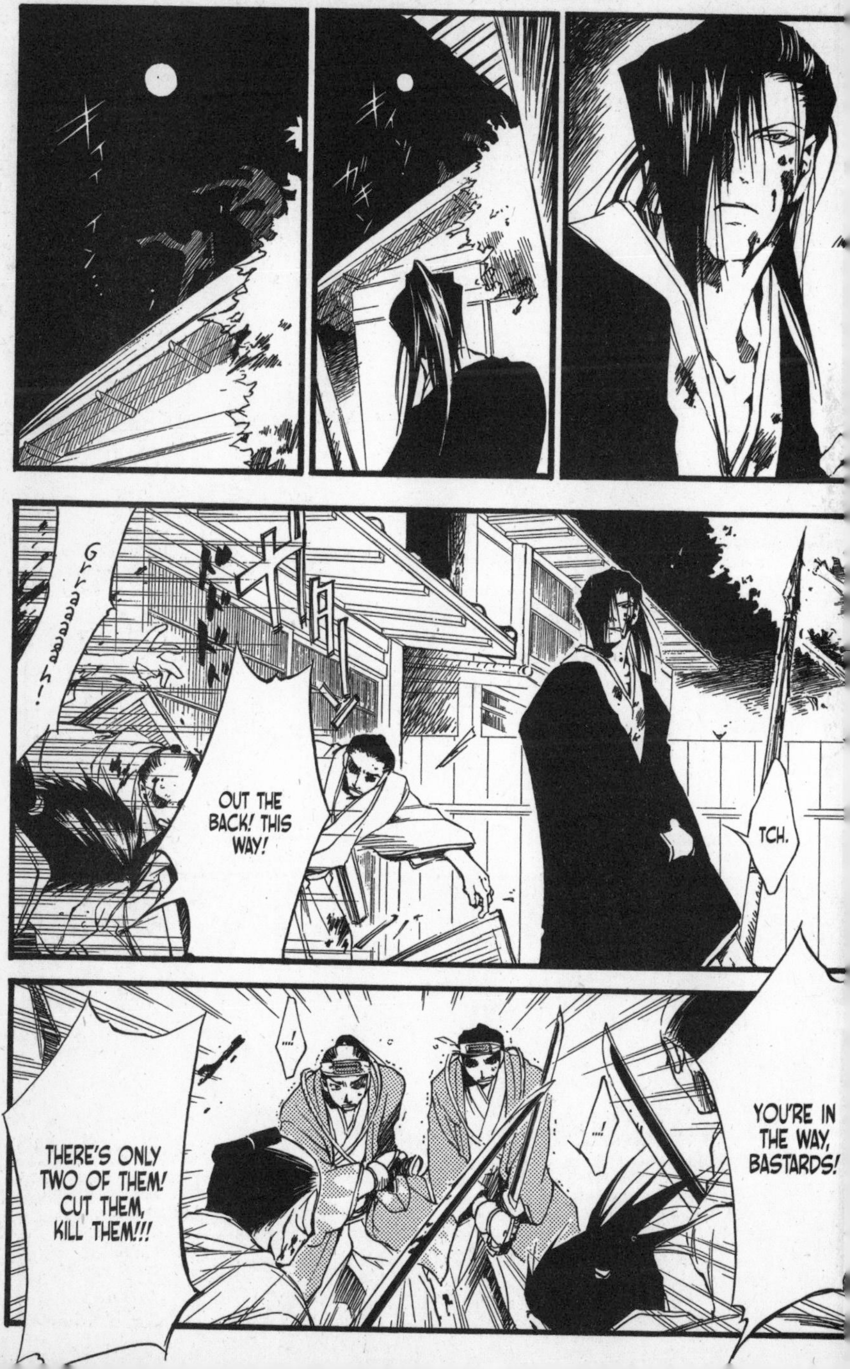
TCH.
OUT THE BACK! THIS WAY!
Grraaaaaah!
YOU'RE IN THE WAY, BASTARDS!
...!
...!
THERE'S ONLY TWO OF THEM! CUT THEM, KILL THEM!!!

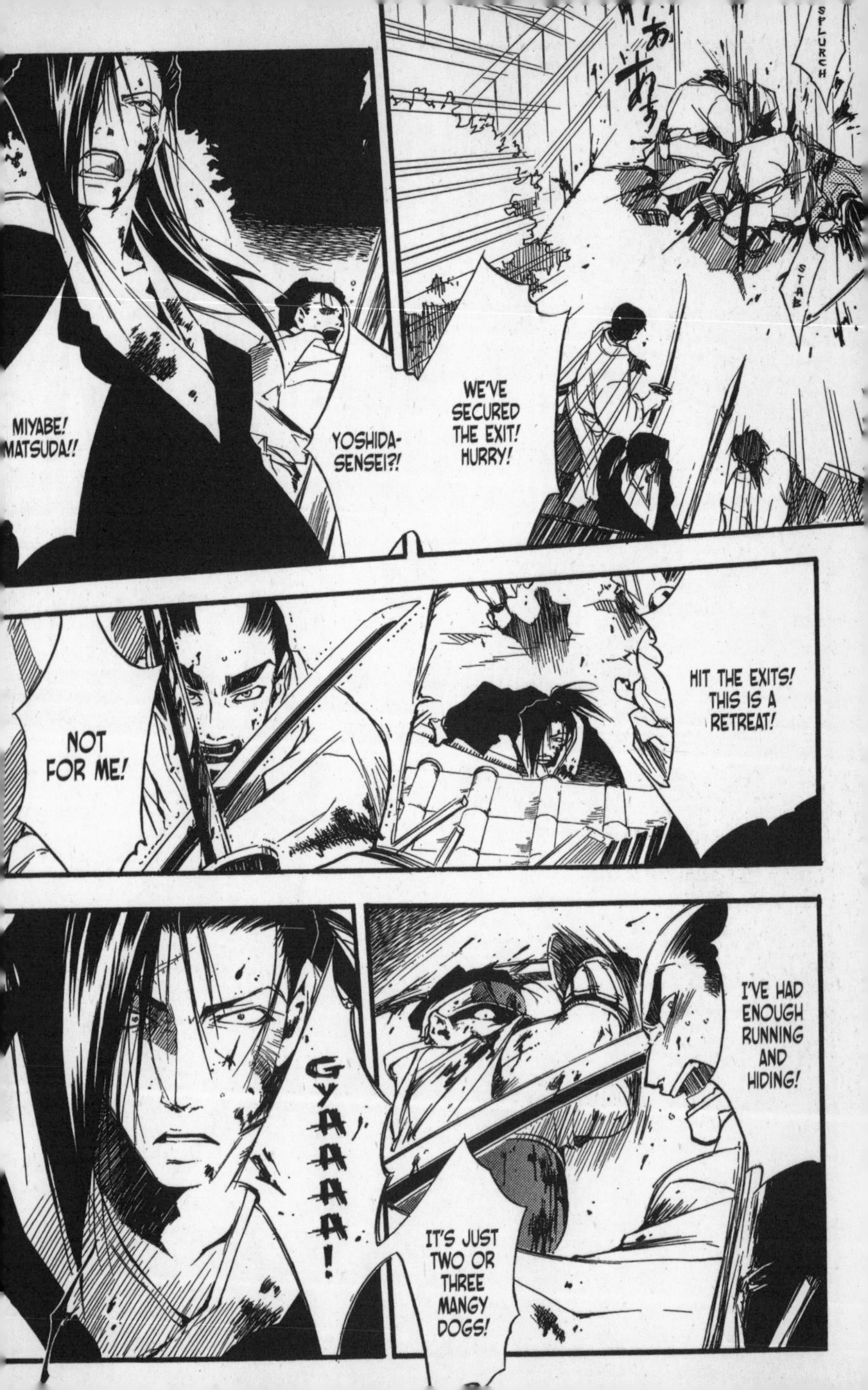
SPLURCH
STAB
WE'VE SECURED THE EXIT! HURRY!
YOSHIDA-SENSEI?!
MIYABE! MATSUDA!!
HIT THE EXITS! THIS IS A RETREAT!
NOT FOR ME!
I'VE HAD ENOUGH RUNNING AND HIDING!
IT'S JUST TWO OR THREE MANGY DOGS!
GYAAAA!

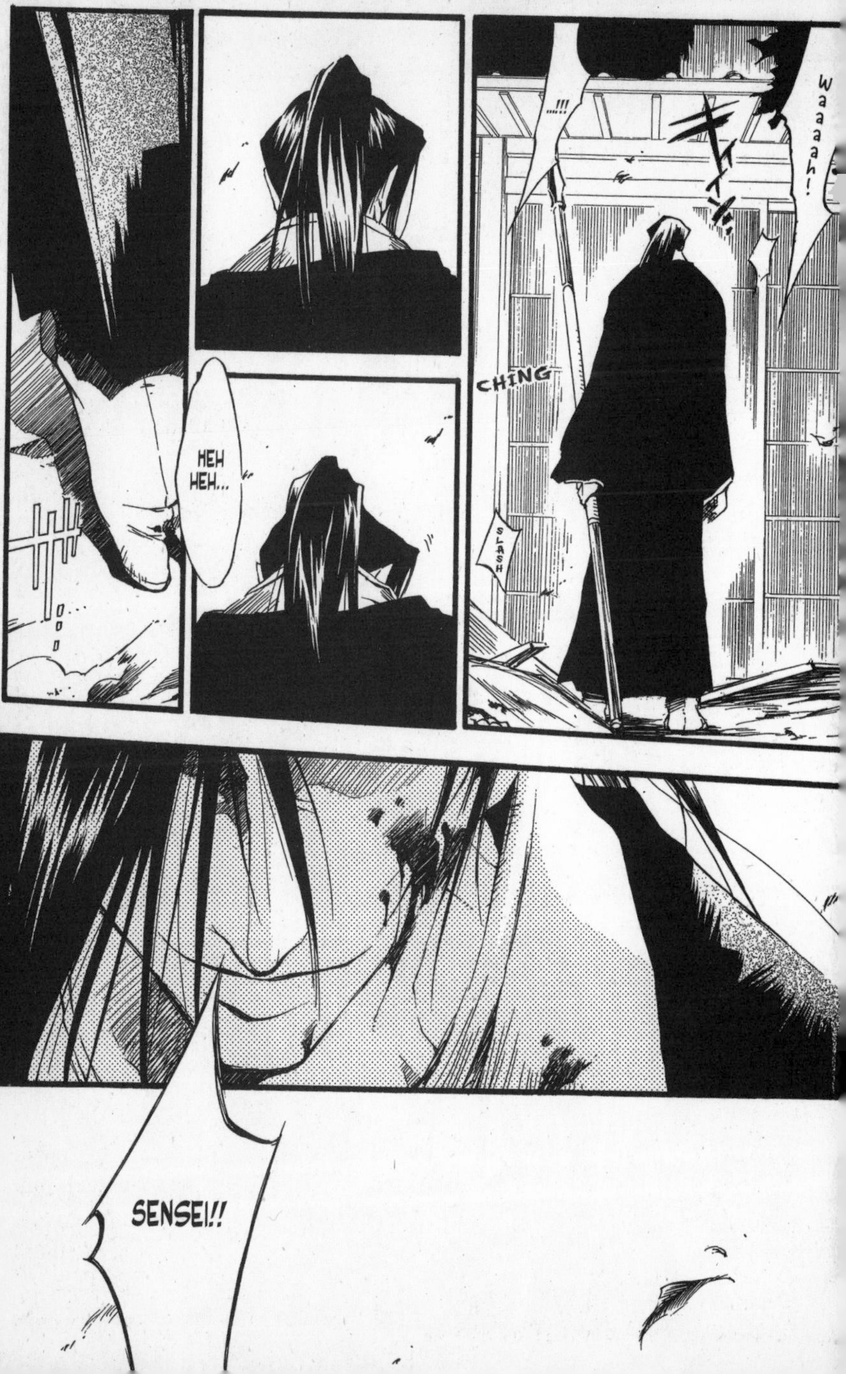
Waaaaah!
...!!!
CHING
SLASH
HEH HEH...
SENSEI!!

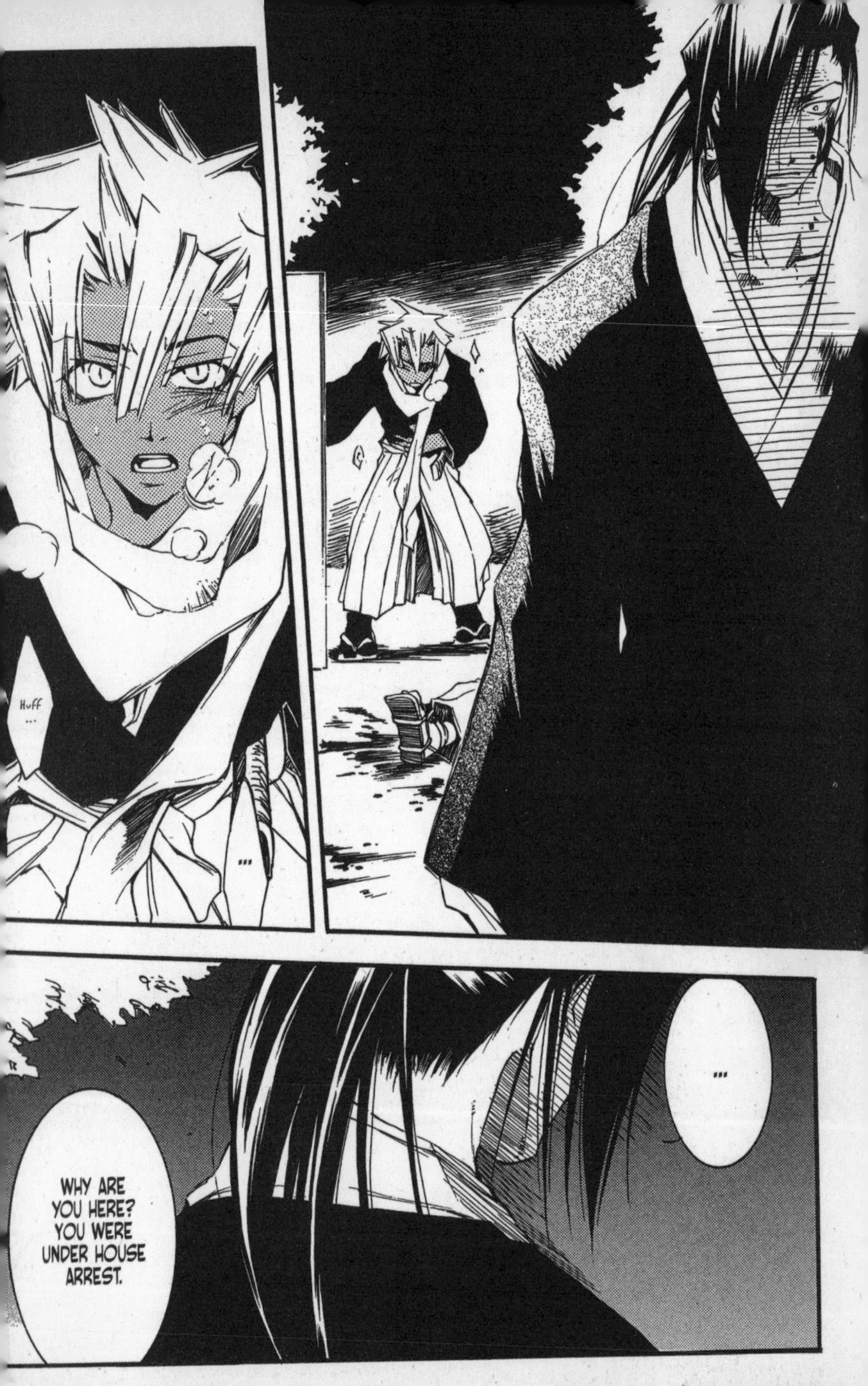
Huff ...
...
...
WHY ARE YOU HERE? YOU WERE UNDER HOUSE ARREST.

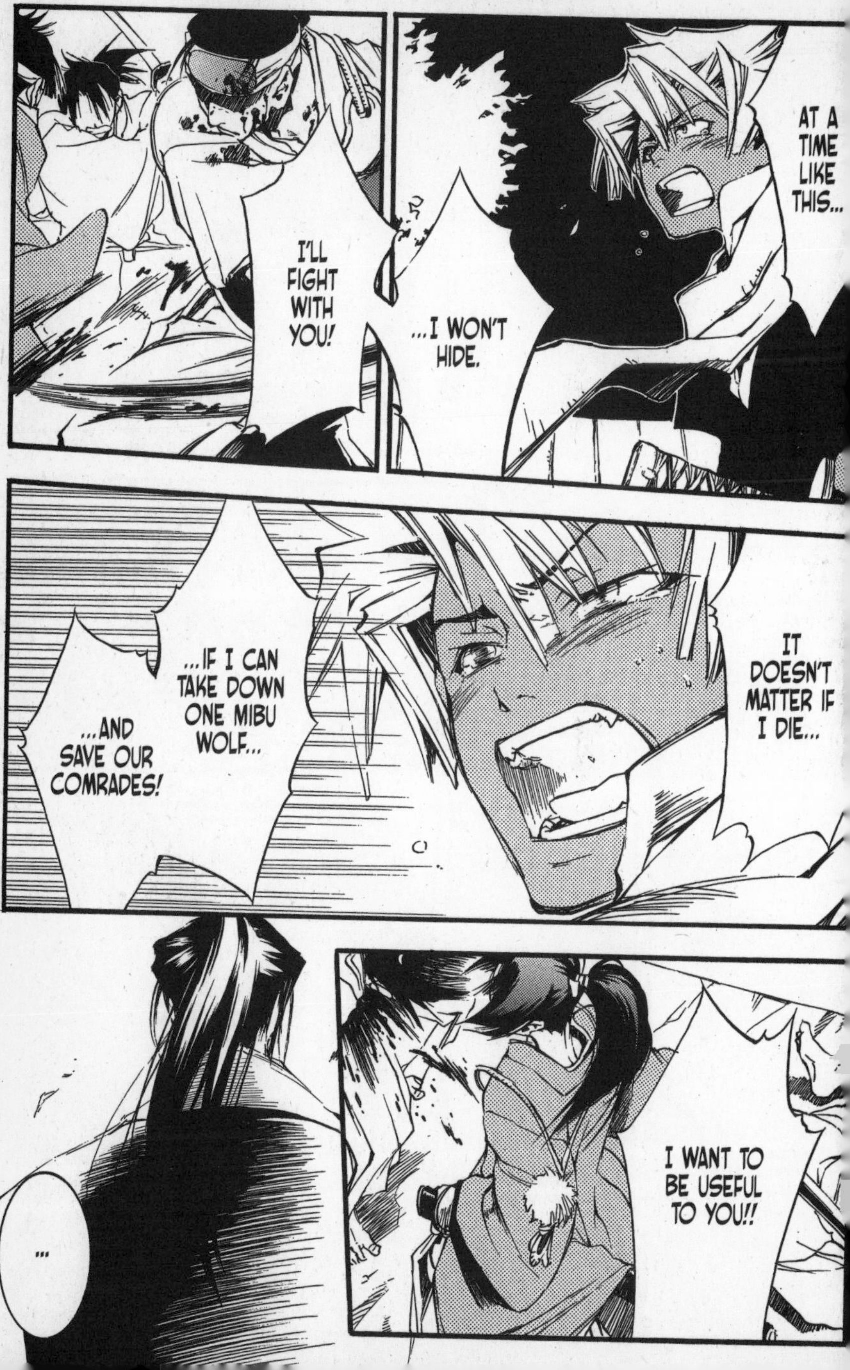
AT A TIME LIKE THIS...
...I WON'T HIDE.
I'LL FIGHT WITH YOU!
IT DOESN'T MATTER IF I DIE...
...IF I CAN TAKE DOWN ONE MIBU WOLF...
...AND SAVE OUR COMRADES!
I WANT TO BE USEFUL TO YOU!!
...

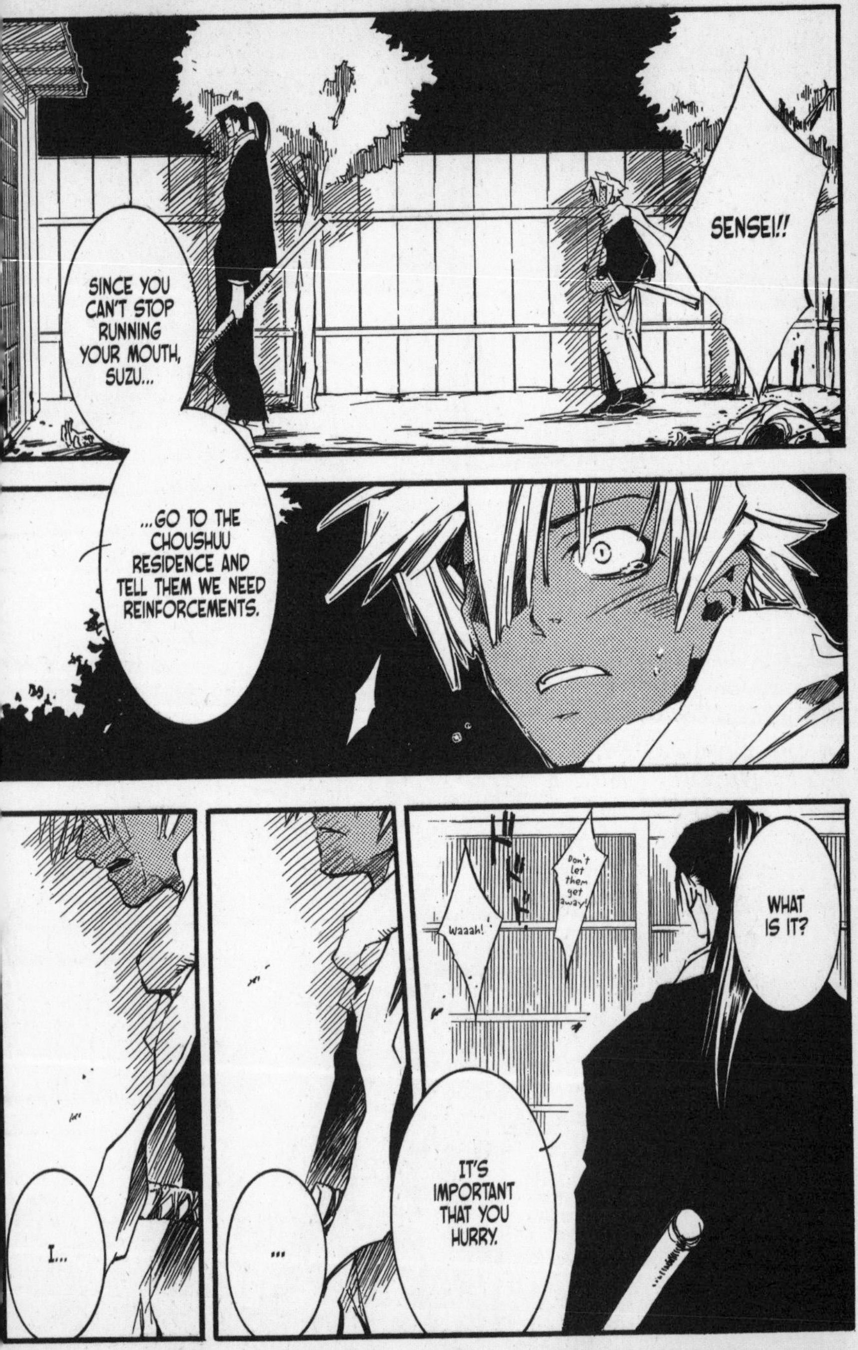
SENSEI!!
SINCE YOU CAN'T STOP RUNNING YOUR MOUTH, SUZU...
...GO TO THE CHOUSHUU RESIDENCE AND TELL THEM WE NEED REINFORCEMENTS.
WHAT IS IT?
Don't let them get away!
Waaah!
IT'S IMPORTANT THAT YOU HURRY.
...
I...

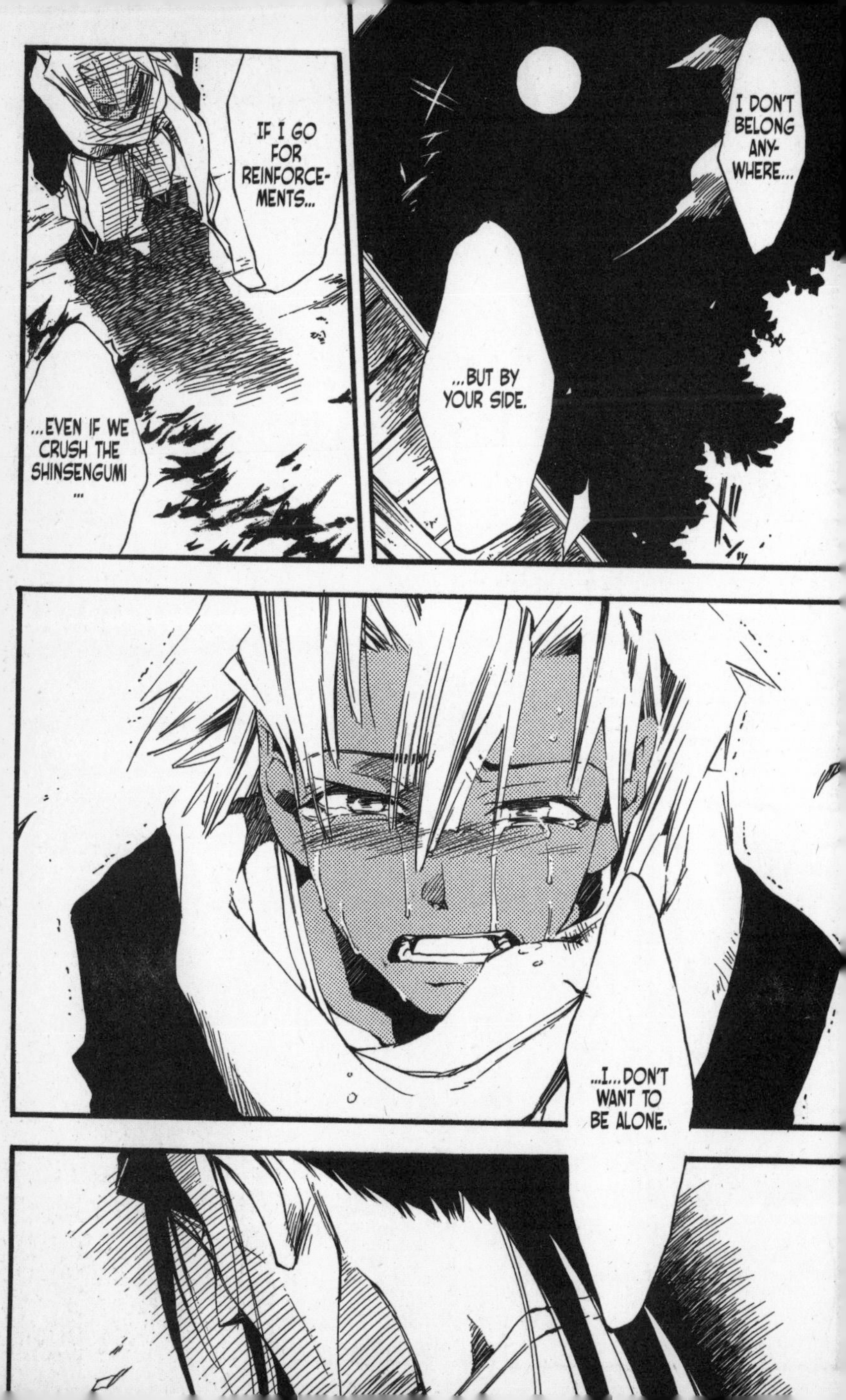
I DON'T BELONG ANYWHERE...
...BUT BY YOUR SIDE.
IF I GO FOR REINFORCEMENTS...
...EVEN IF WE CRUSH THE SHINSENGUMI...
...I...DON'T WANT TO BE ALONE.

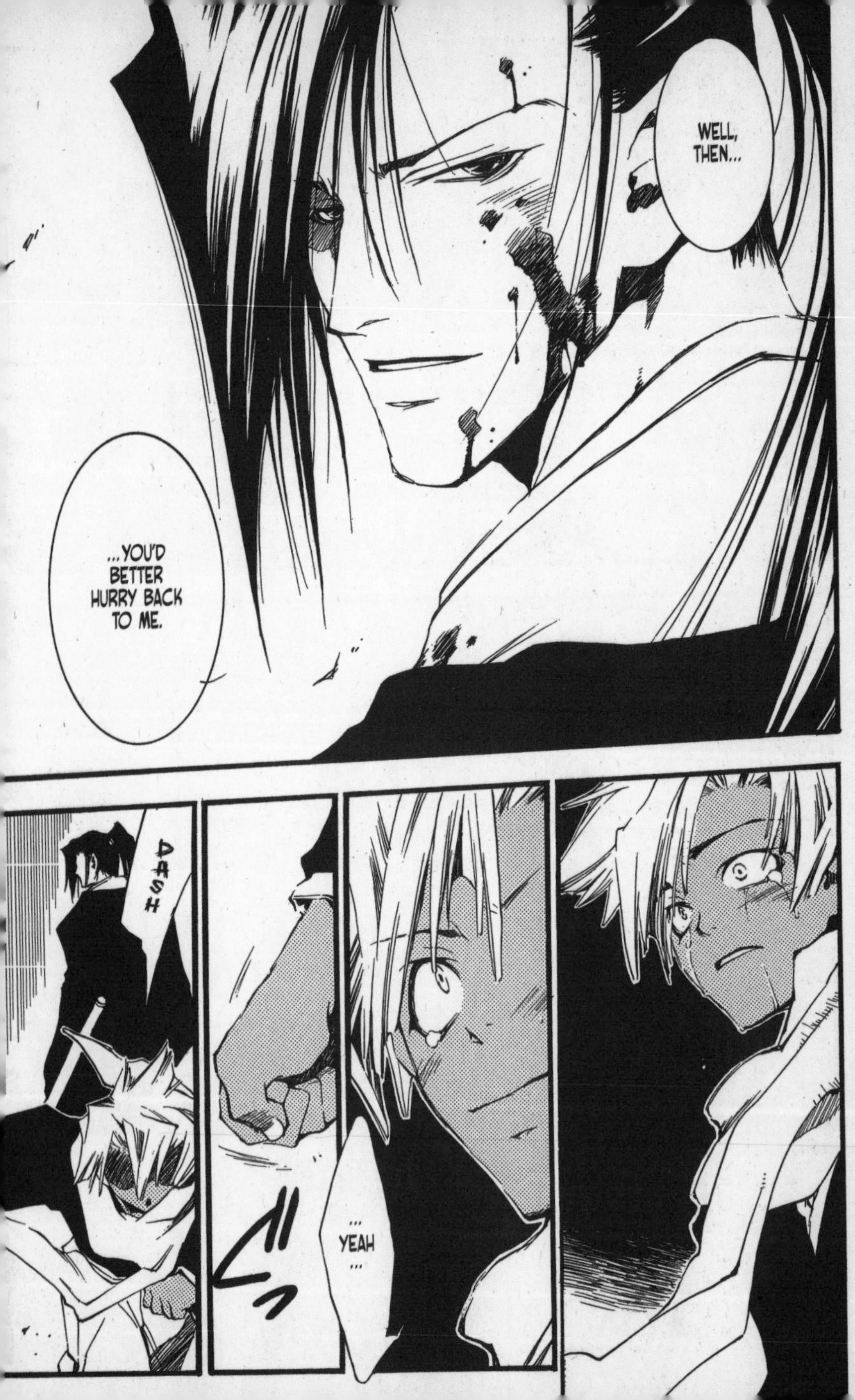
WELL, THEN...
...YOU'D BETTER HURRY BACK TO ME.
... YEAH ...
DASH

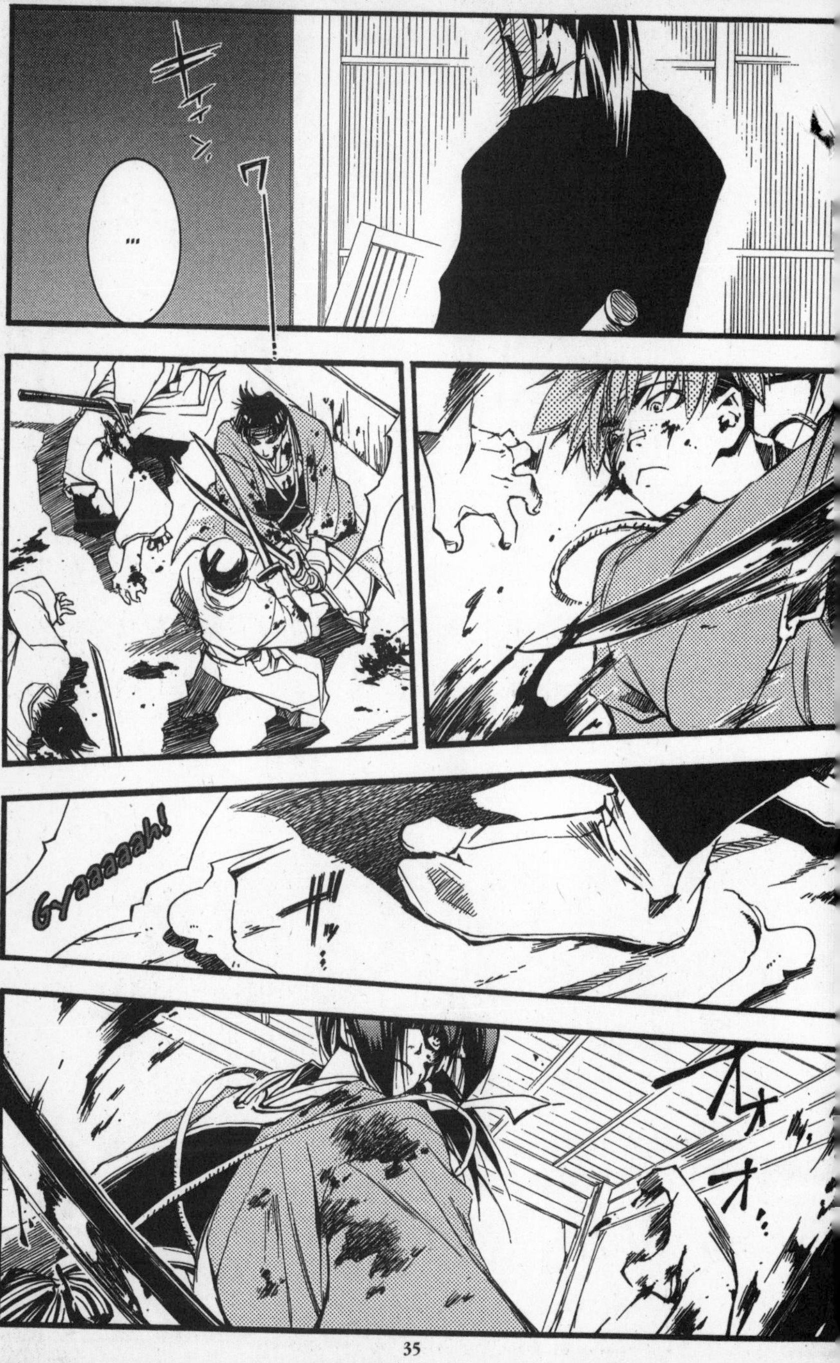
...
Gyaaaaah!

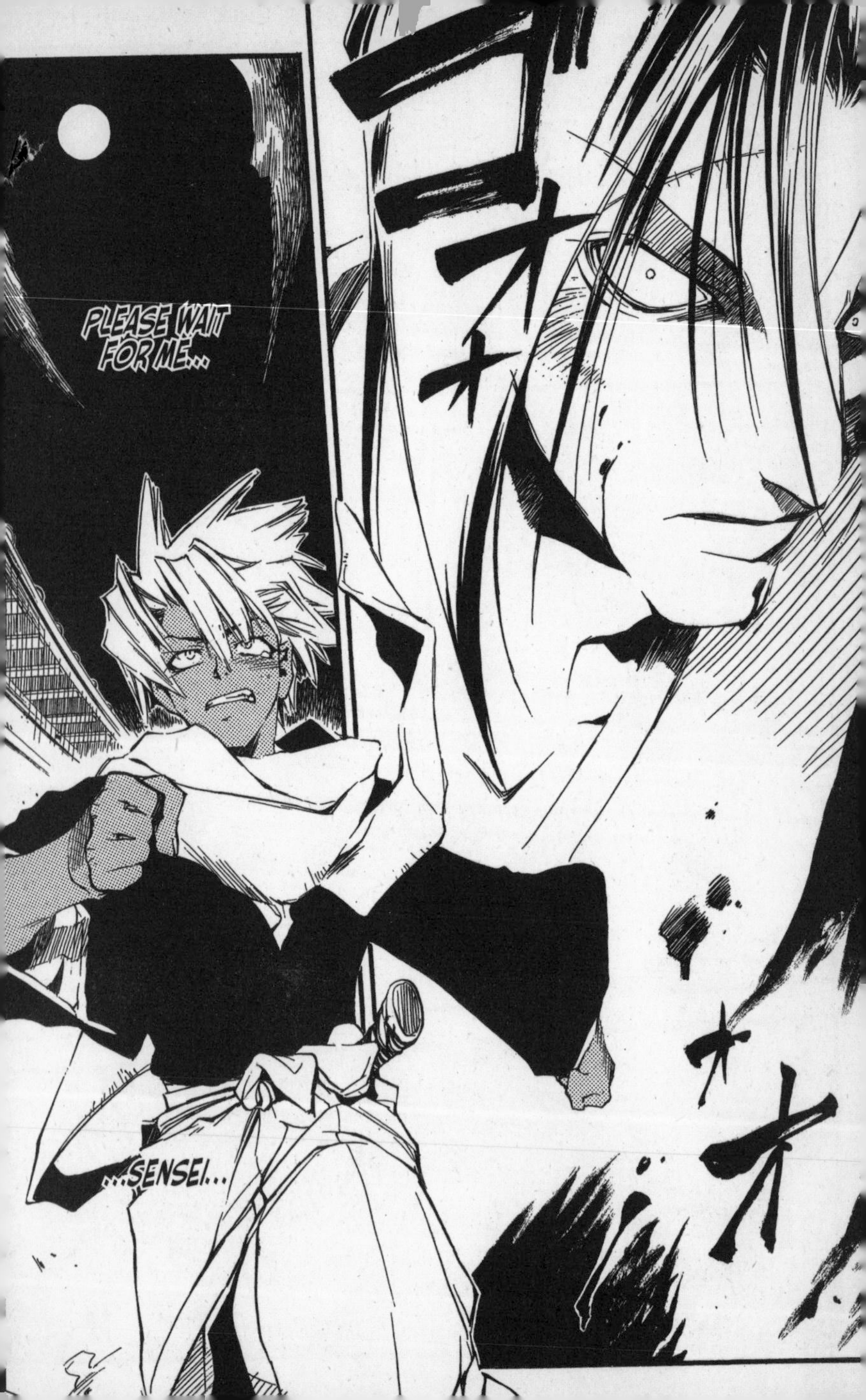
PLEASE WAIT FOR ME...
...SENSEI...

Act.25
A Hard Day's Night (Scene 2)

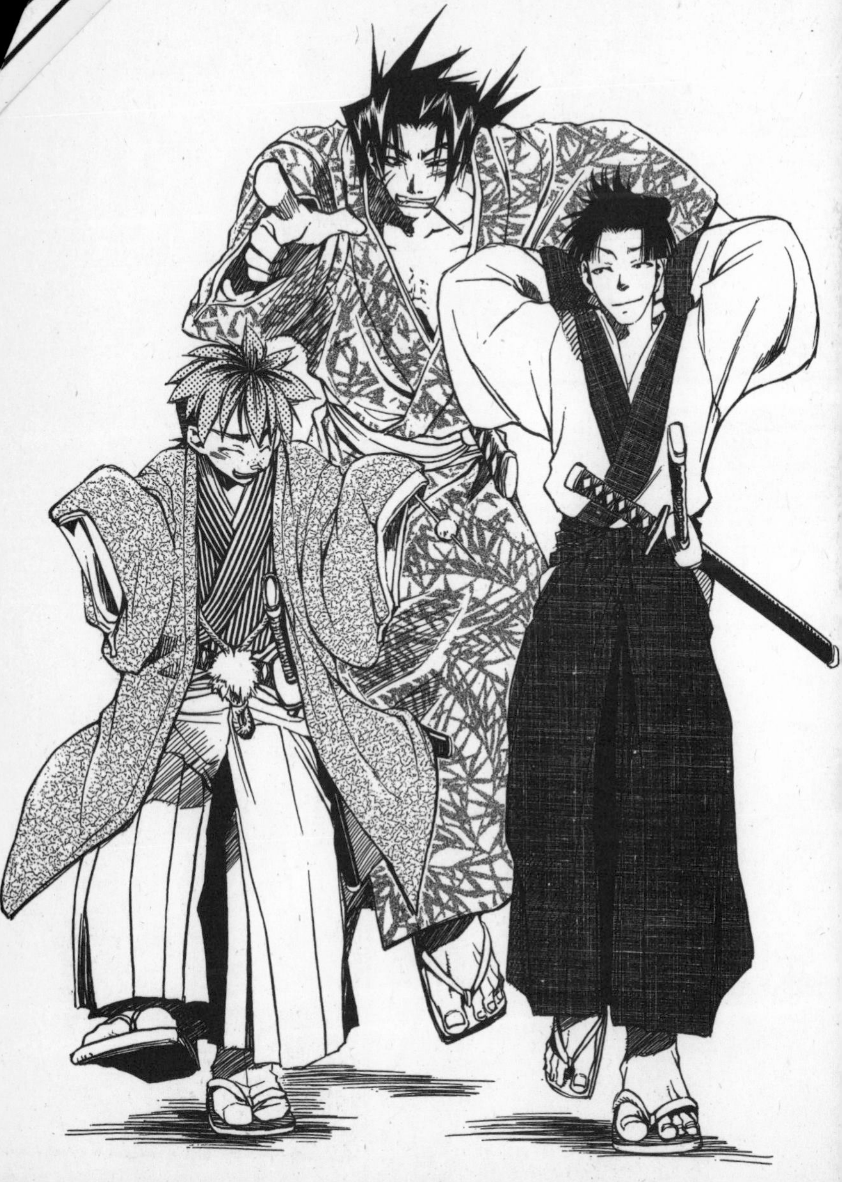

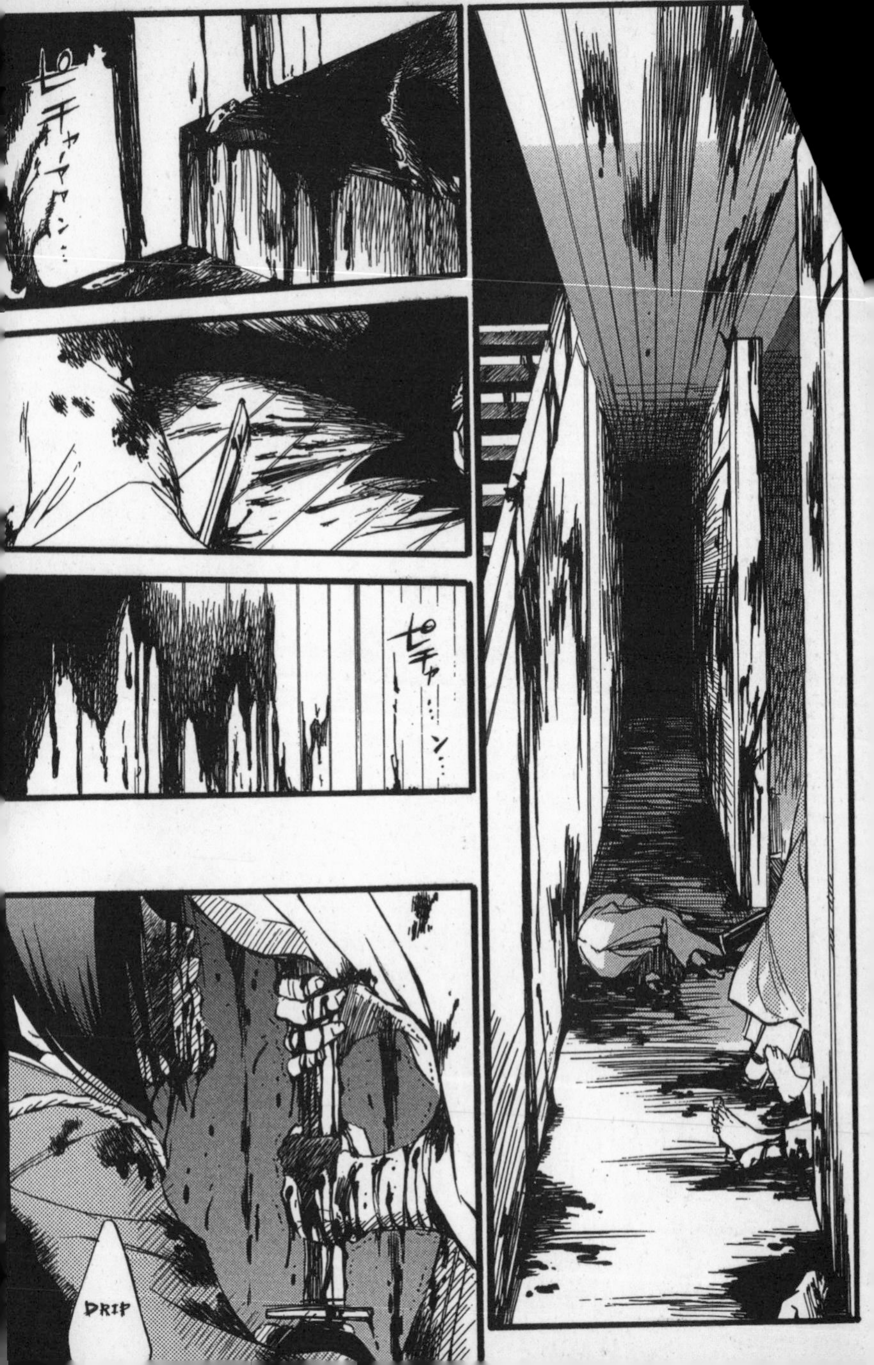
ピチャーアーン…
ピチャ…ン…
DRIP

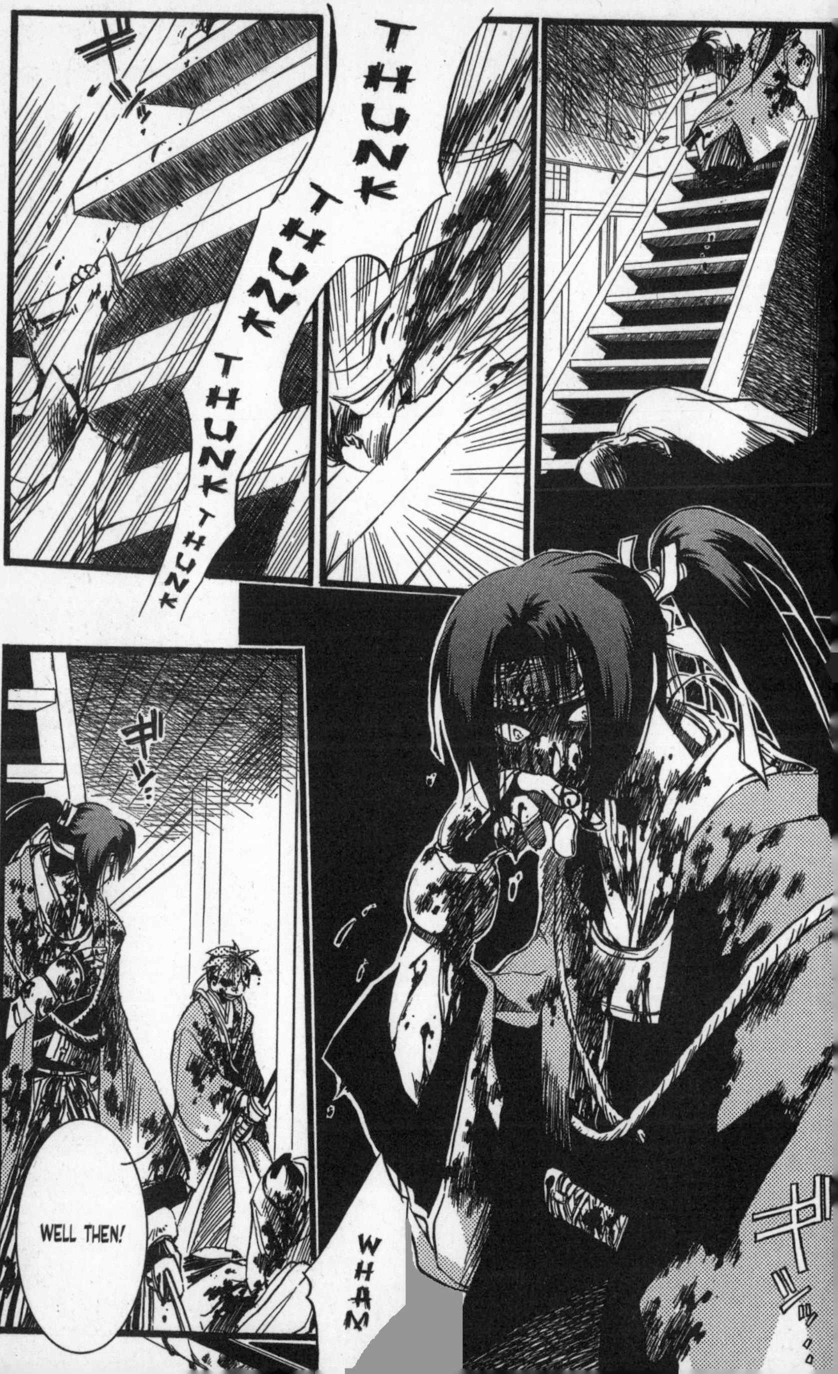
THUNK
THUNK
THUNK
THUNK
WHAM
WELL THEN!

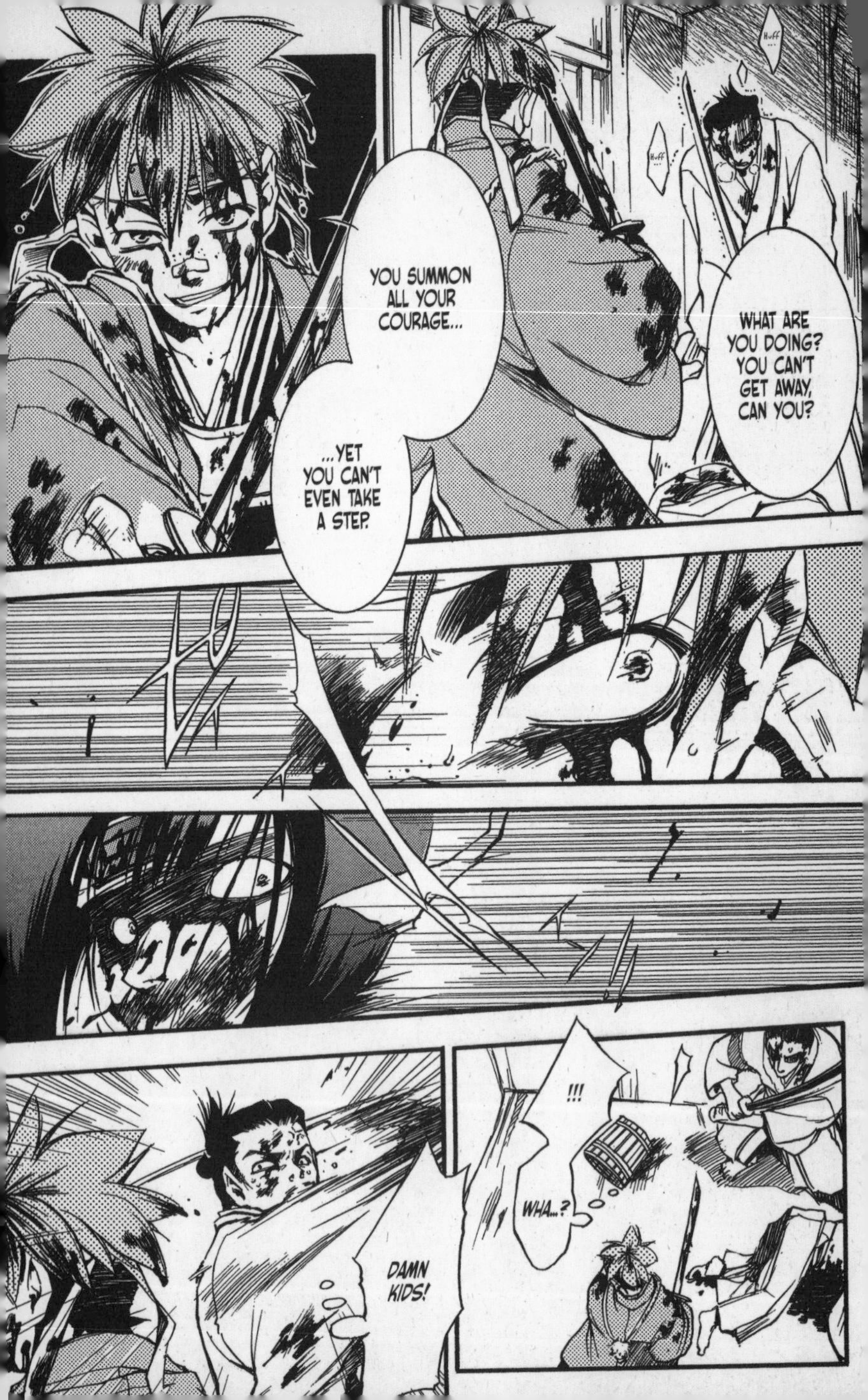
Huff...
Huff...
WHAT ARE YOU DOING? YOU CAN'T GET AWAY, CAN YOU?
YOU SUMMON ALL YOUR COURAGE...
...YET YOU CAN'T EVEN TAKE A STEP.
!!!
WHA...?
DAMN KIDS!

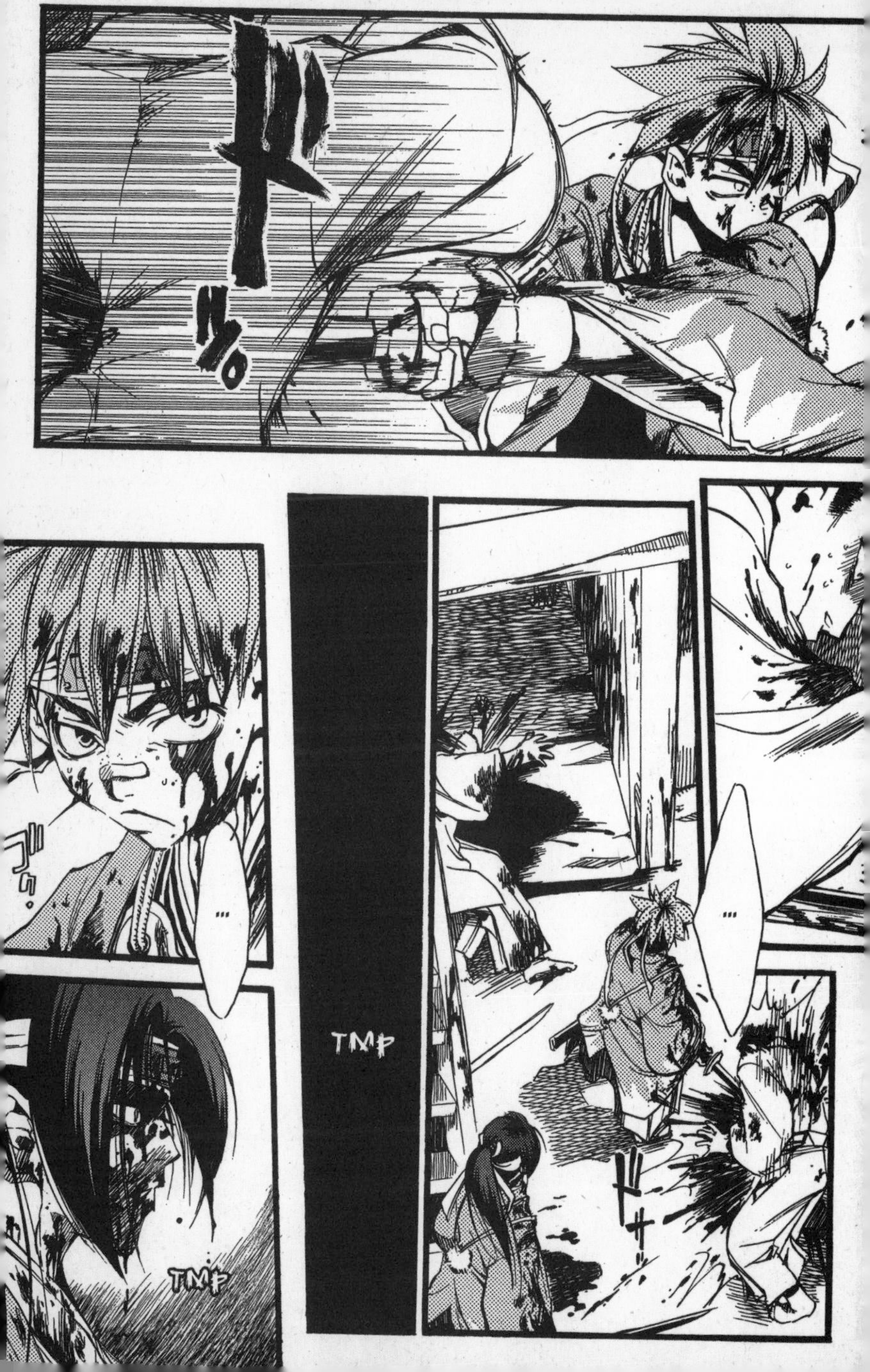
...
TMP
...
ゴク
TMP

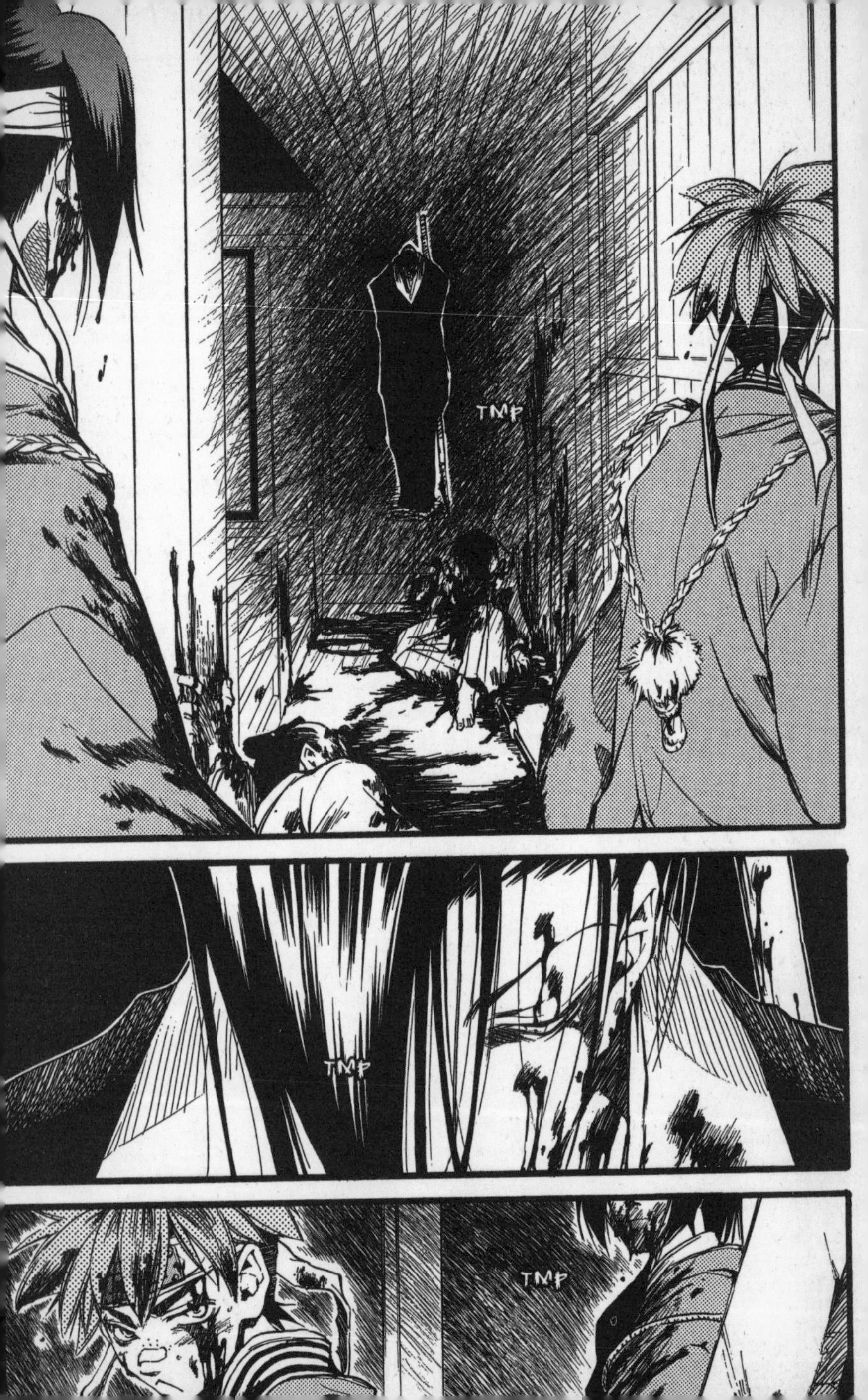
TMP
TMP
TMP

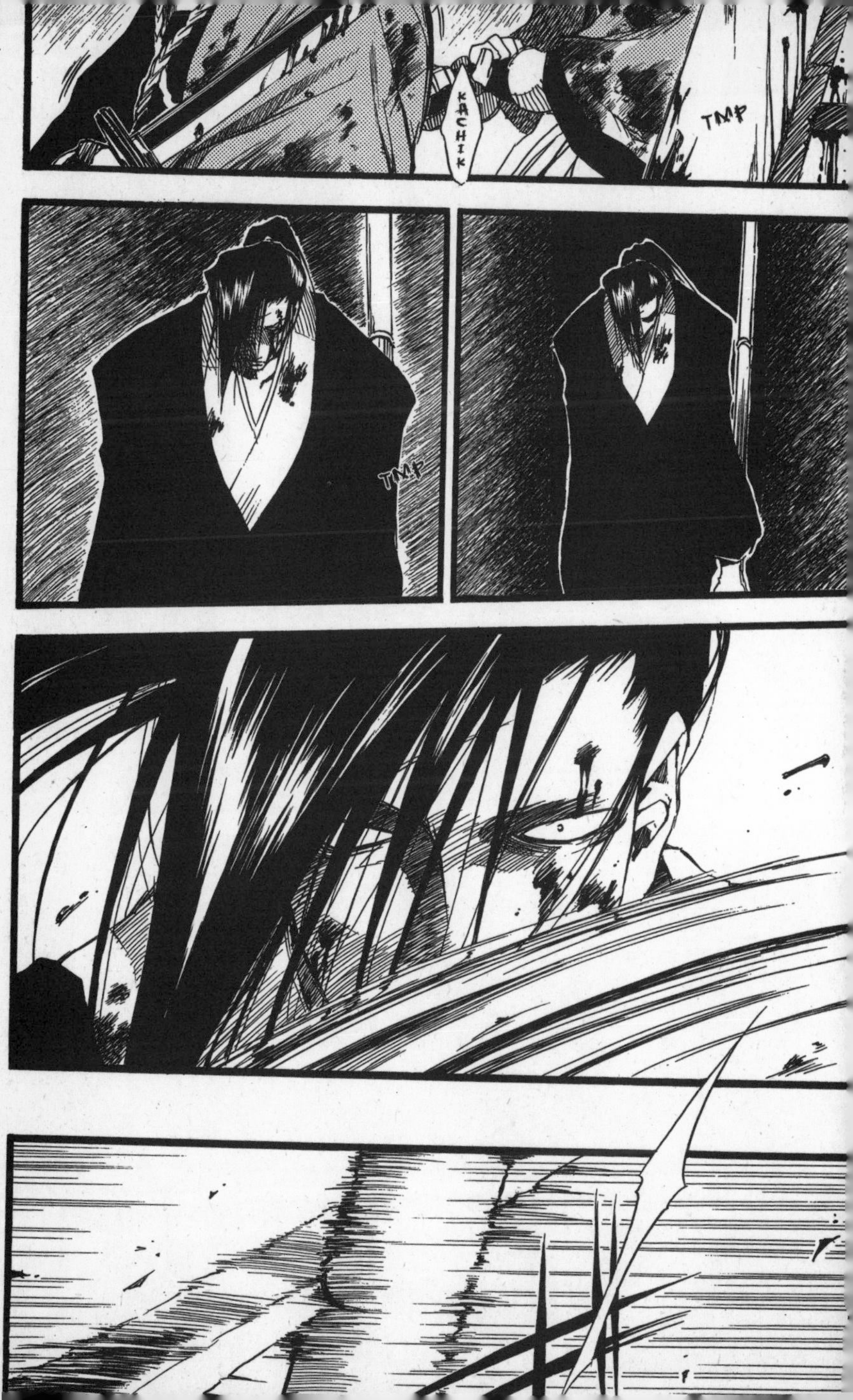
TMP
KACHIK
TMP

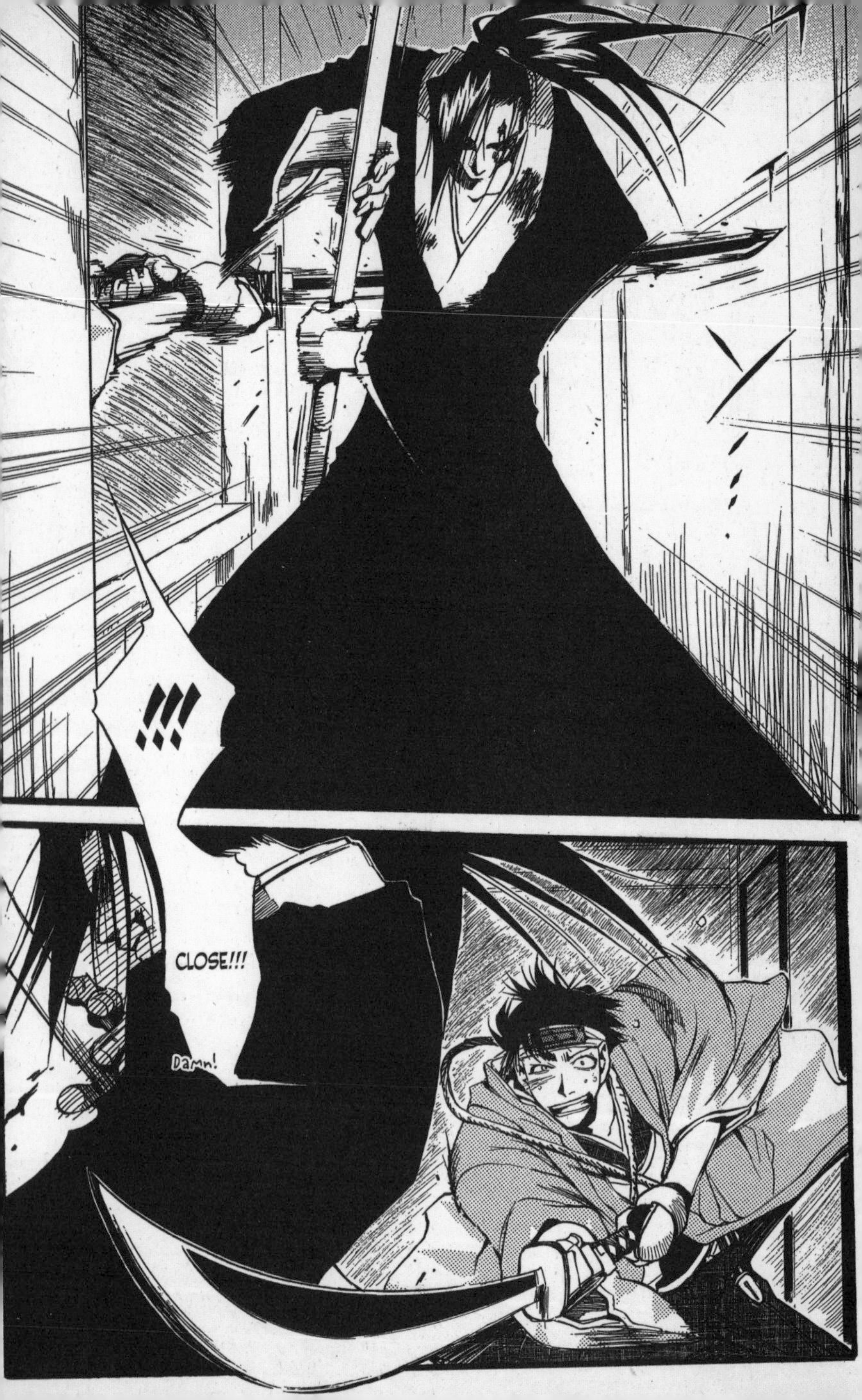
!!!
CLOSE!!!
Damn!

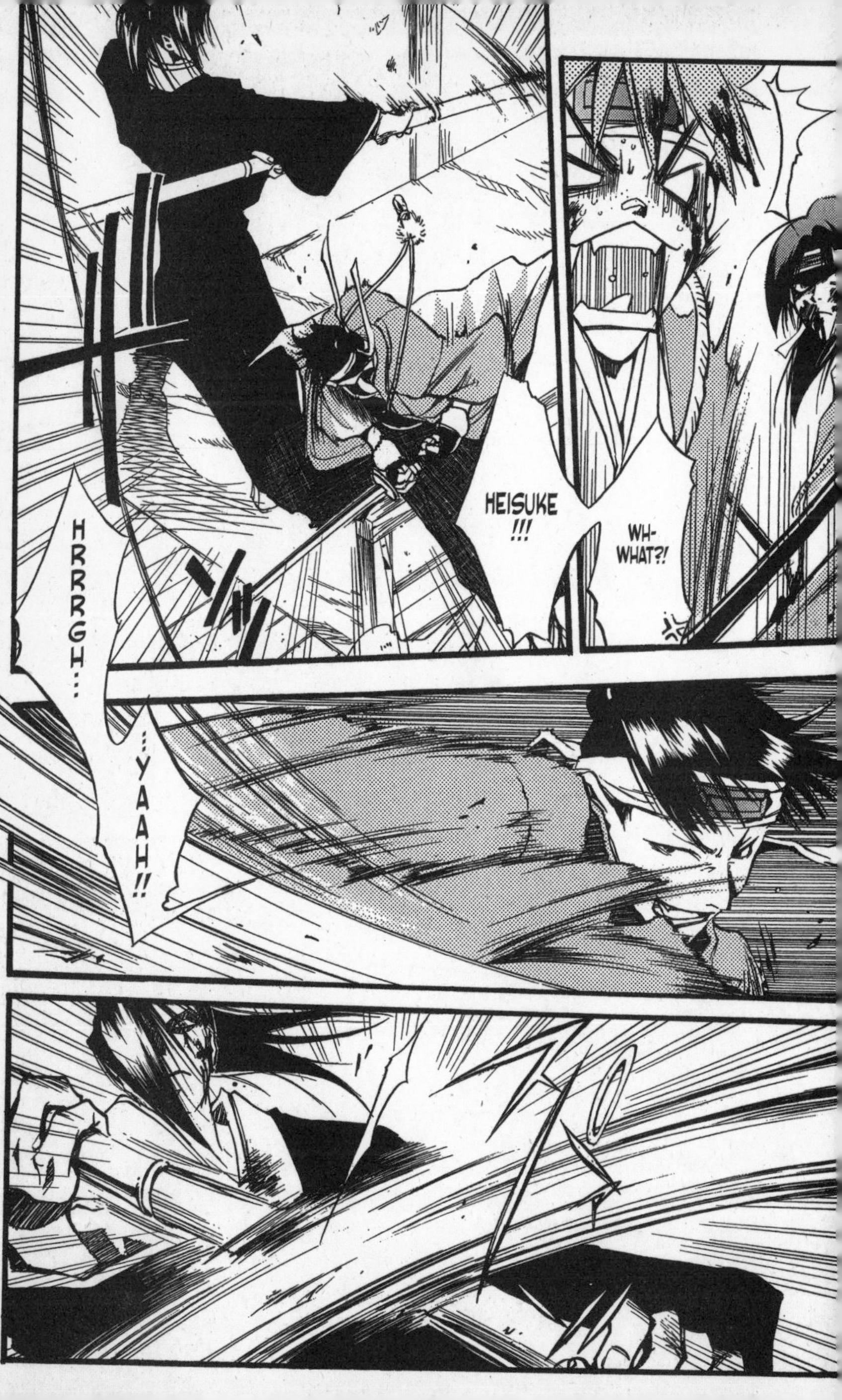
WH-WHAT?!
HEISUKE!!!
HRRRGH...
...YAAAH!!

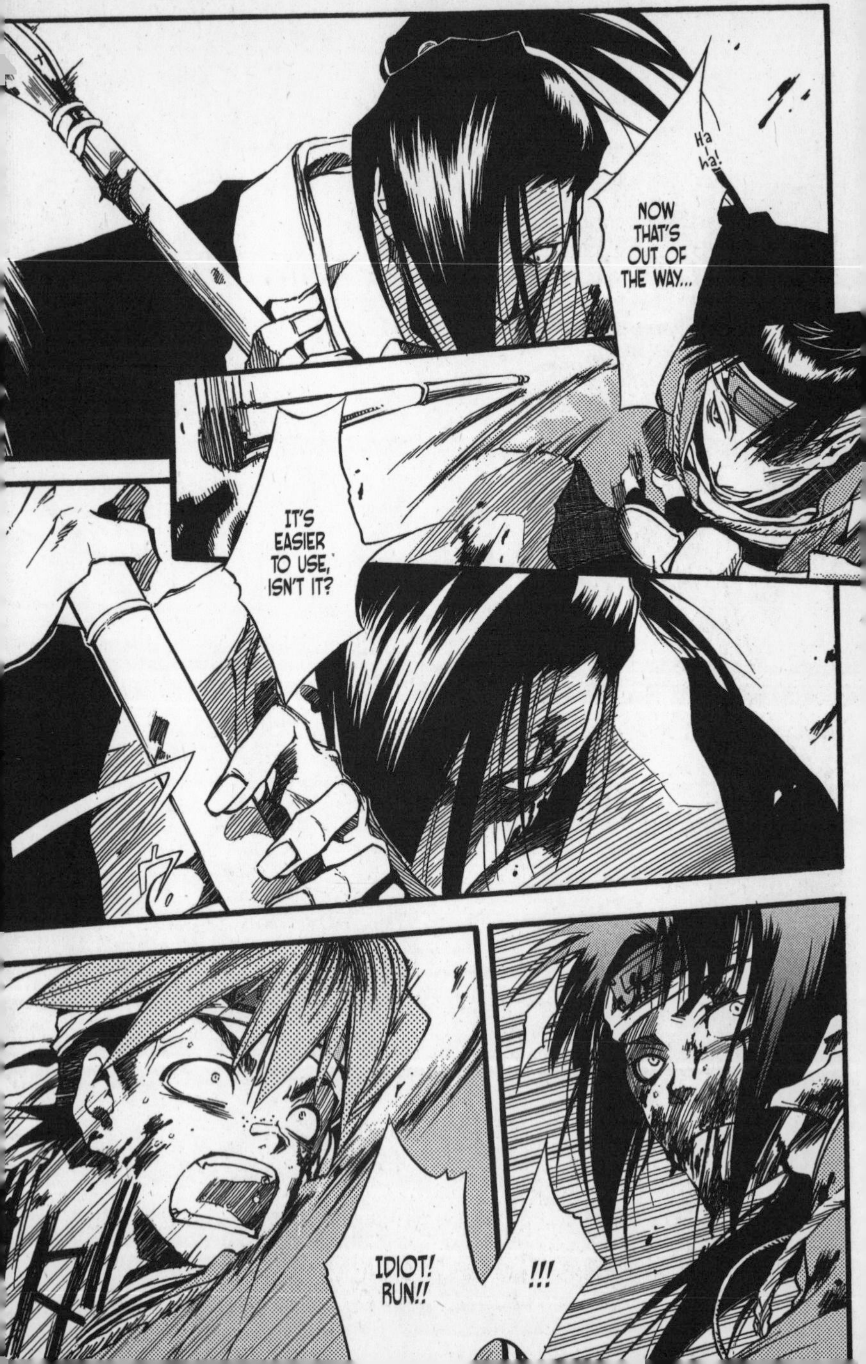
Ha ha!
NOW THAT'S OUT OF THE WAY...
IT'S EASIER TO USE, ISN'T IT?
!!!
IDIOT! RUN!!

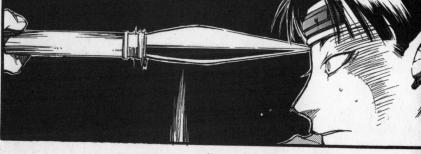

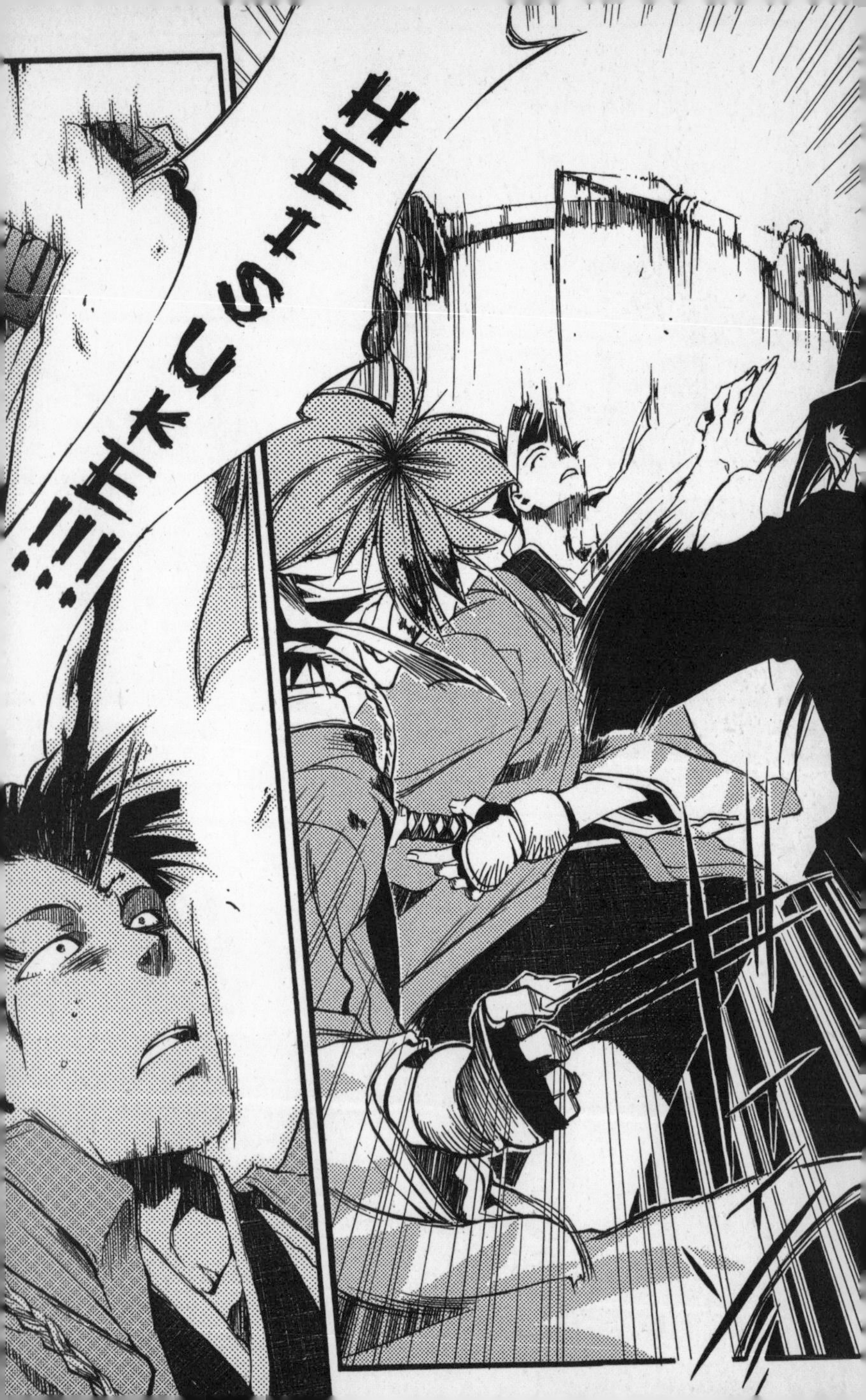
HEISUKE!!!

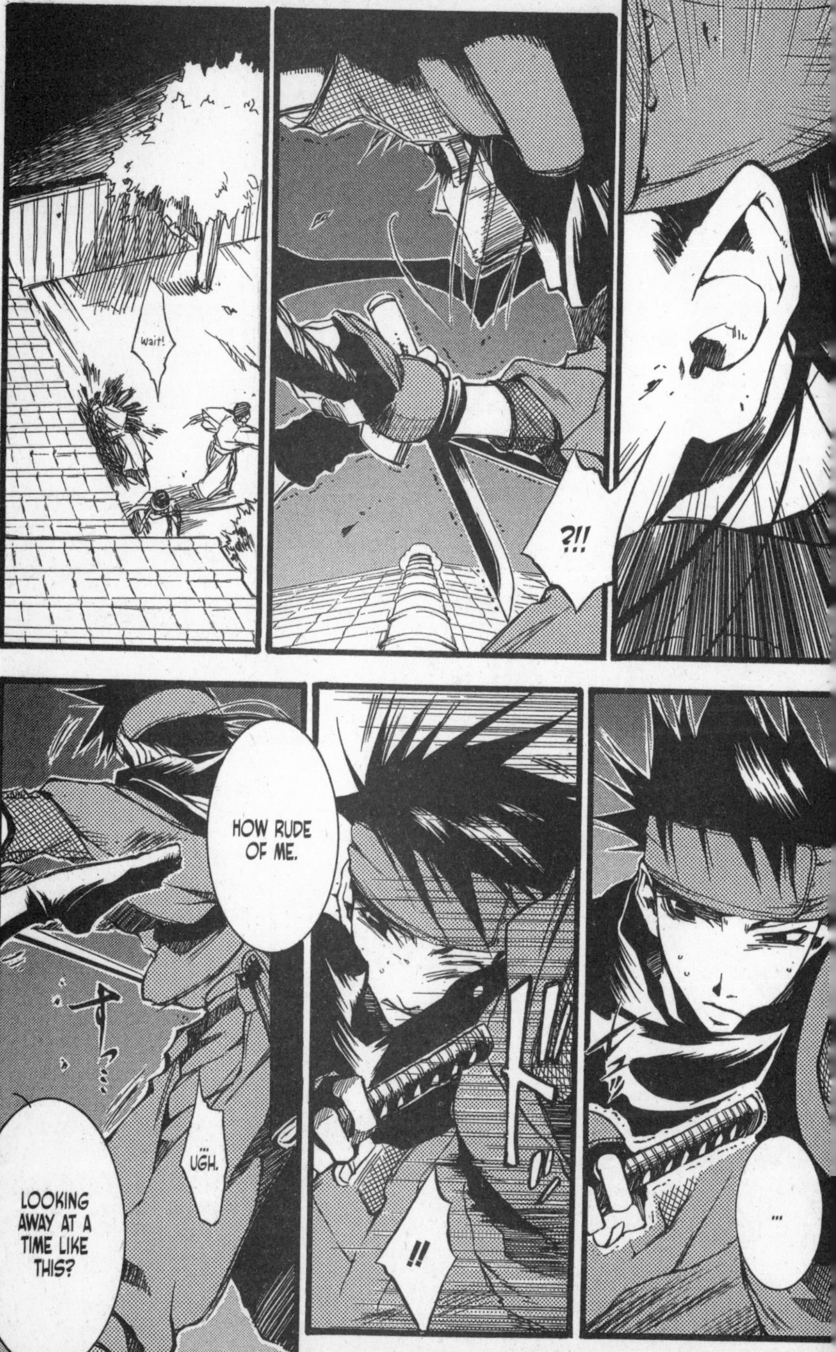
?!!
wait!
...
HOW RUDE OF ME.
!!
...UGH.
LOOKING AWAY AT A TIME LIKE THIS?

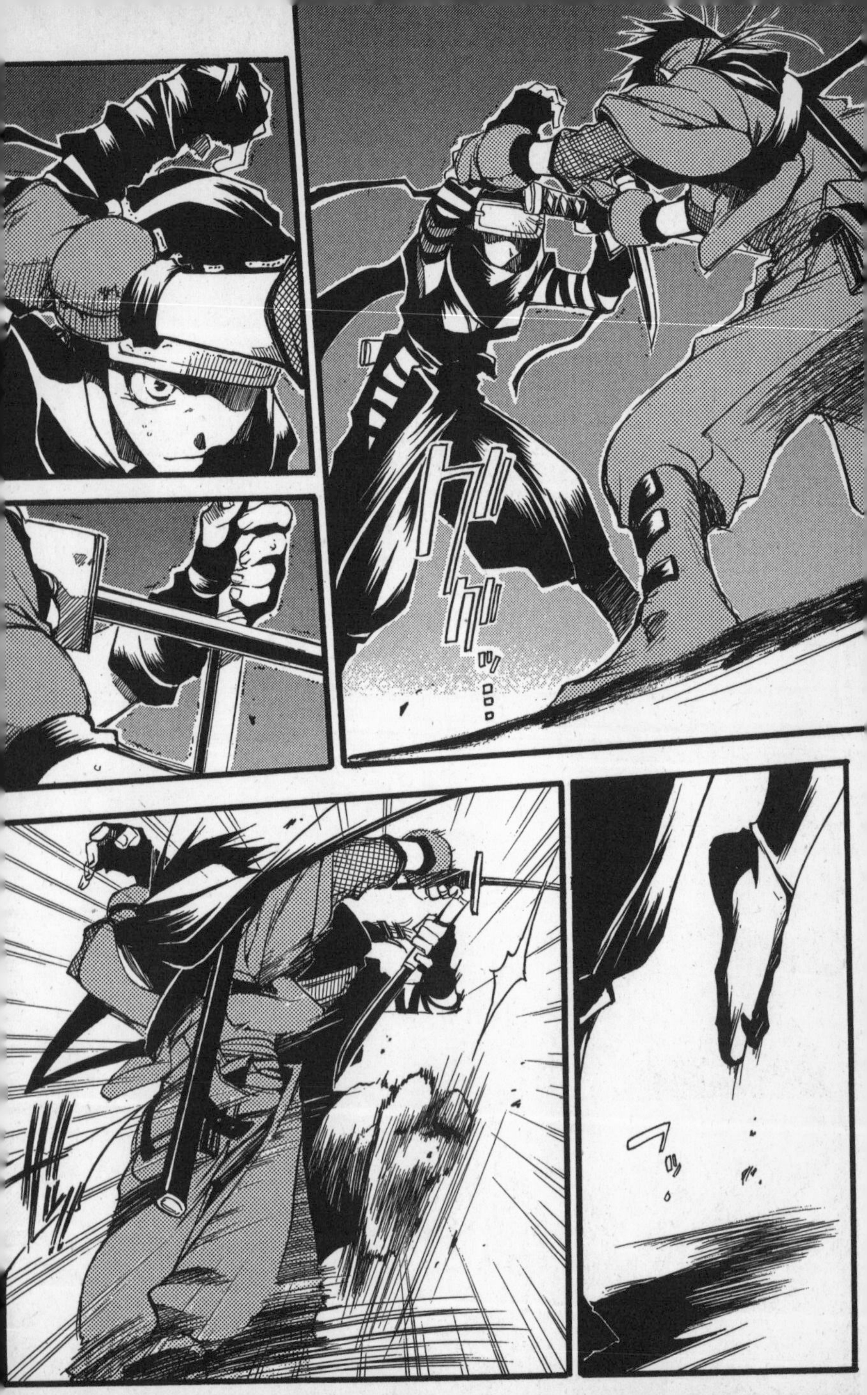

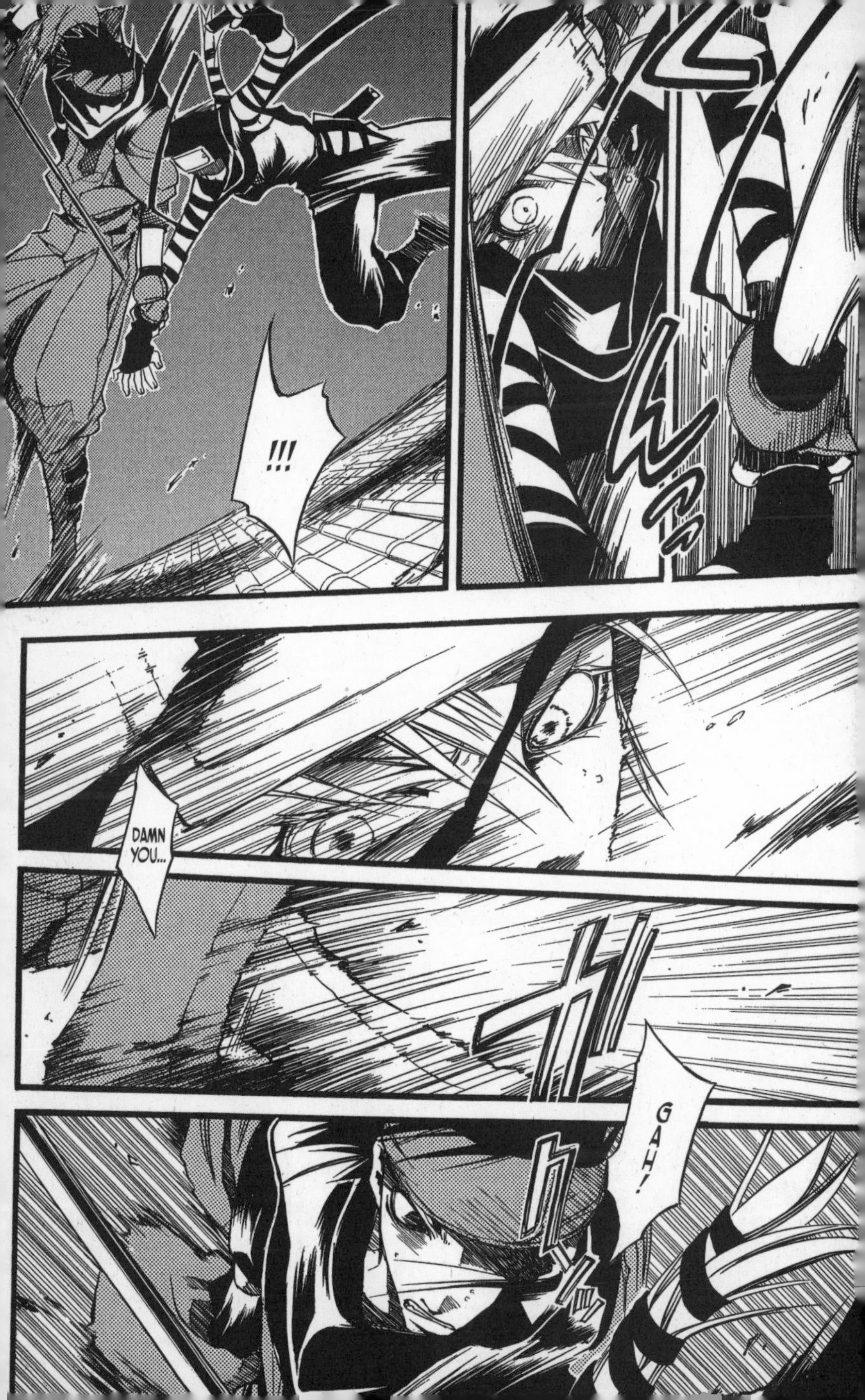
!!!
DAMN YOU...
GAH!

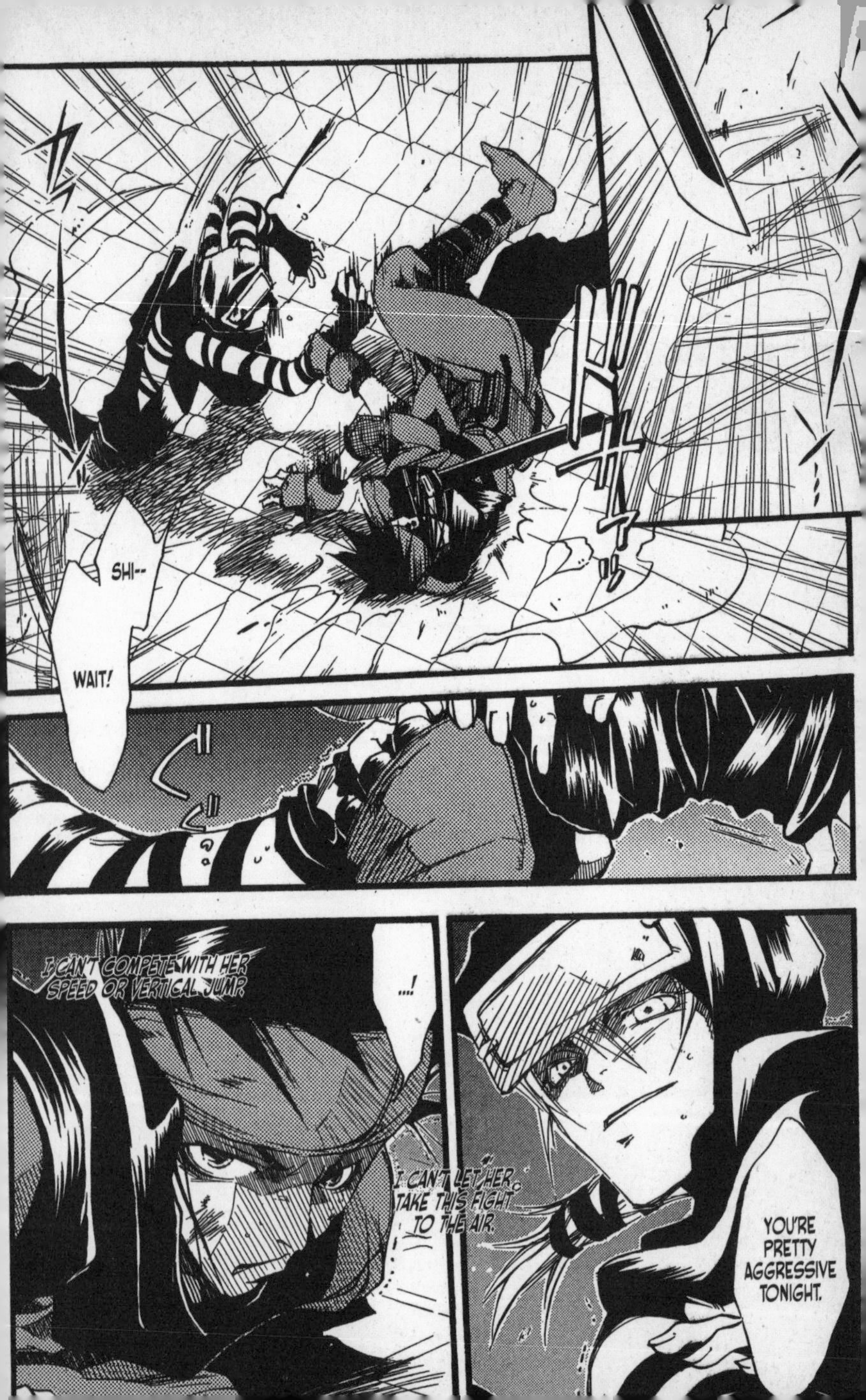
SHI--
WAIT!
YOU'RE PRETTY AGGRESSIVE TONIGHT.
I CAN'T COMPETE WITH HER SPEED OR VERTICAL JUMP.
...!
I CAN'T LET HER TAKE THIS FIGHT TO THE AIR.

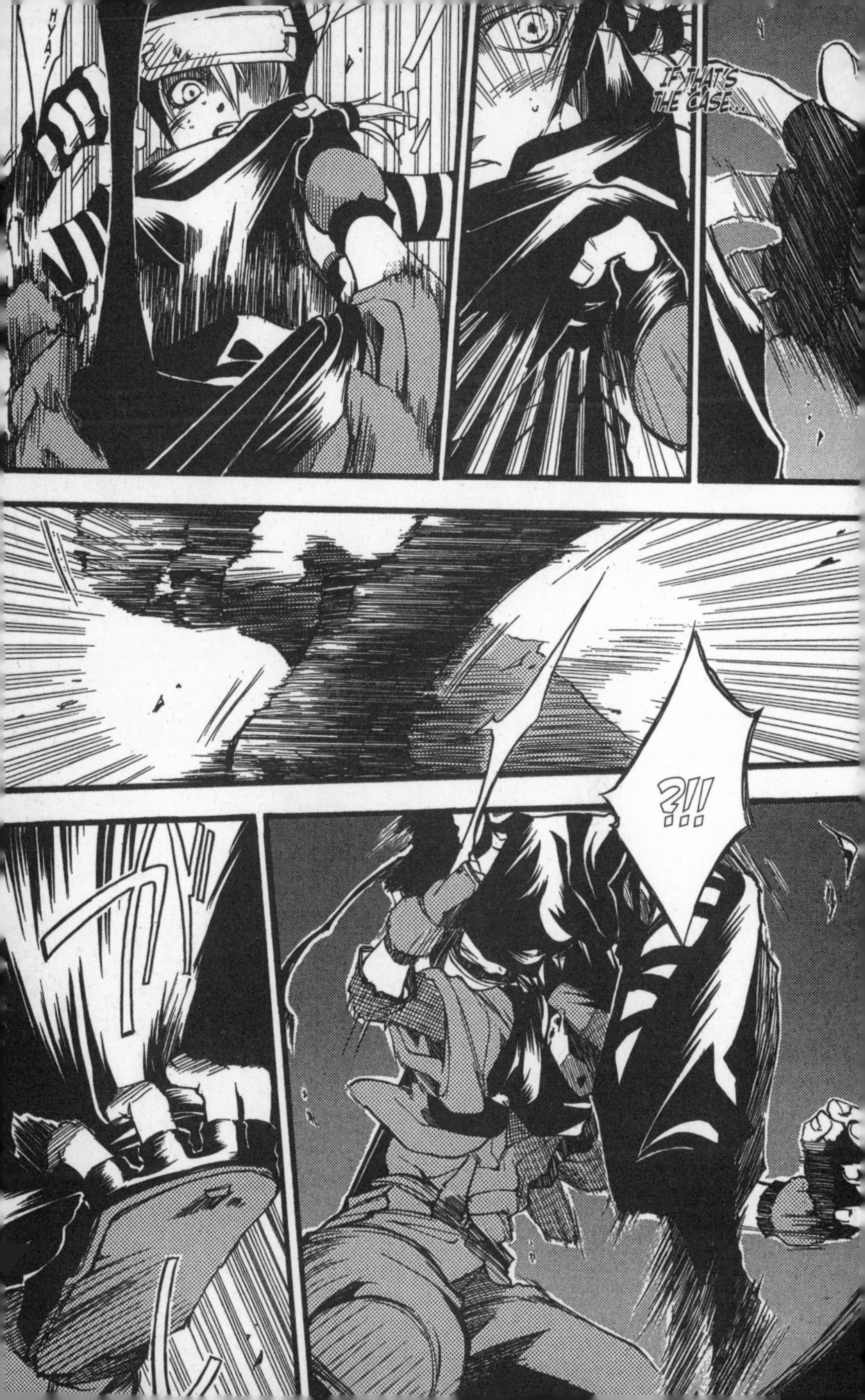
IF THAT'S THE CASE...
HYA!
?!!

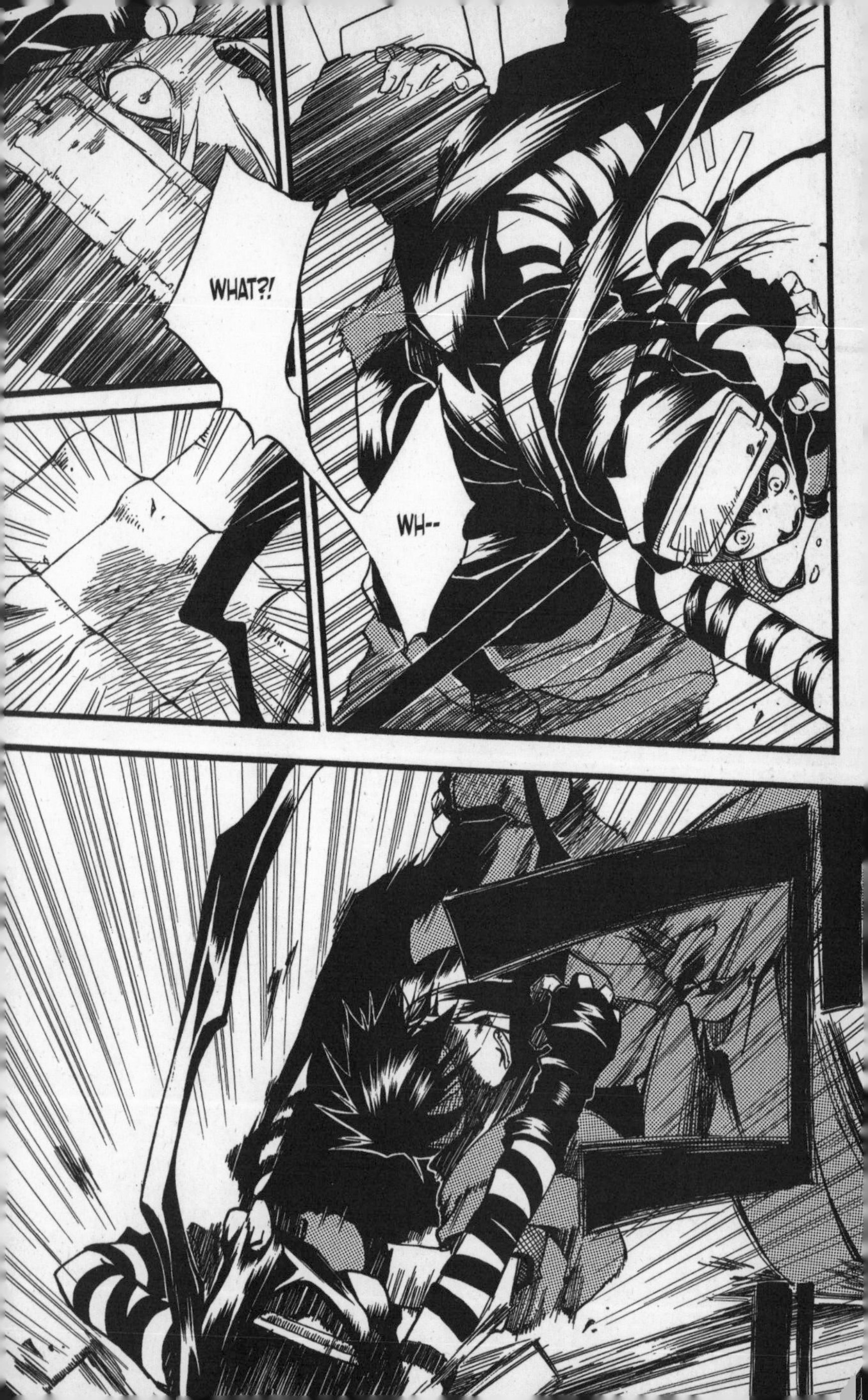
WH--
WHAT?!

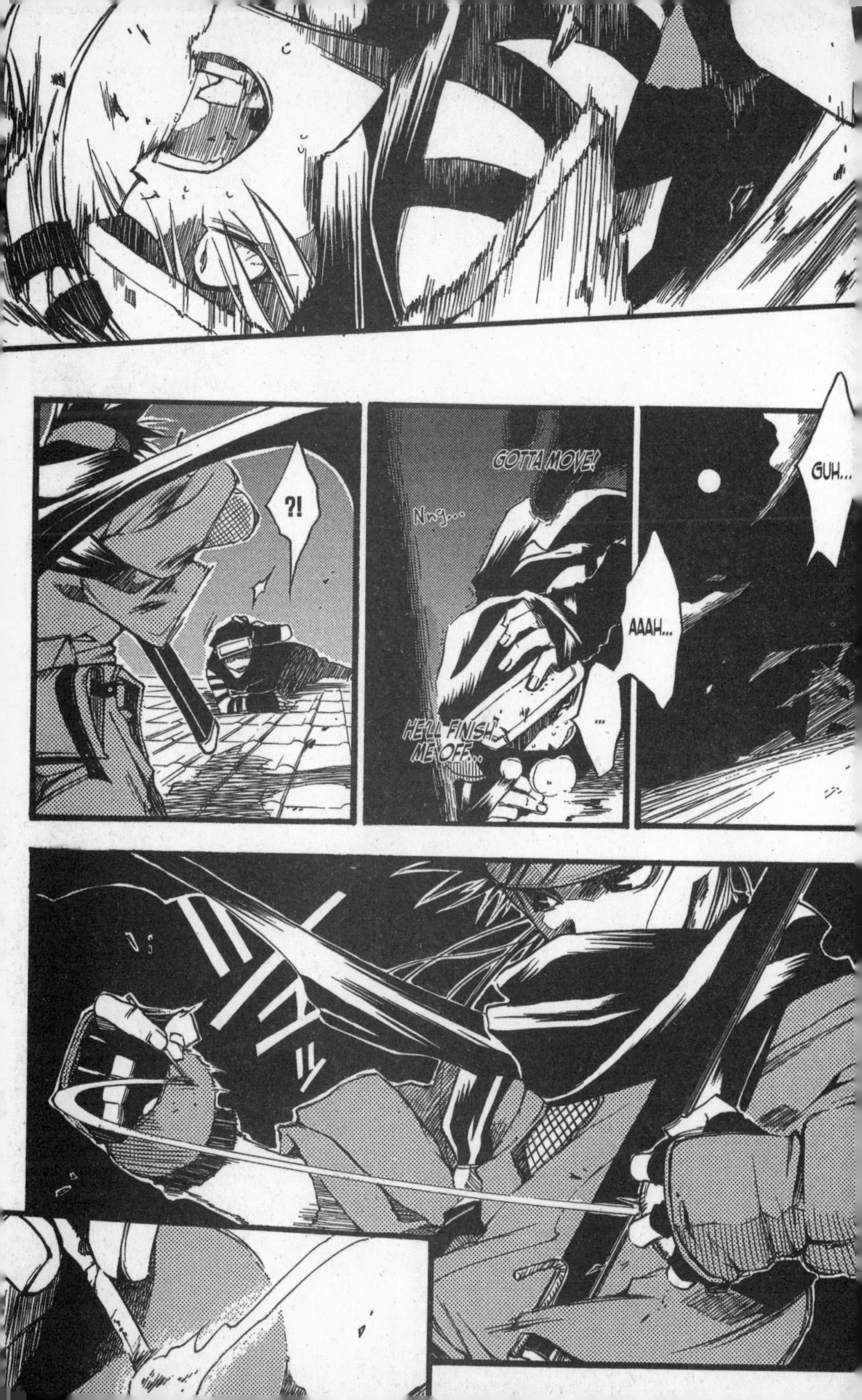
GUH...
AAAH...
GOTTA MOVE!
Nng...
...
HE'LL FINISH ME OFF...
?!

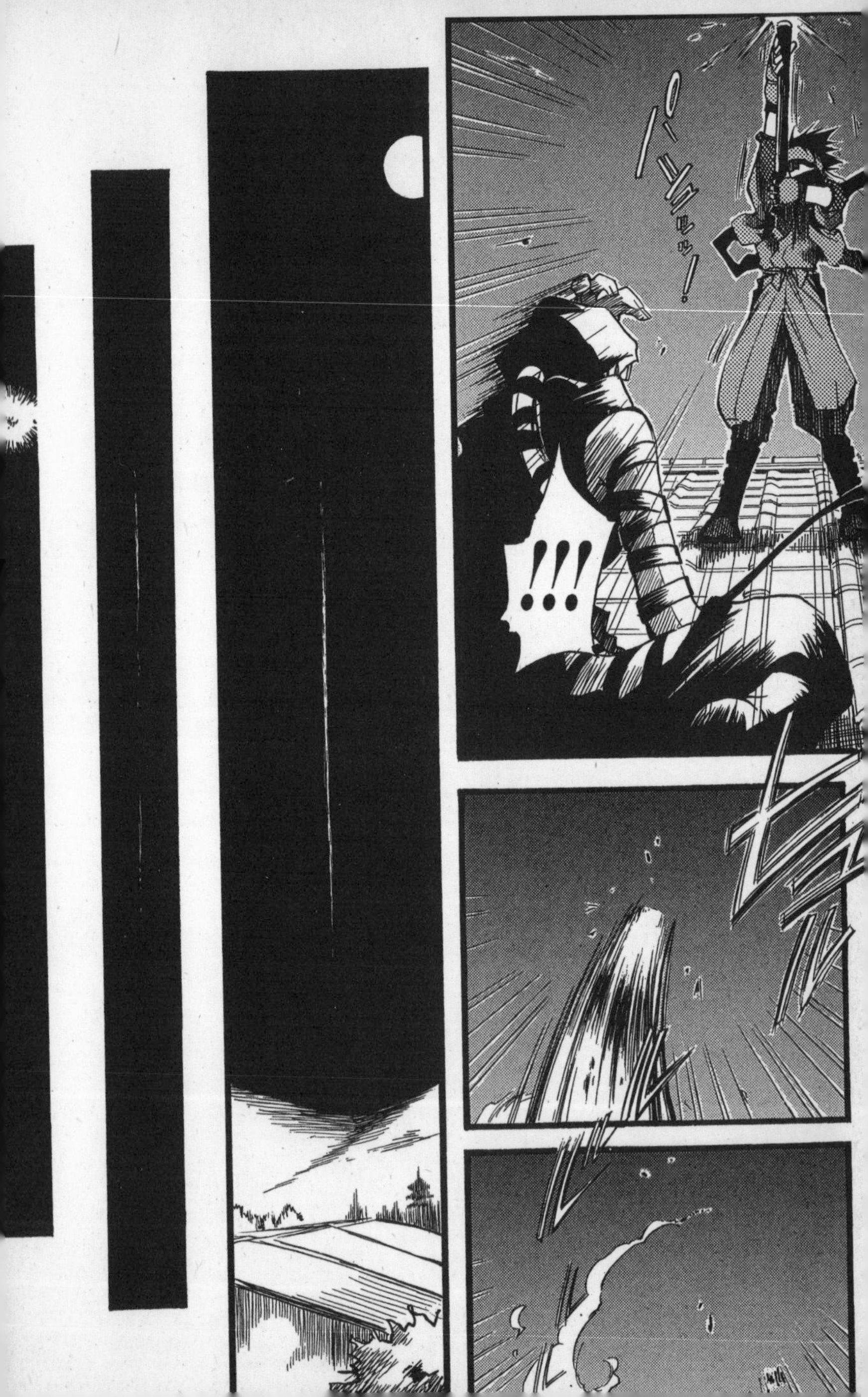
パシュッ!
!!!

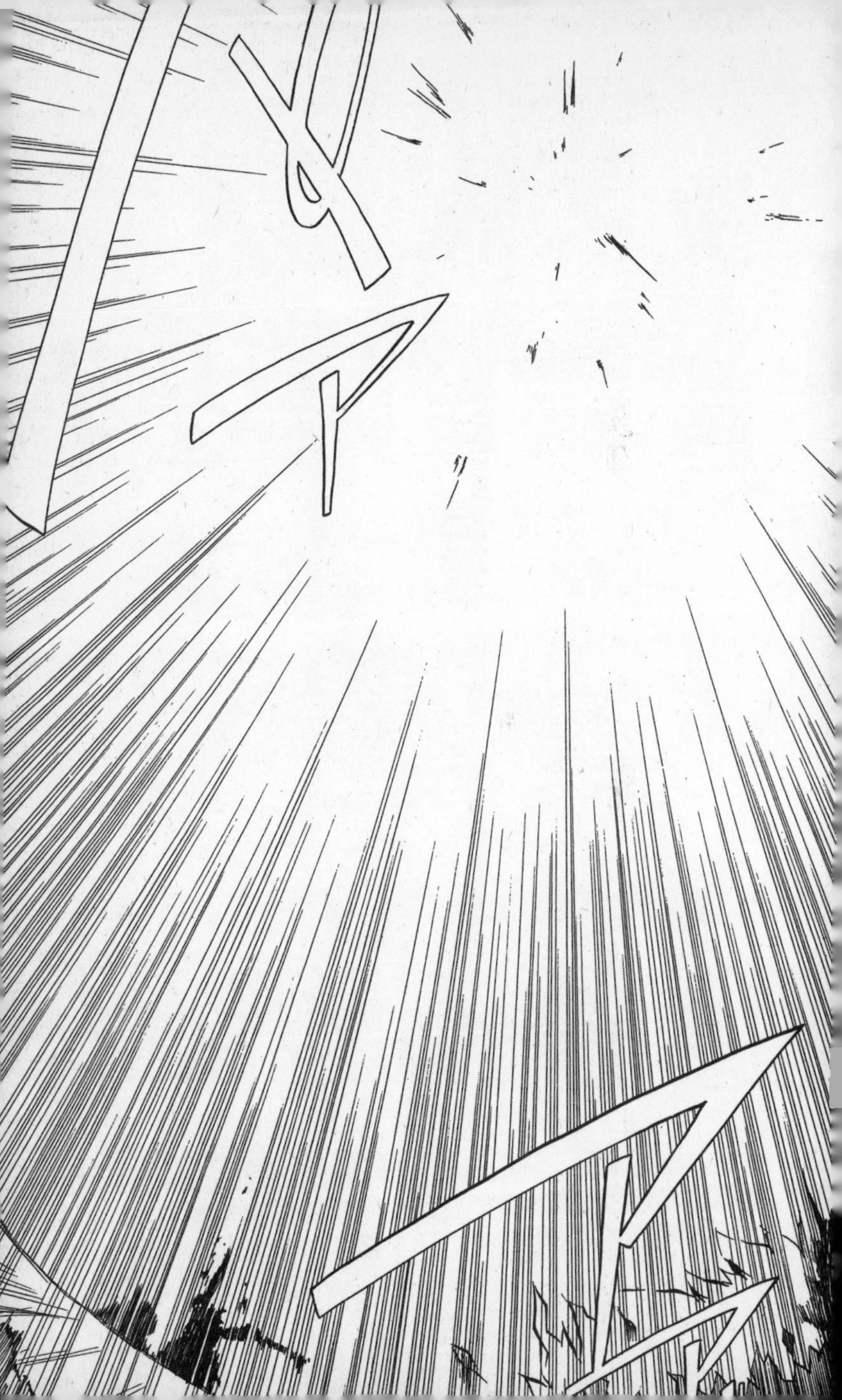

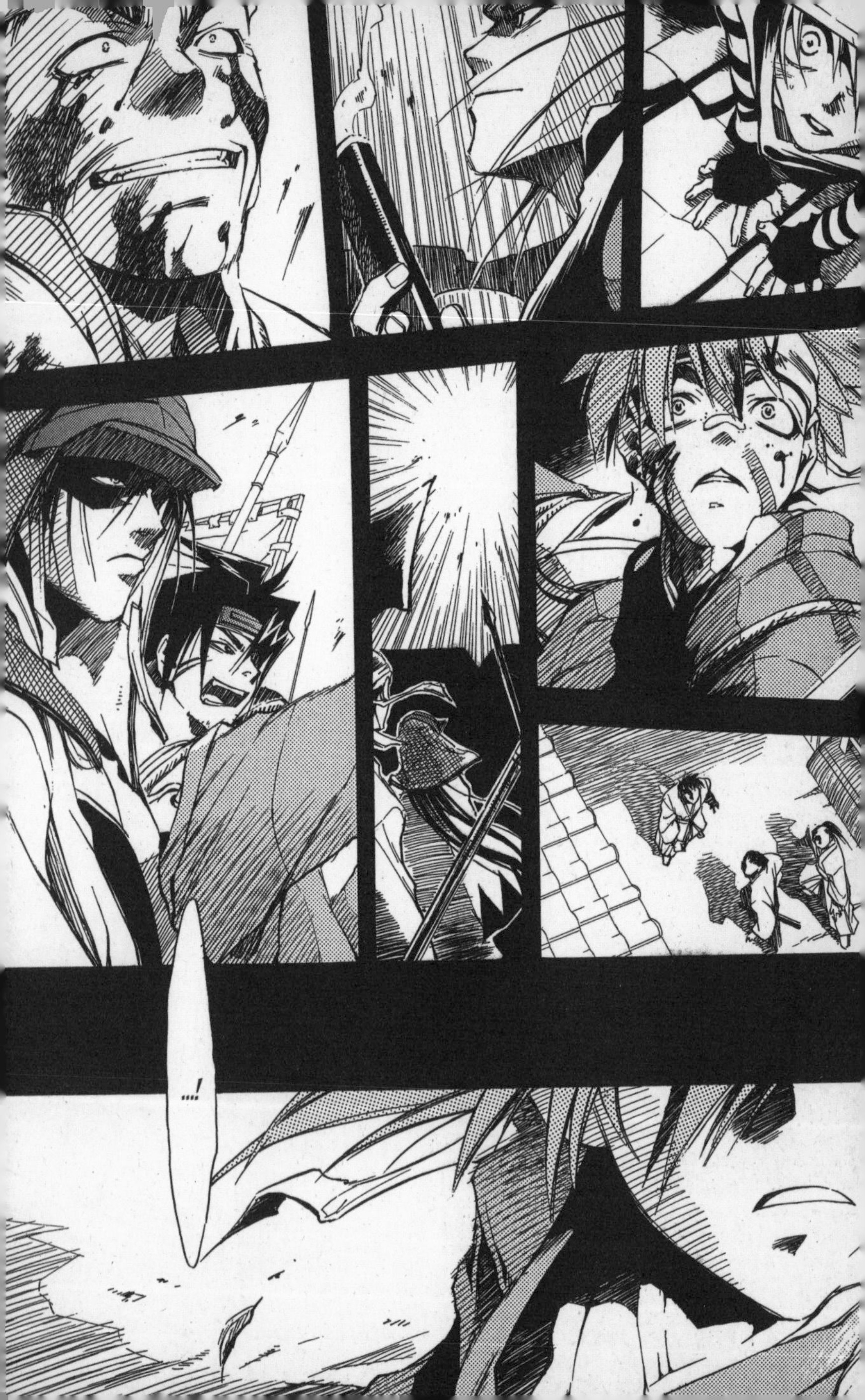
...!

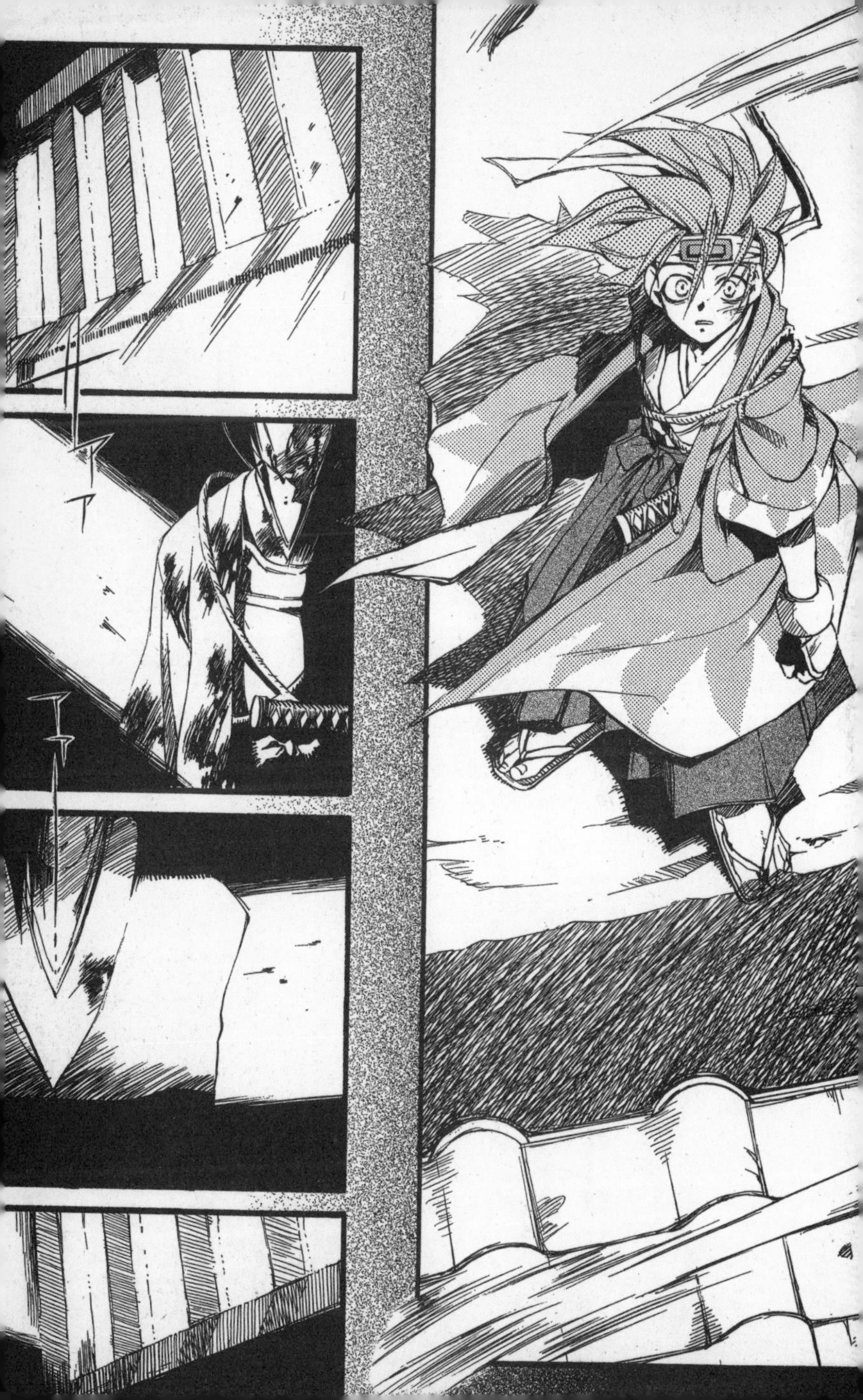

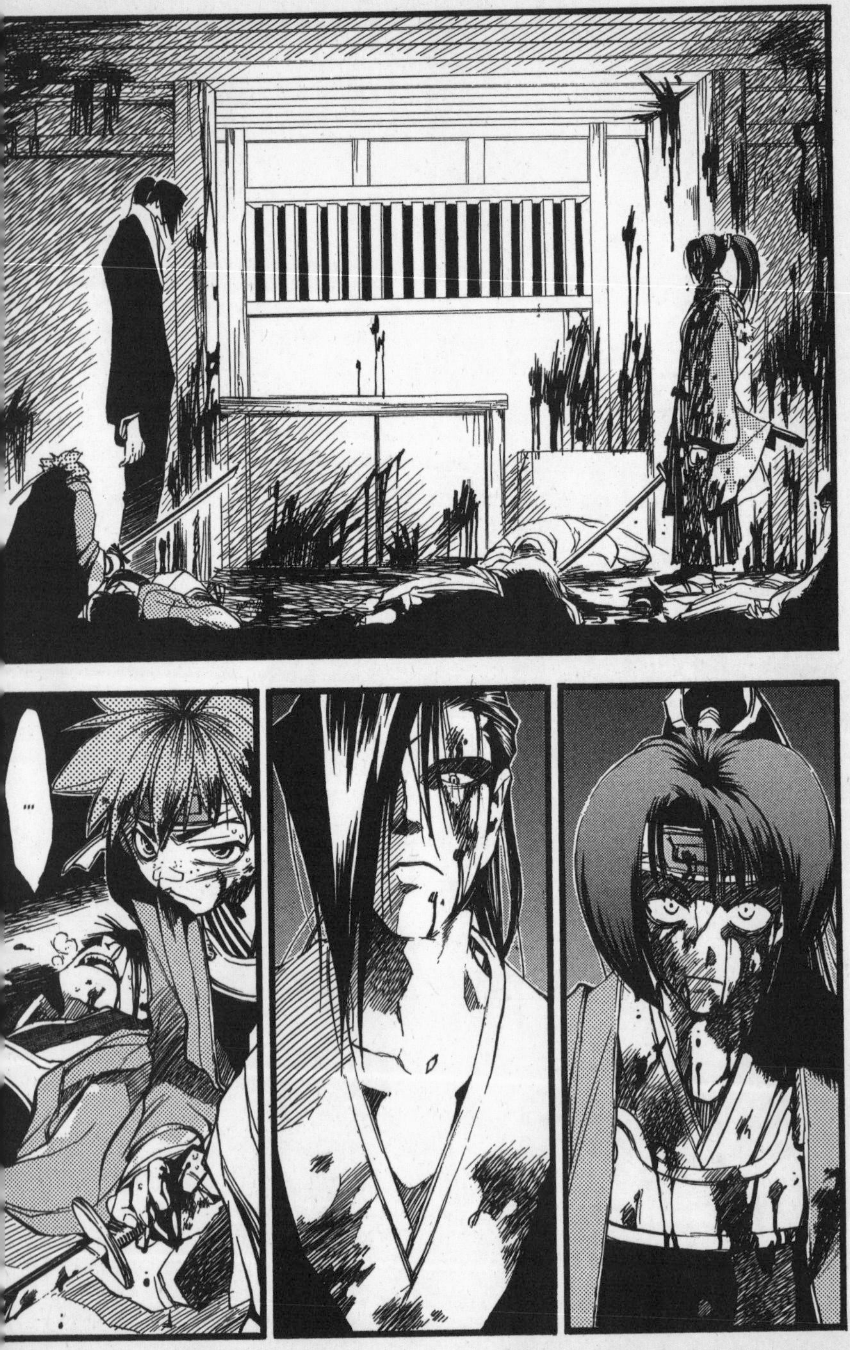
...

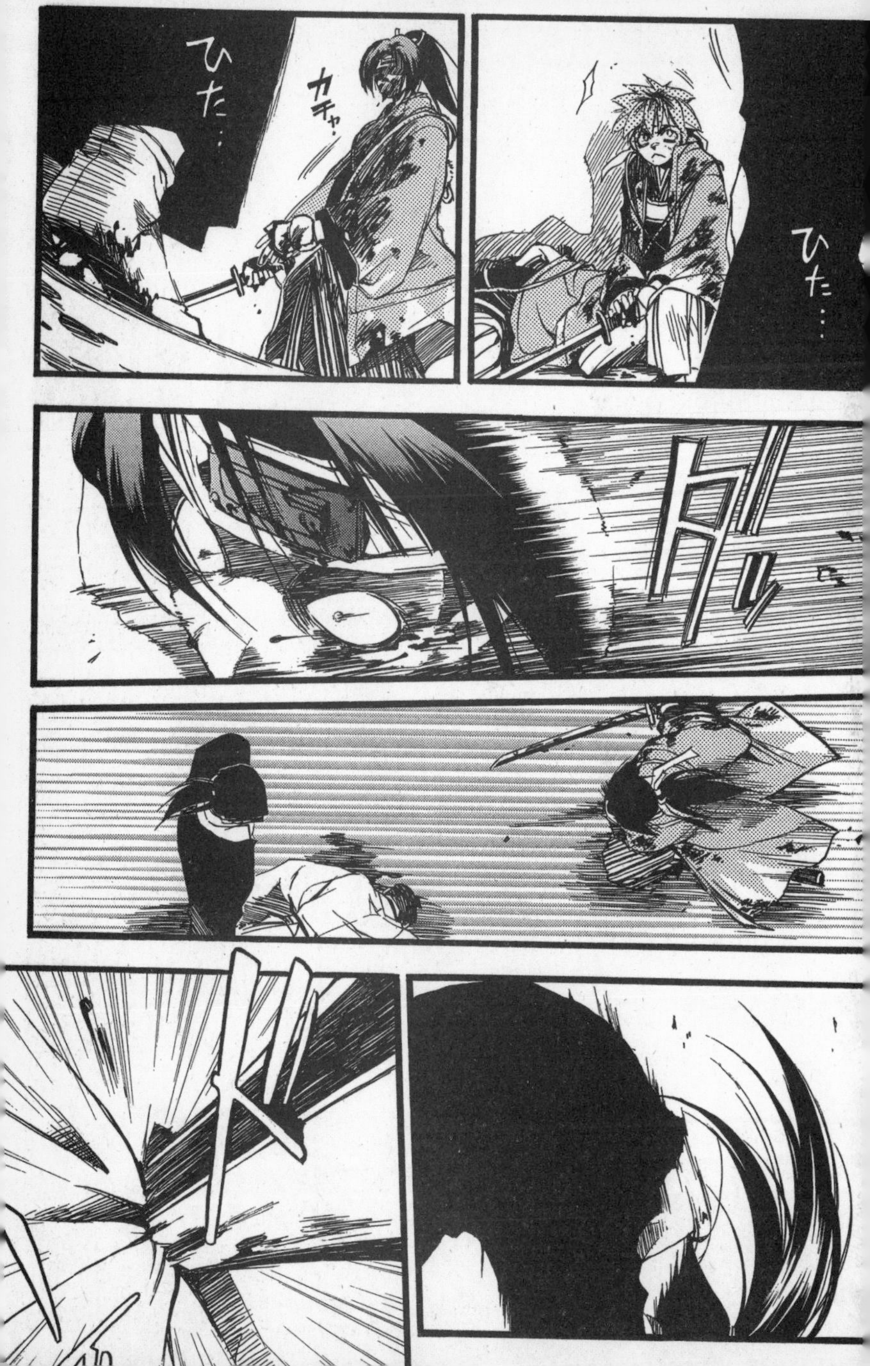
ひた…
カチャ
ひた…
ダッ

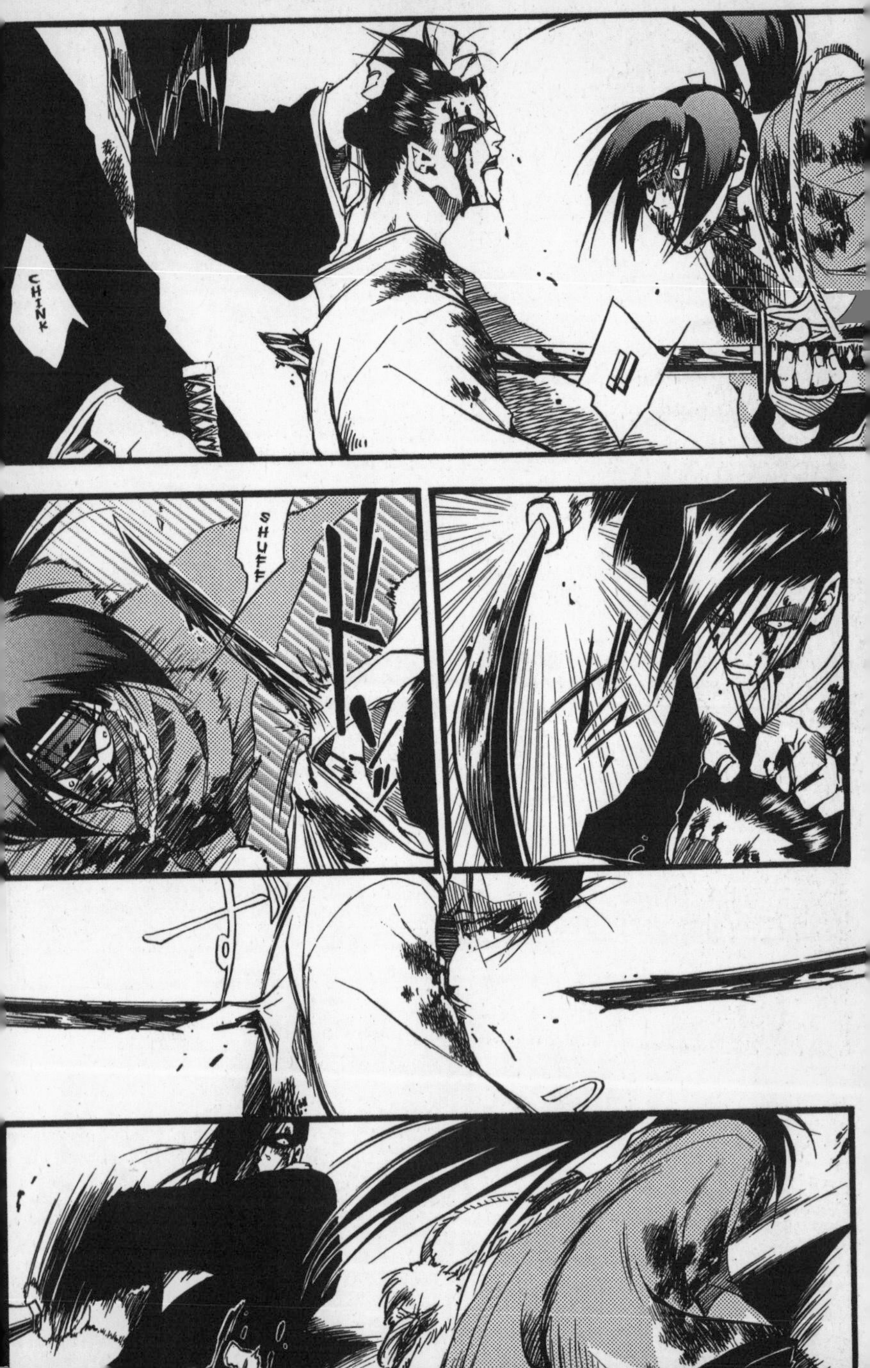
CHINK
SHUFF

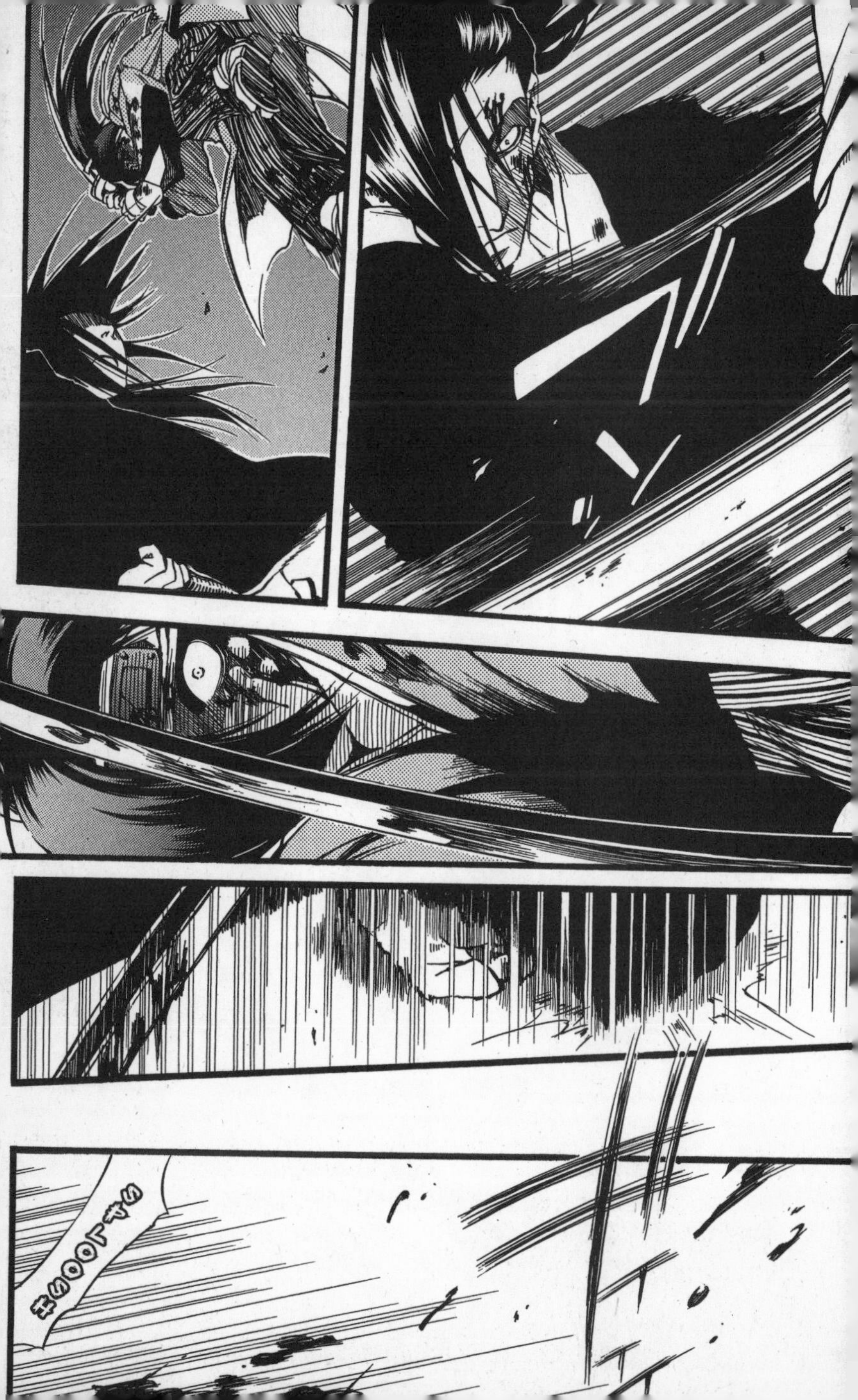

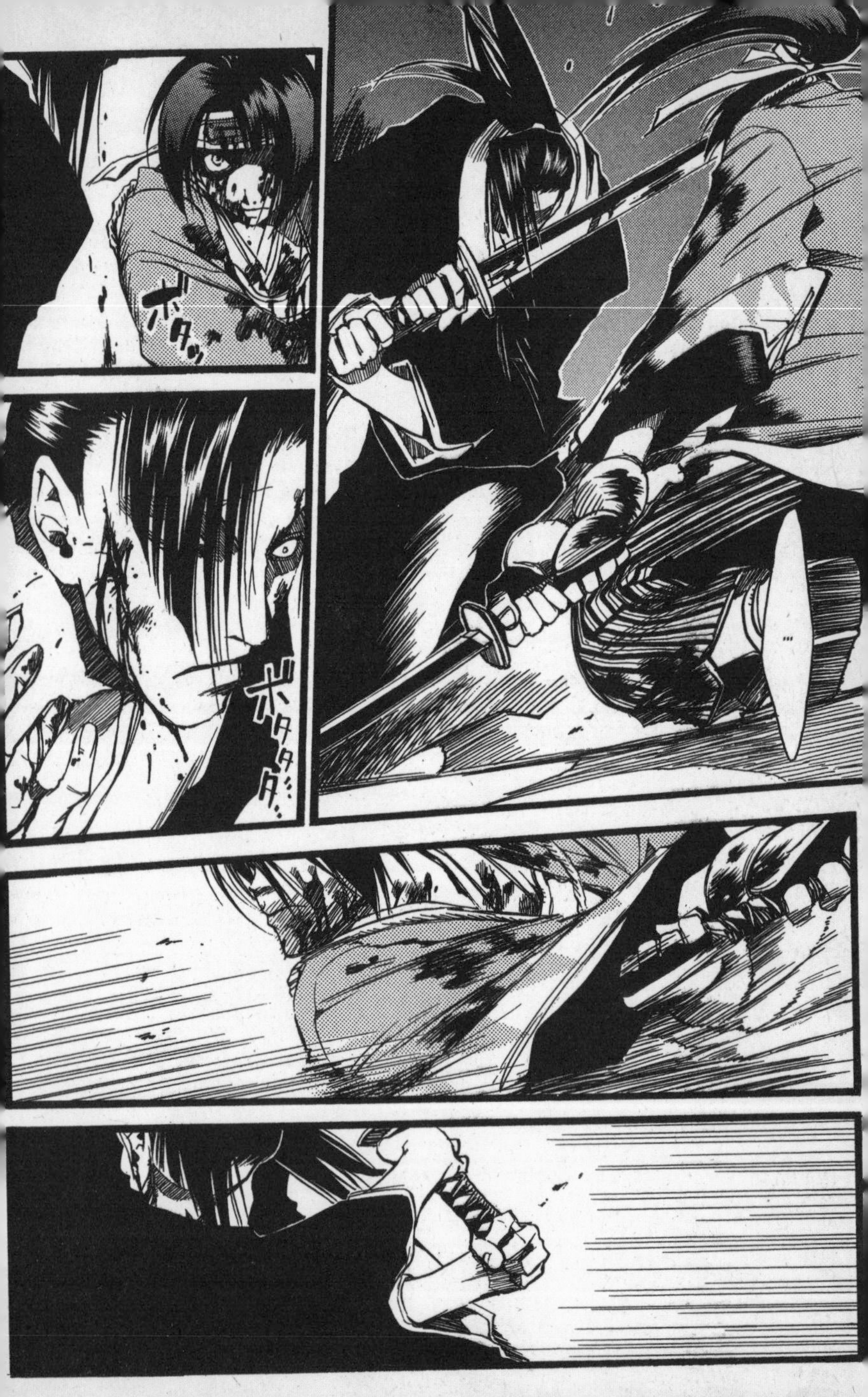
ボタッ
ボタタタ…

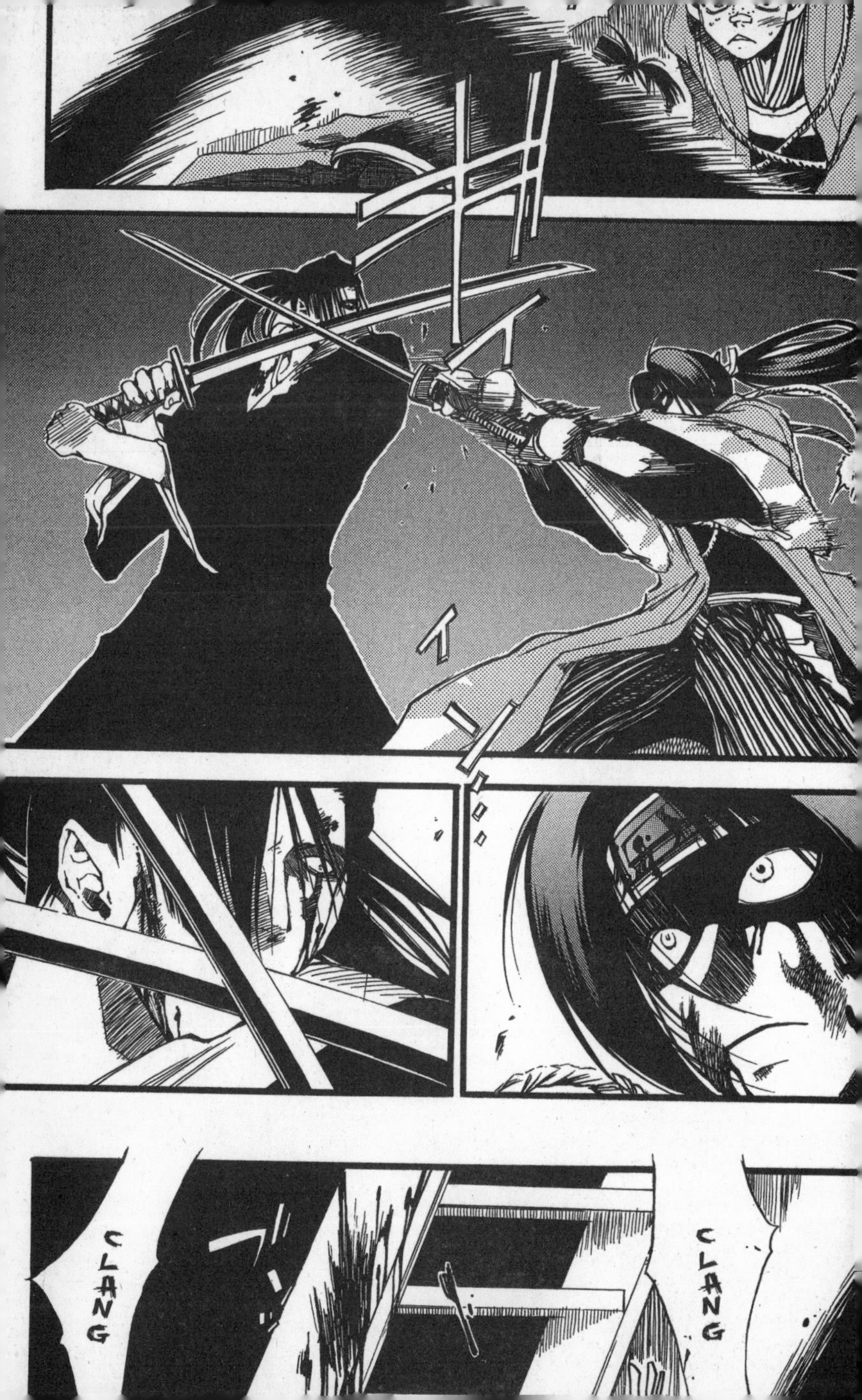
CLANG
CLANG

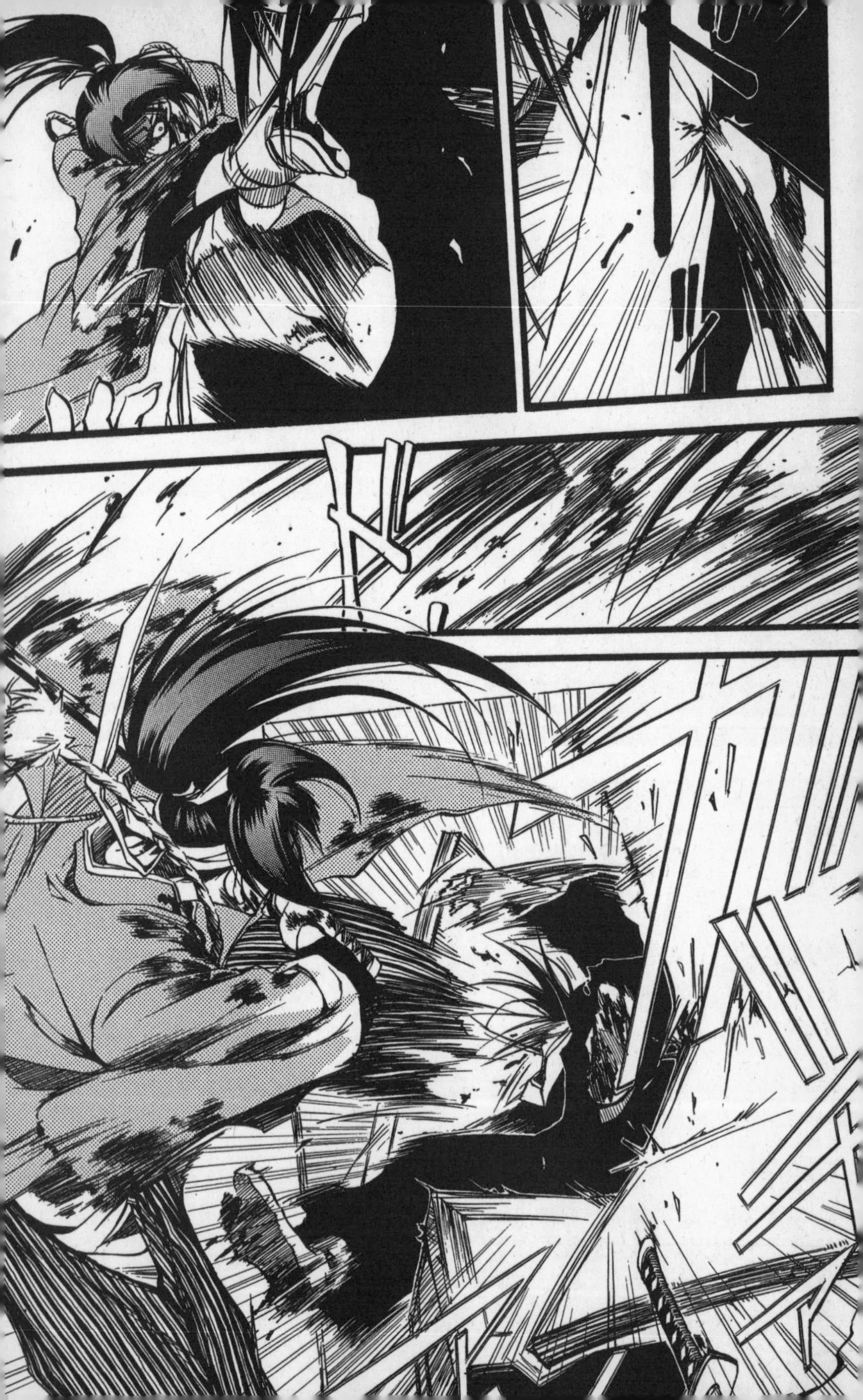

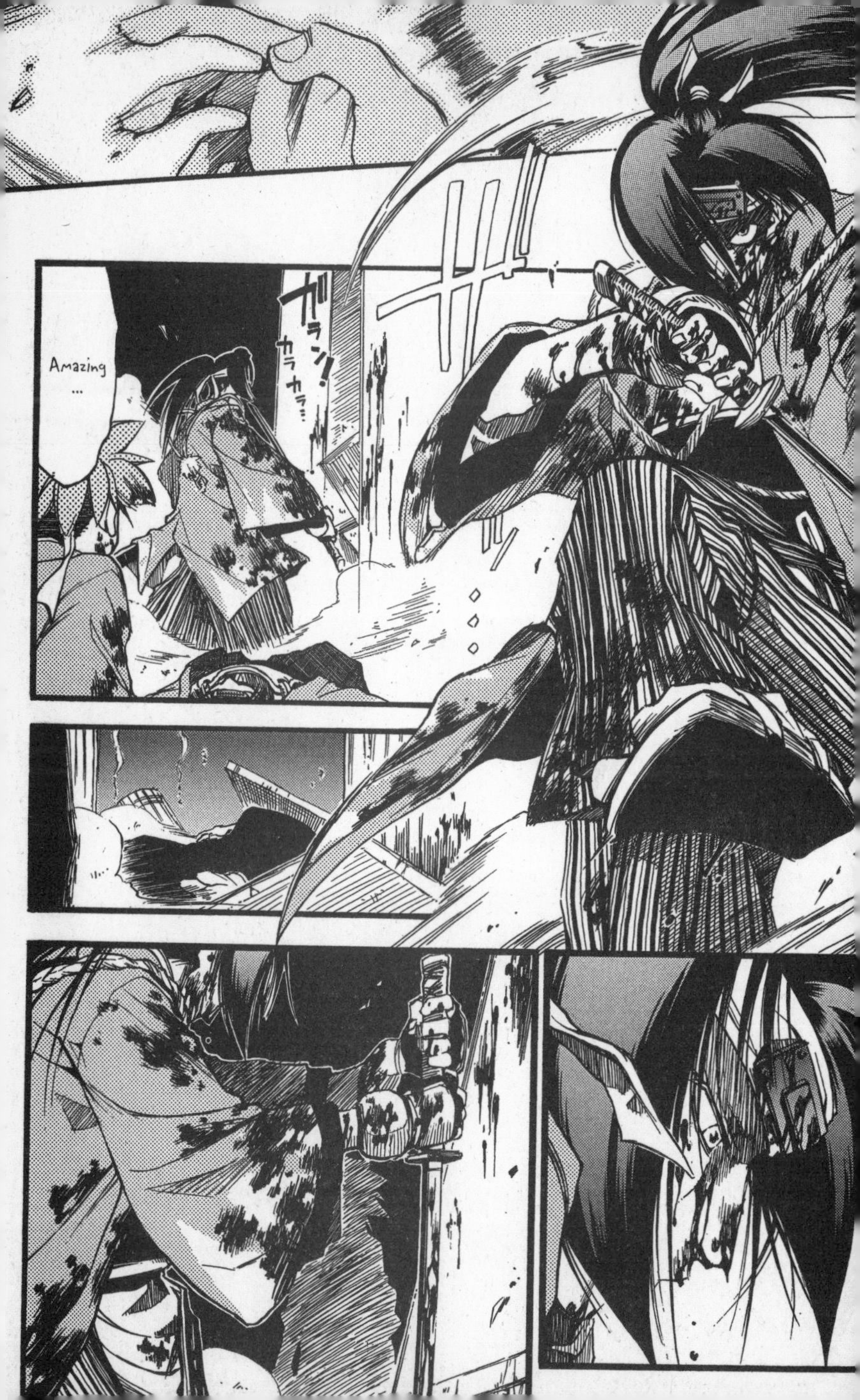
ガラン!!
カラカラ…
Amazing ...

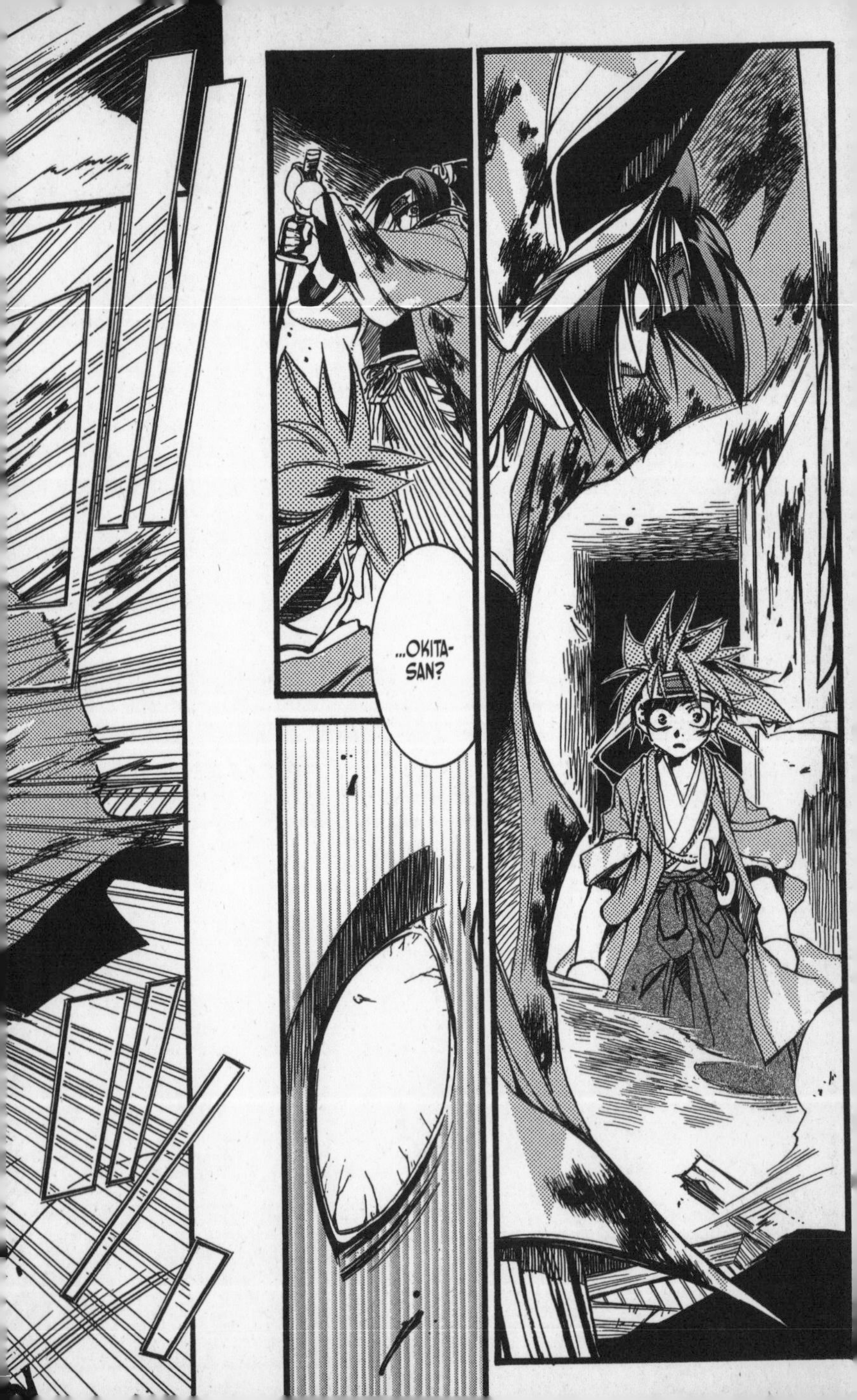
...OKITA-SAN?

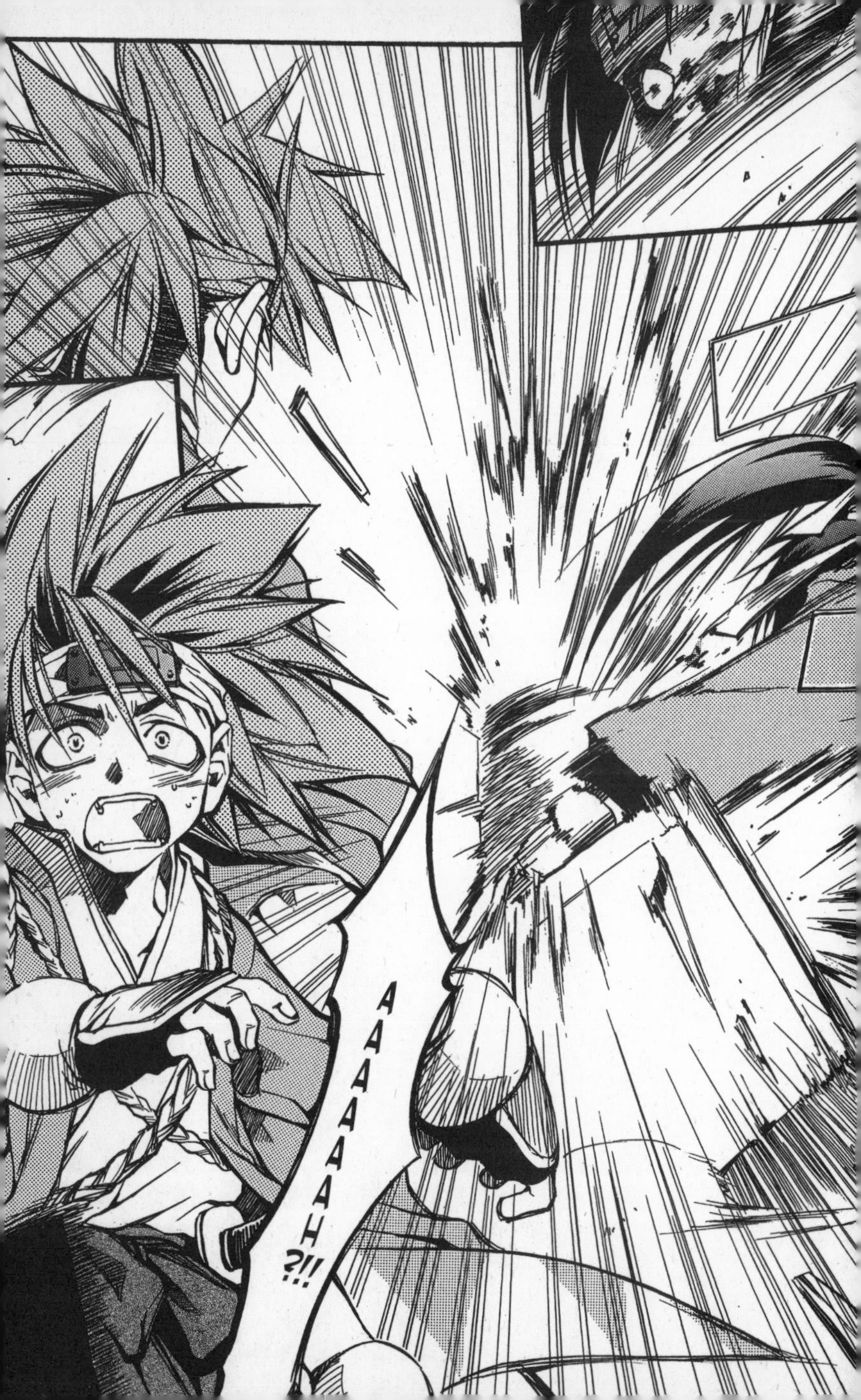
AAAAAAAAH?!!

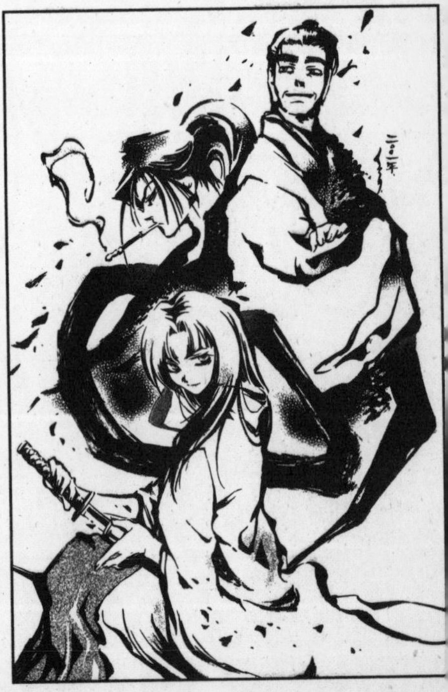
二〇〇一年

Act.26
A Hard Day's Night (Scene 3)

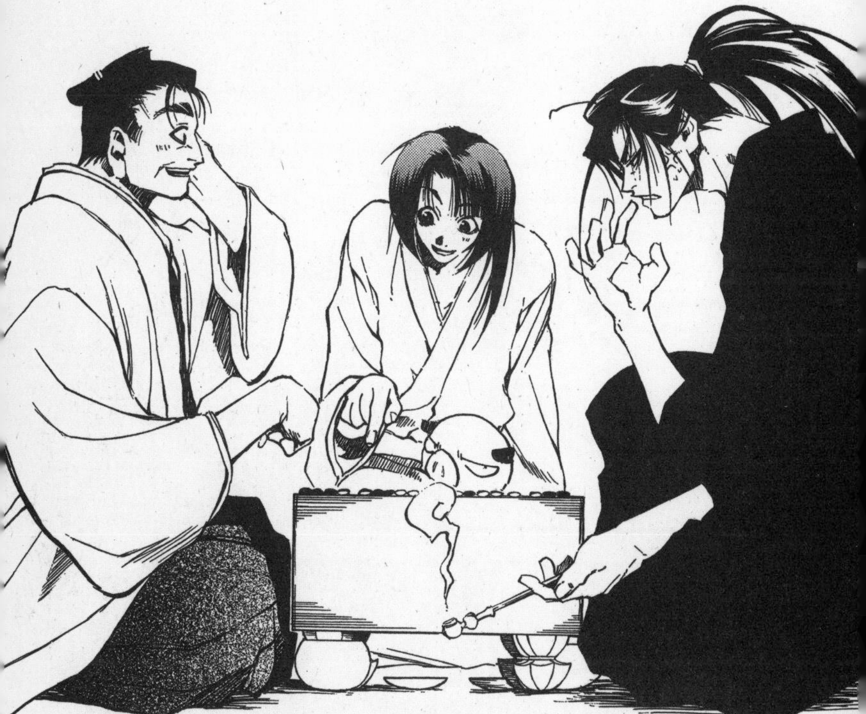

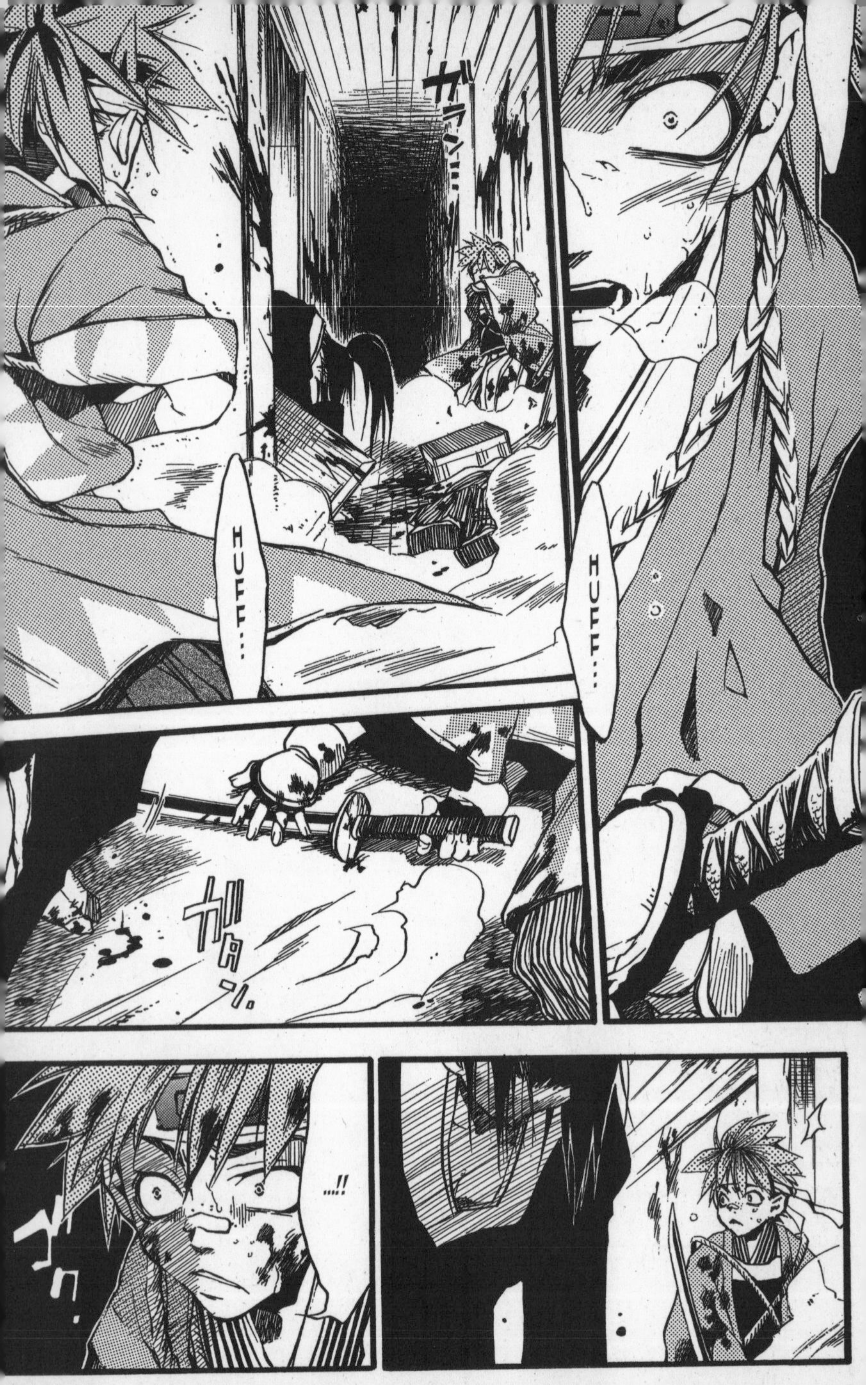
HUFF...
ガラン…
HUFF...
カタッ
...!!

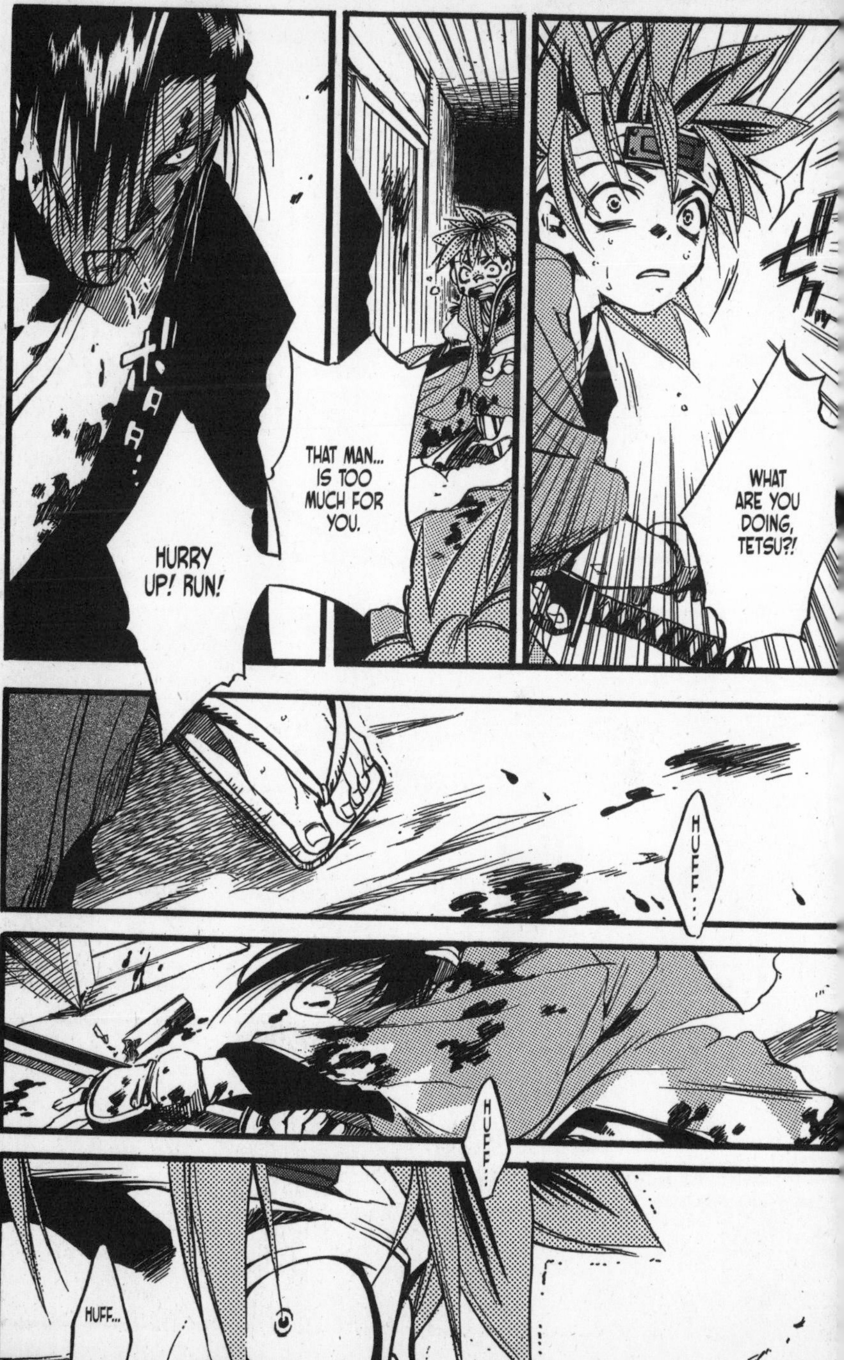
WHAT ARE YOU DOING, TETSU?!
THAT MAN... IS TOO MUCH FOR YOU.
HURRY UP! RUN!
HUFF...
HUFF...
HUFF...

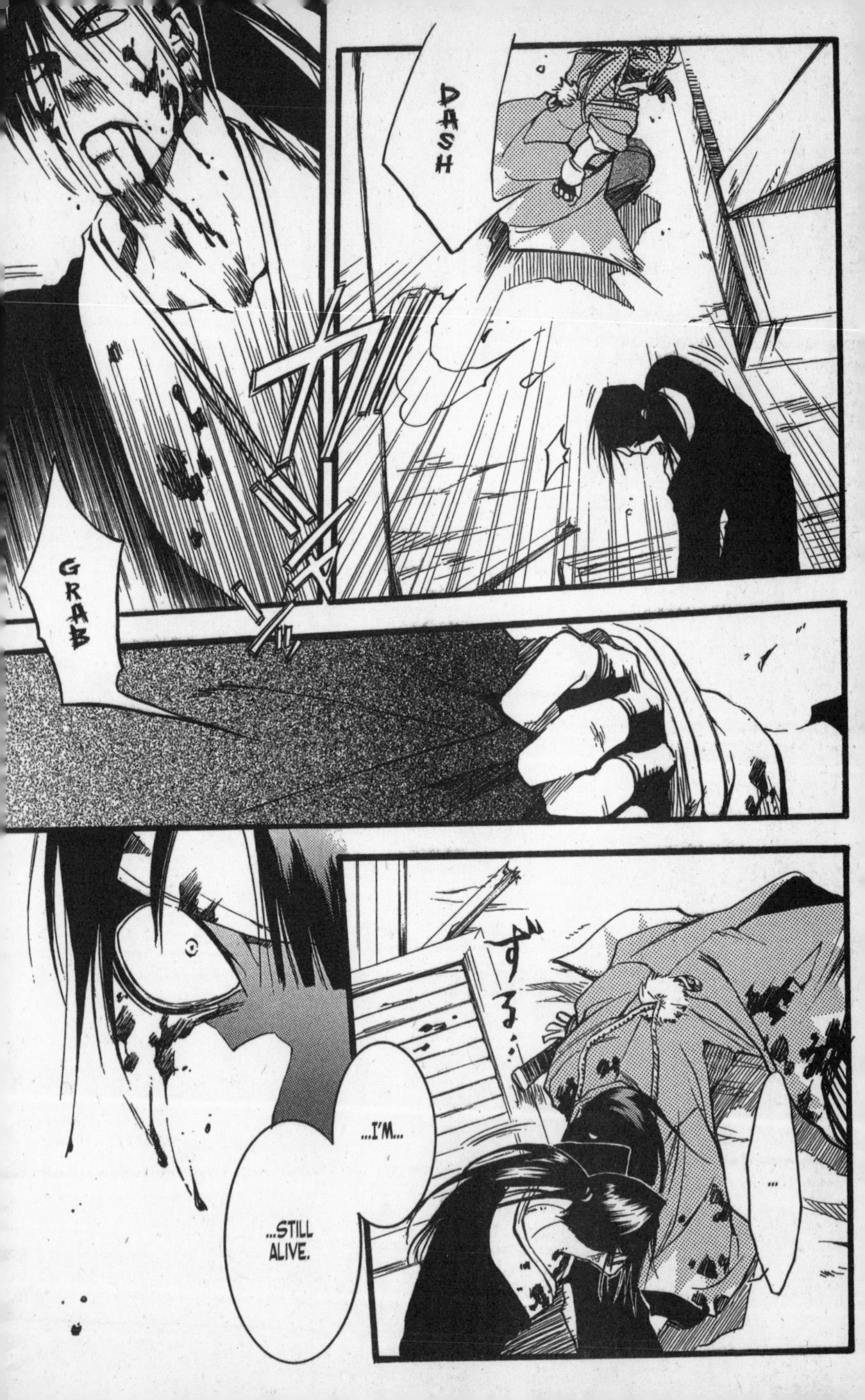
DASH
GRAB
...
...I'M...
...STILL ALIVE.

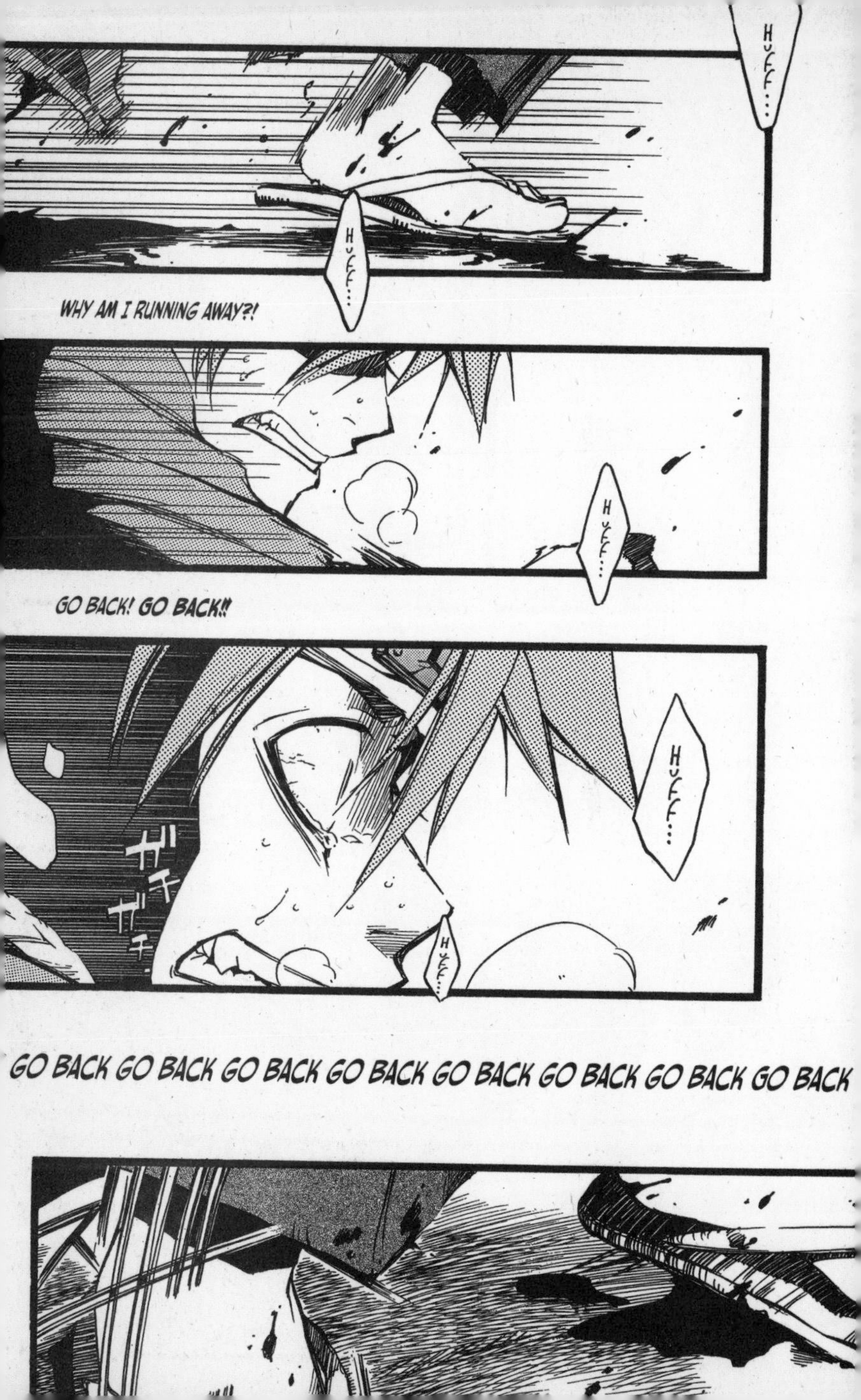
HUFF...
HUFF...
WHY AM I RUNNING AWAY?!
HUFF...
GO BACK! GO BACK!!
HUFF...
HUFF...
ガチガチ
GO BACK GO BACK GO BACK GO BACK GO BACK GO BACK GO BACK GO BACK

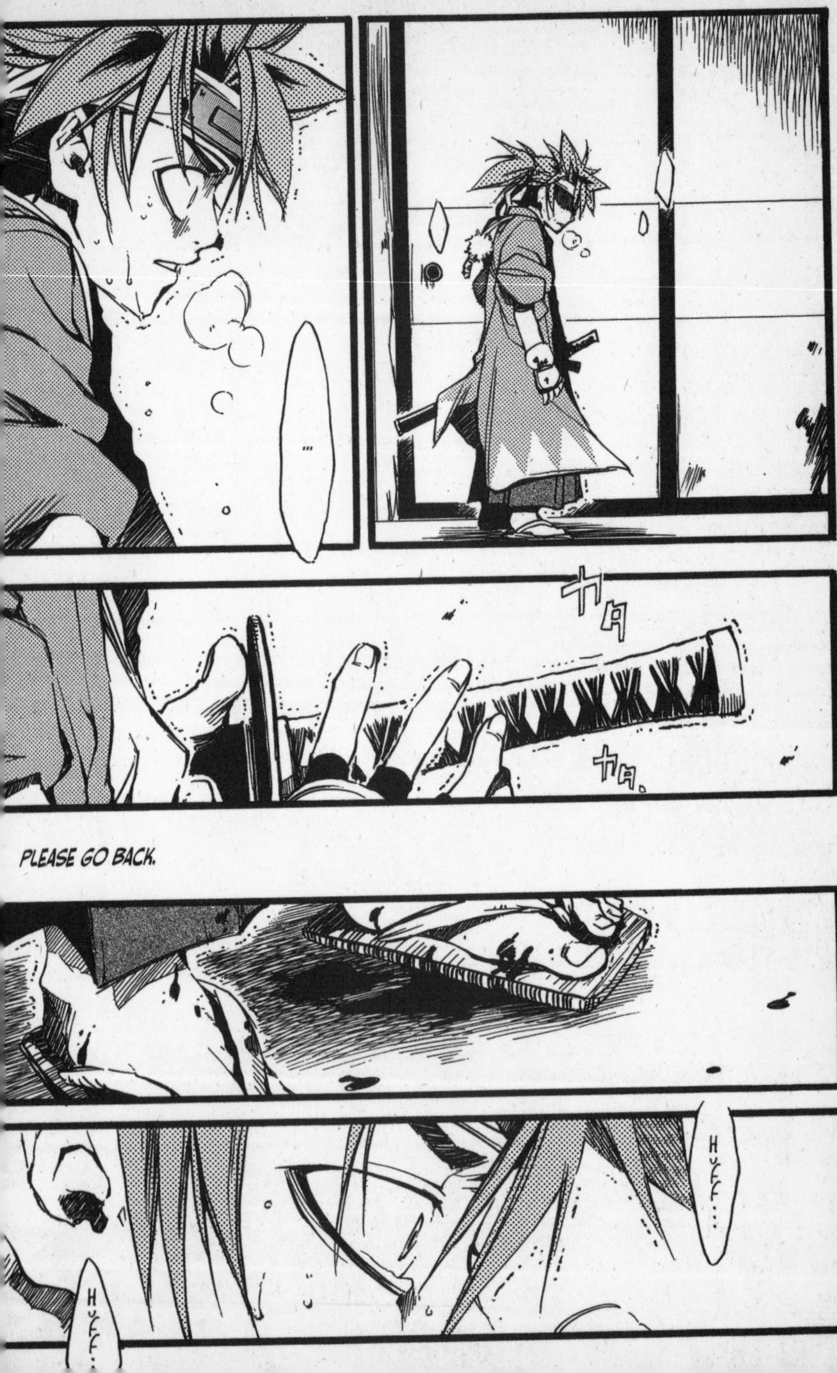
...
カタ
カタ。
PLEASE GO BACK.
HUFF...
HUFF...

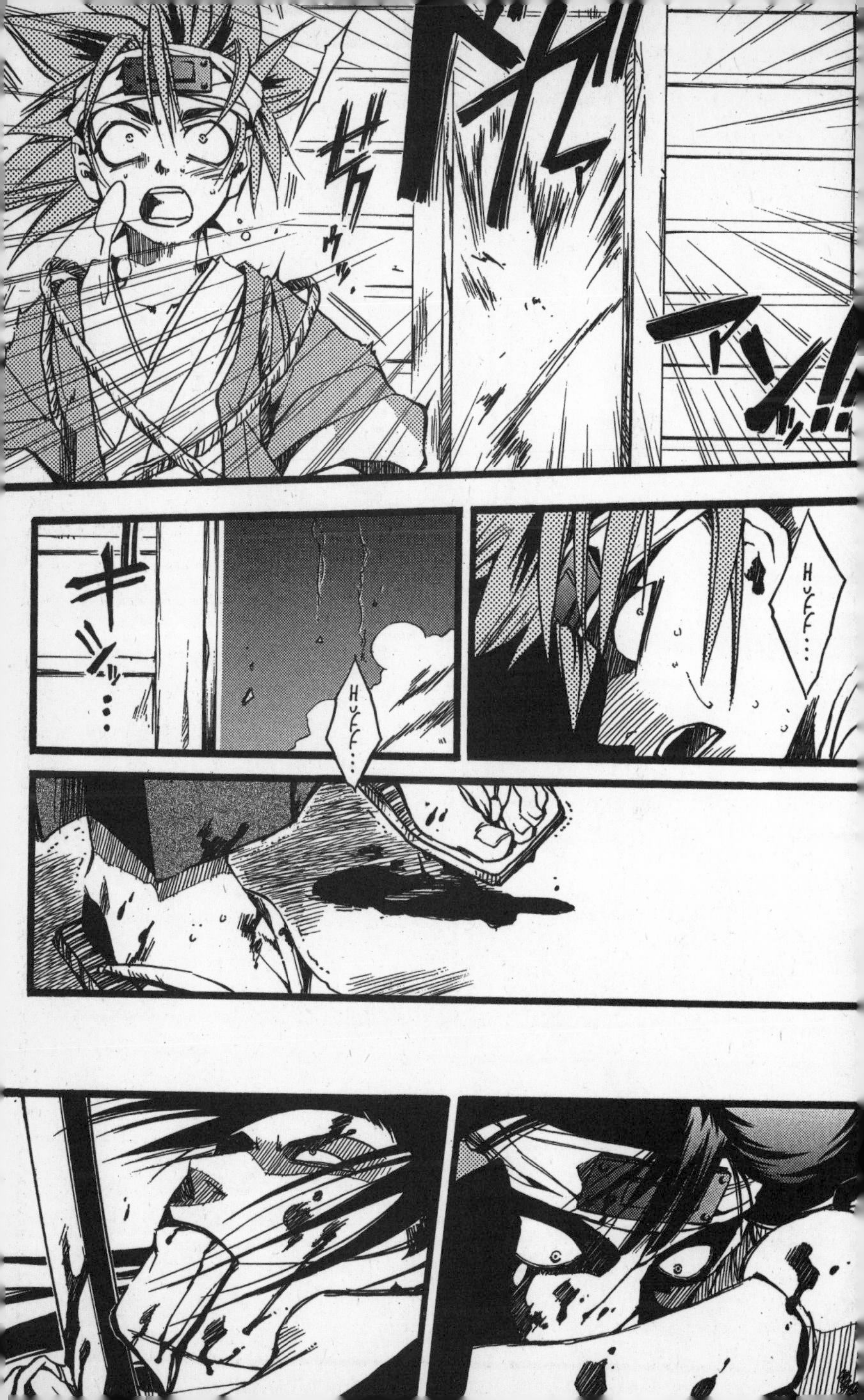
ドガアン!!
ザッ
HUFF...
ギシッ...
HUFF...

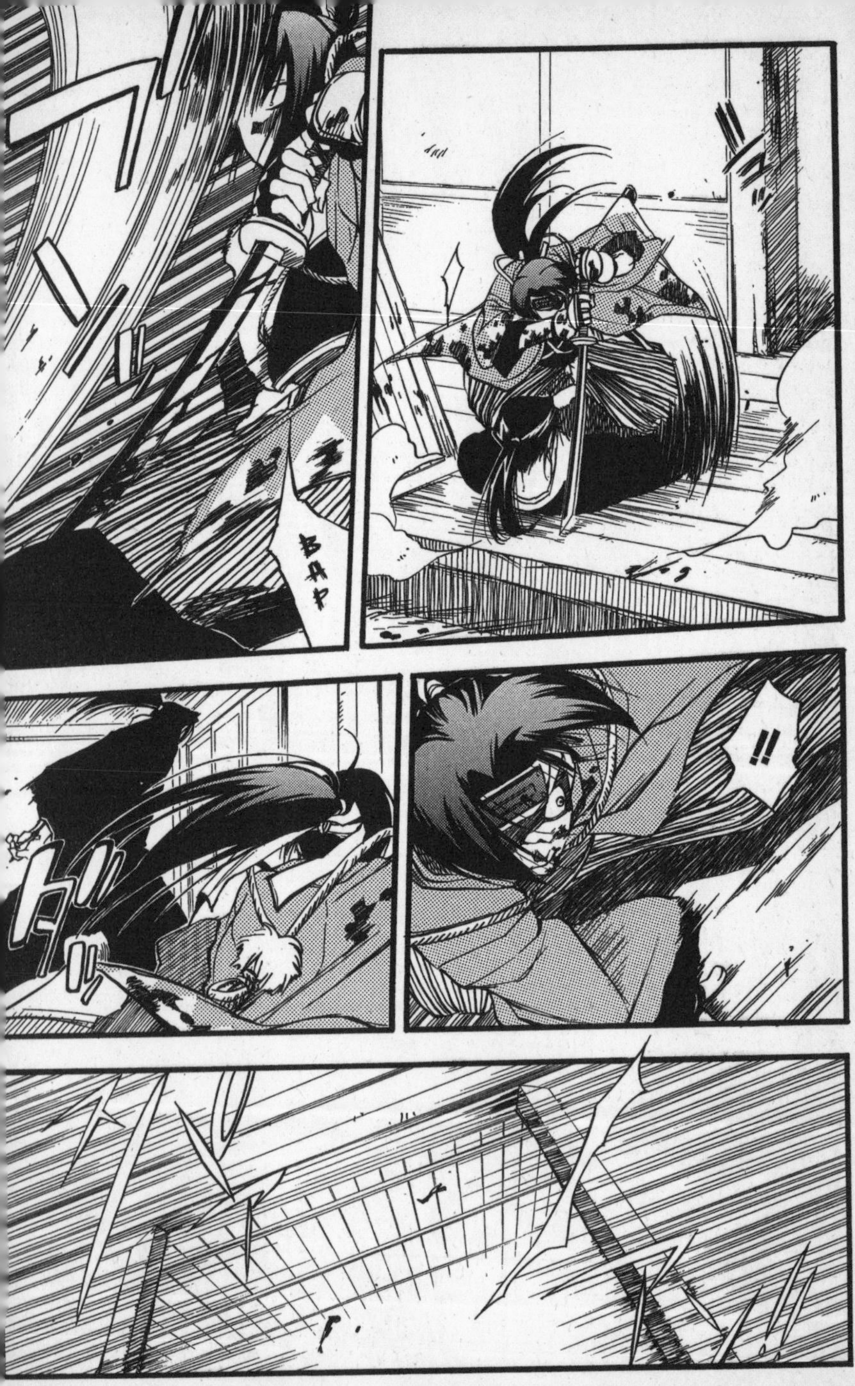
BAP
!!

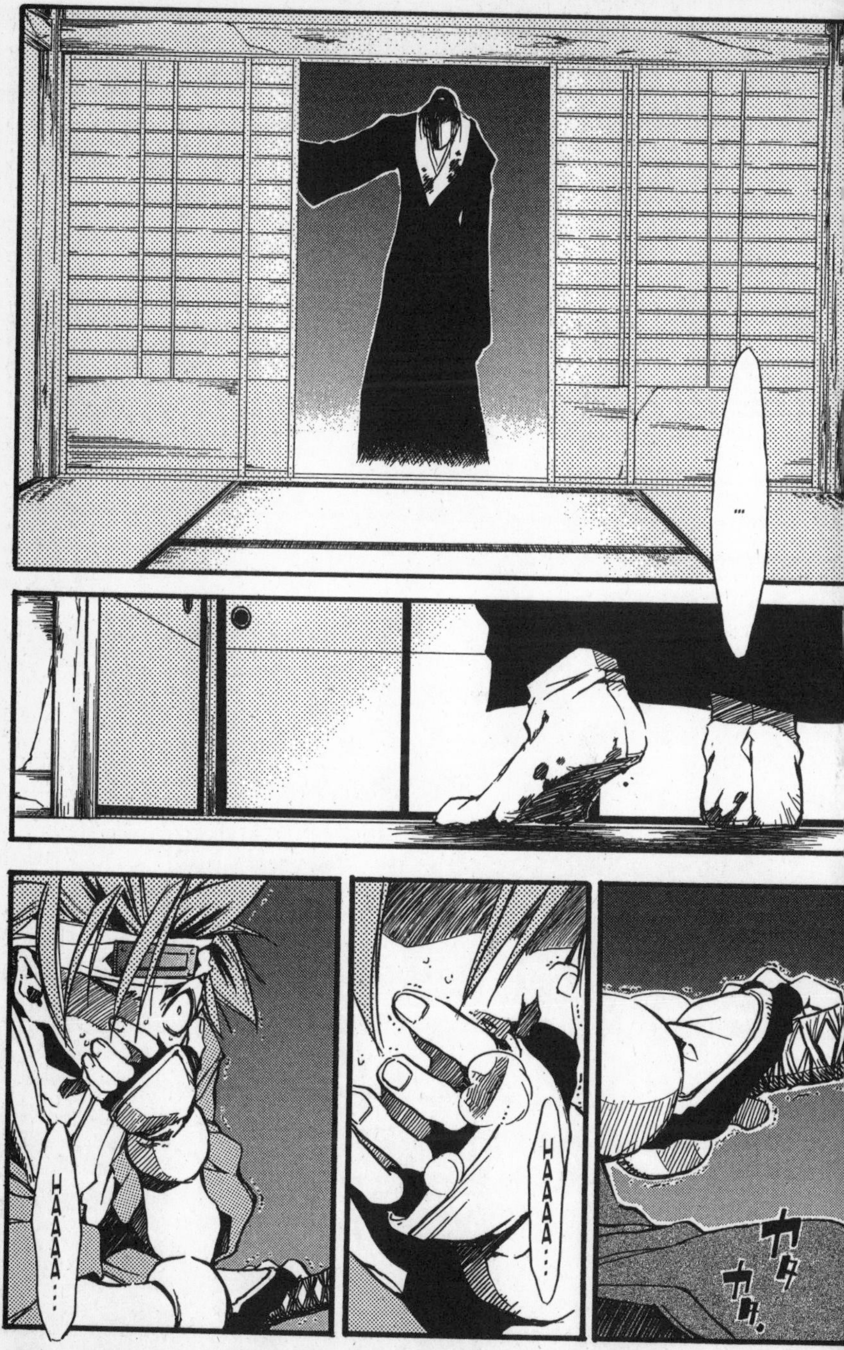
...
カタ
カタ.
HAAAA...
HAAAA...

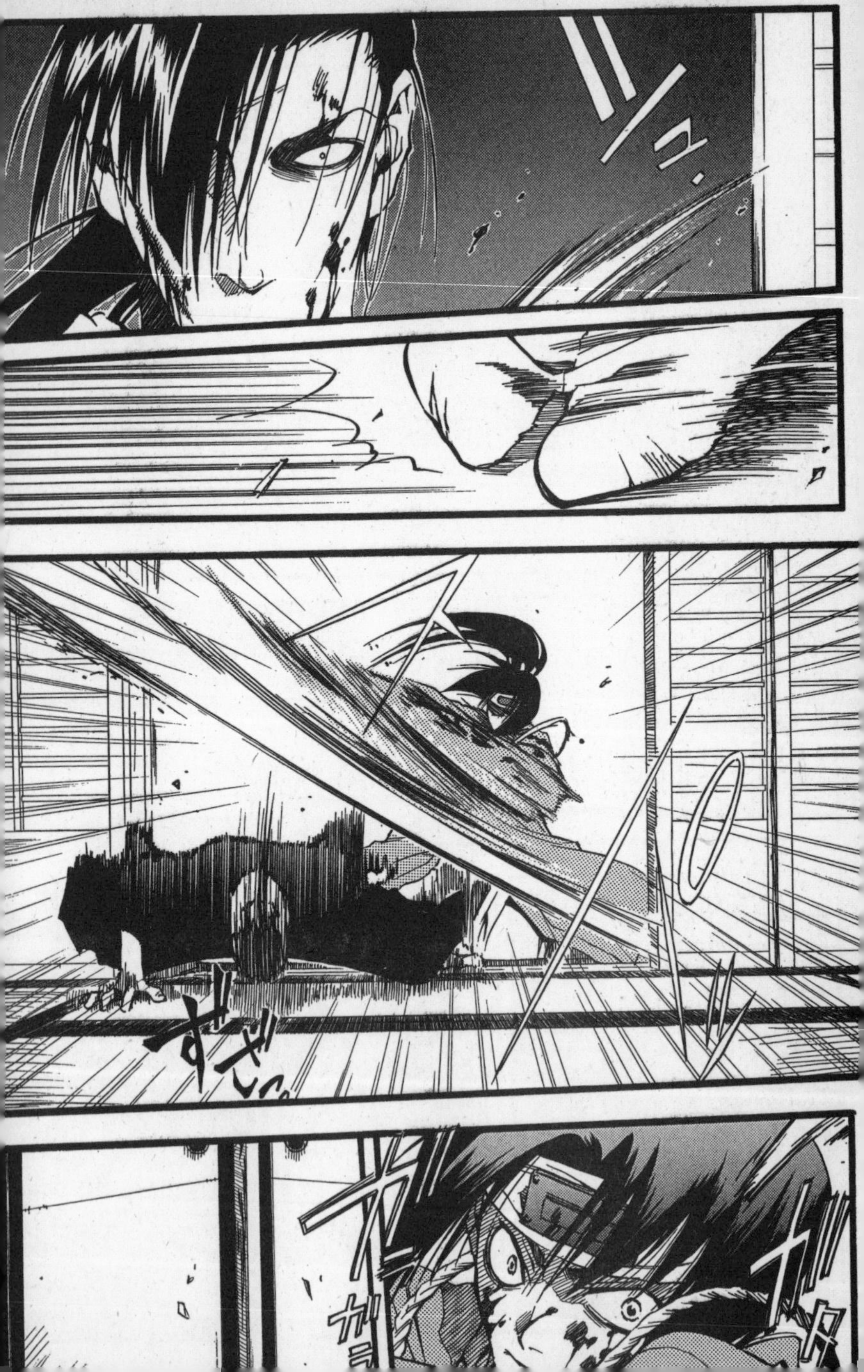

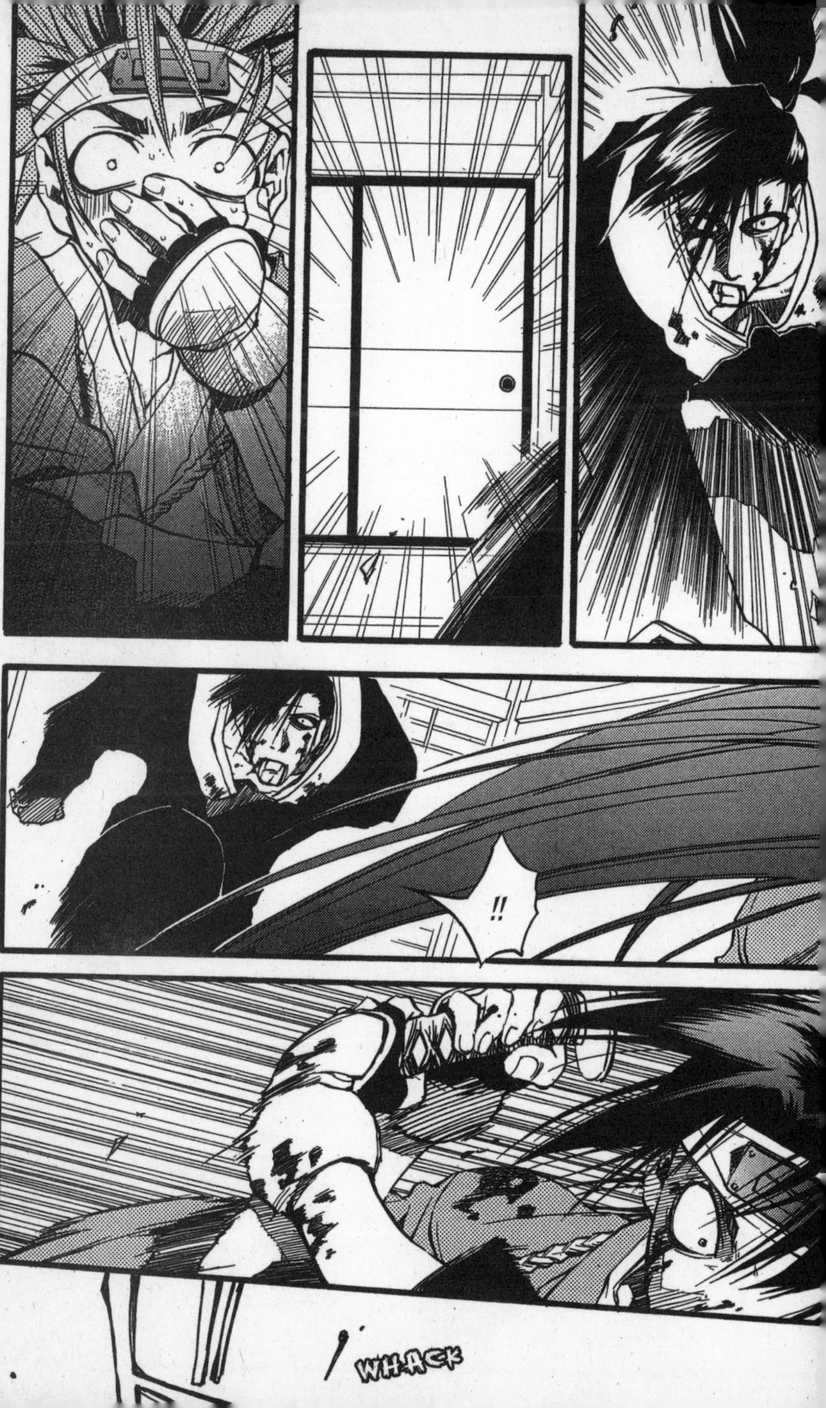
!!
WHACK

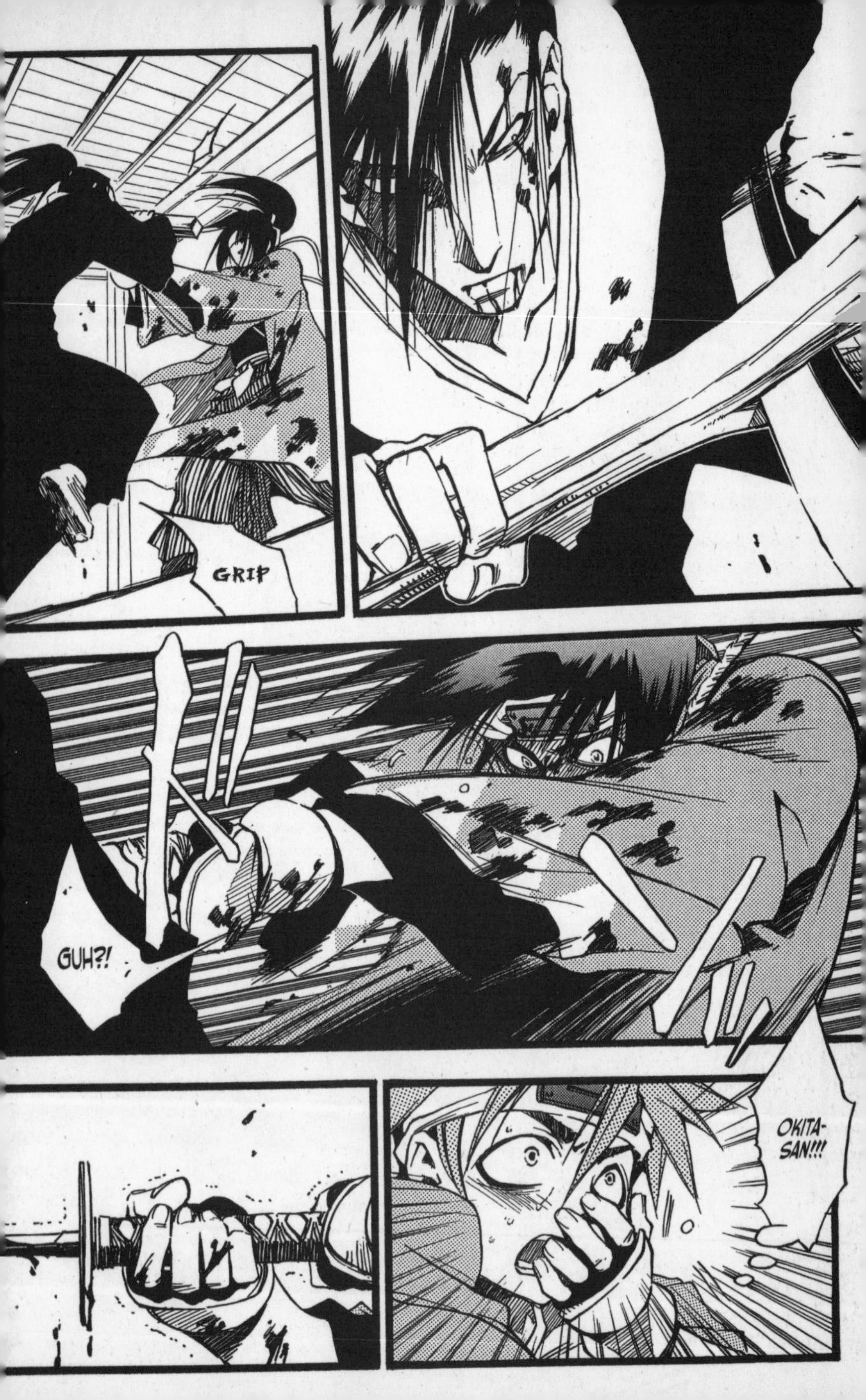
GRIP
GUH?!
OKITA-SAN!!!

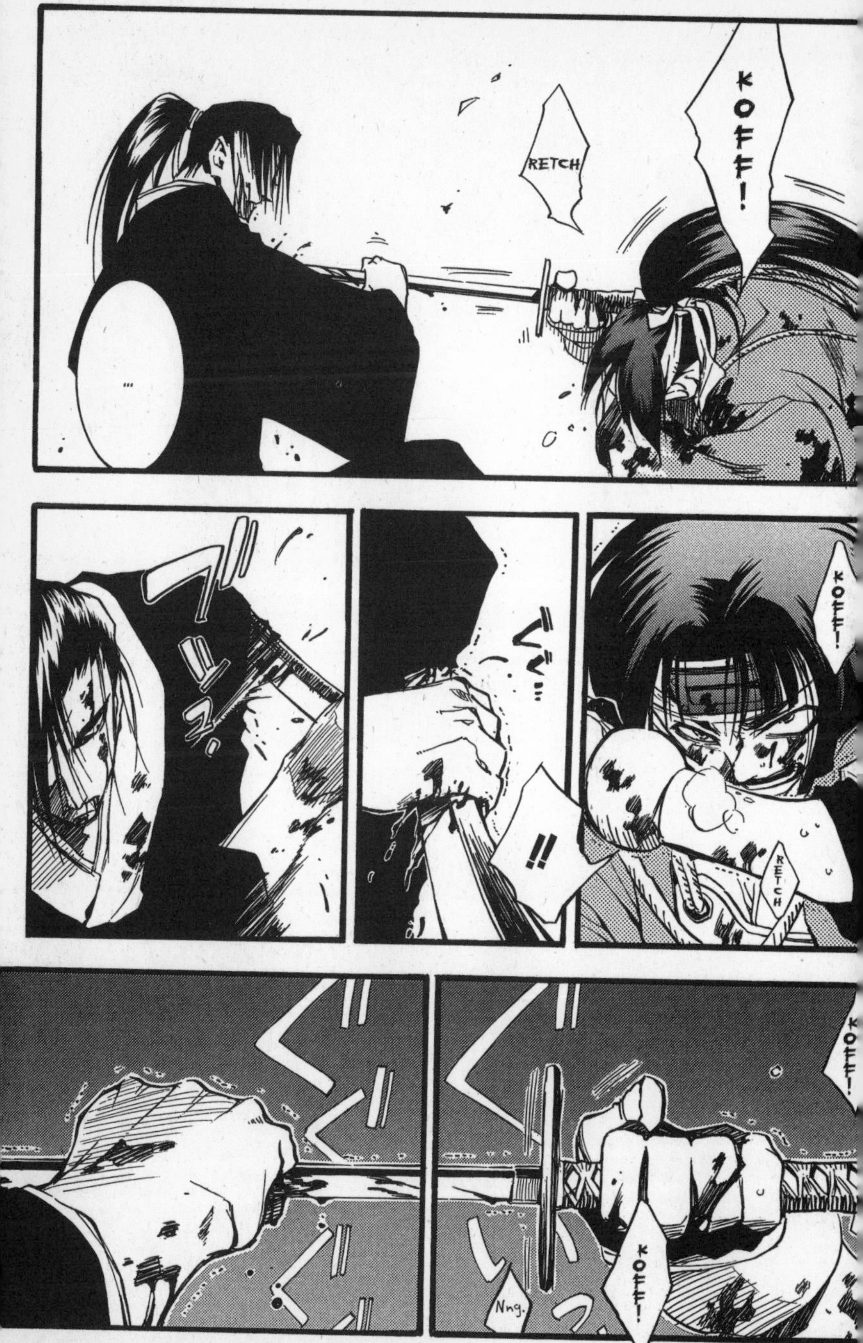
KOFF!
RETCH
...
KOFF!
RETCH
!!
KOFF!
KOFF!
Nng.

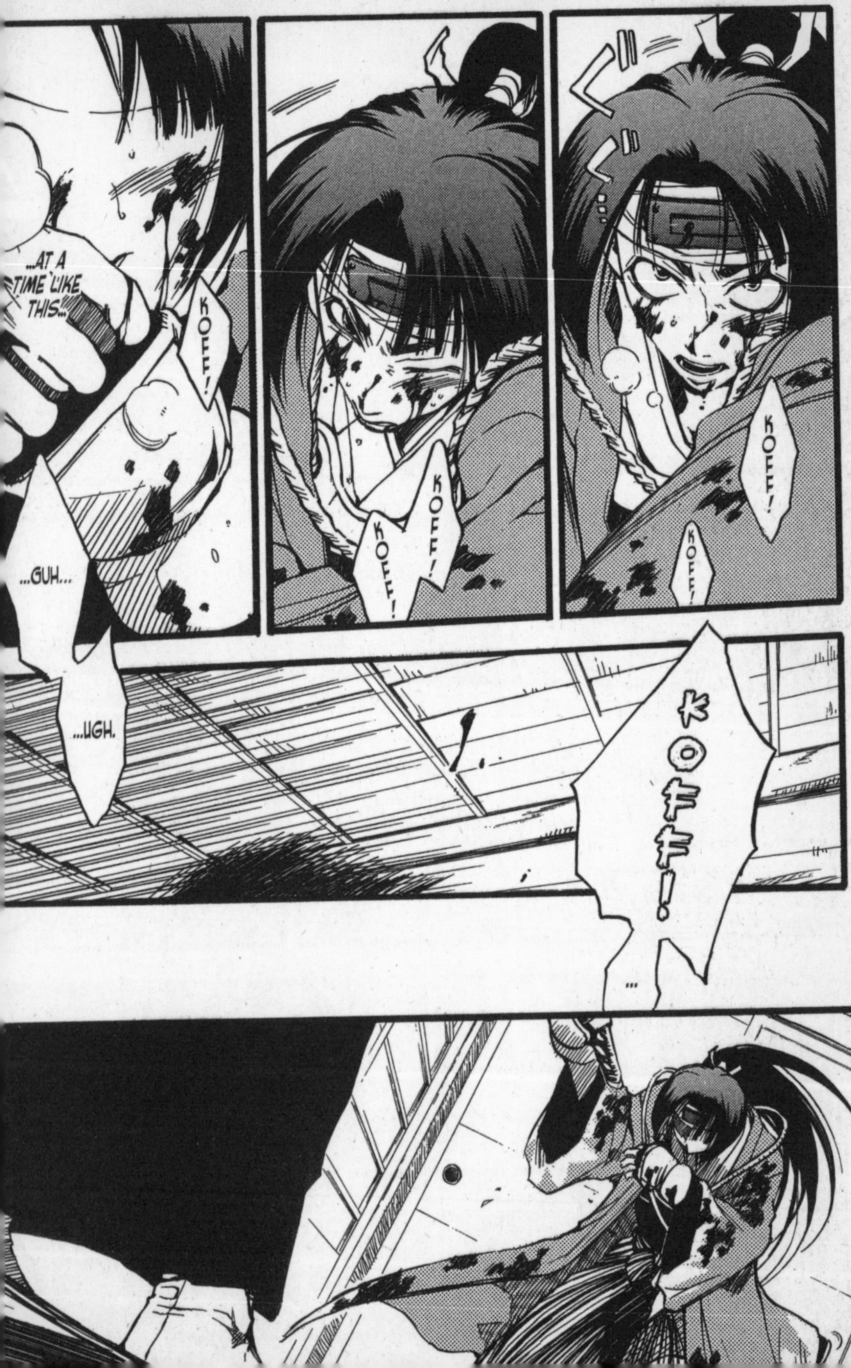
KOFF!
KOFF!
KOFF!
KOFF!
KOFF!
...AT A TIME LIKE THIS...
...GUH...
...UGH.
KOFF!
...

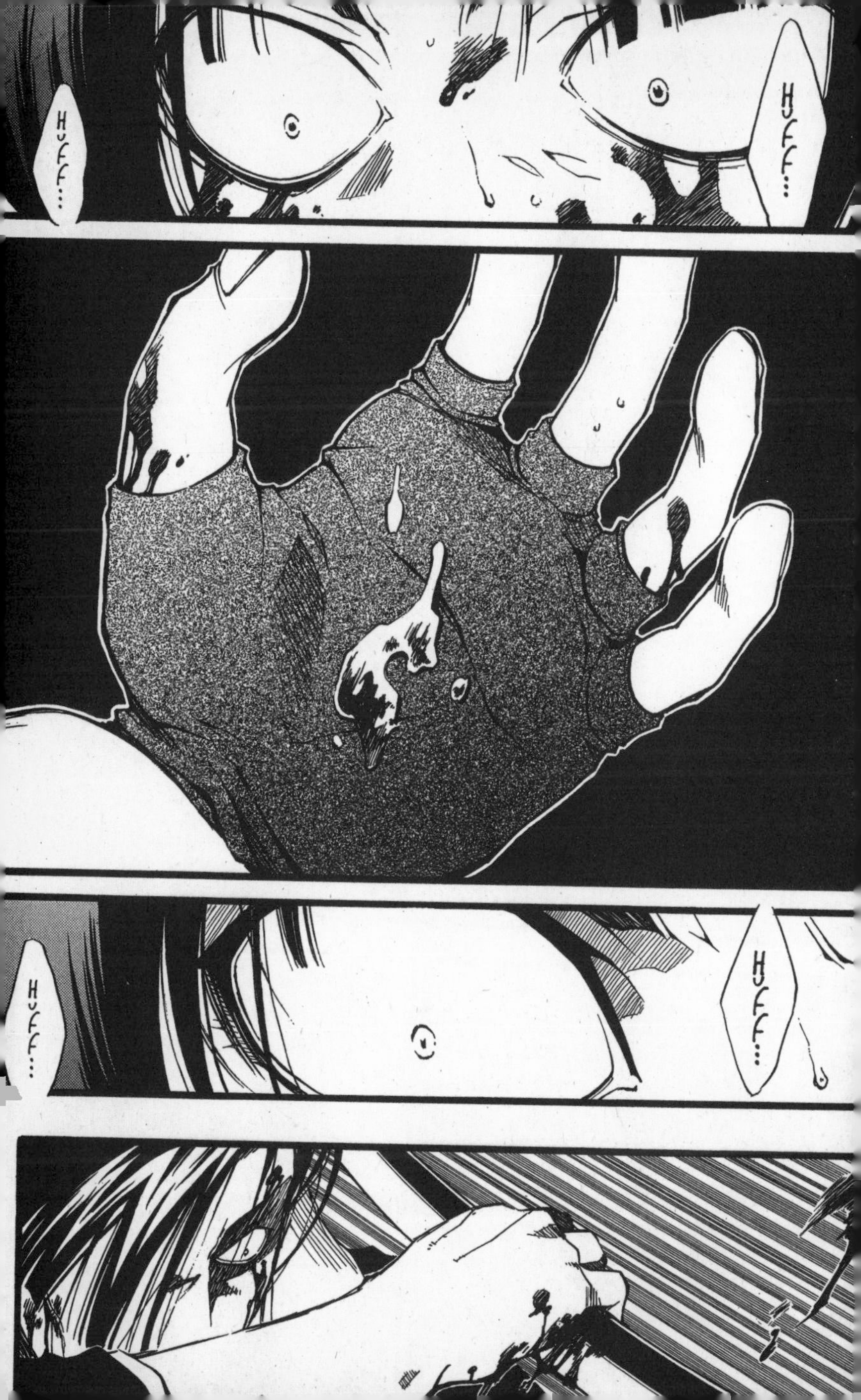
HUFF...
HUFF...
HUFF...
HUFF...

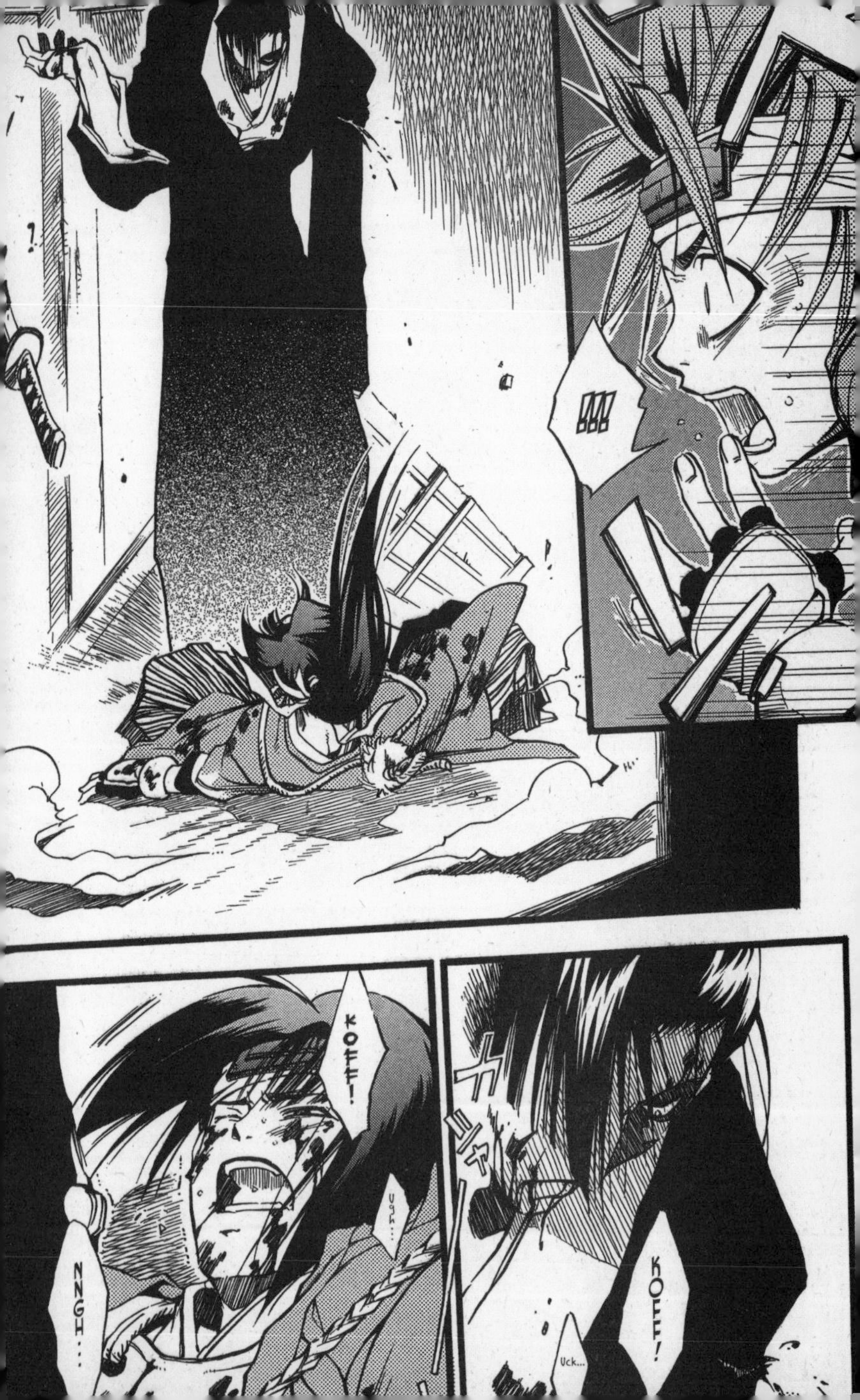
!!!
!?
Hk...
KOFF!
Uck...
カシャ
KOFF!
Ugh...
NNGH...

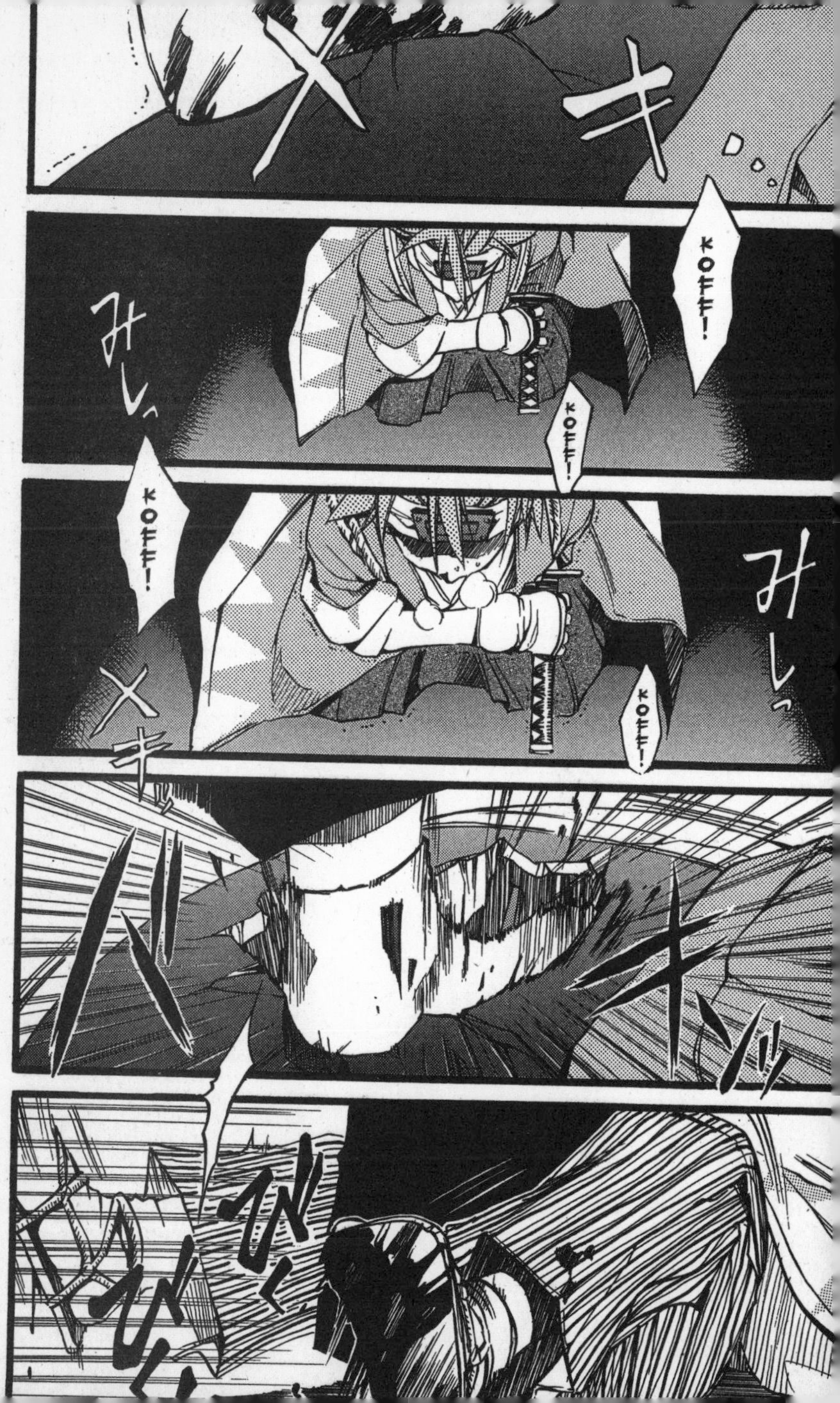
メキ
KOFF!
KOFF!
みしっ
みしっ
KOFF!
KOFF!
メキ

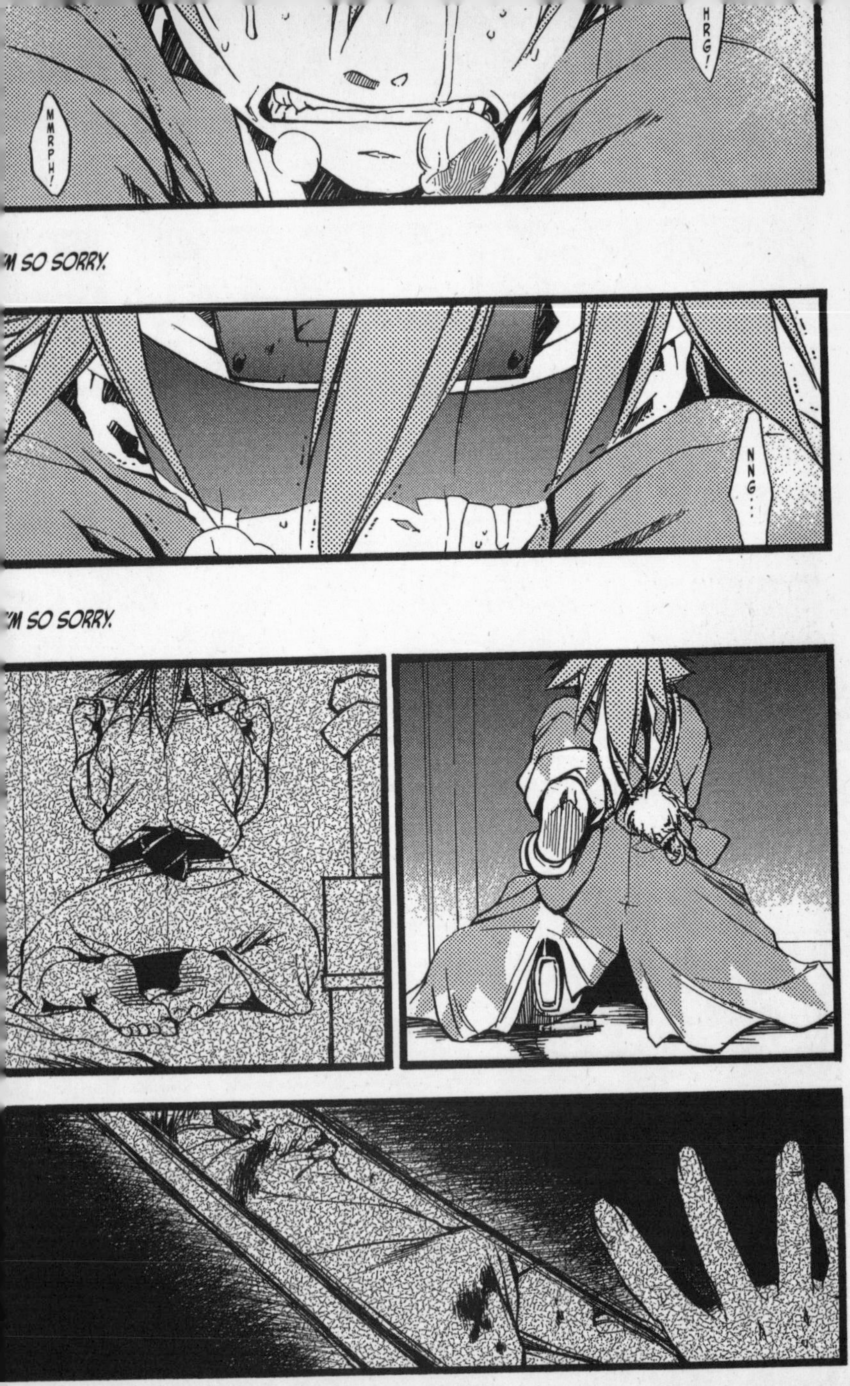
HRG!
MMRPH!
'M SO SORRY.
NNG...
'M SO SORRY.

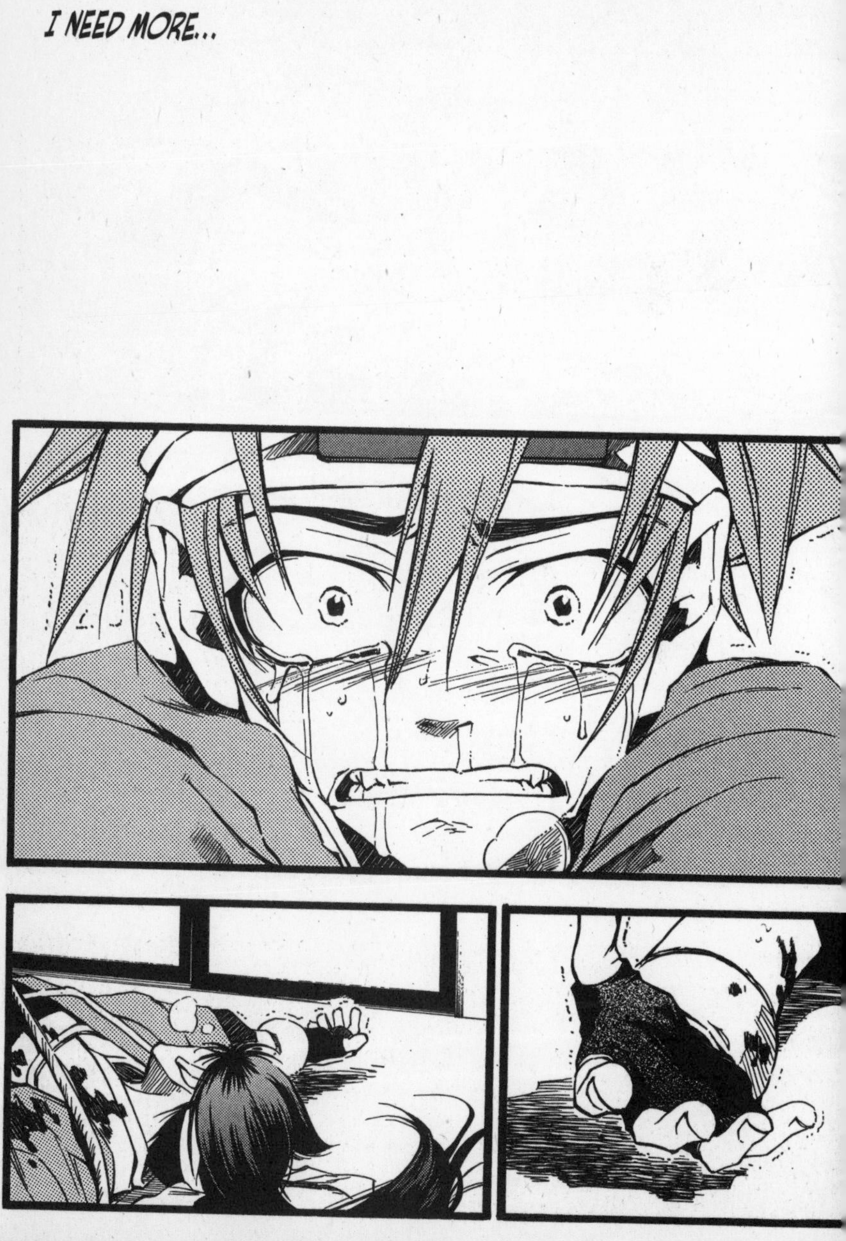
I NEED MORE...

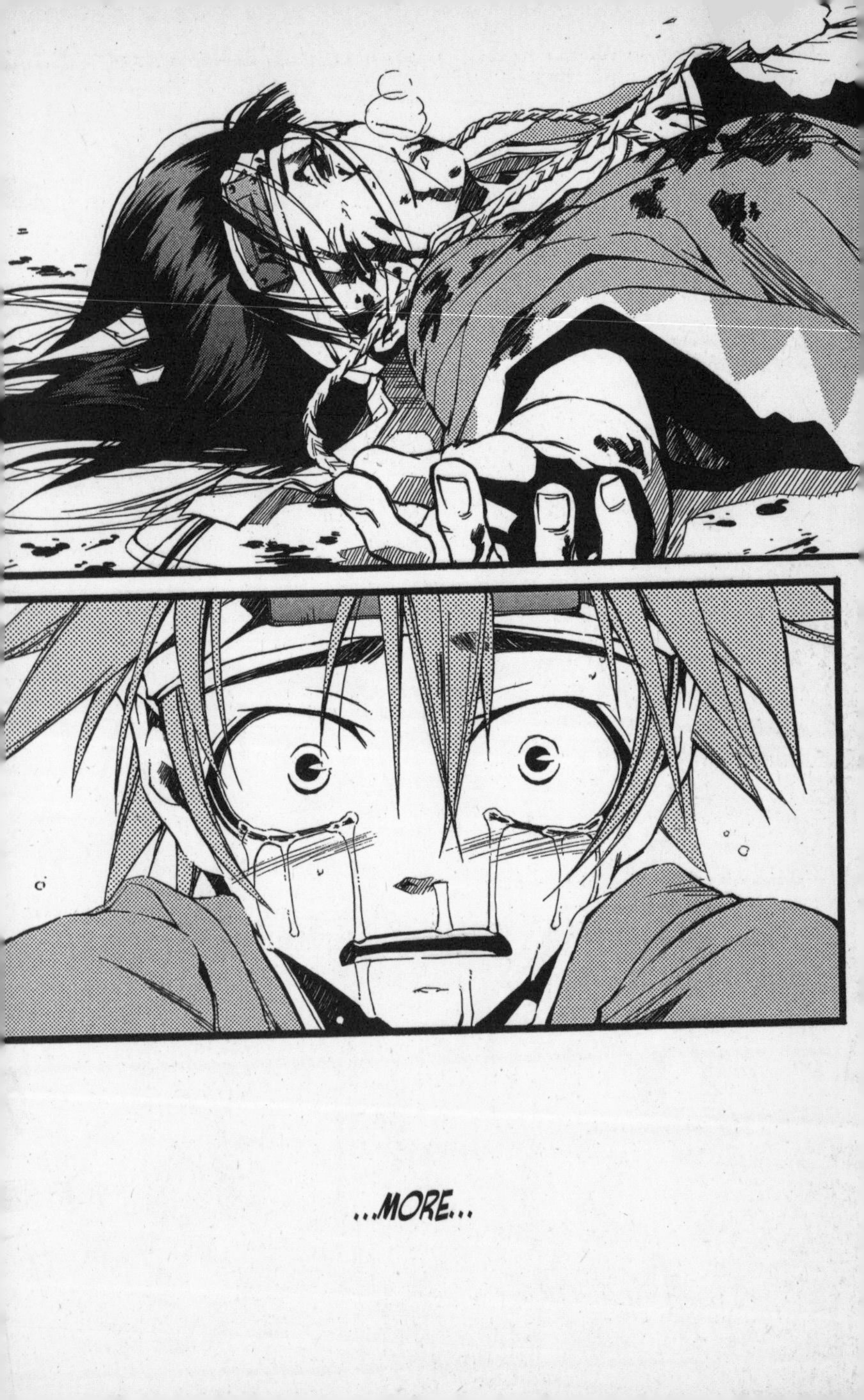
...MORE...

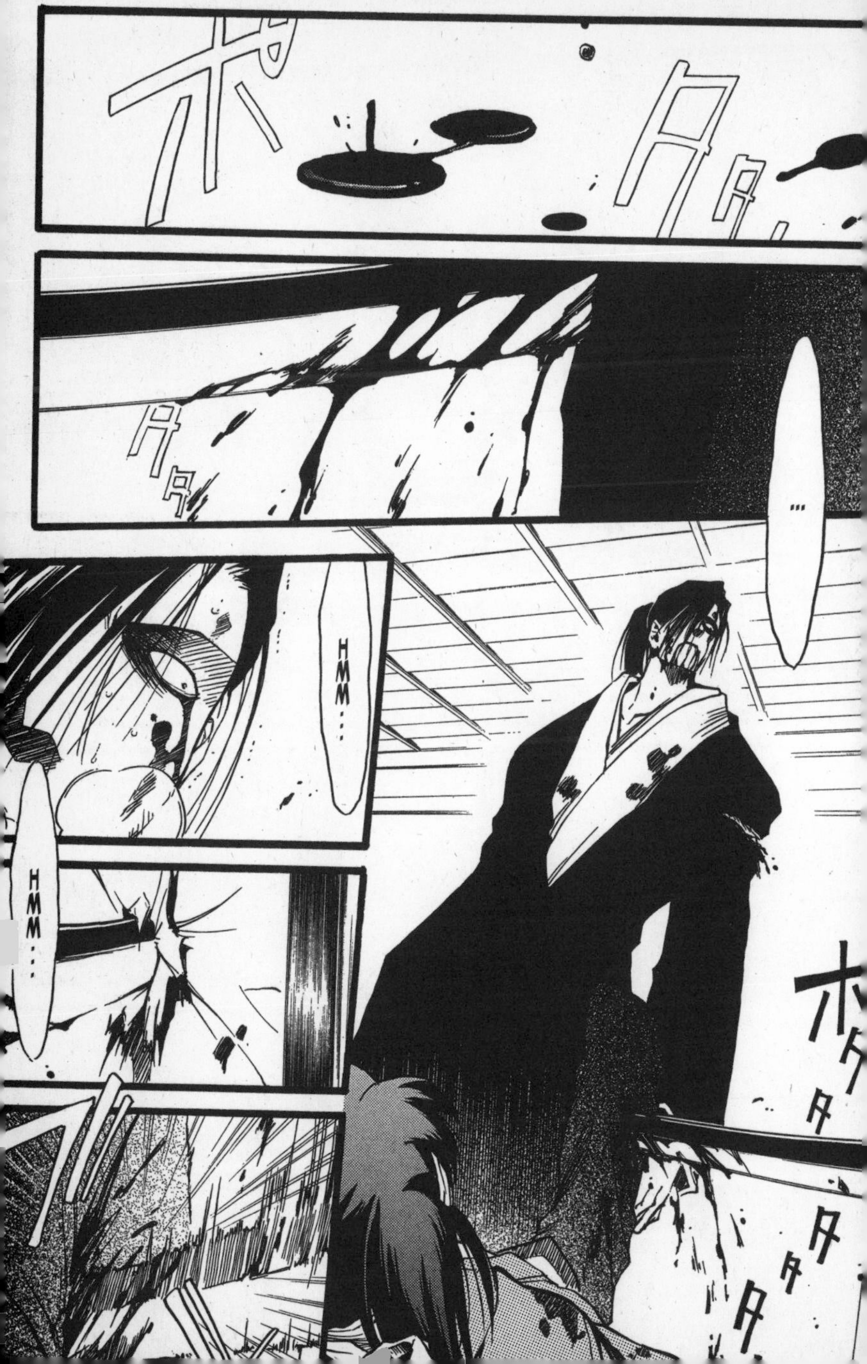
...
HMM...
HMM...

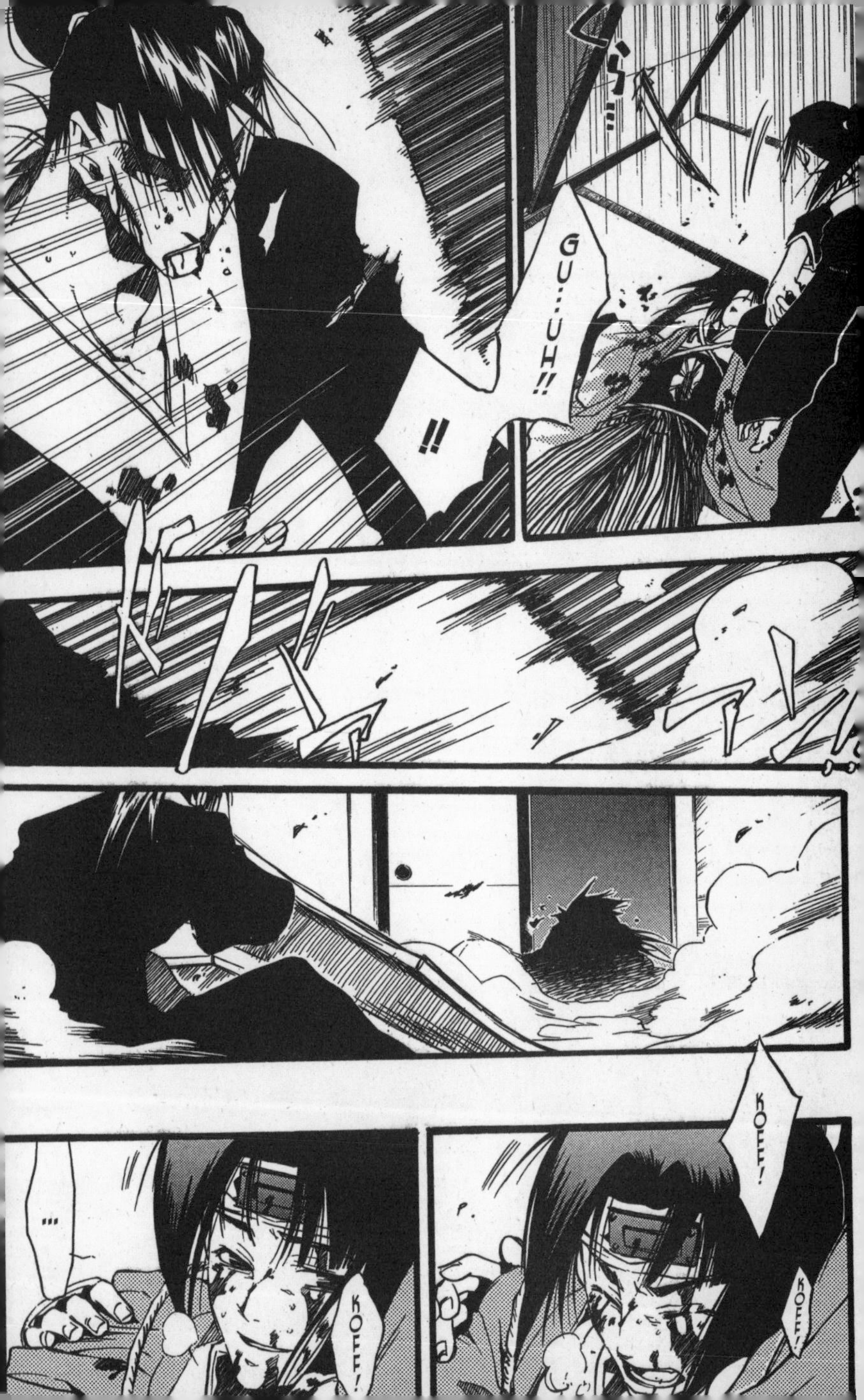
GU...UH!!
!!
KOFF!
P.
KOFF!
...
KOFF!

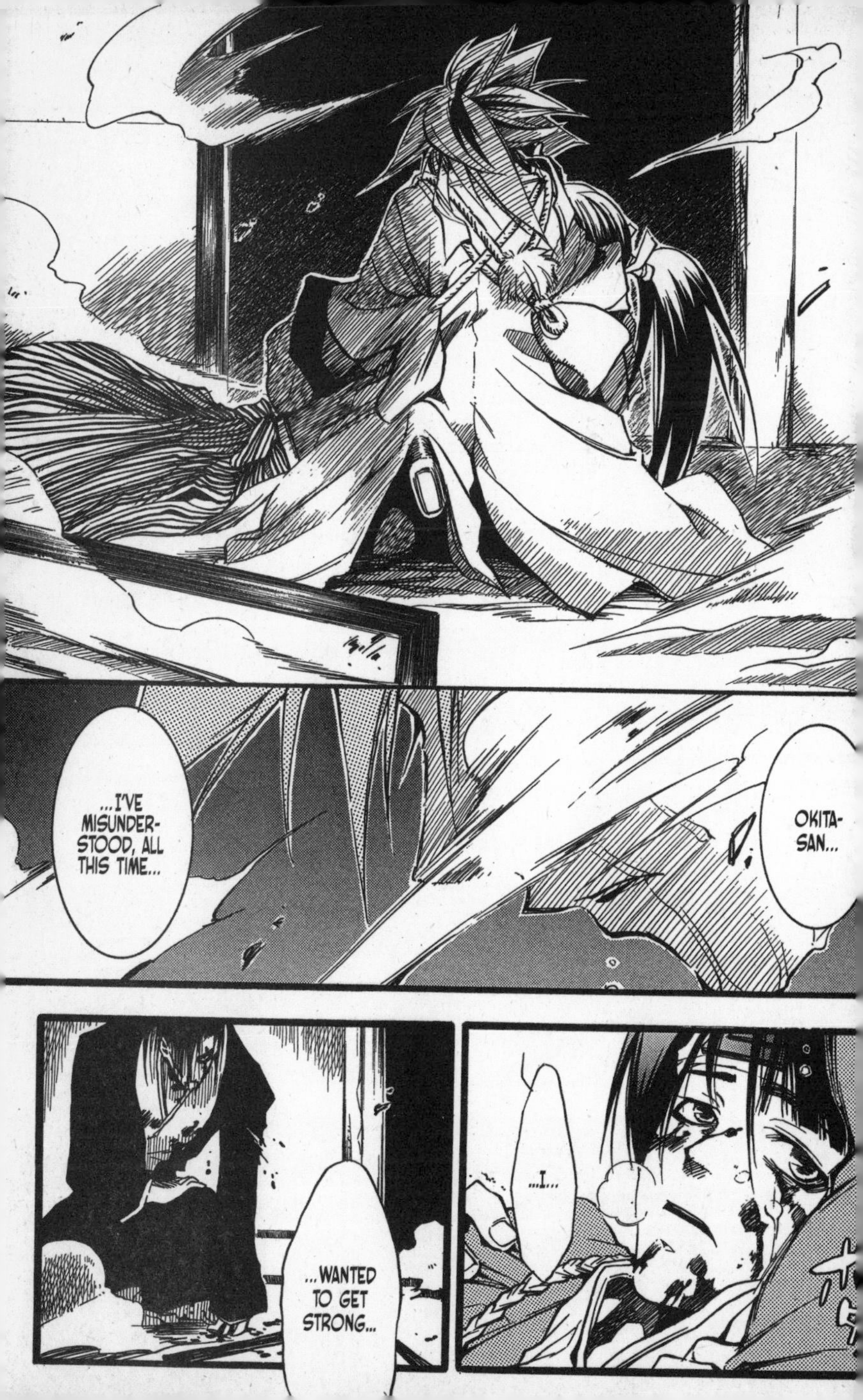
OKITA-SAN...
...I'VE MISUNDERSTOOD, ALL THIS TIME...
...I...
...WANTED TO GET STRONG...

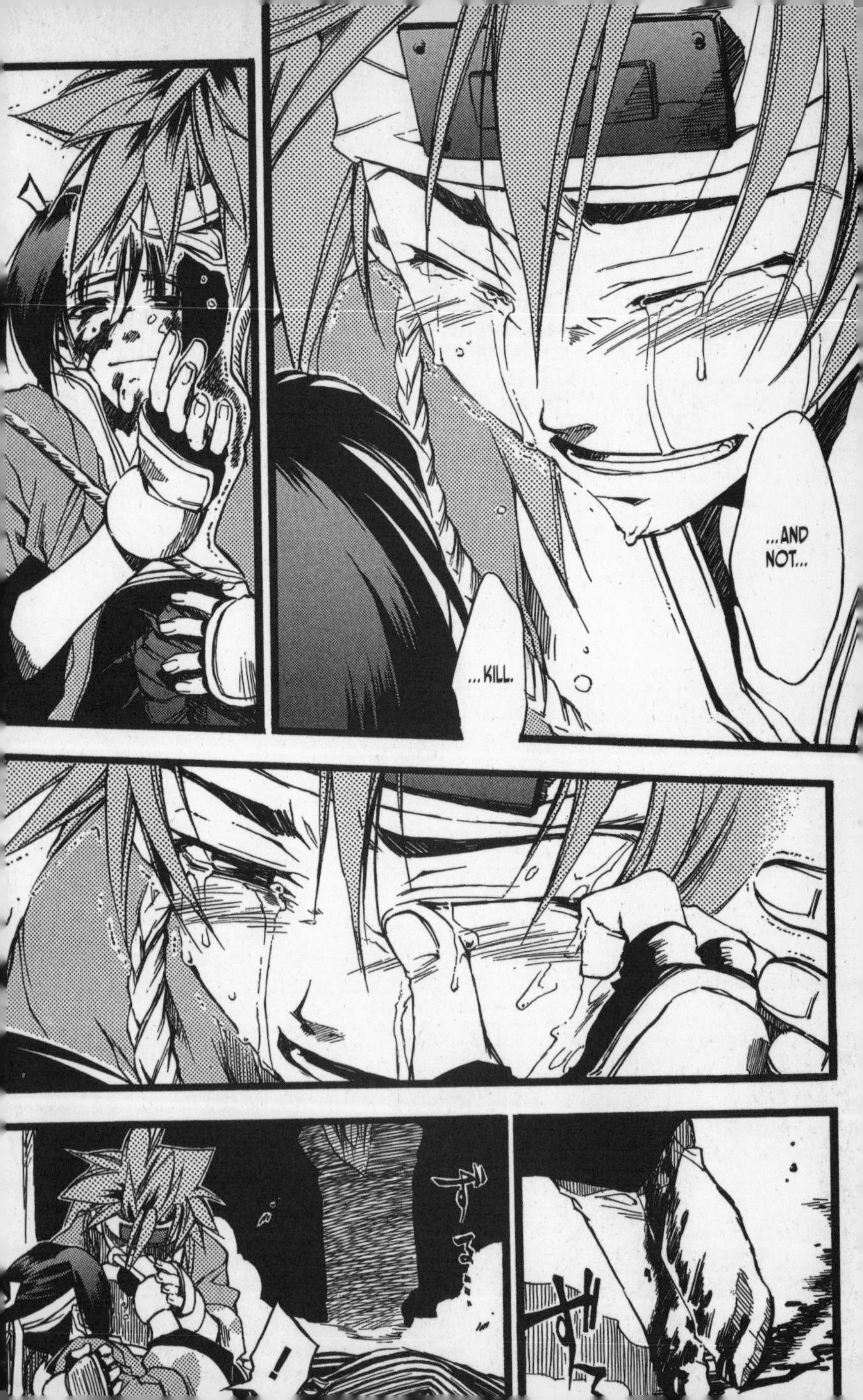
...AND NOT...
...KILL.
!

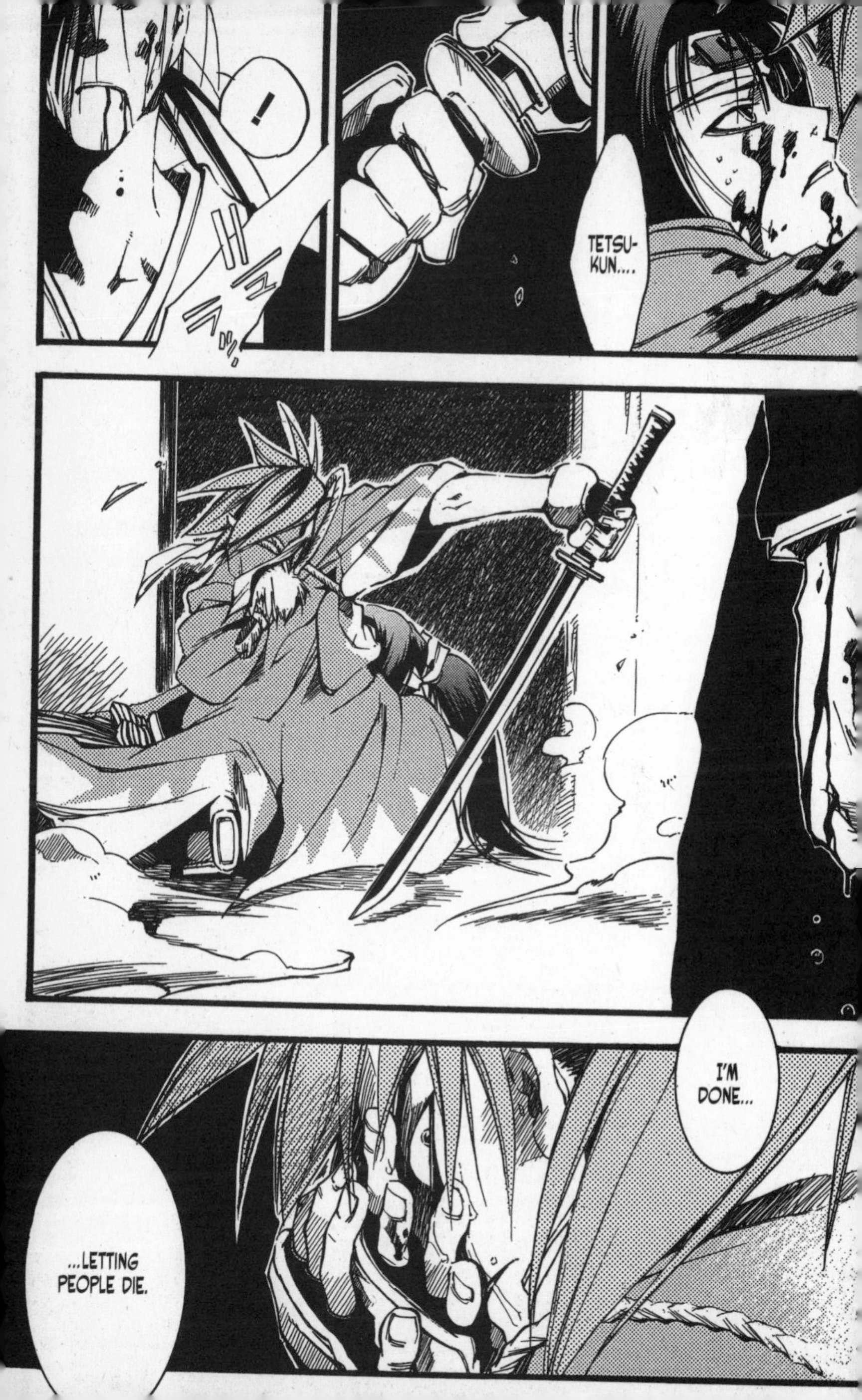
TETSU-KUN....
!
I'M DONE...
...LETTING PEOPLE DIE.

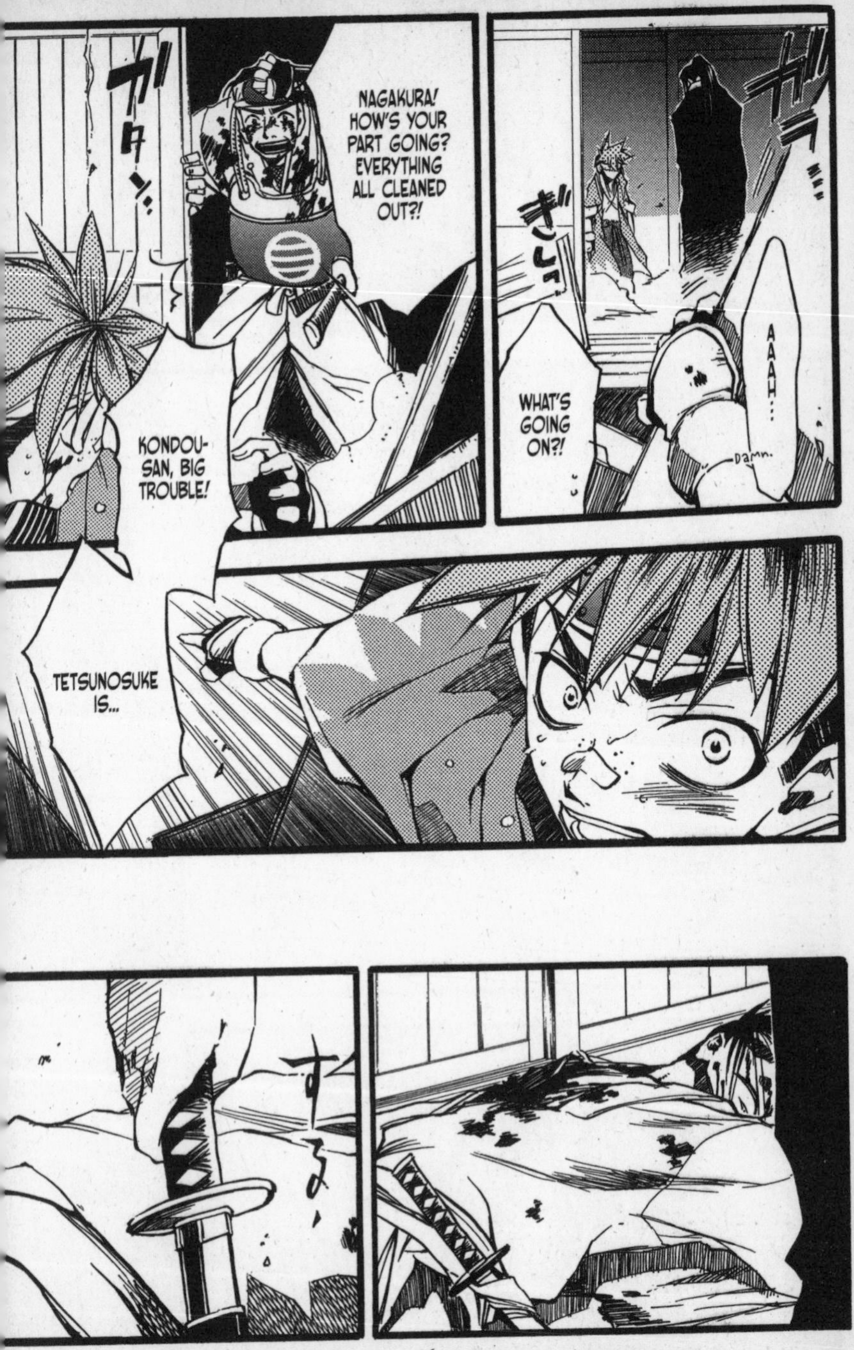
AAAH...
Damn.
WHAT'S GOING ON?!
NAGAKURA! HOW'S YOUR PART GOING? EVERYTHING ALL CLEANED OUT?!
KONDOU-SAN, BIG TROUBLE!
TETSUNOSUKE IS...

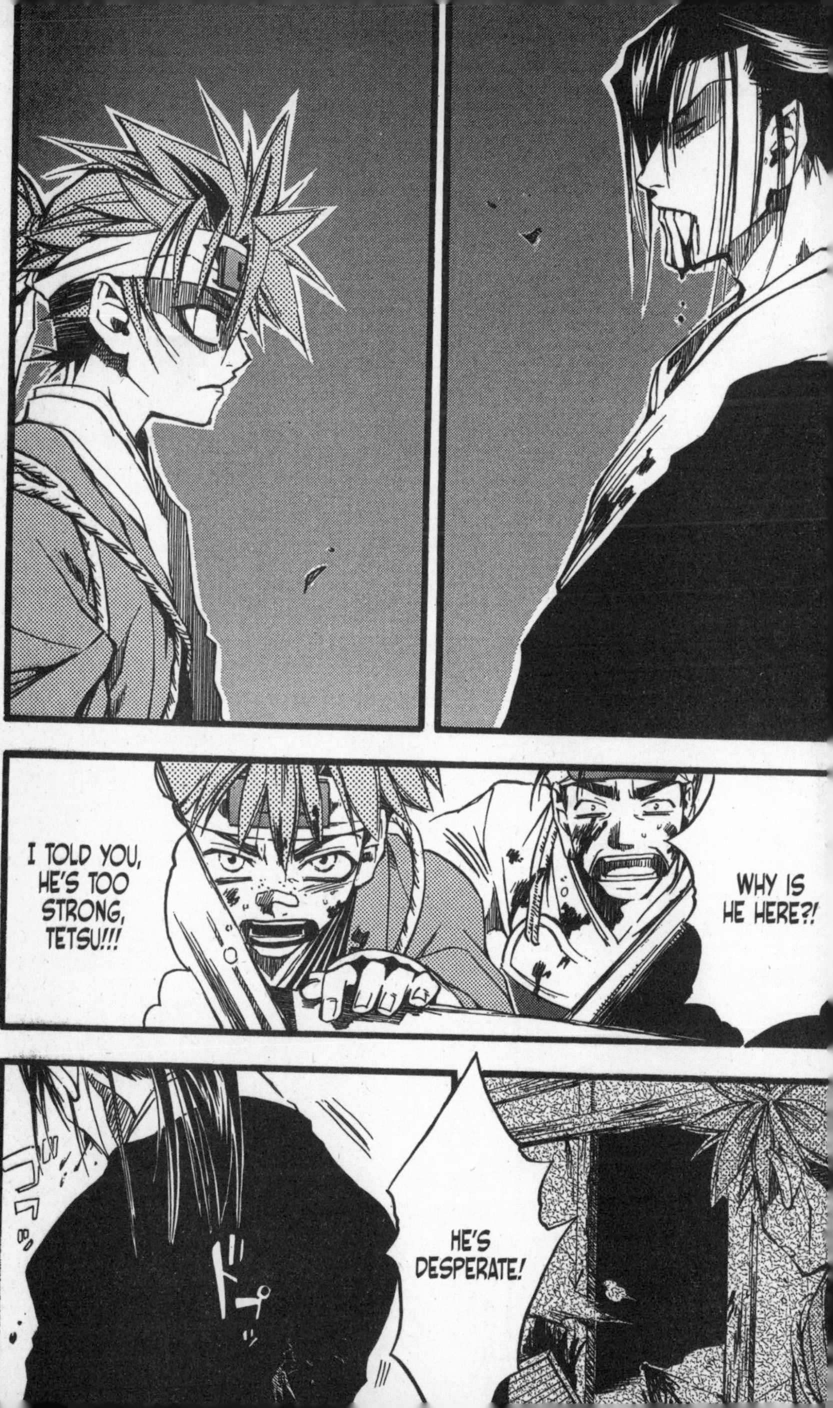
WHY IS HE HERE?!
I TOLD YOU, HE'S TOO STRONG, TETSU!!!
HE'S DESPERATE!

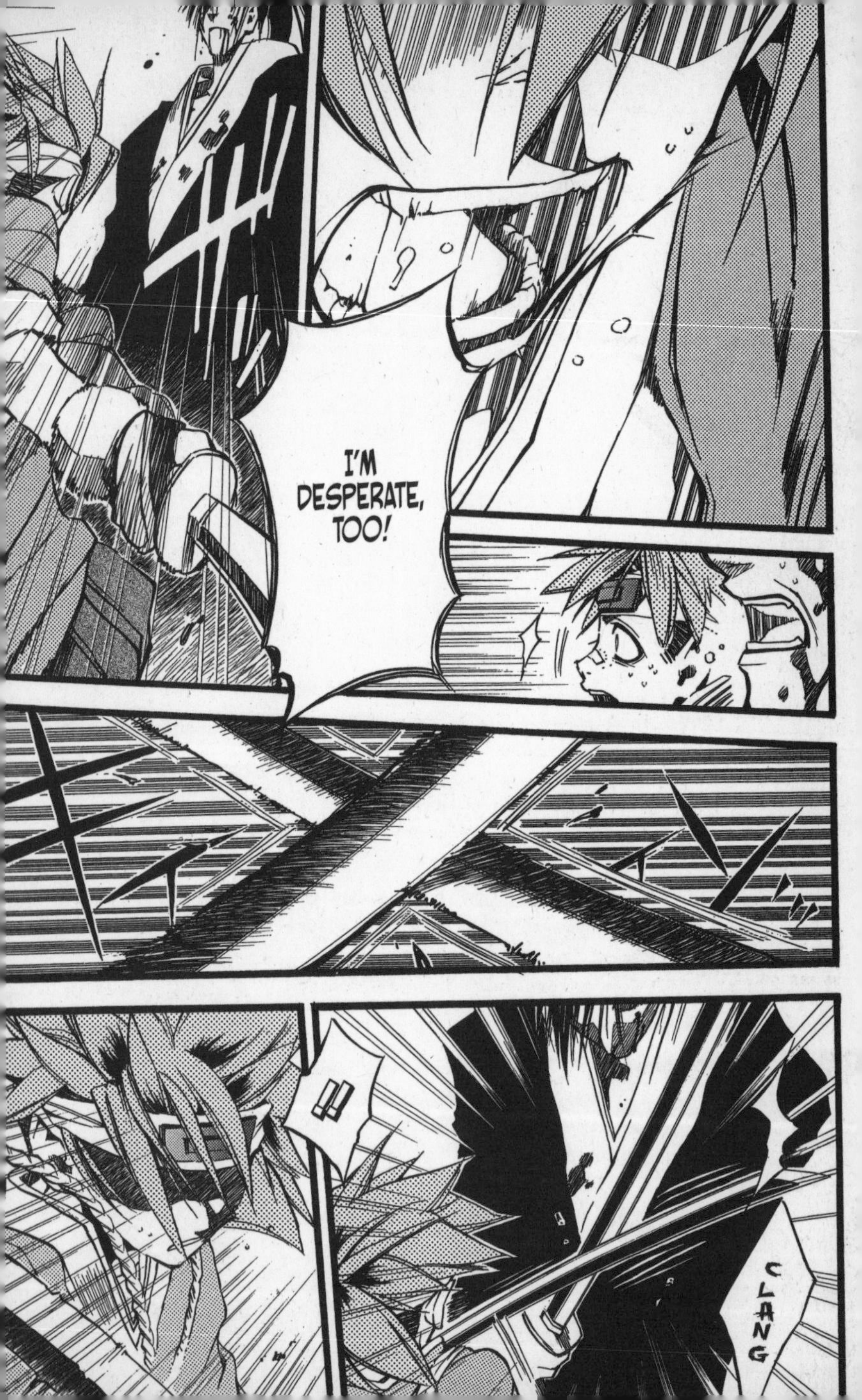
I'M DESPERATE, TOO!
!!
CLANG

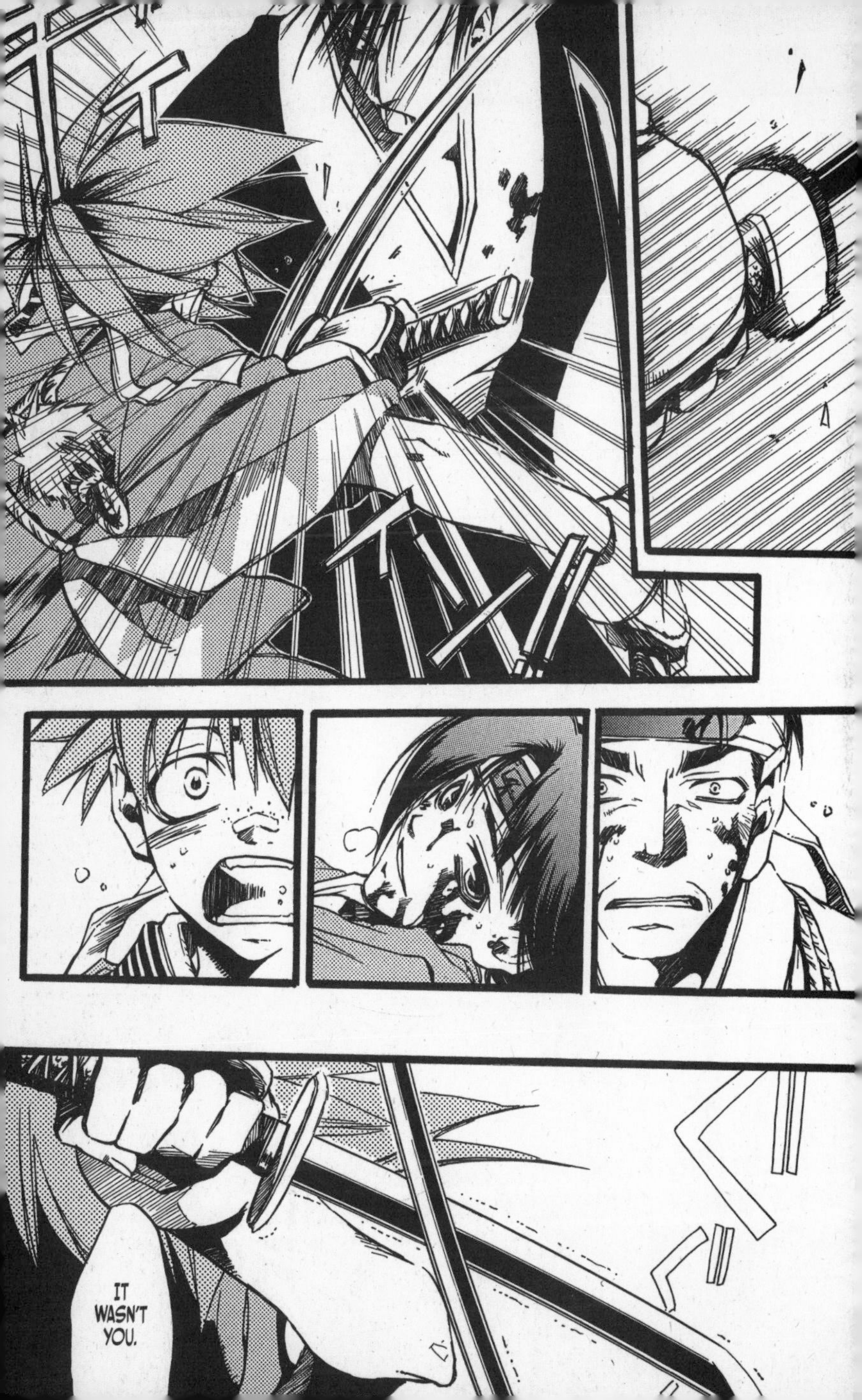
IT WASN'T YOU.

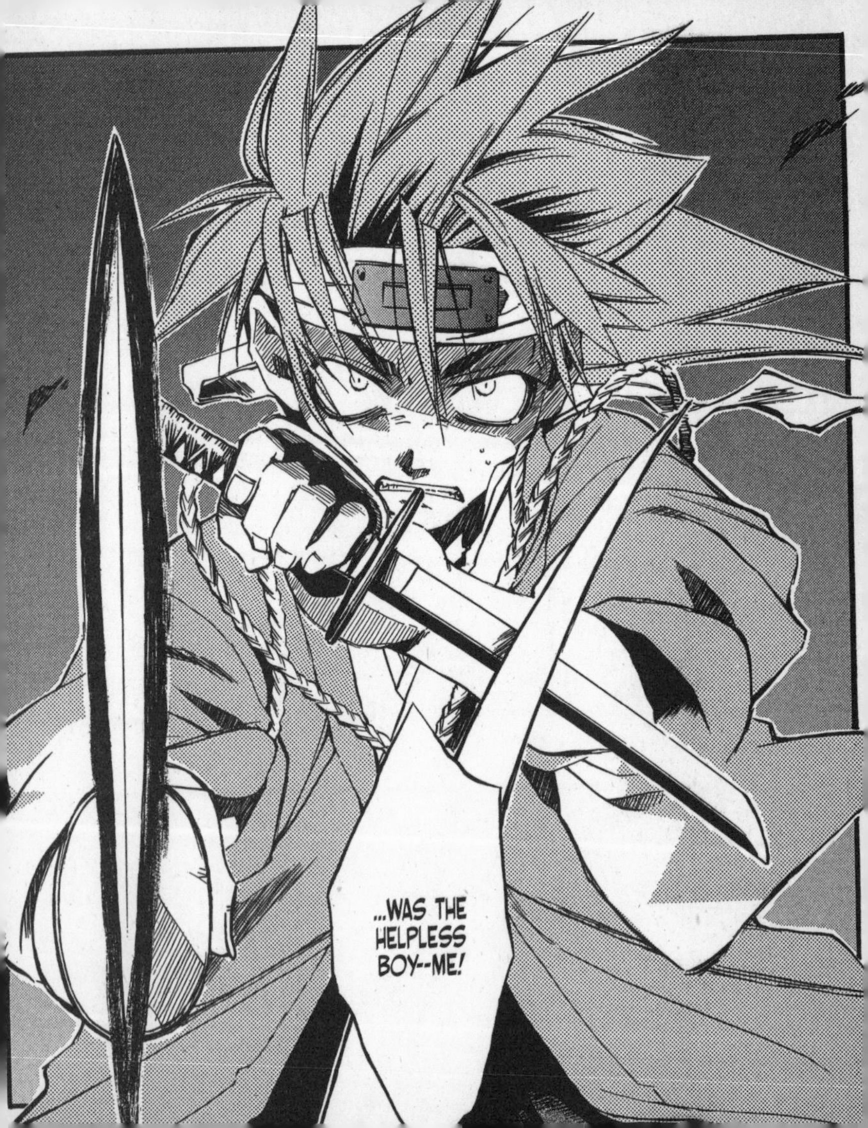
...WAS THE HELPLESS BOY--ME!

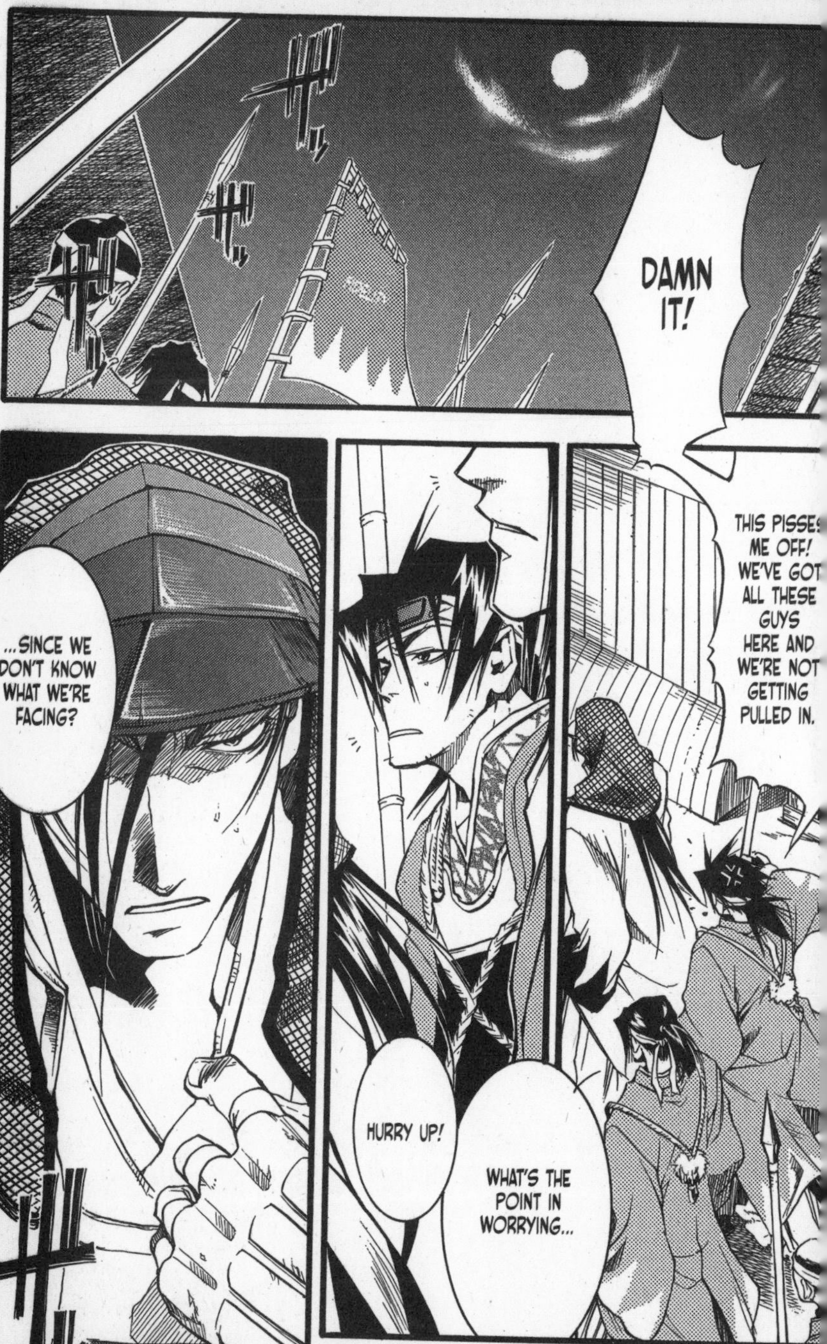
DAMN IT!
THIS PISSES ME OFF! WE'VE GOT ALL THESE GUYS HERE AND WE'RE NOT GETTING PULLED IN.
HURRY UP!
WHAT'S THE POINT IN WORRYING...
...SINCE WE DON'T KNOW WHAT WE'RE FACING?

Act.27
A Hard Day's Night (Scene 4)

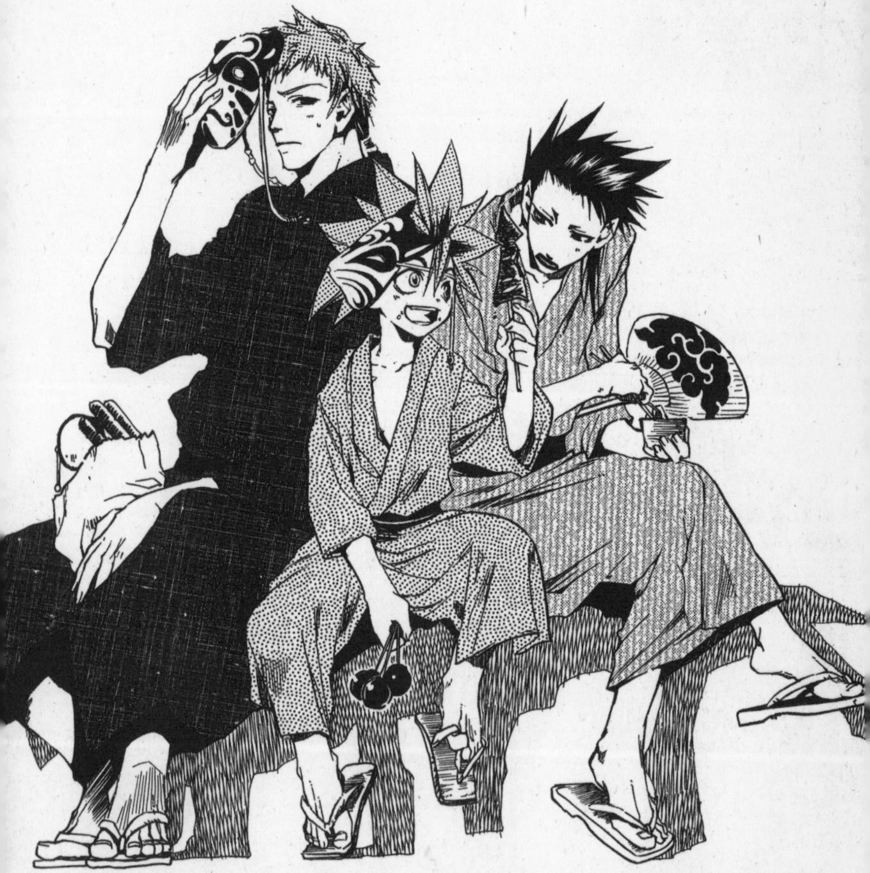

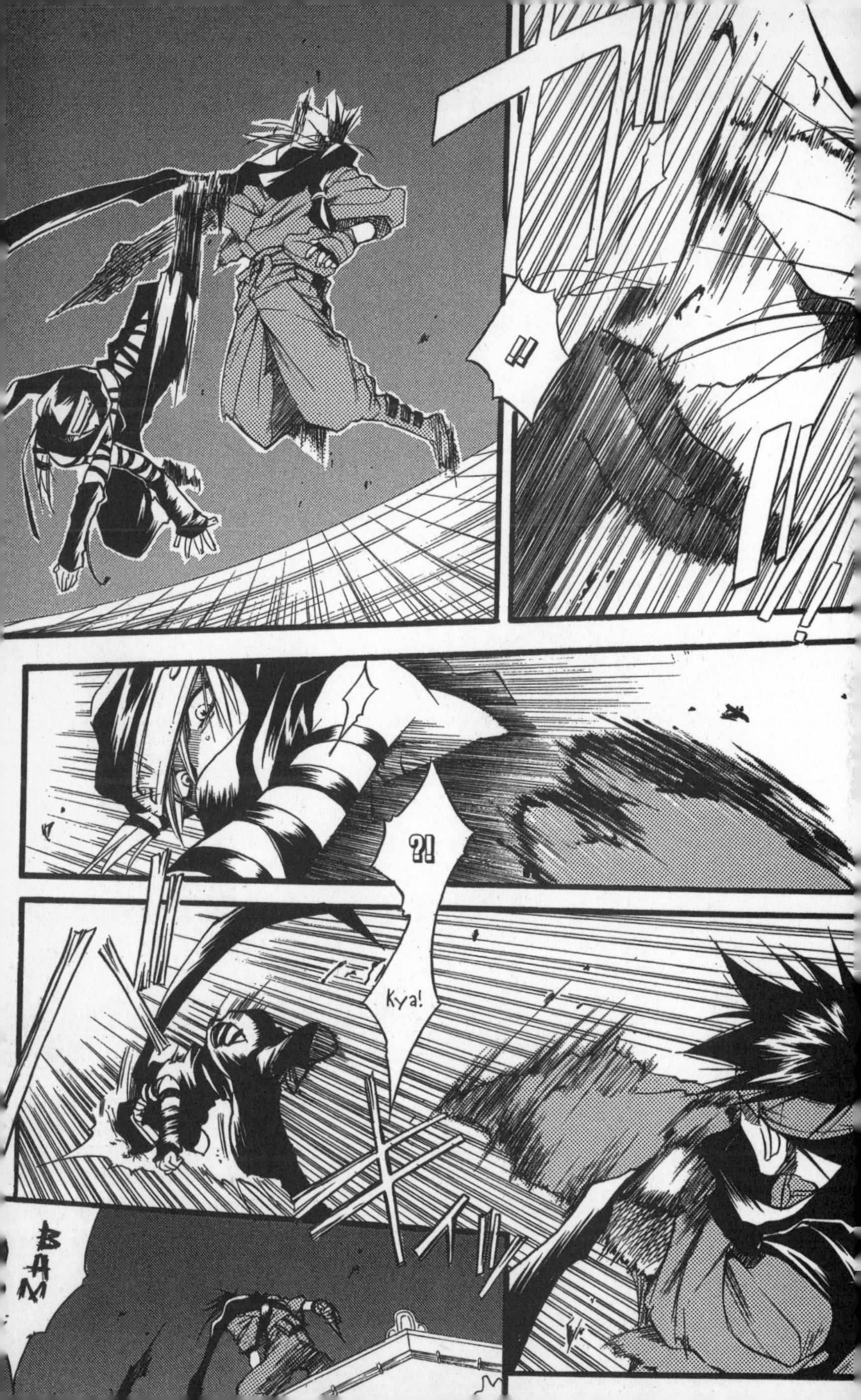
!!
?!
Kya!
BAM

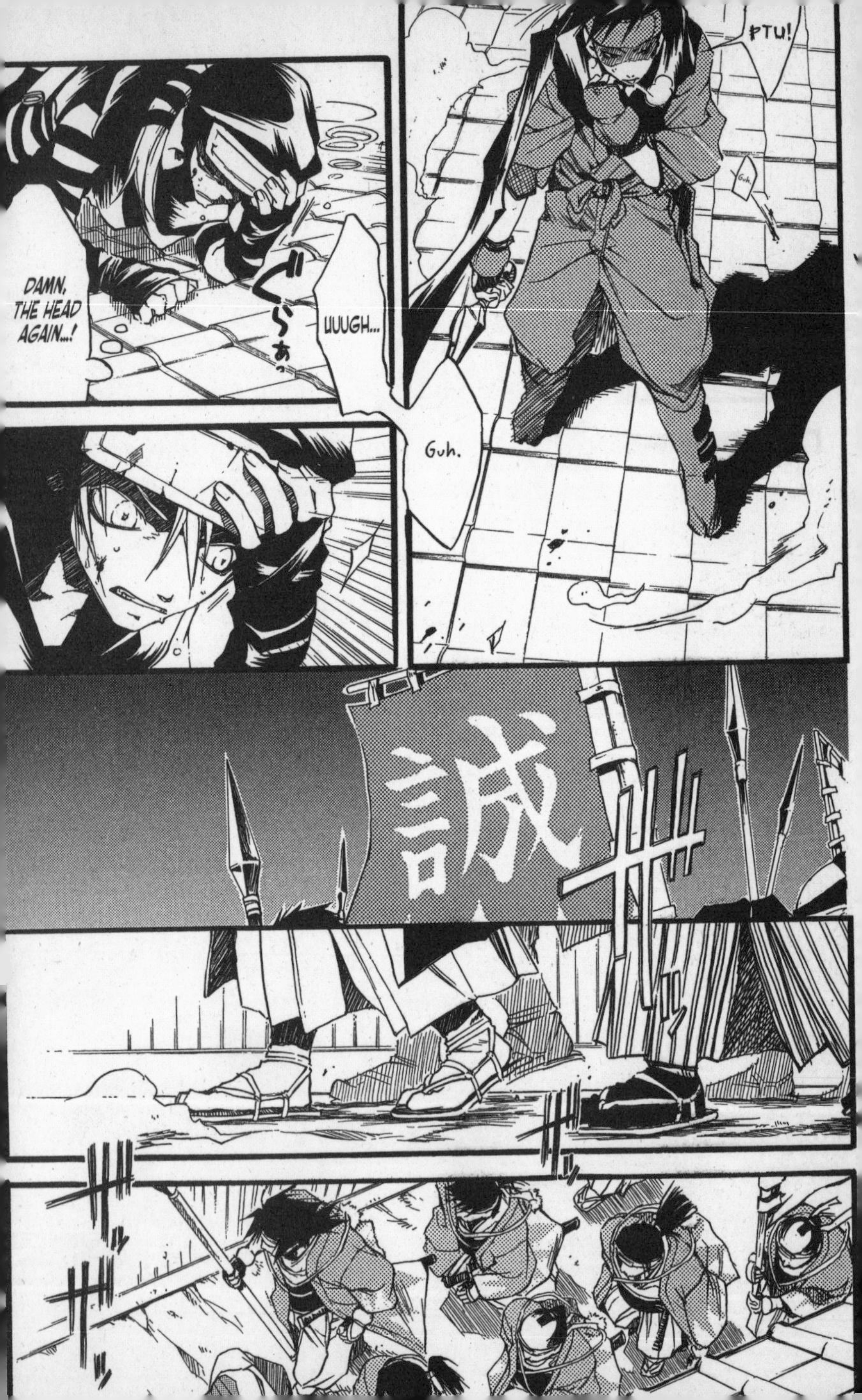
PTU!
Guh.
Guh.
UUUGH...
ぐらぁっ
DAMN, THE HEAD AGAIN...!
誠

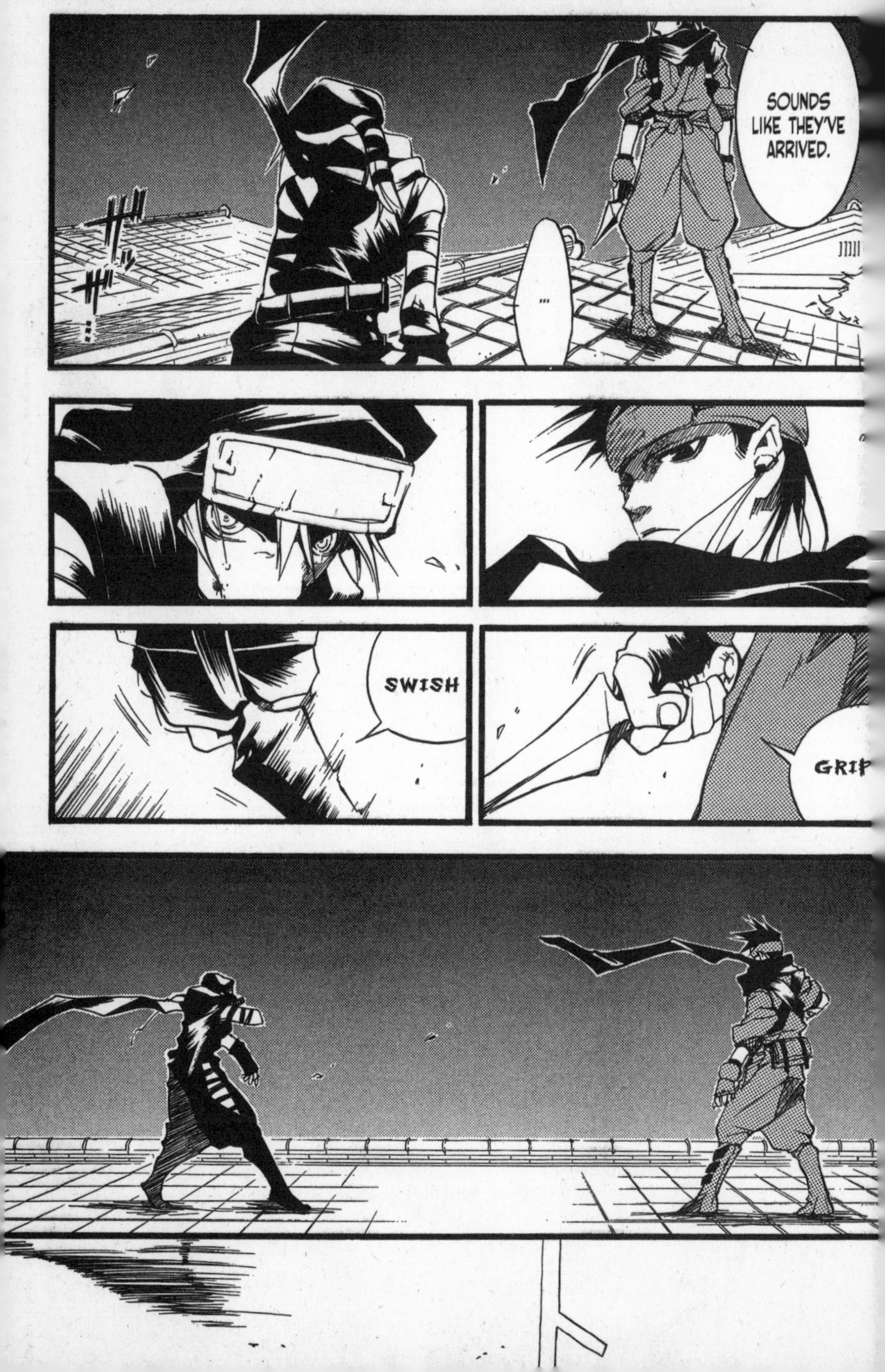
SOUNDS LIKE THEY'VE ARRIVED.
...
GRIP
SWISH

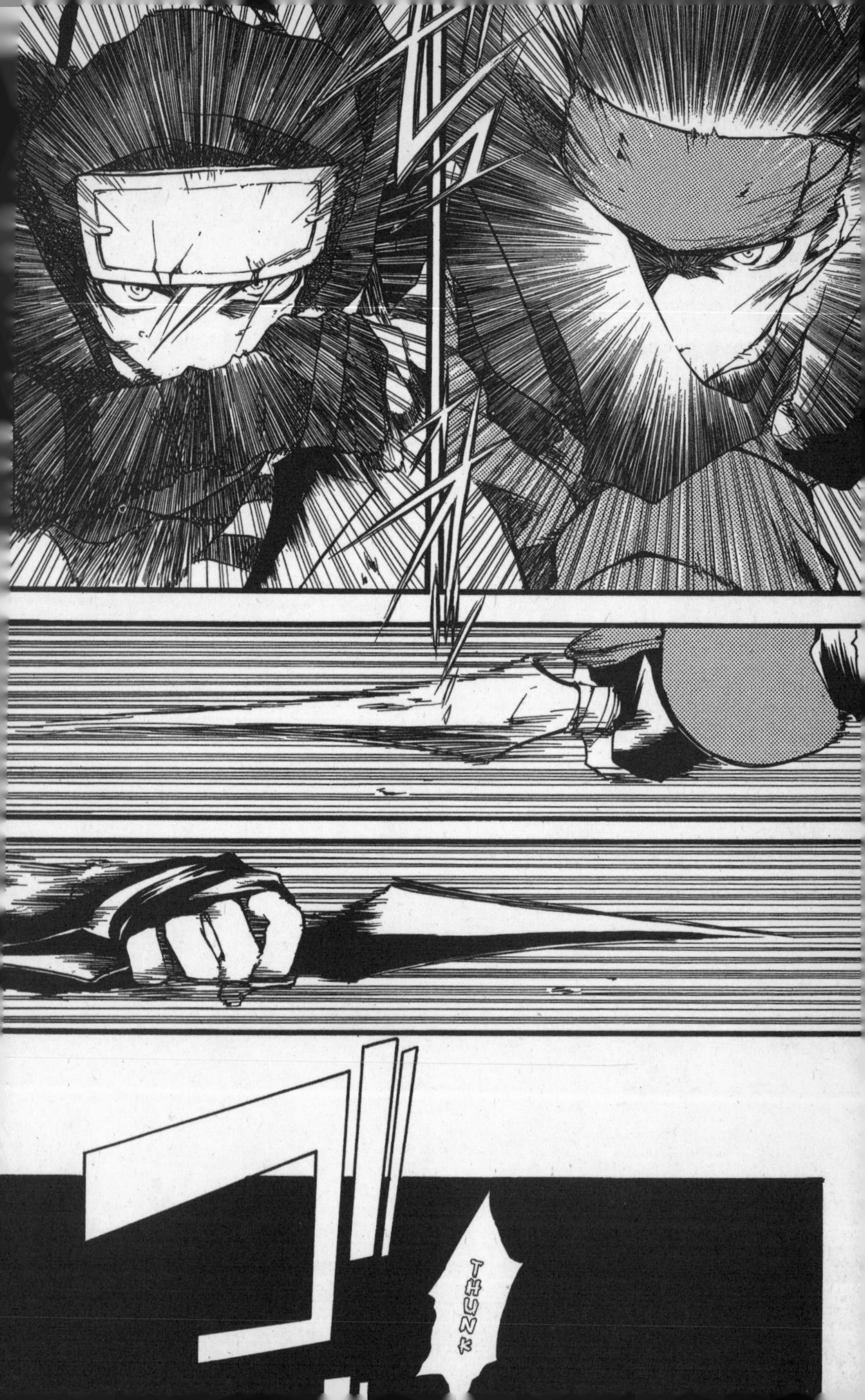
THUNK

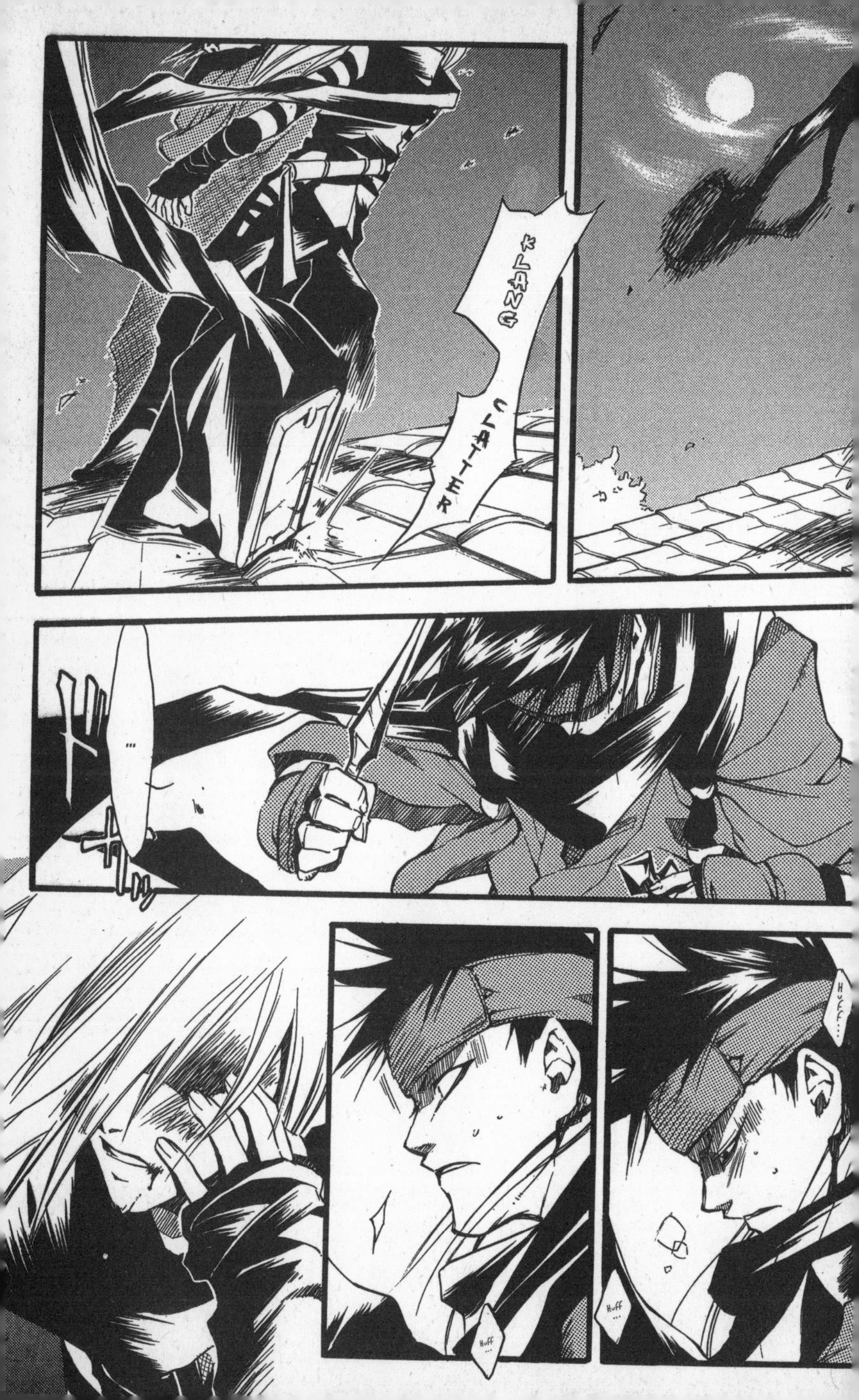
KLANG
CLATTER
...
Huff...
Huff...
Huff...

IMPOSSIBLE... A BARBARIAN NINJA?

BLONDE...

WHY DON'T YOU KILL ME?

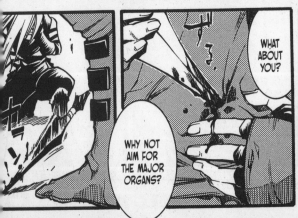

WHAT ABOUT YOU?

WHY NOT AIM FOR THE MAJOR ORGANS?

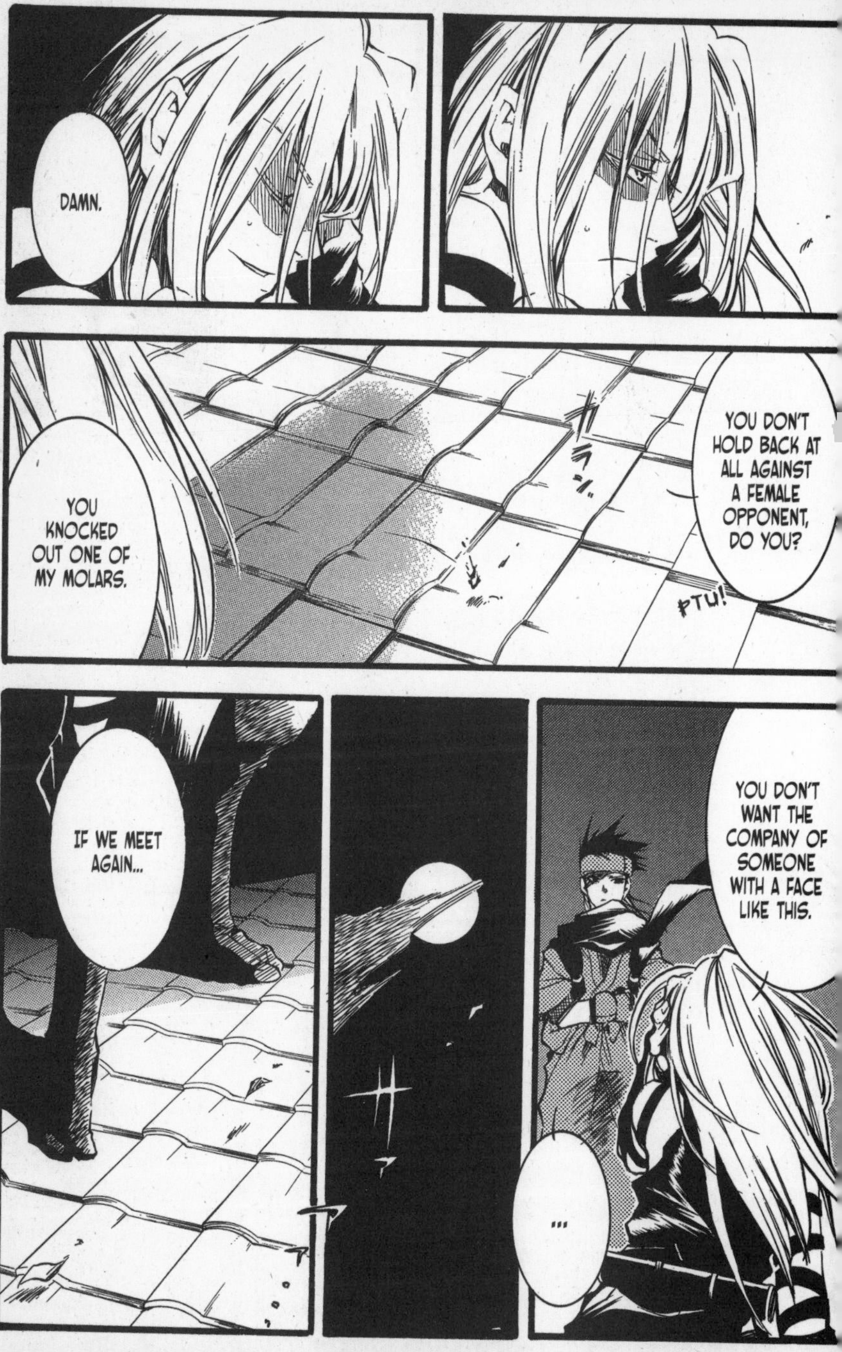
DAMN.
YOU DON'T HOLD BACK AT ALL AGAINST A FEMALE OPPONENT, DO YOU?
PTU!
YOU KNOCKED OUT ONE OF MY MOLARS.
YOU DON'T WANT THE COMPANY OF SOMEONE WITH A FACE LIKE THIS.
...
IF WE MEET AGAIN...

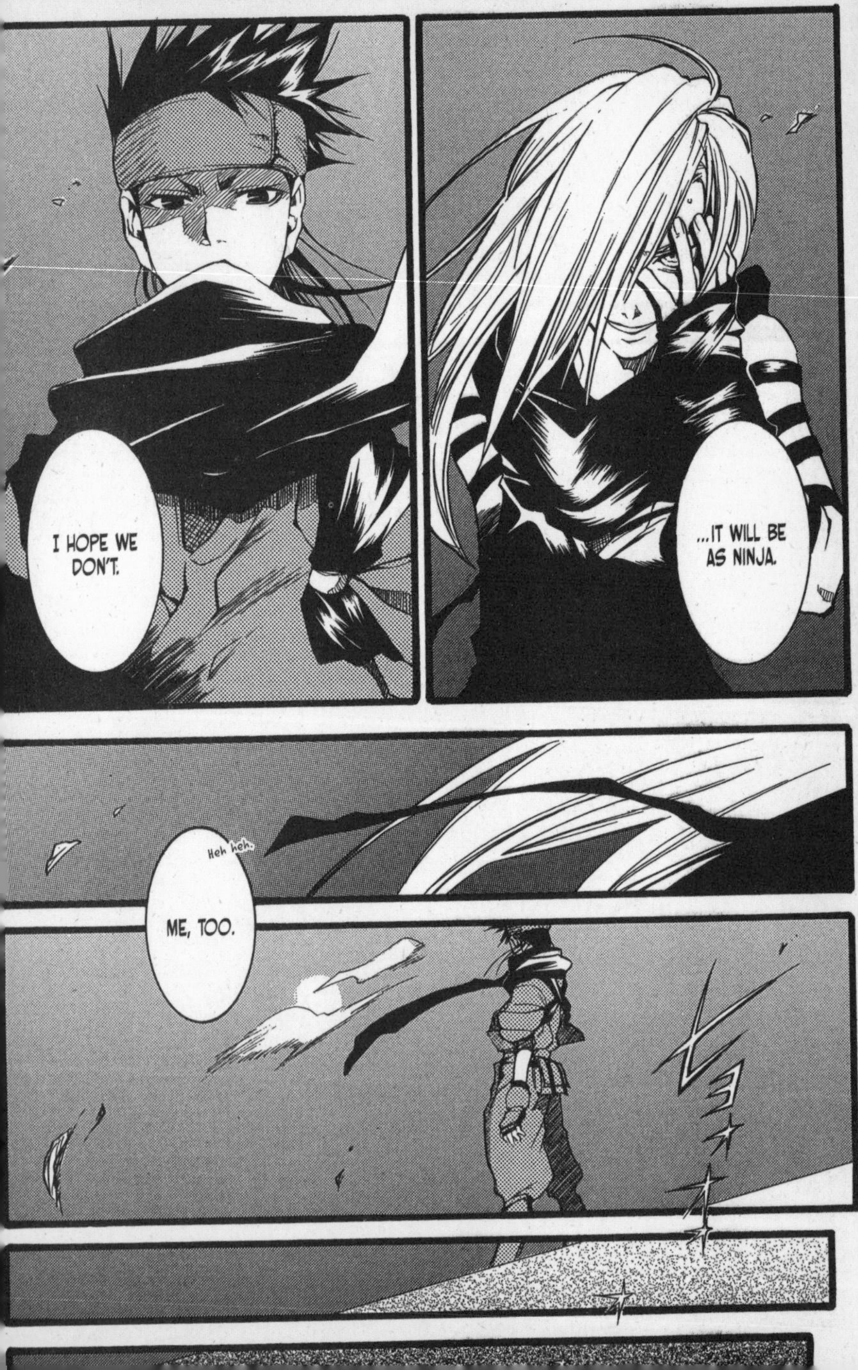
...IT WILL BE AS NINJA.
I HOPE WE DON'T.
Heh heh.
ME, TOO.

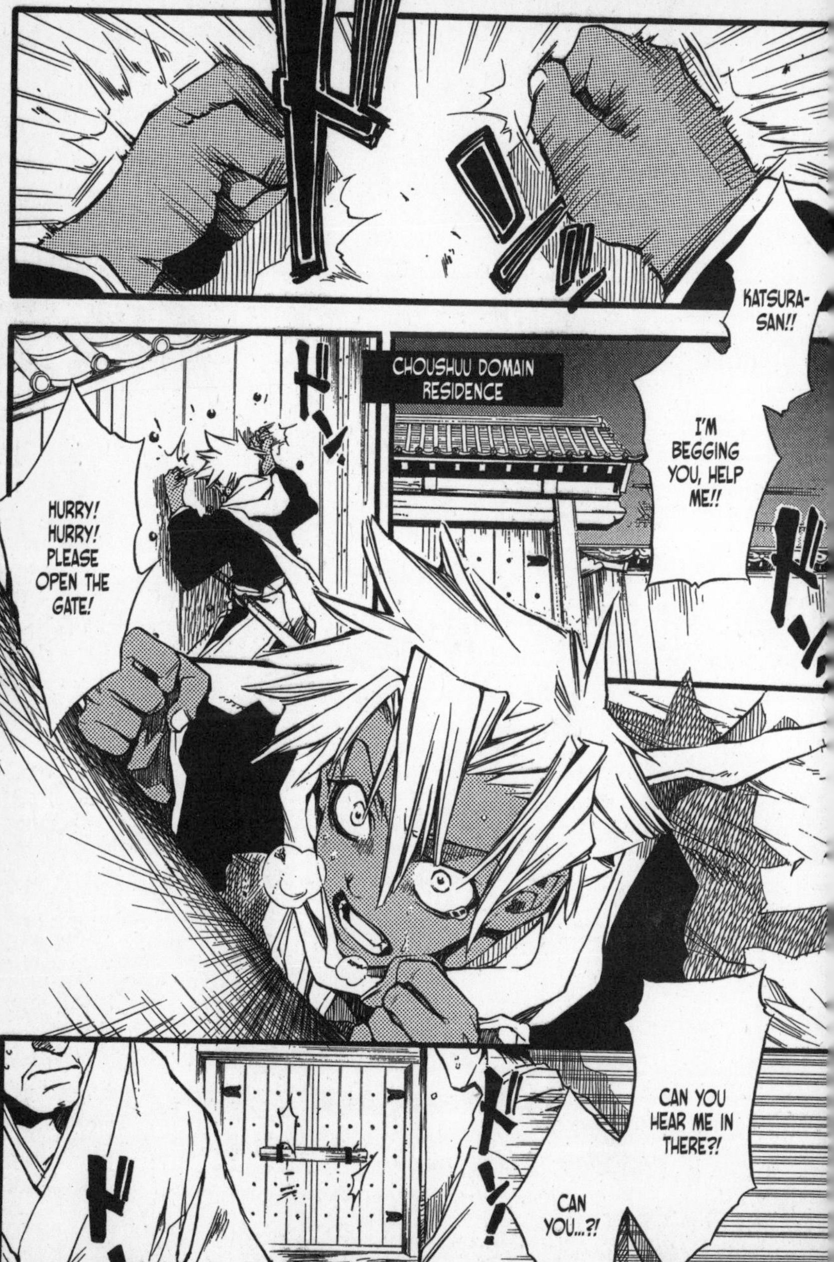
KATSURA-SAN!!
CHOUSHUU DOMAIN RESIDENCE
I'M BEGGING YOU, HELP ME!!
HURRY! HURRY! PLEASE OPEN THE GATE!
CAN YOU HEAR ME IN THERE?!
CAN YOU...?!

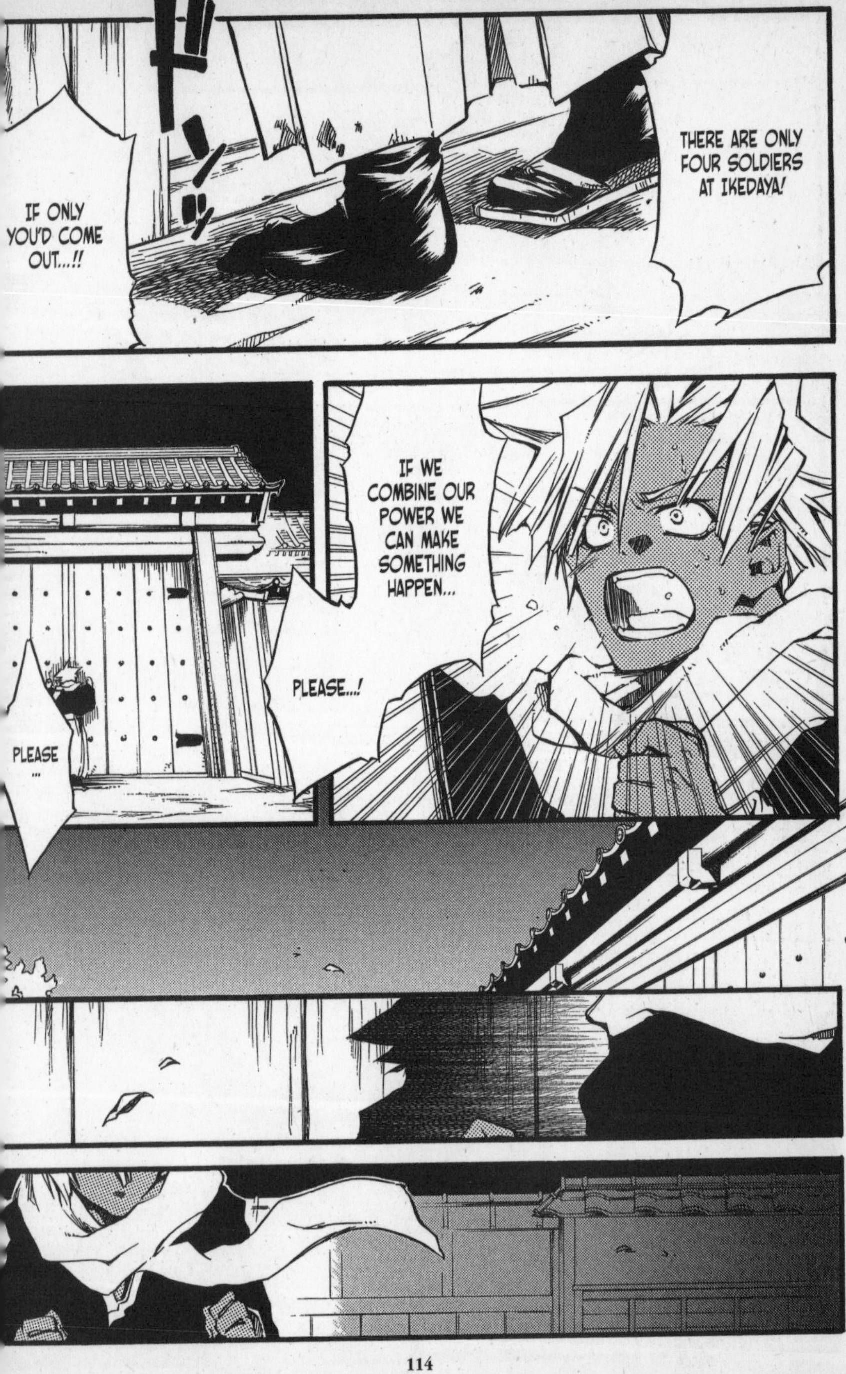
THERE ARE ONLY FOUR SOLDIERS AT IKEDAYA!
IF ONLY YOU'D COME OUT...!!
IF WE COMBINE OUR POWER WE CAN MAKE SOMETHING HAPPEN...
PLEASE...!
PLEASE ...

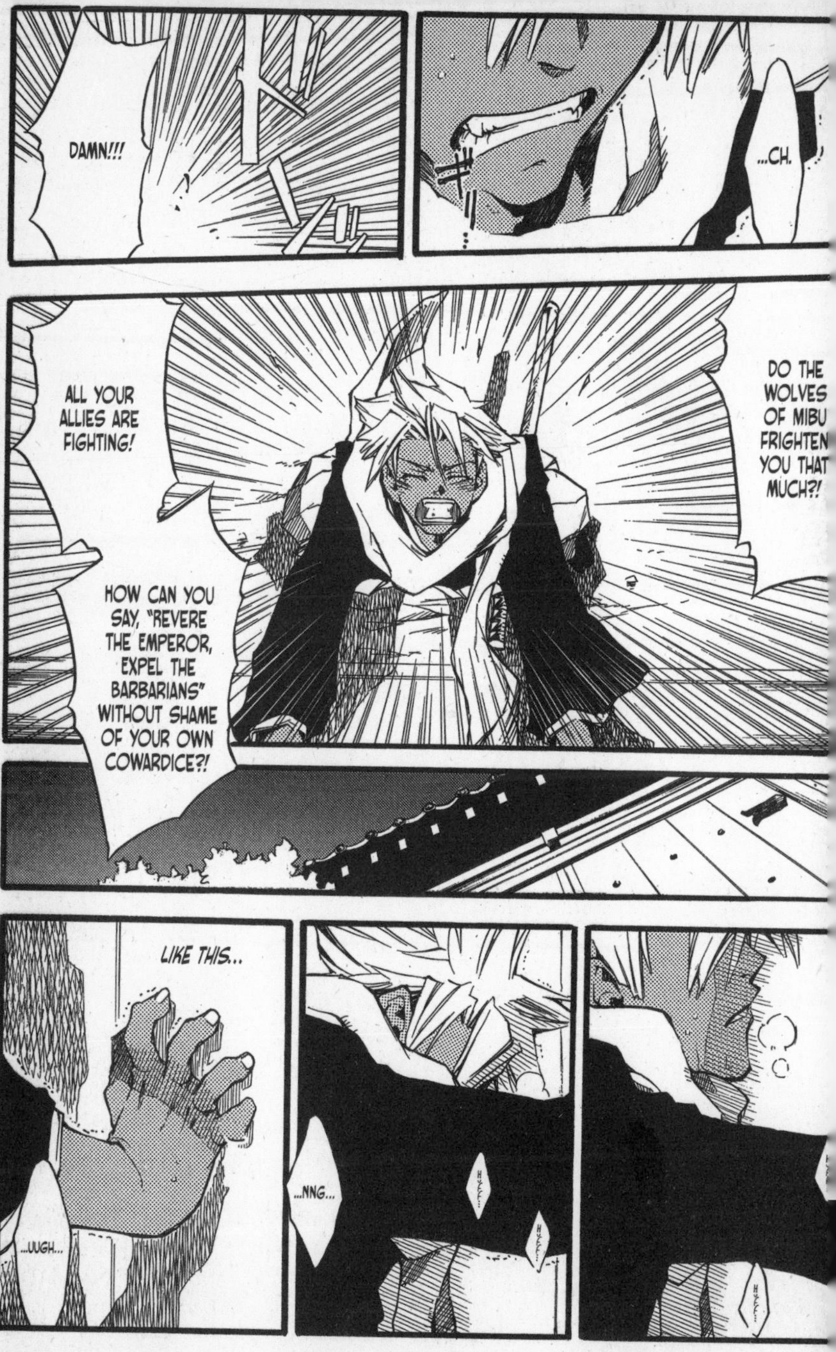
...CH.
DAMN!!!
DO THE WOLVES OF MIBU FRIGHTEN YOU THAT MUCH?!
ALL YOUR ALLIES ARE FIGHTING!
HOW CAN YOU SAY, "REVERE THE EMPEROR, EXPEL THE BARBARIANS" WITHOUT SHAME OF YOUR OWN COWARDICE?!
HUFF...
...NNG...
HUFF...
HUFF...
LIKE THIS...
...UUGH...

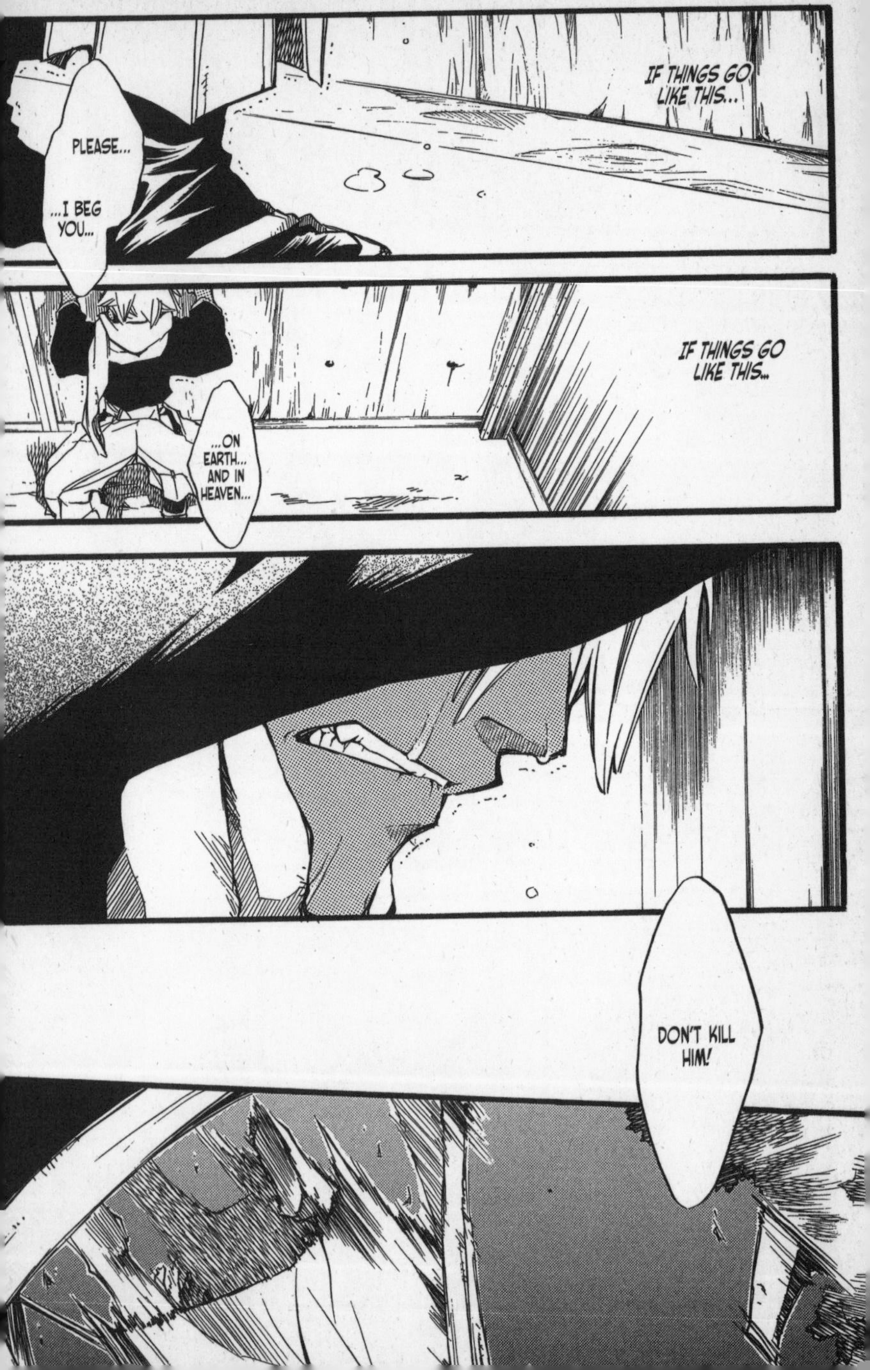
IF THINGS GO LIKE THIS...
PLEASE...
...I BEG YOU...
IF THINGS GO LIKE THIS...
...ON EARTH... AND IN HEAVEN...
DON'T KILL HIM!

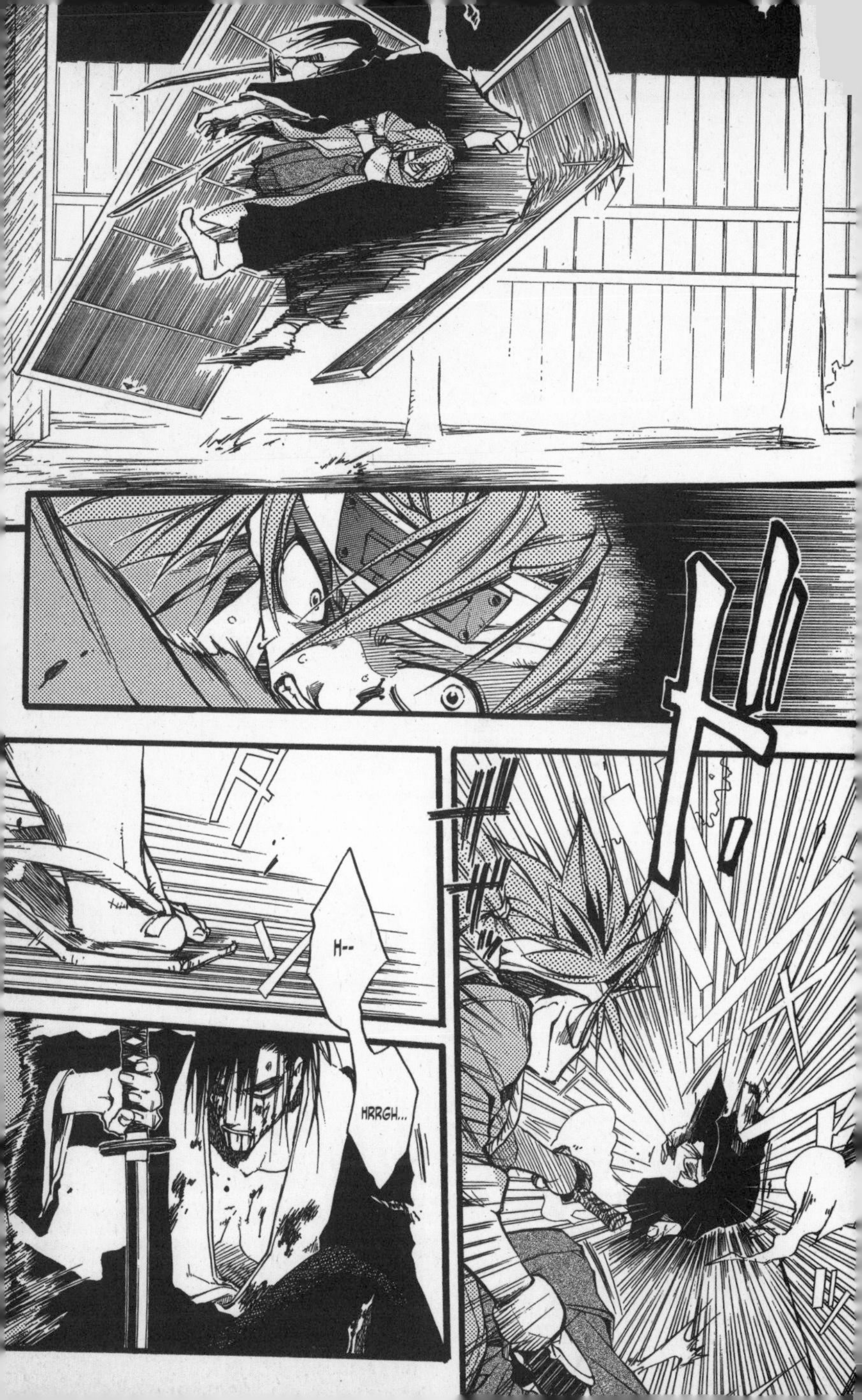
H--
HRRGH...

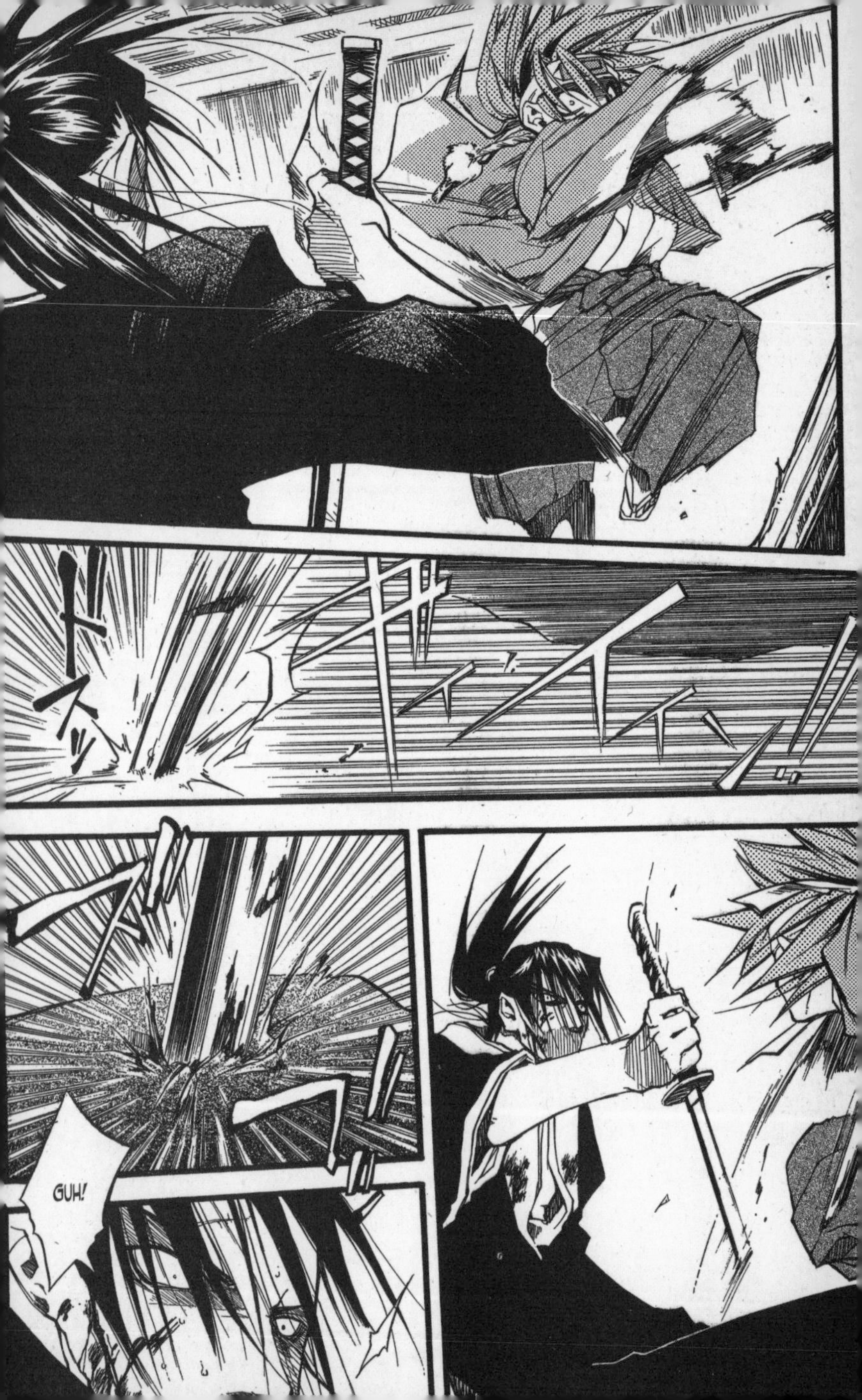
ドスッ!!
GUH!

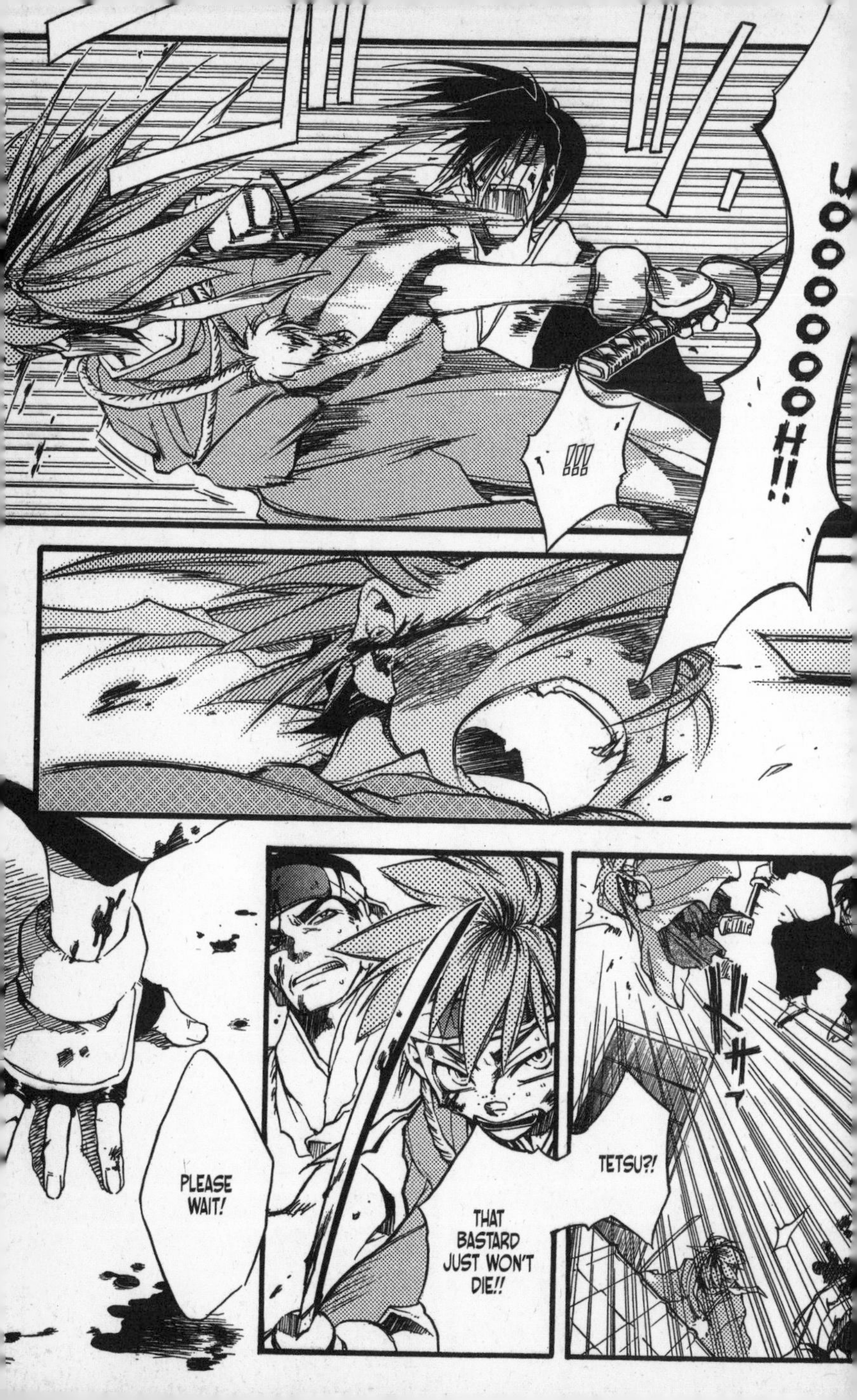
UOOOOOOOOH!!
!!!
TETSU?!
THAT BASTARD JUST WON'T DIE!!
PLEASE WAIT!

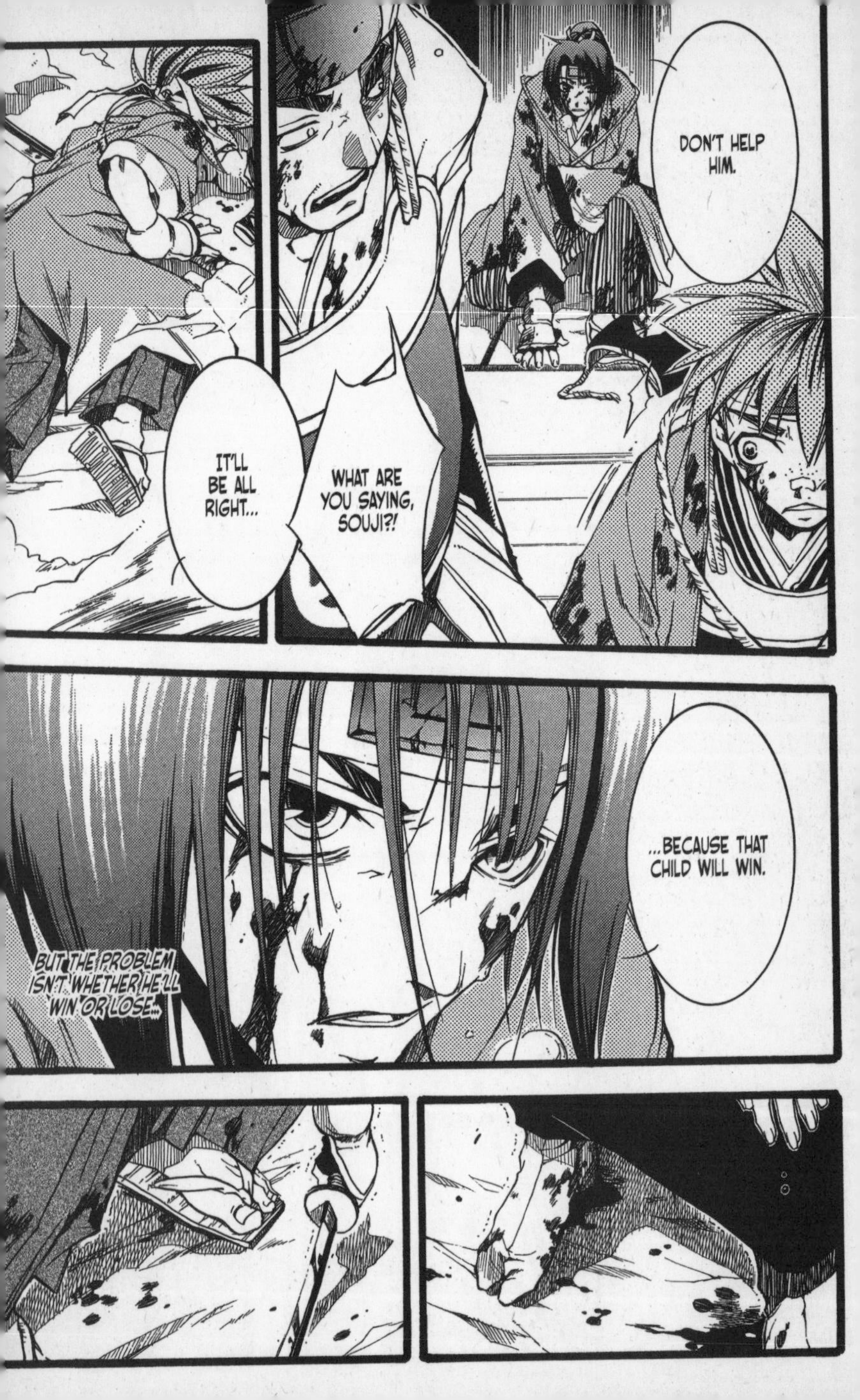
DON'T HELP HIM.
WHAT ARE YOU SAYING, SOUJI?!
IT'LL BE ALL RIGHT...
...BECAUSE THAT CHILD WILL WIN.
BUT THE PROBLEM ISN'T WHETHER HE'LL WIN OR LOSE...

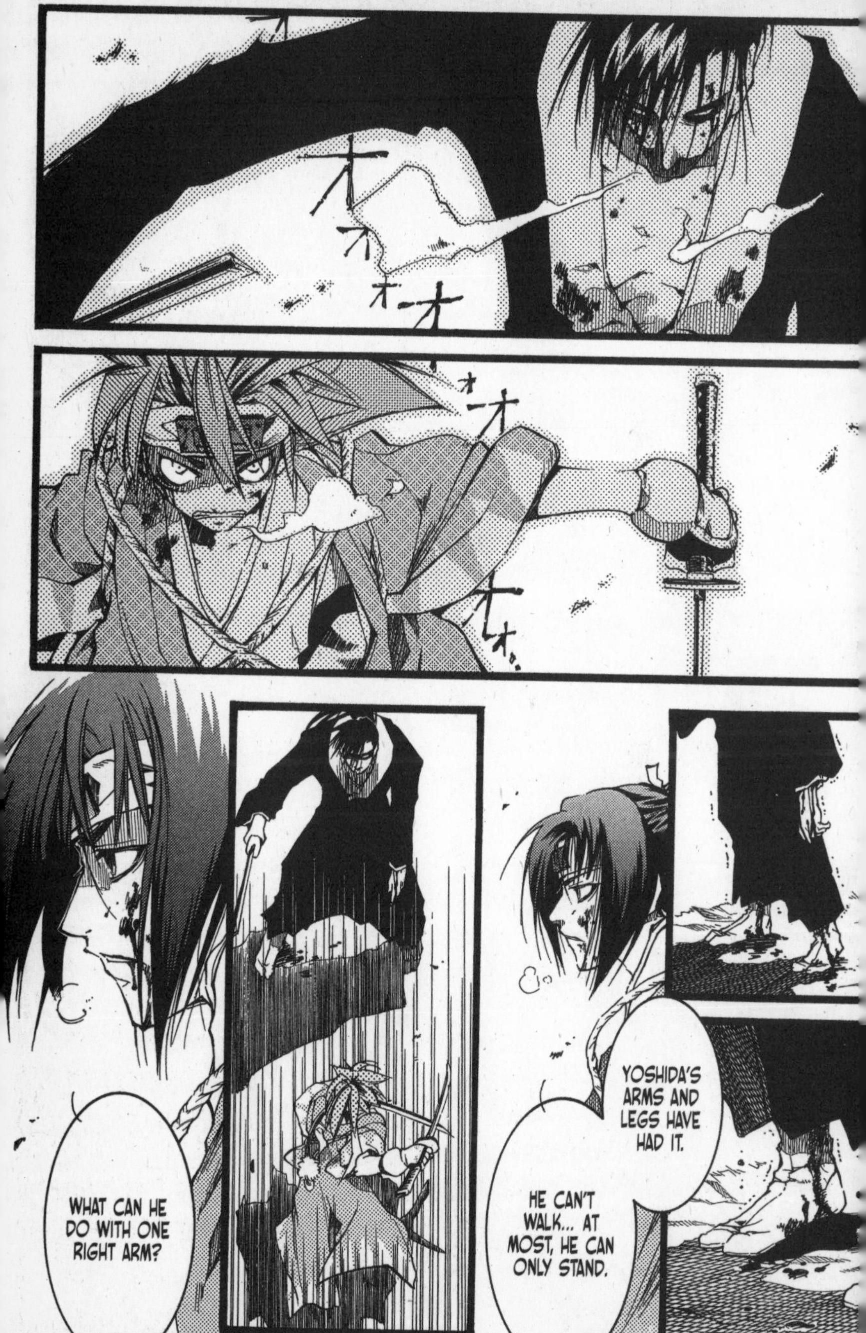
オオオオ
オオ
オォォ…
YOSHIDA'S ARMS AND LEGS HAVE HAD IT.
HE CAN'T WALK... AT MOST, HE CAN ONLY STAND.
WHAT CAN HE DO WITH ONE RIGHT ARM?

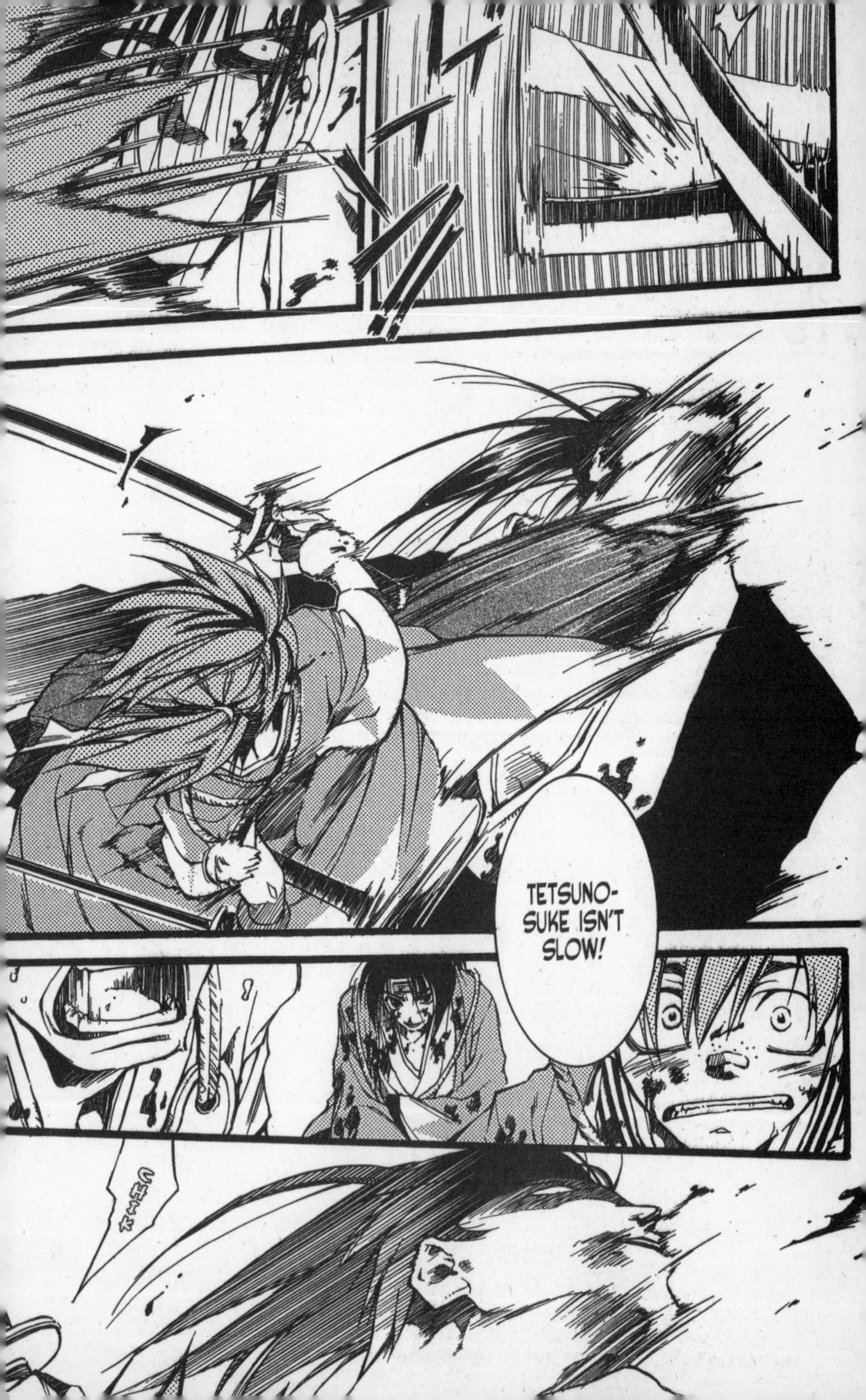
TETSUNO-SUKE ISN'T SLOW!
CHIK

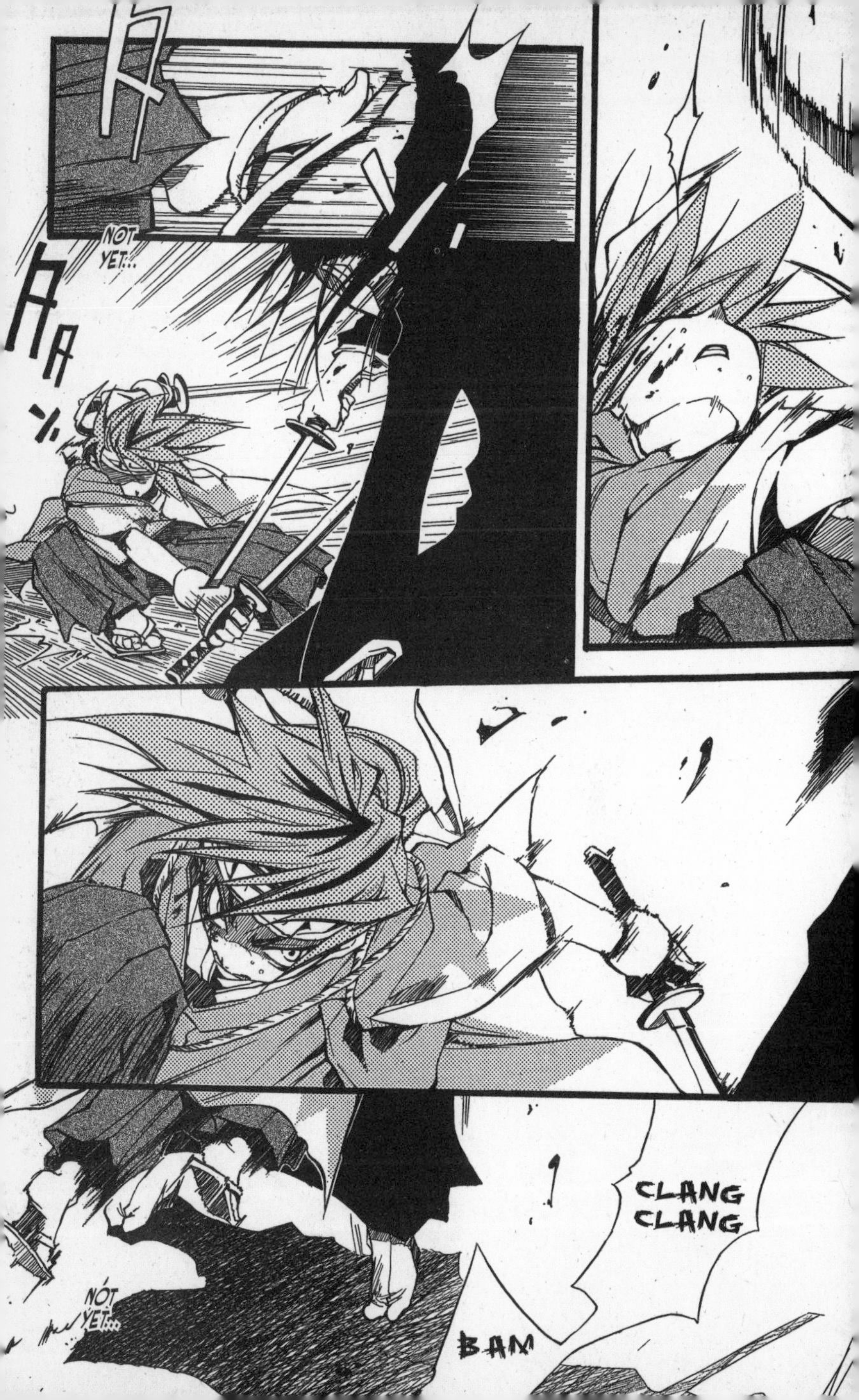
NOT YET...
CLANG
CLANG
NOT YET...
BAM

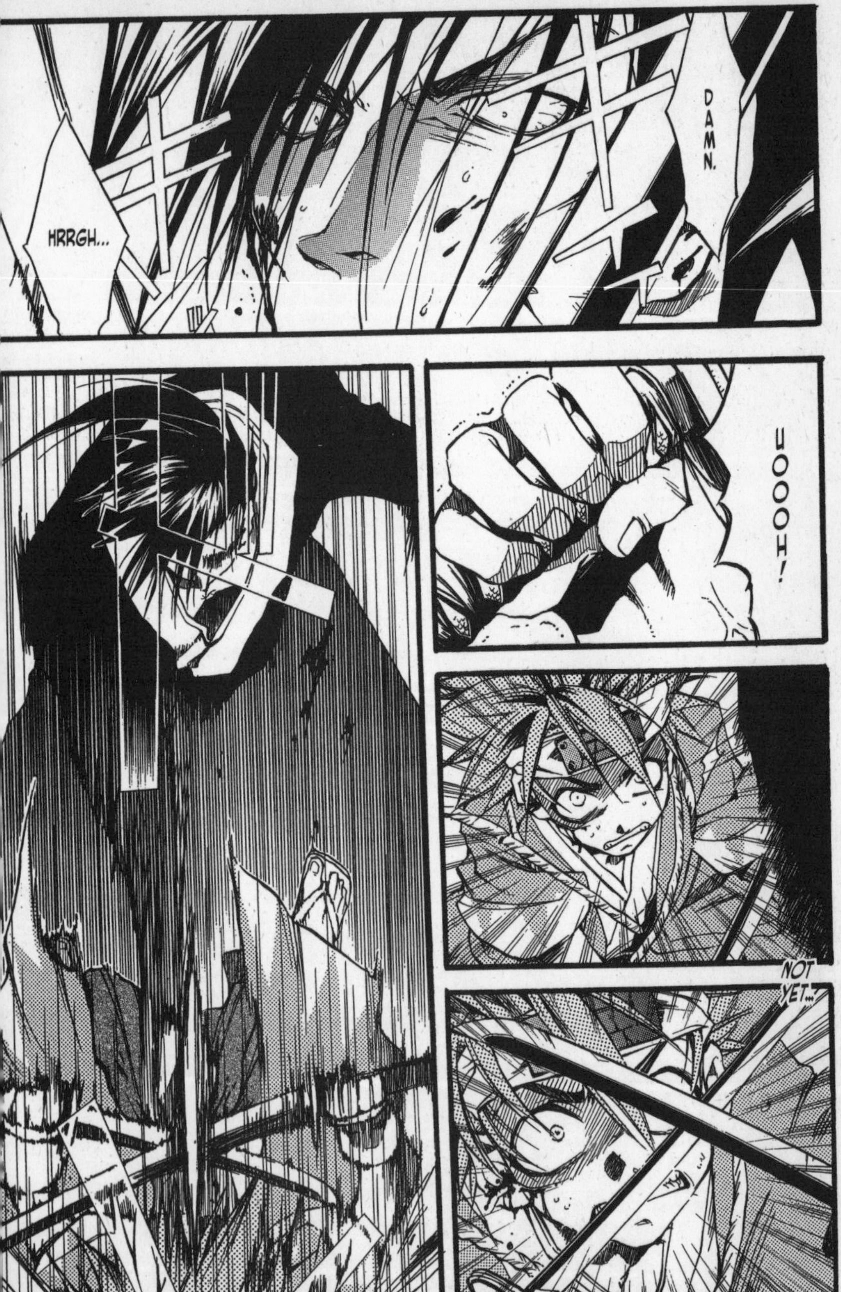
DAMN.
HRRGH...
UOOOH!
NOT YET...!

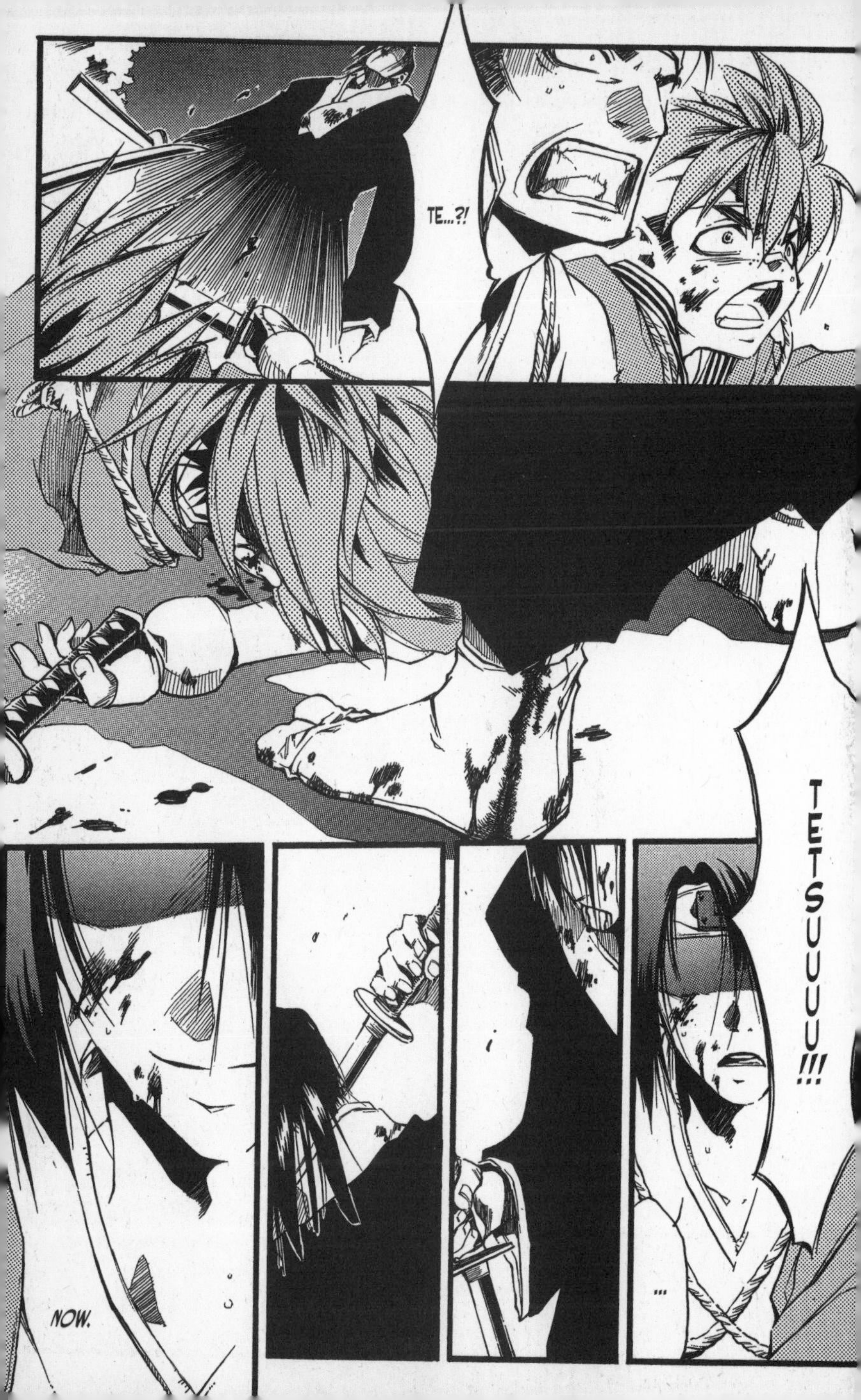
TE...?!
TETSUUUU!!!
...
NOW.

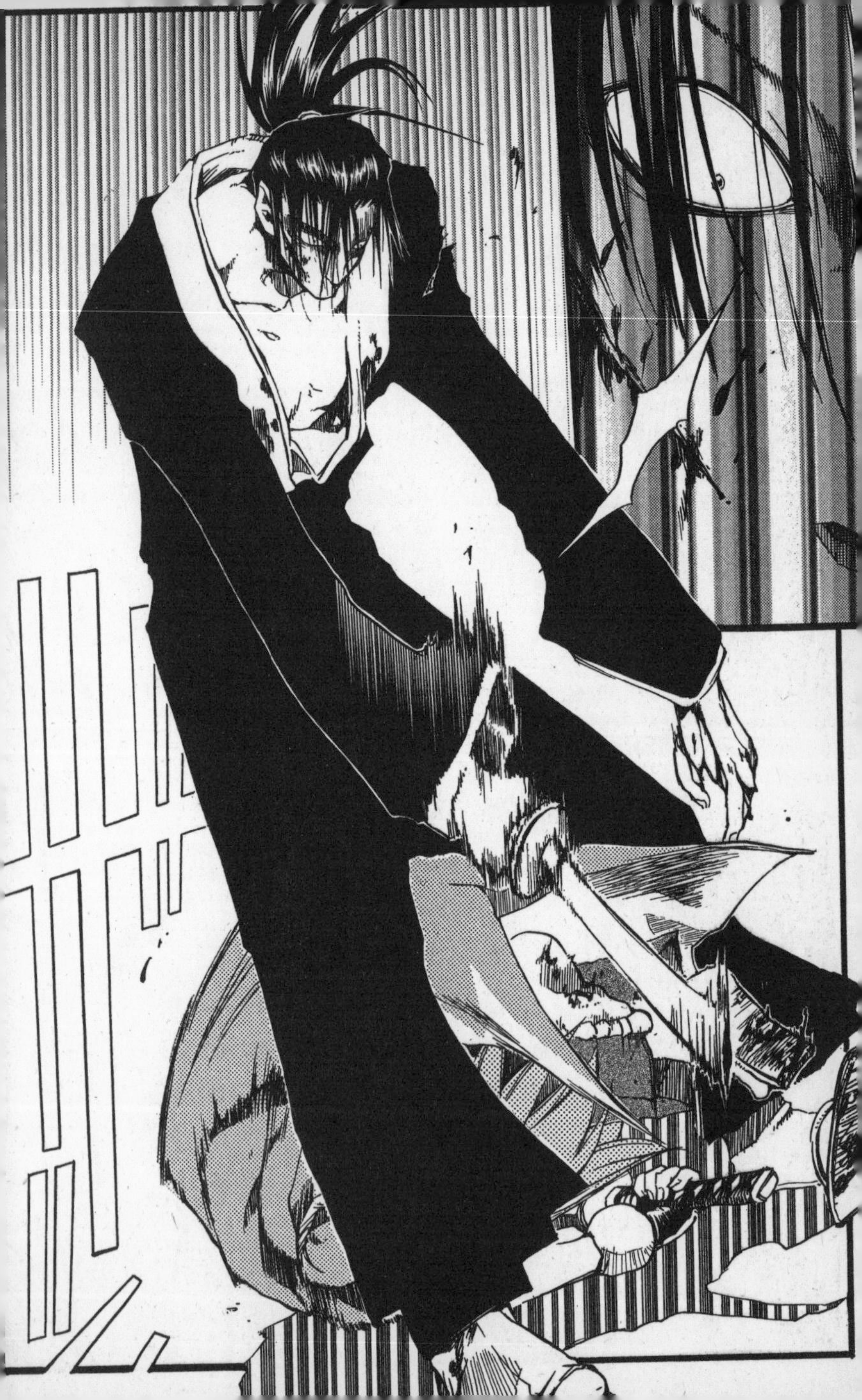

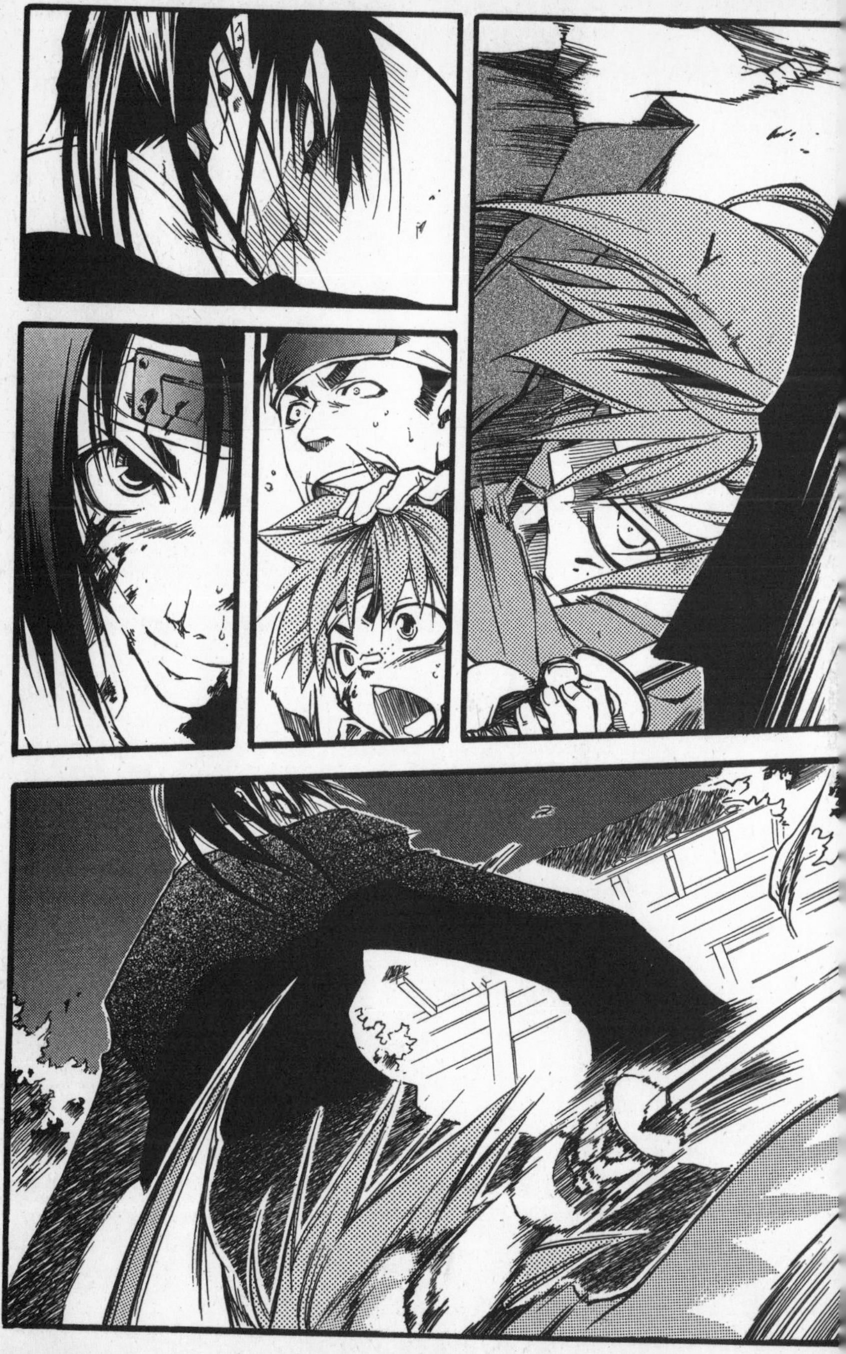

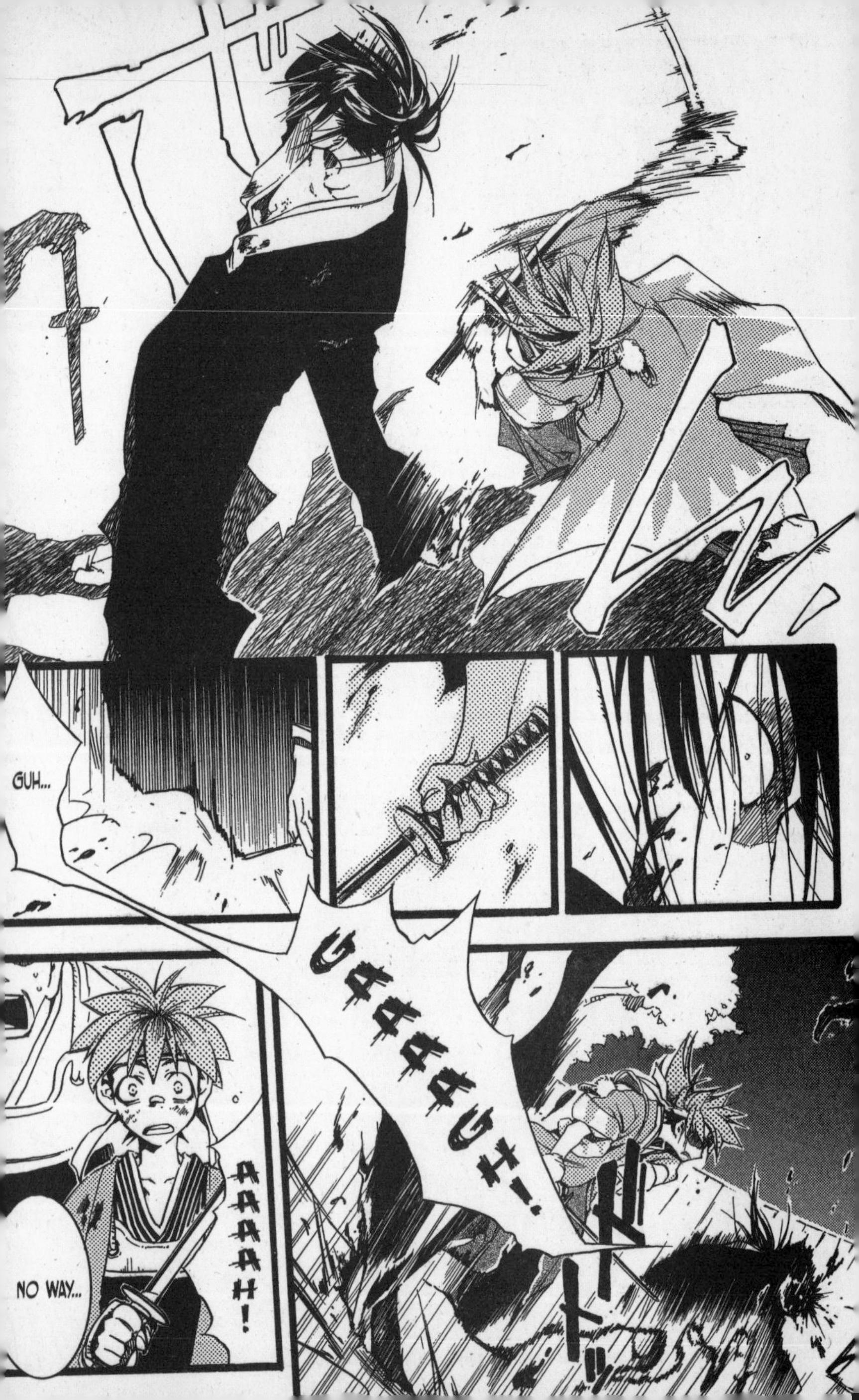
GUH...
UAAAAGH!!
AAAAAH!
NO WAY...

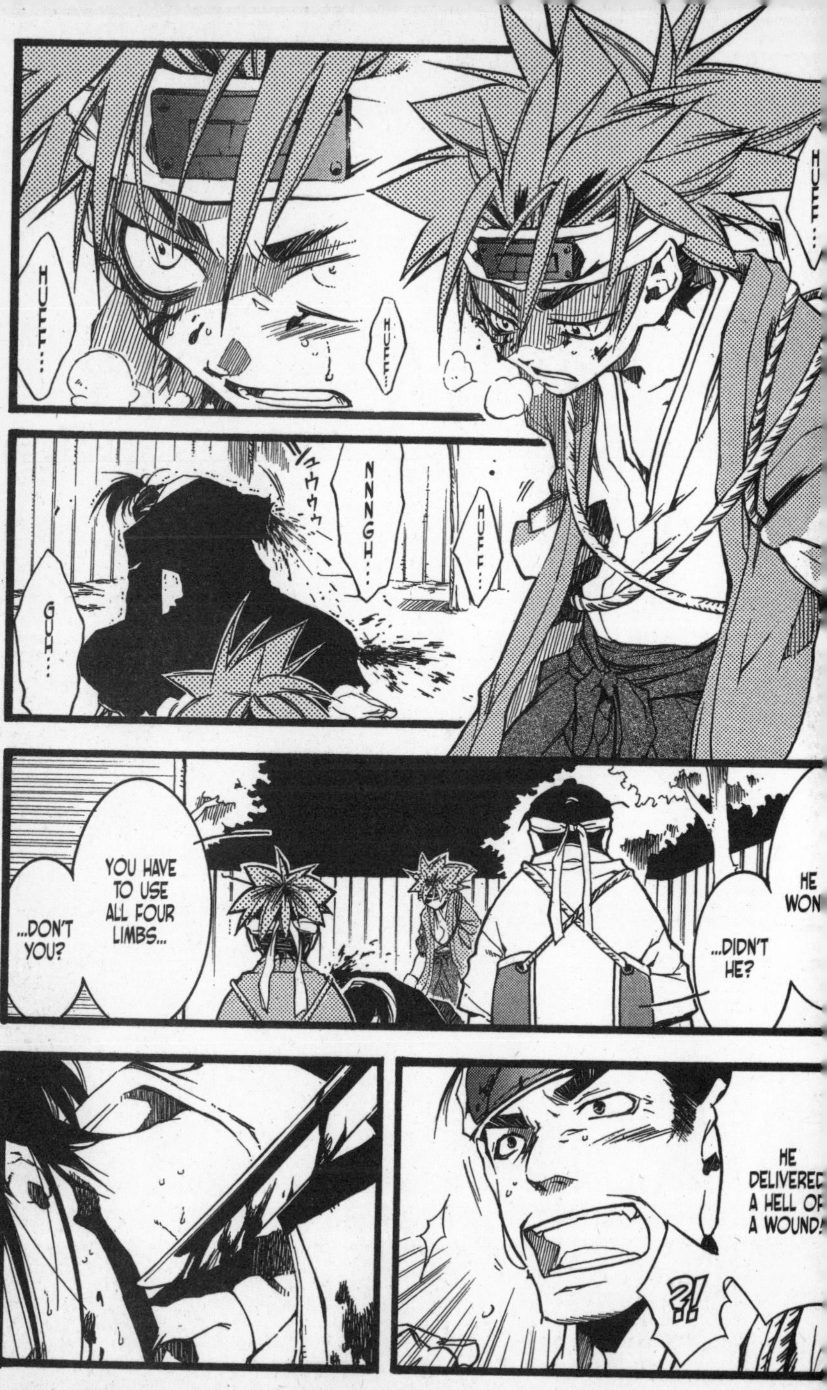
HUFF...
HUFF...
HUFF...
HUFF...
NNNGH...
シュウウウ
GUH...
HE WON
...DIDN'T HE?
YOU HAVE TO USE ALL FOUR LIMBS...
...DON'T YOU?
HE DELIVERED A HELL OF A WOUND!
?!

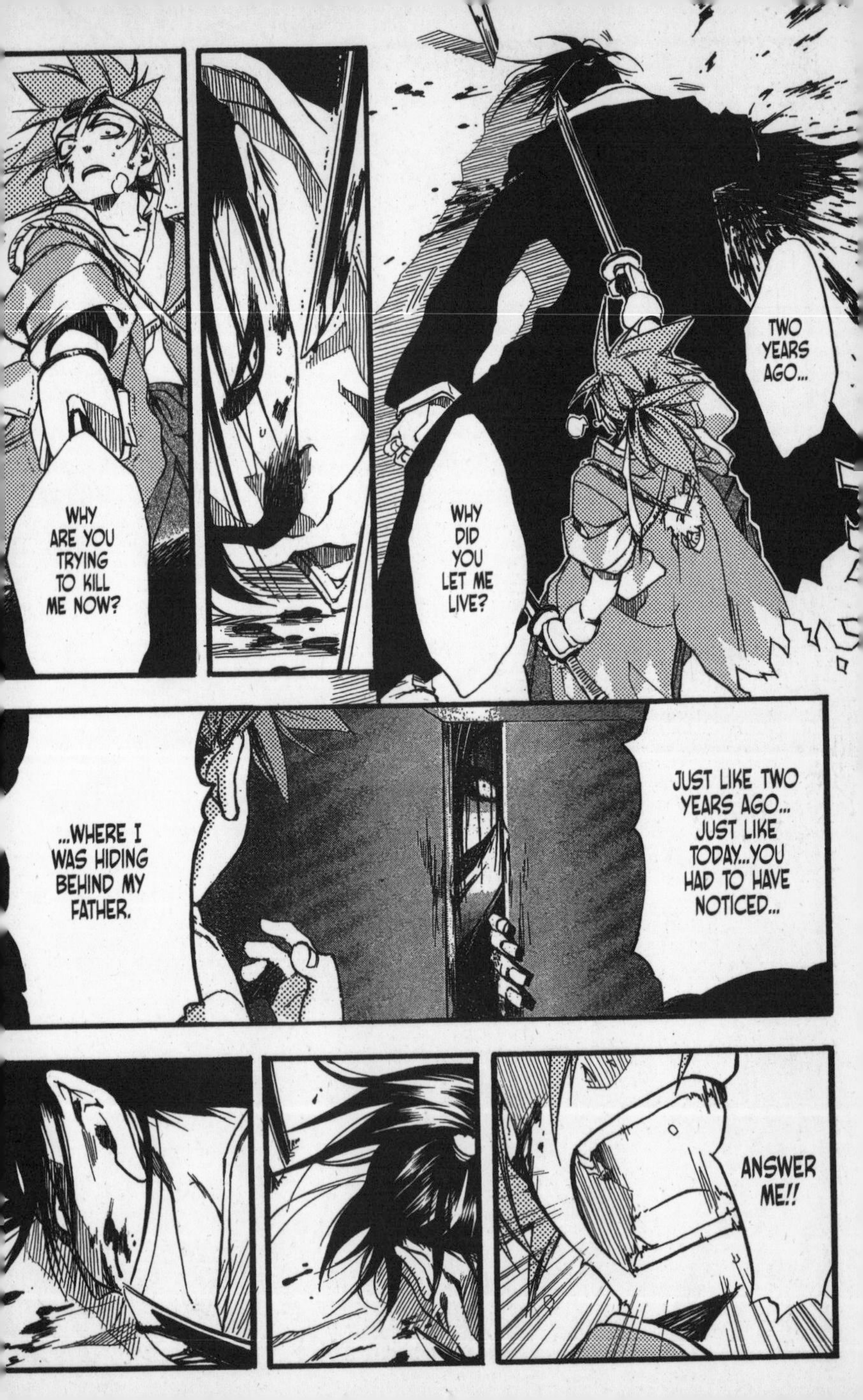
TWO YEARS AGO...
WHY DID YOU LET ME LIVE?
WHY ARE YOU TRYING TO KILL ME NOW?
JUST LIKE TWO YEARS AGO... JUST LIKE TODAY...YOU HAD TO HAVE NOTICED...
...WHERE I WAS HIDING BEHIND MY FATHER.
ANSWER ME!!

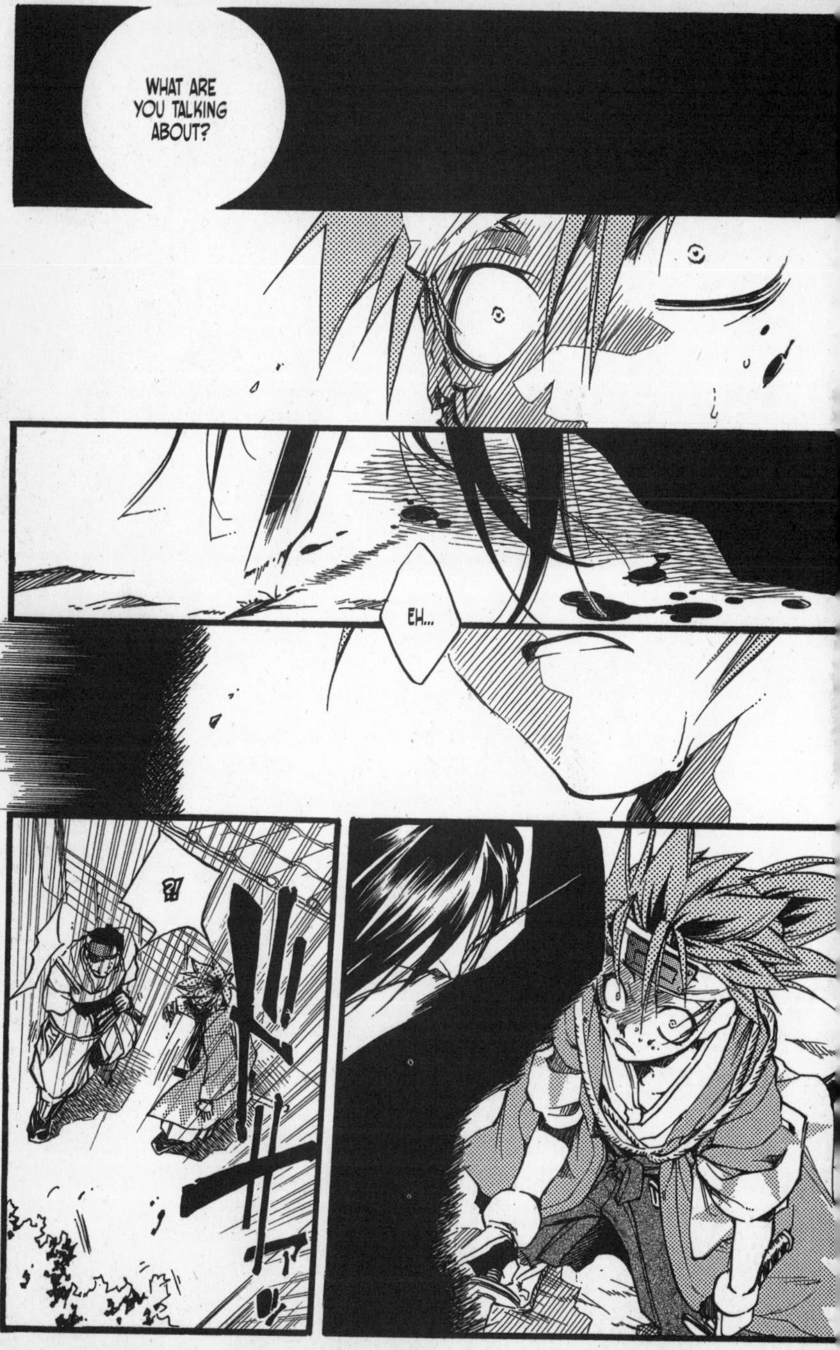
WHAT ARE YOU TALKING ABOUT?
EH...
?!

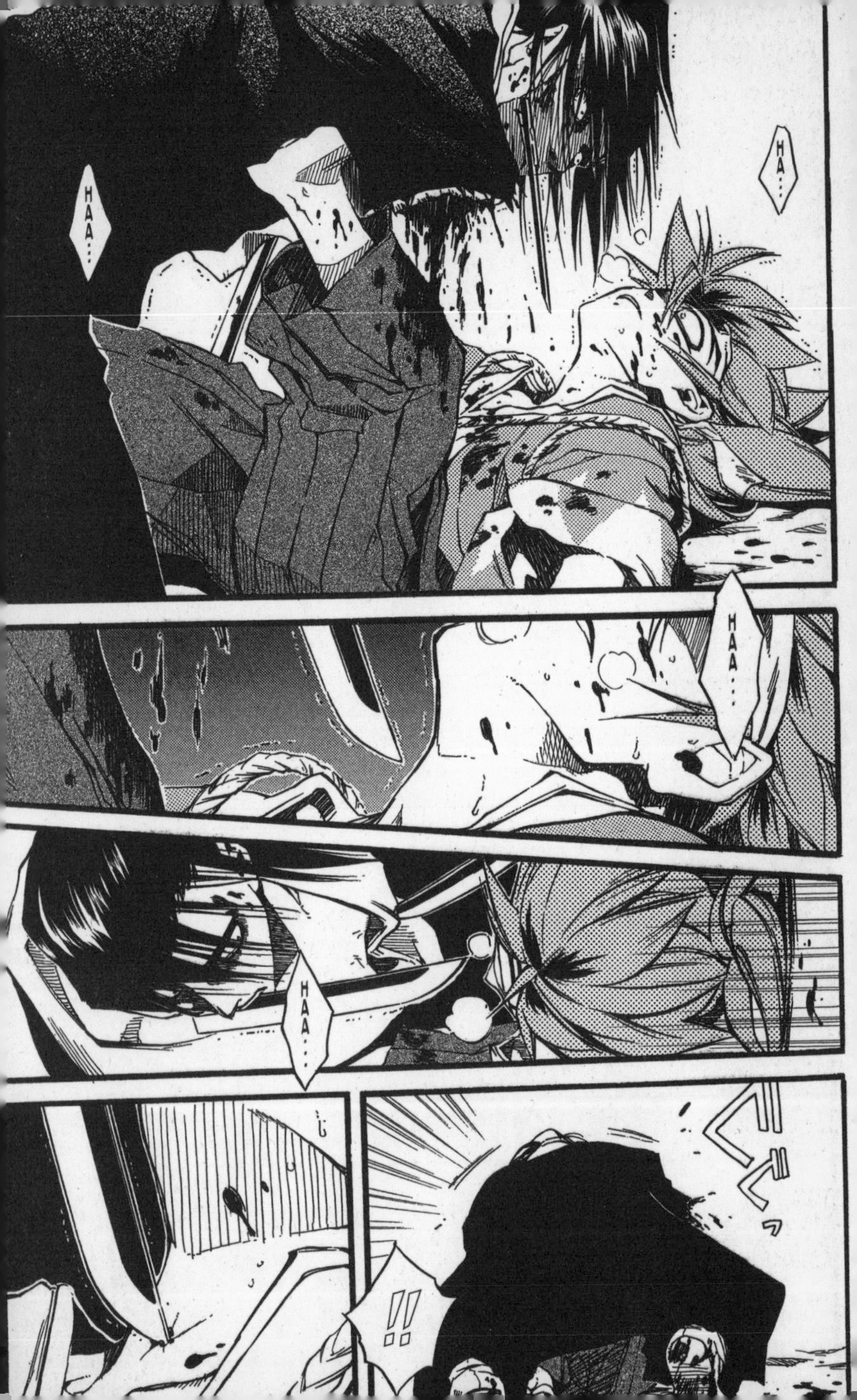
HA...
HAA...
HAA...
HAA...
!!

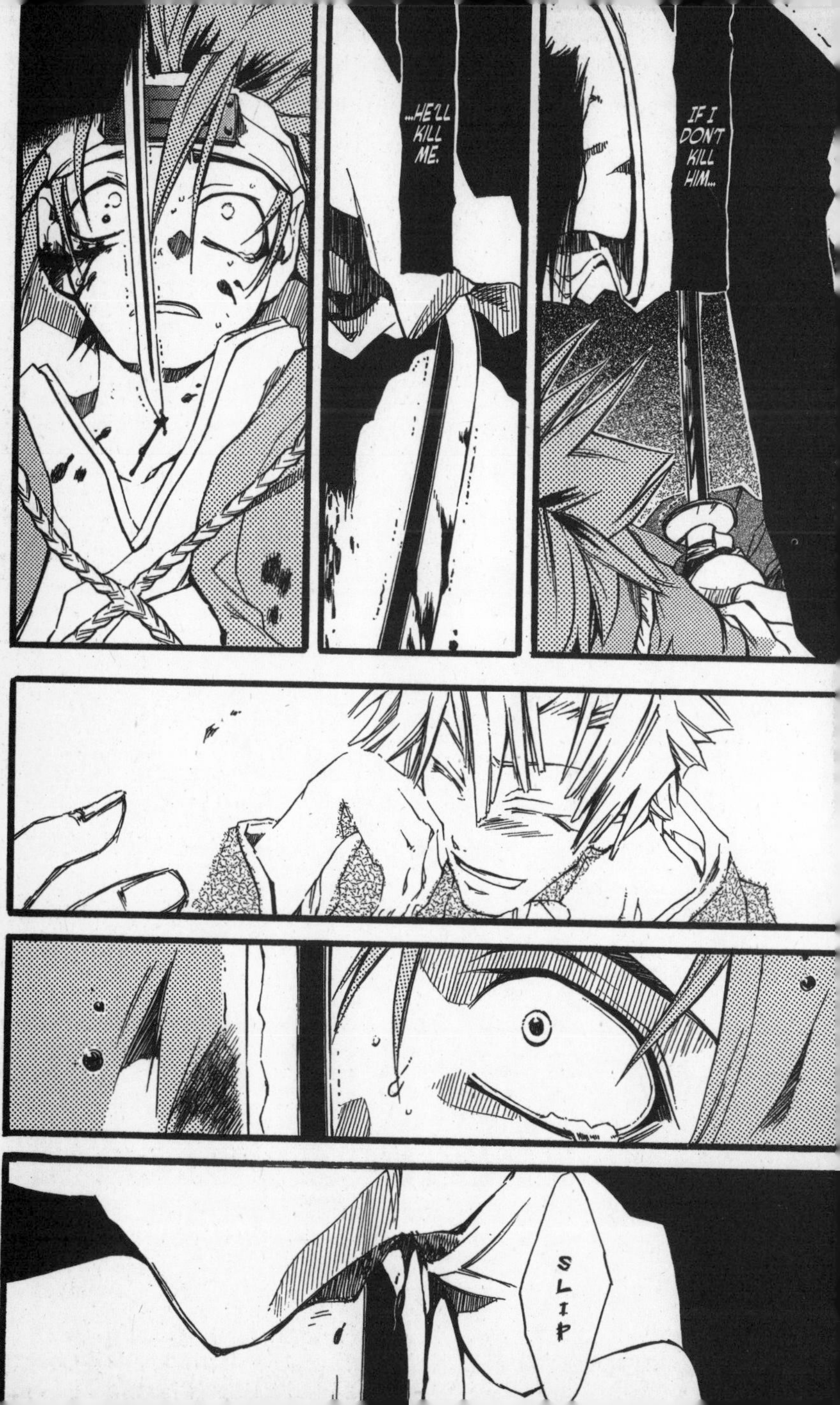
IF I DON'T KILL HIM...
...HE'LL KILL ME.
SLIP

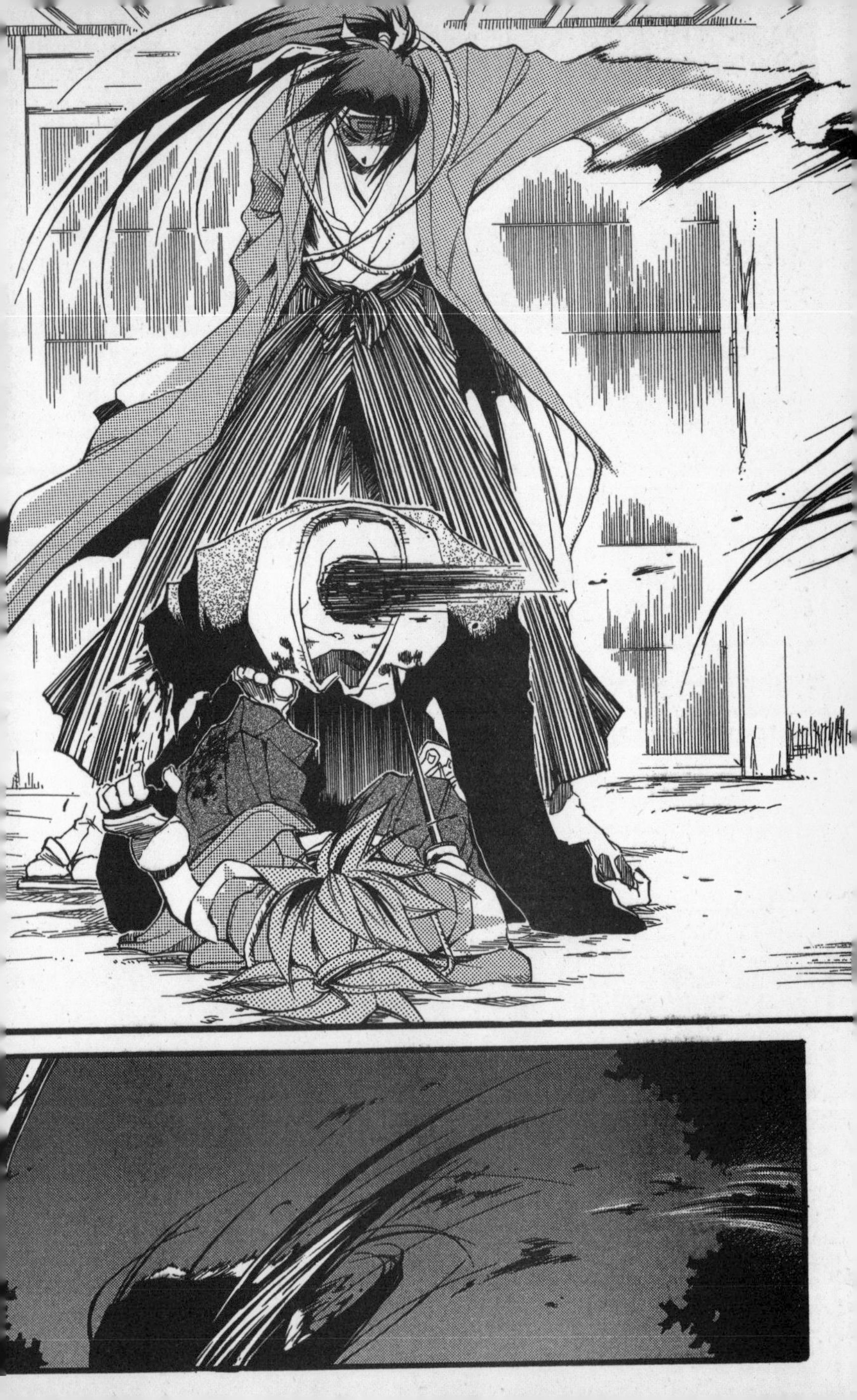

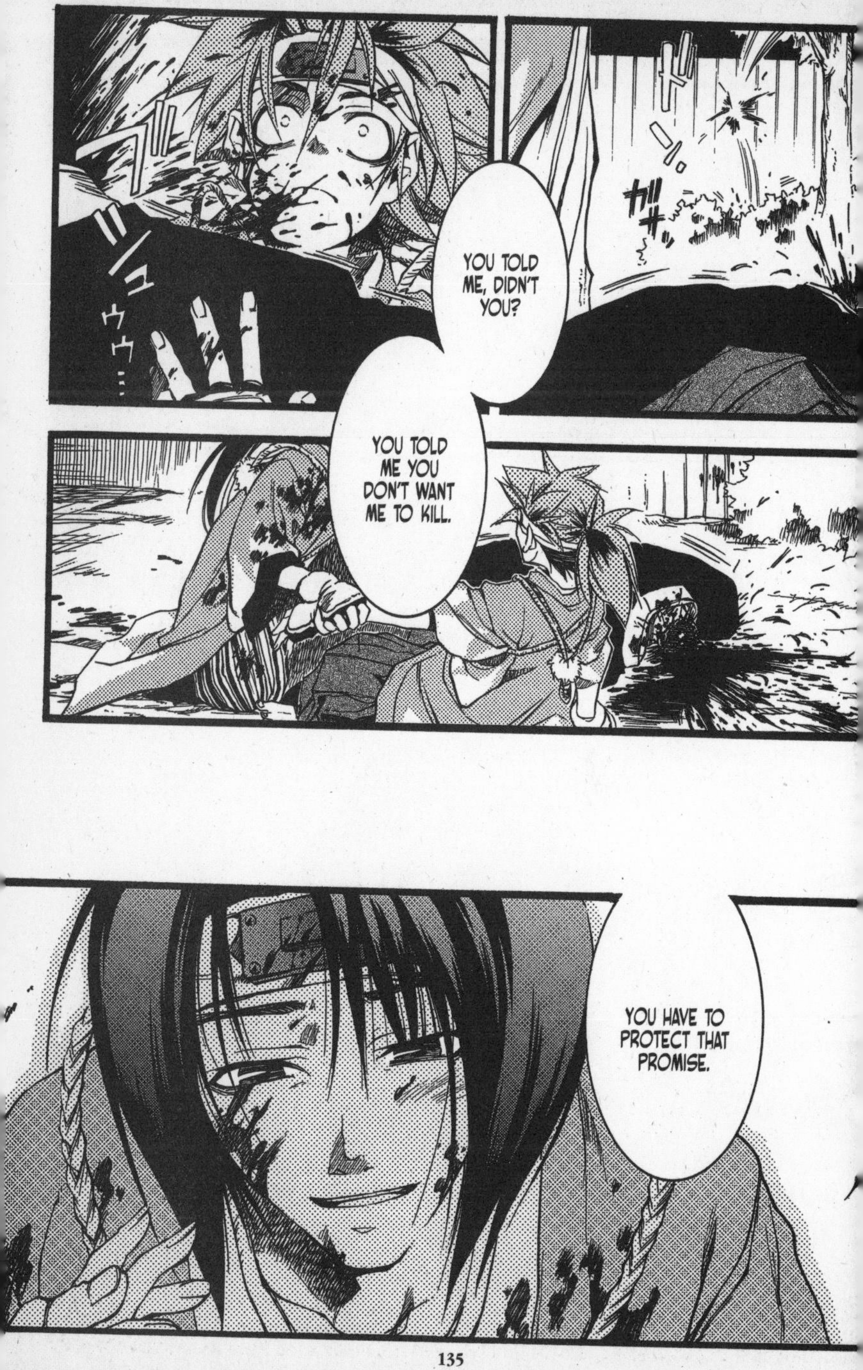
YOU TOLD ME, DIDN'T YOU?
YOU TOLD ME YOU DON'T WANT ME TO KILL.
YOU HAVE TO PROTECT THAT PROMISE.

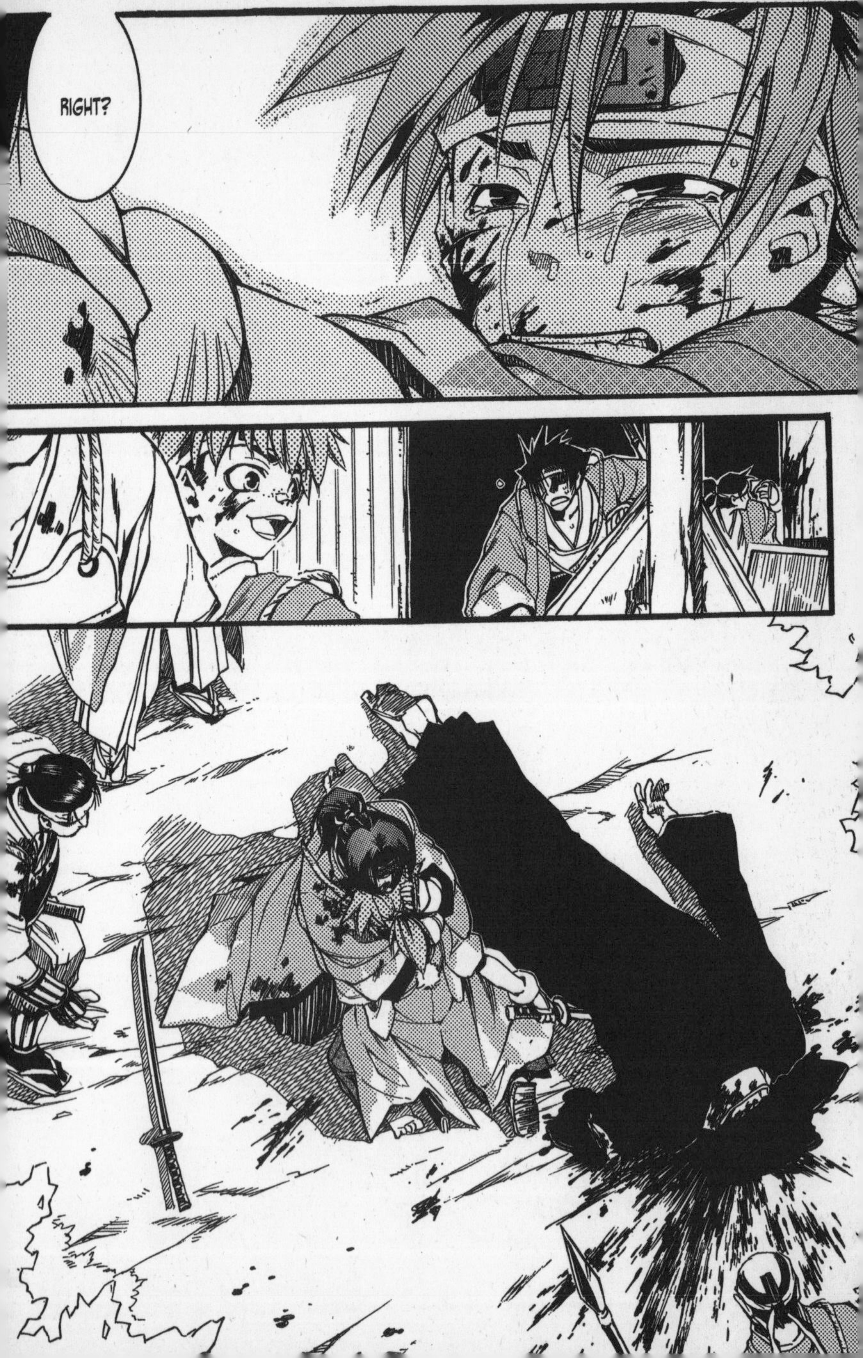
RIGHT?

Act.28
A Hard Day's Night (Final Scene)

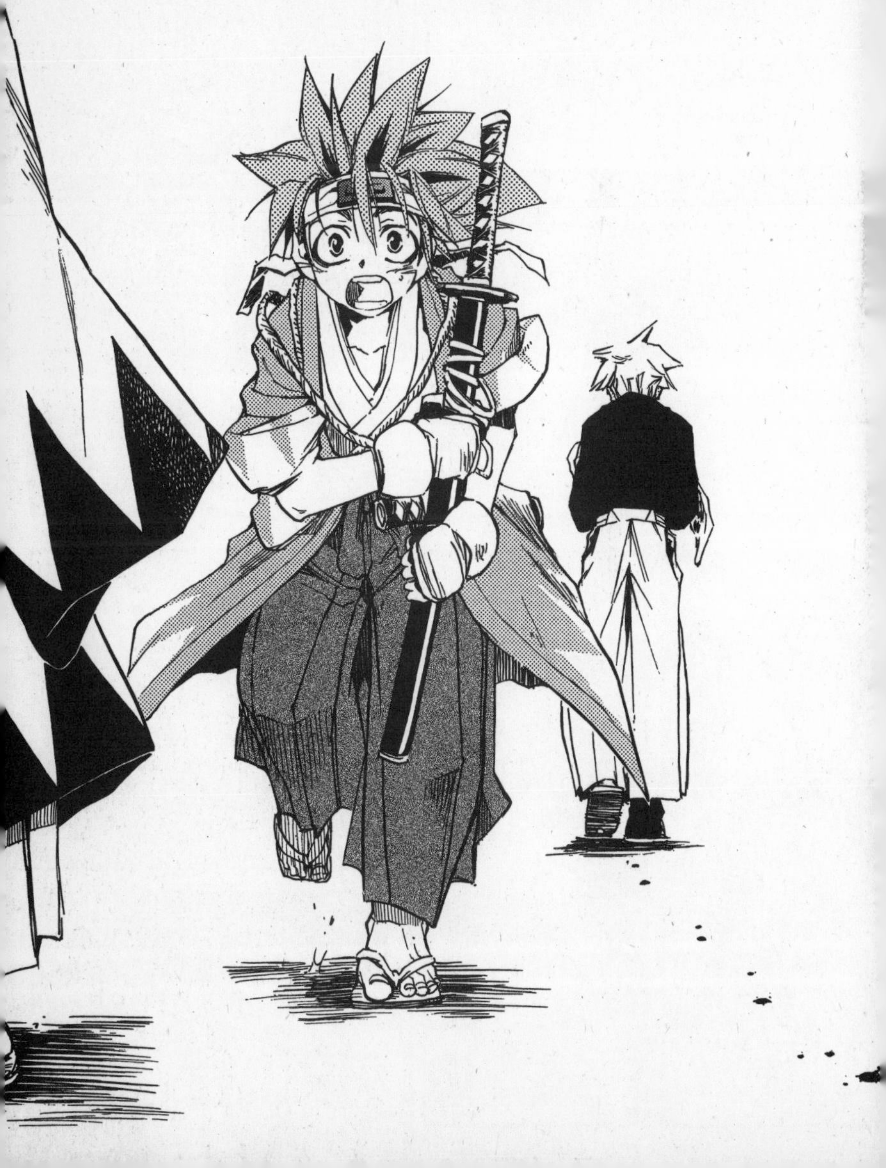

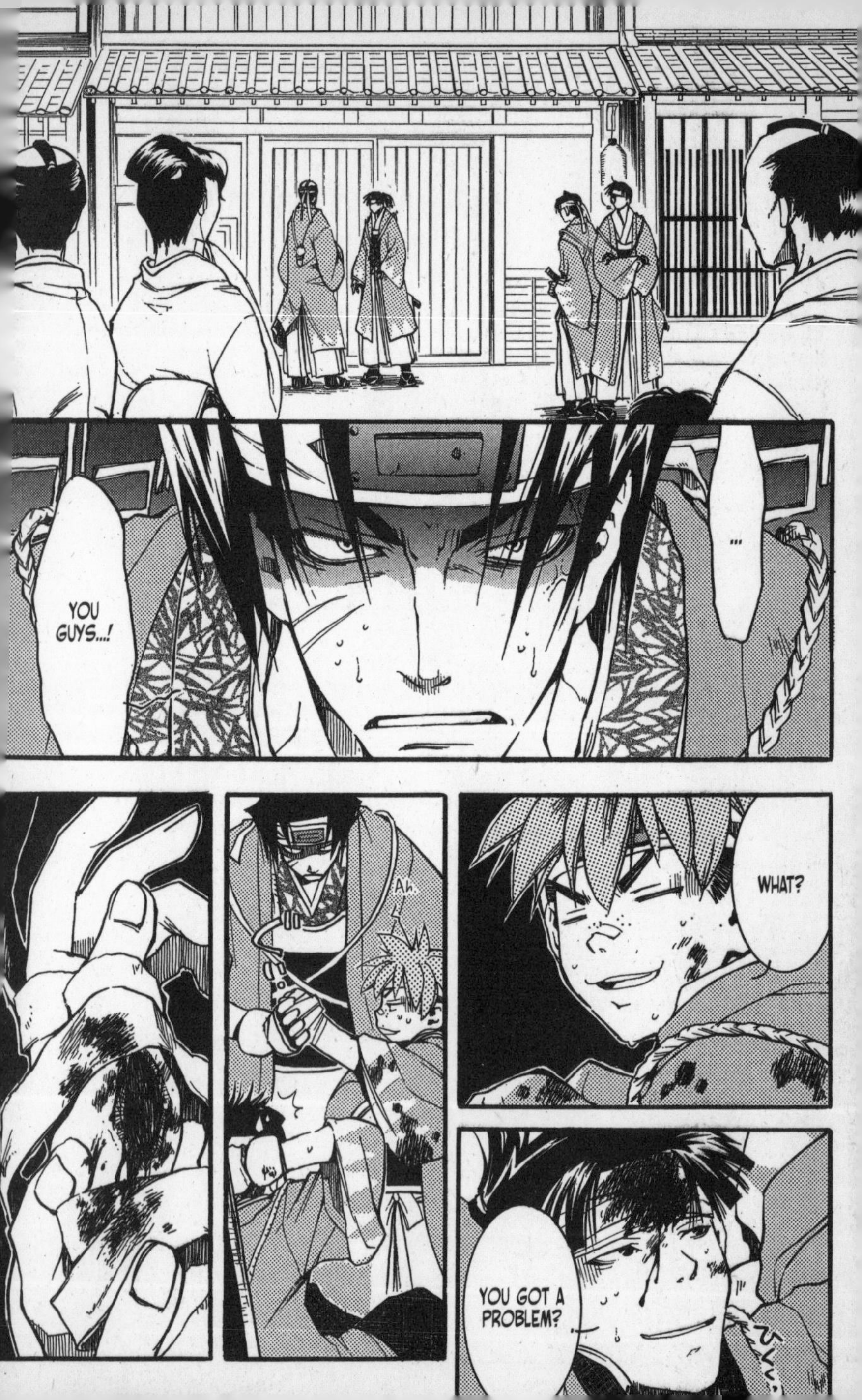
...
YOU GUYS...!
WHAT?
YOU GOT A PROBLEM?
Ah

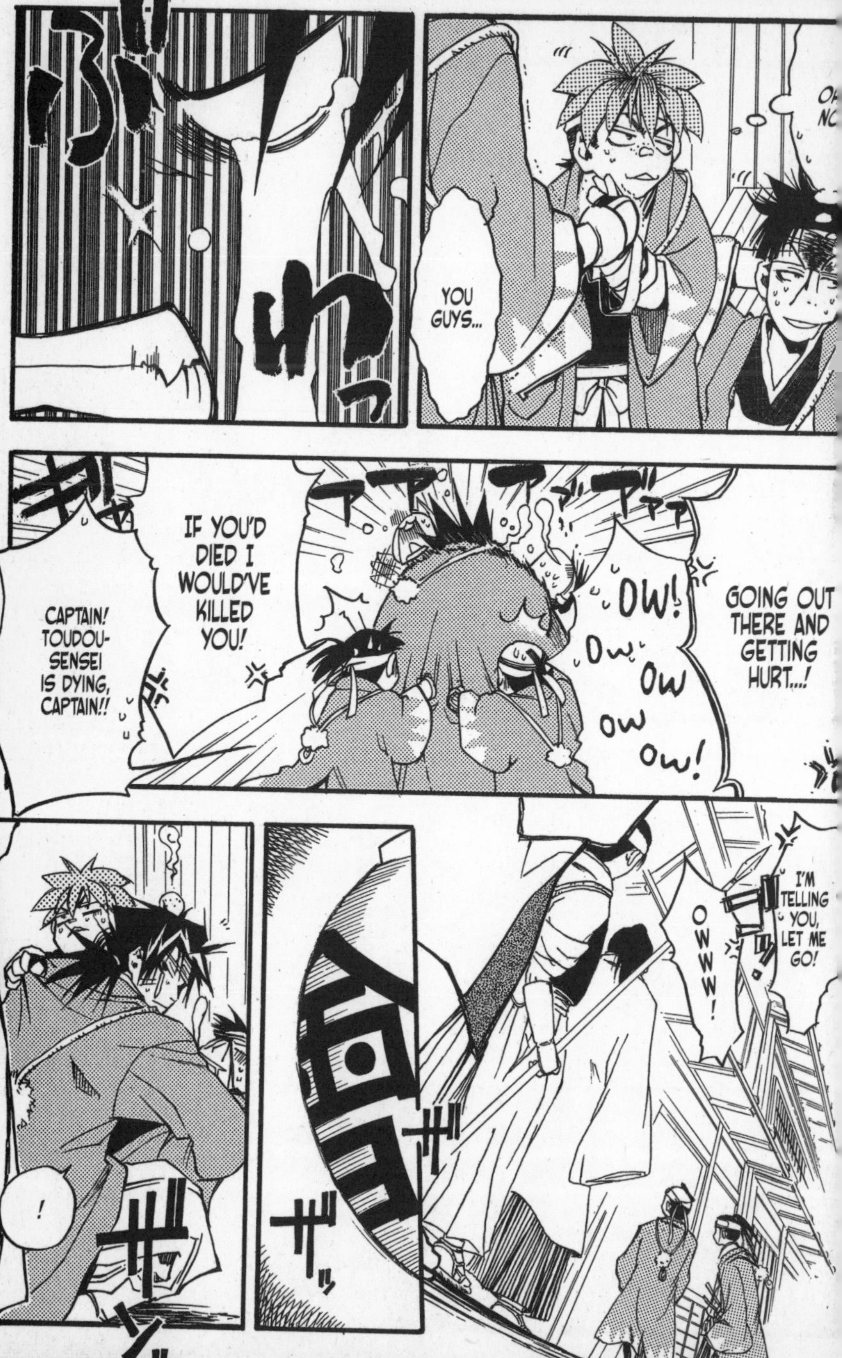

YOU GUYS...
GOING OUT THERE AND GETTING HURT...!
OW! OW OW OW OW!
IF YOU'D DIED I WOULD'VE KILLED YOU!
CAPTAIN! TOUDOU-SENSEI IS DYING, CAPTAIN!!
I'M TELLING YOU, LET ME GO!
OWWW!
!

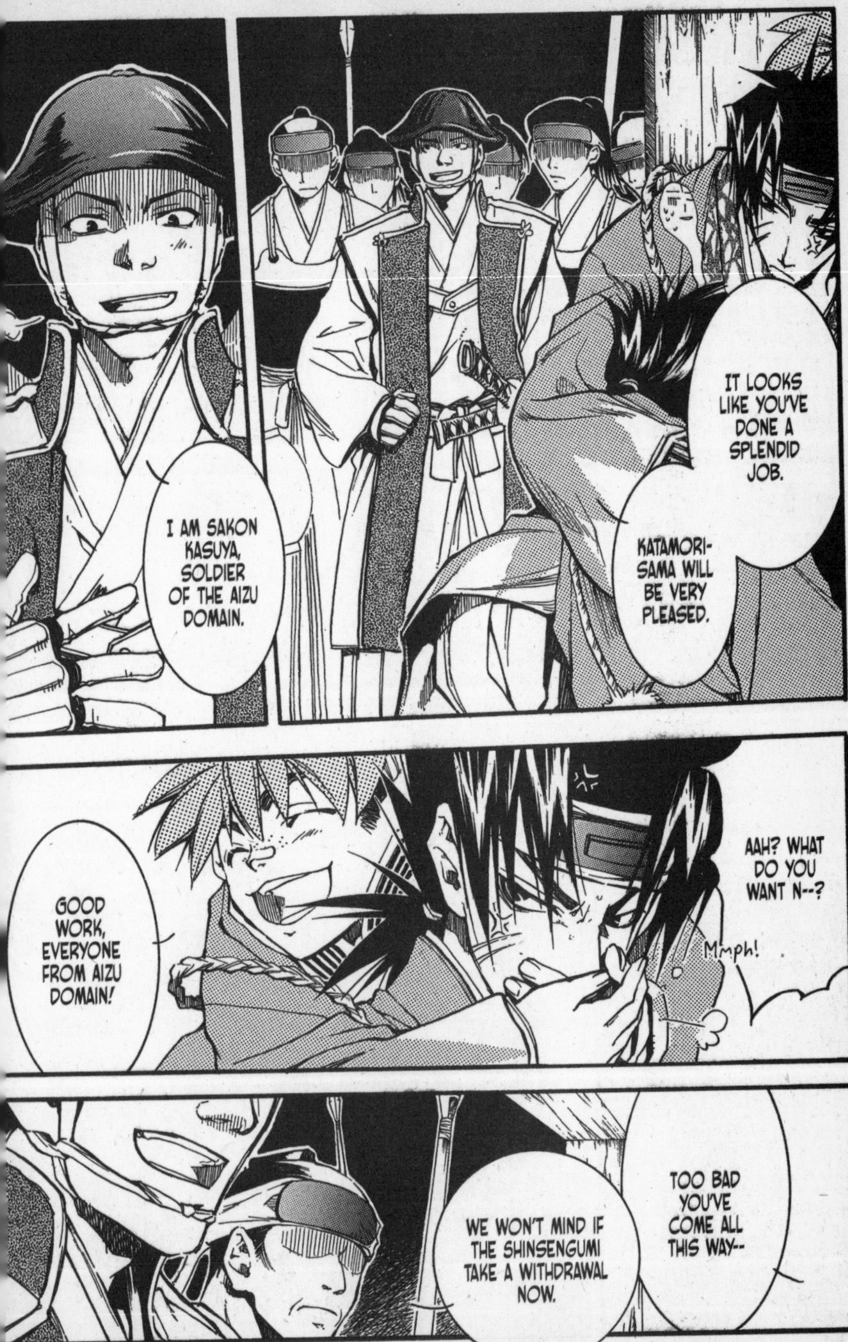
IT LOOKS LIKE YOU'VE DONE A SPLENDID JOB.
KATAMORI-SAMA WILL BE VERY PLEASED.
I AM SAKON KASUYA, SOLDIER OF THE AIZU DOMAIN.
AAH? WHAT DO YOU WANT N--?
Mmph!
GOOD WORK, EVERYONE FROM AIZU DOMAIN!
TOO BAD YOU'VE COME ALL THIS WAY--
WE WON'T MIND IF THE SHINSENGUMI TAKE A WITHDRAWAL NOW.

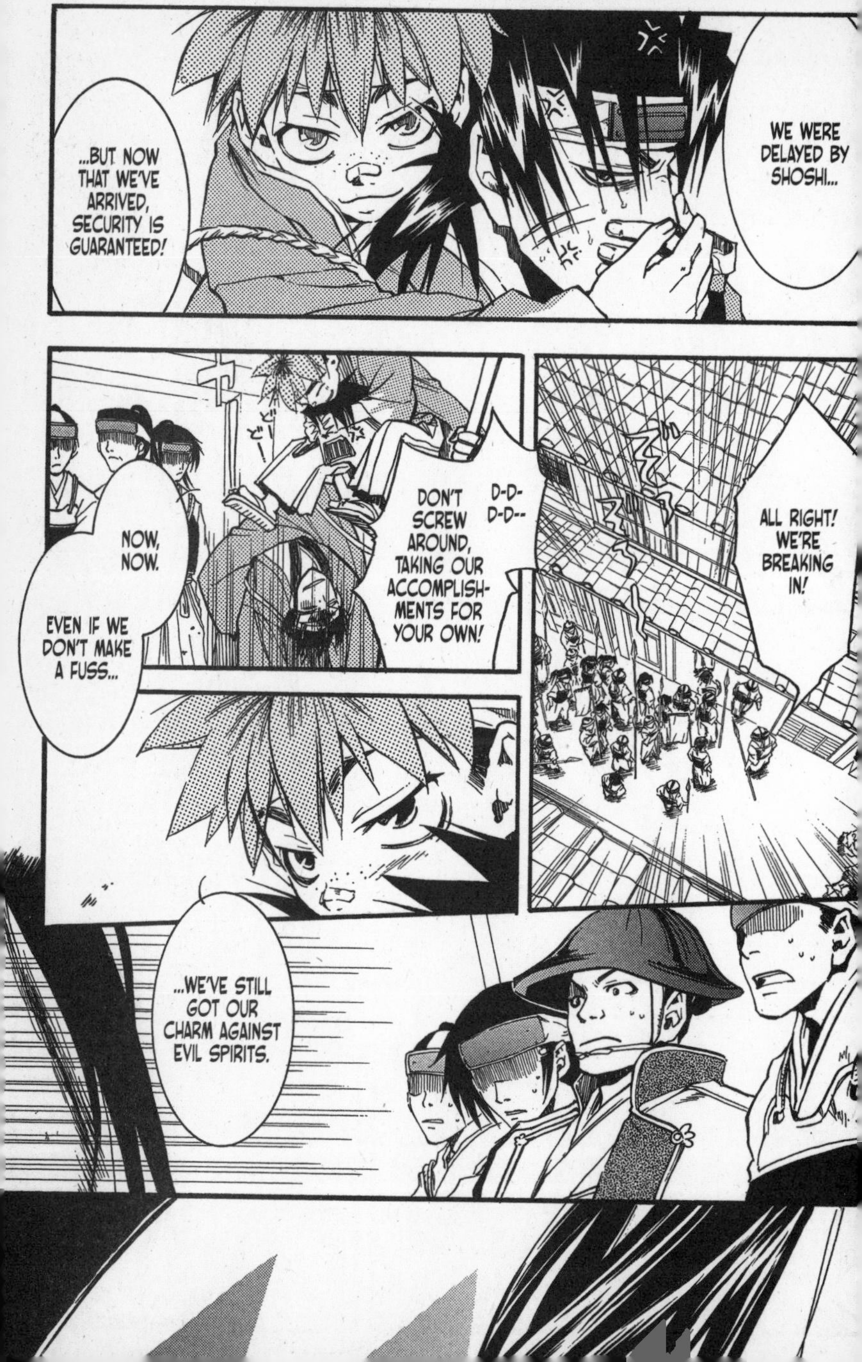
WE WERE DELAYED BY SHOSHI...
...BUT NOW THAT WE'VE ARRIVED, SECURITY IS GUARANTEED!
ALL RIGHT! WE'RE BREAKING IN!
D-D-D-D--
DON'T SCREW AROUND, TAKING OUR ACCOMPLISHMENTS FOR YOUR OWN!
NOW, NOW.
EVEN IF WE DON'T MAKE A FUSS...
...WE'VE STILL GOT OUR CHARM AGAINST EVIL SPIRITS.

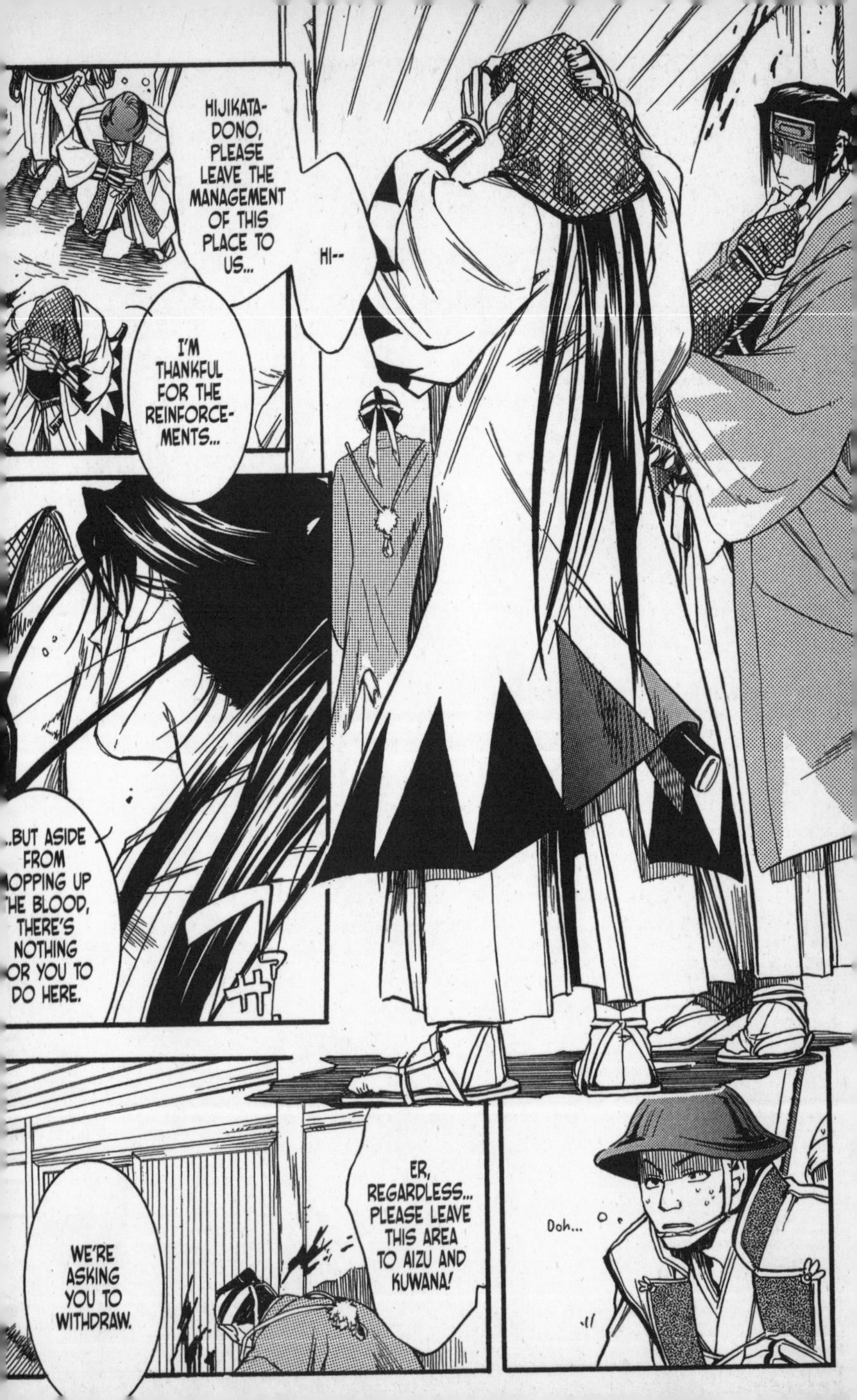
HI--
HIJIKATA-DONO, PLEASE LEAVE THE MANAGEMENT OF THIS PLACE TO US...
I'M THANKFUL FOR THE REINFORCEMENTS...
..BUT ASIDE FROM OPPING UP HE BLOOD, THERE'S NOTHING OR YOU TO DO HERE.
Doh...
ER, REGARDLESS... PLEASE LEAVE THIS AREA TO AIZU AND KUWANA!
WE'RE ASKING YOU TO WITHDRAW.

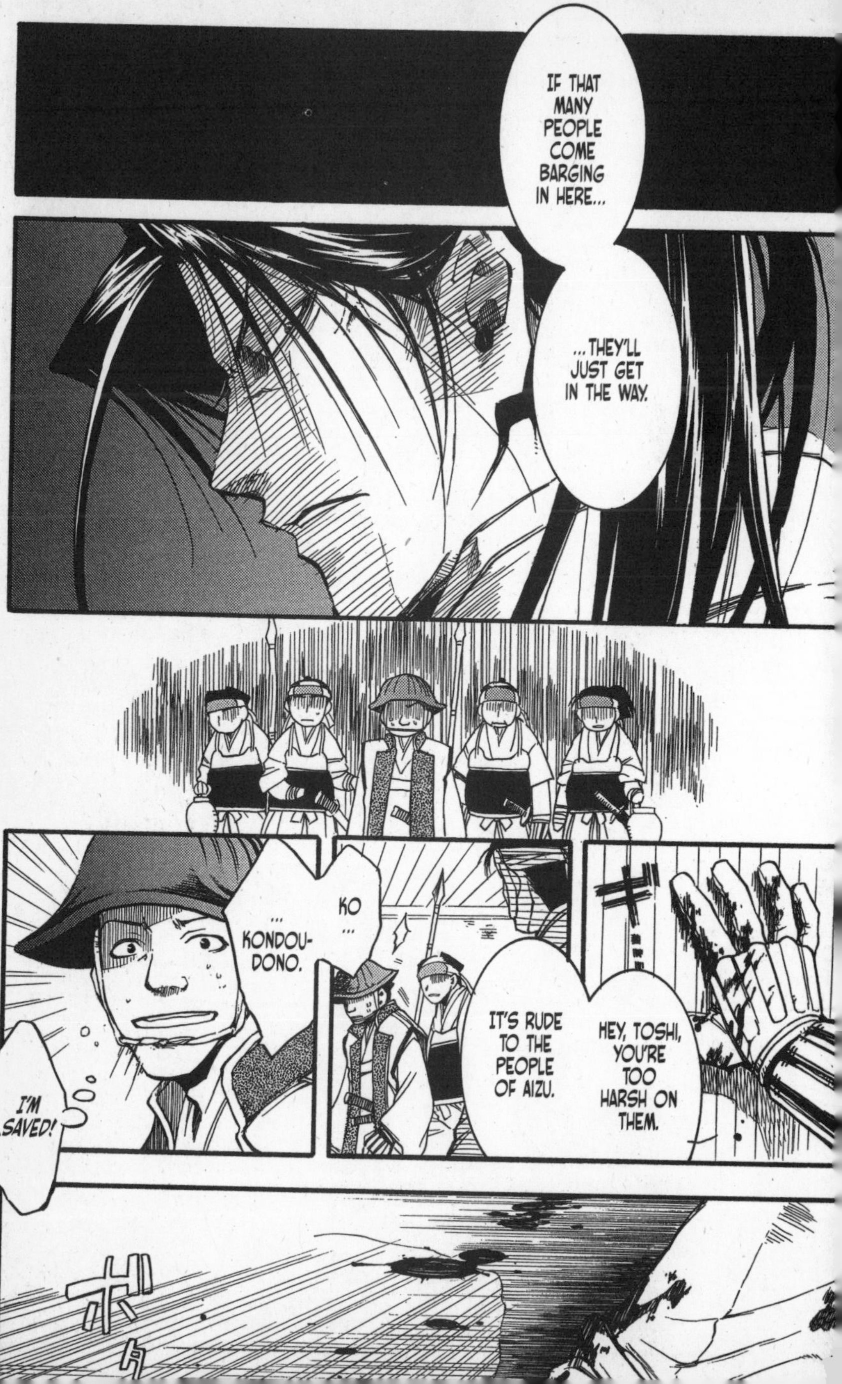
IF THAT MANY PEOPLE COME BARGING IN HERE...
...THEY'LL JUST GET IN THE WAY.
HEY, TOSHI, YOU'RE TOO HARSH ON THEM.
IT'S RUDE TO THE PEOPLE OF AIZU.
KO ...
... KONDOU-DONO.
I'M SAVED!
ボタ

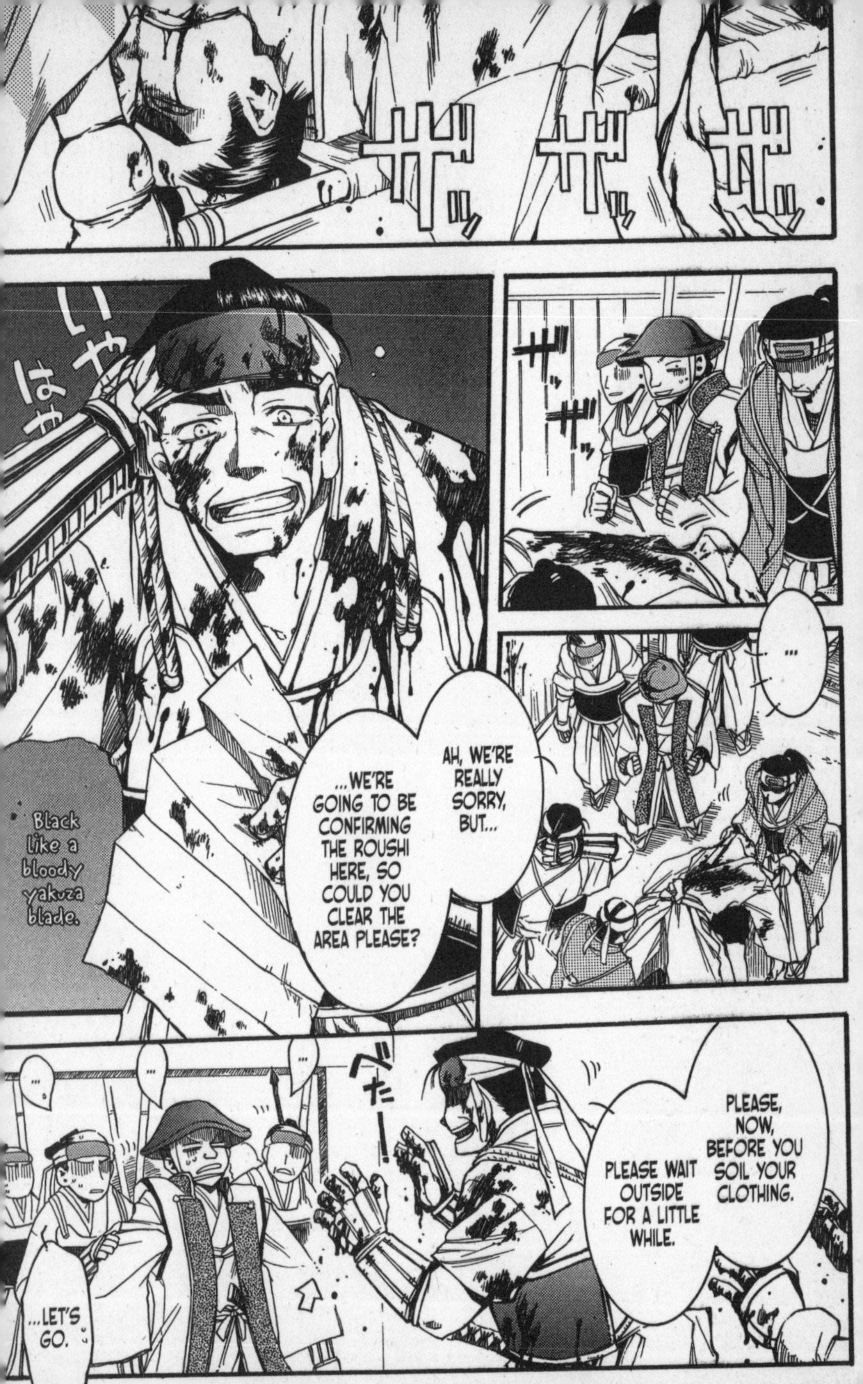
ザッ
ザッ
ザッ
ザッ
ザッ
...
いやはや
AH, WE'RE REALLY SORRY, BUT...
...WE'RE GOING TO BE CONFIRMING THE ROUSHI HERE, SO COULD YOU CLEAR THE AREA PLEASE?
Black like a bloody yakuza blade.
PLEASE, NOW, BEFORE YOU SOIL YOUR CLOTHING.
PLEASE WAIT OUTSIDE FOR A LITTLE WHILE.
べたー!
...
...
...
...LET'S GO.

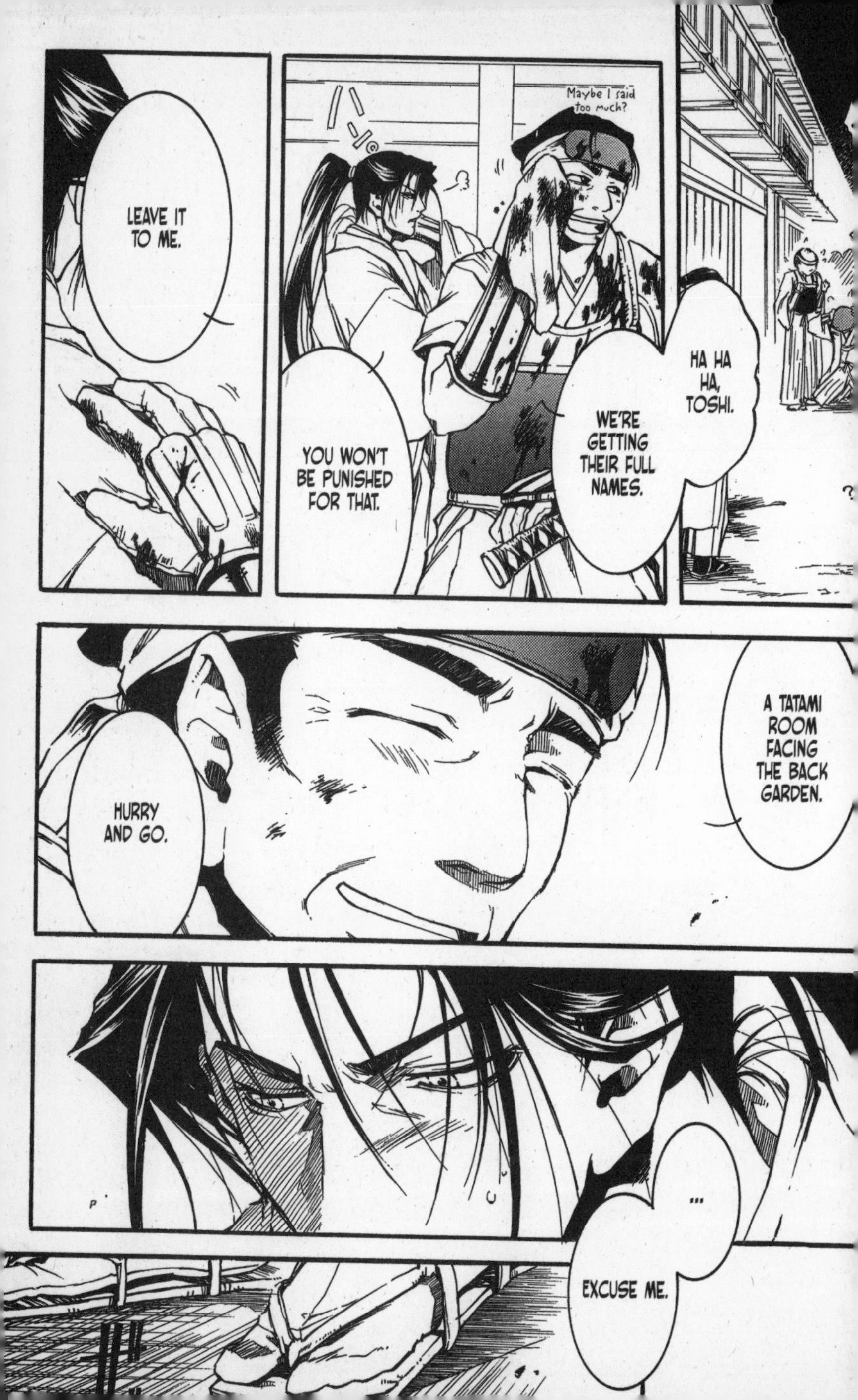
Maybe I said too much?
HA HA HA, TOSHI.
WE'RE GETTING THEIR FULL NAMES.
YOU WON'T BE PUNISHED FOR THAT.
LEAVE IT TO ME.
A TATAMI ROOM FACING THE BACK GARDEN.
HURRY AND GO.
...
EXCUSE ME.

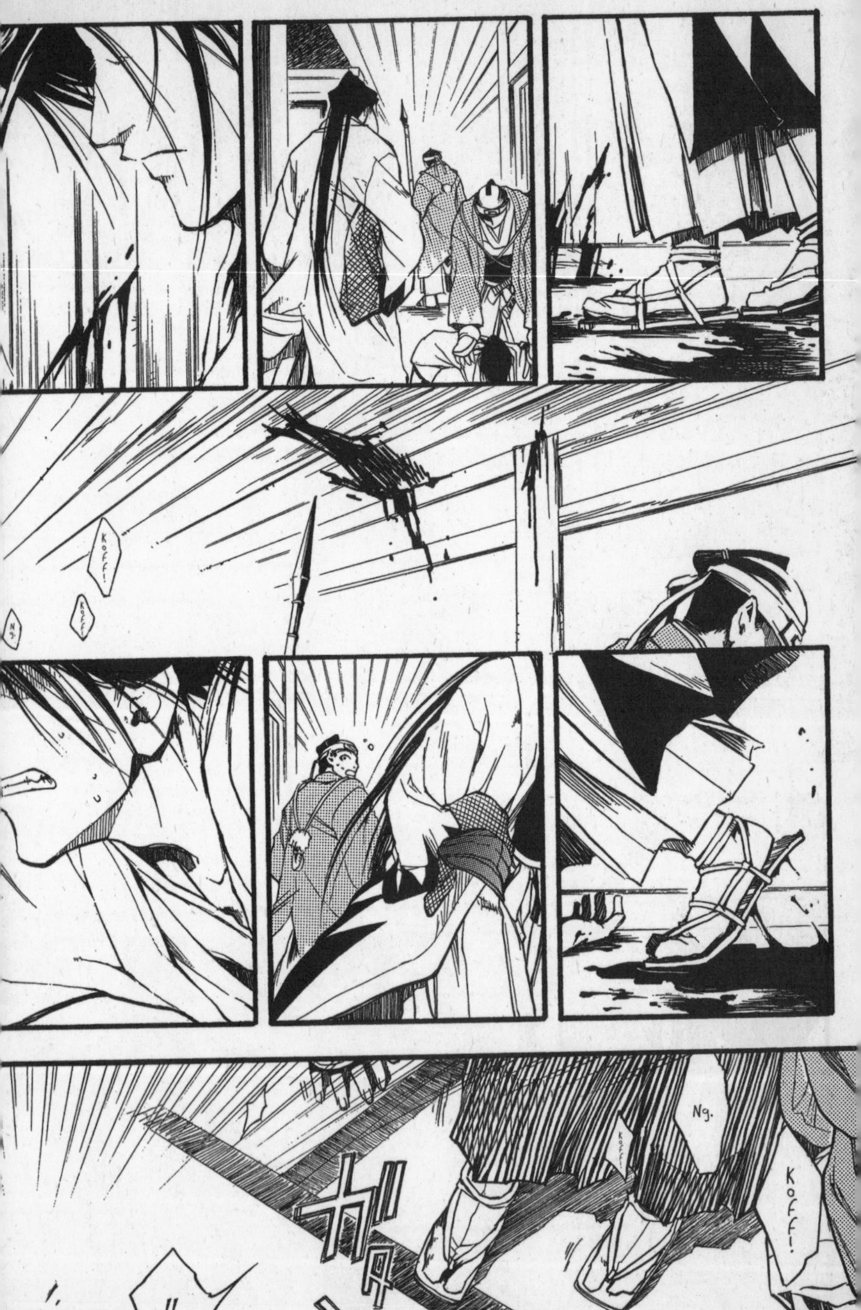
Koff!
Koff!
Ng.
Koff!
Ng.
Koff!
ガタッ
!!

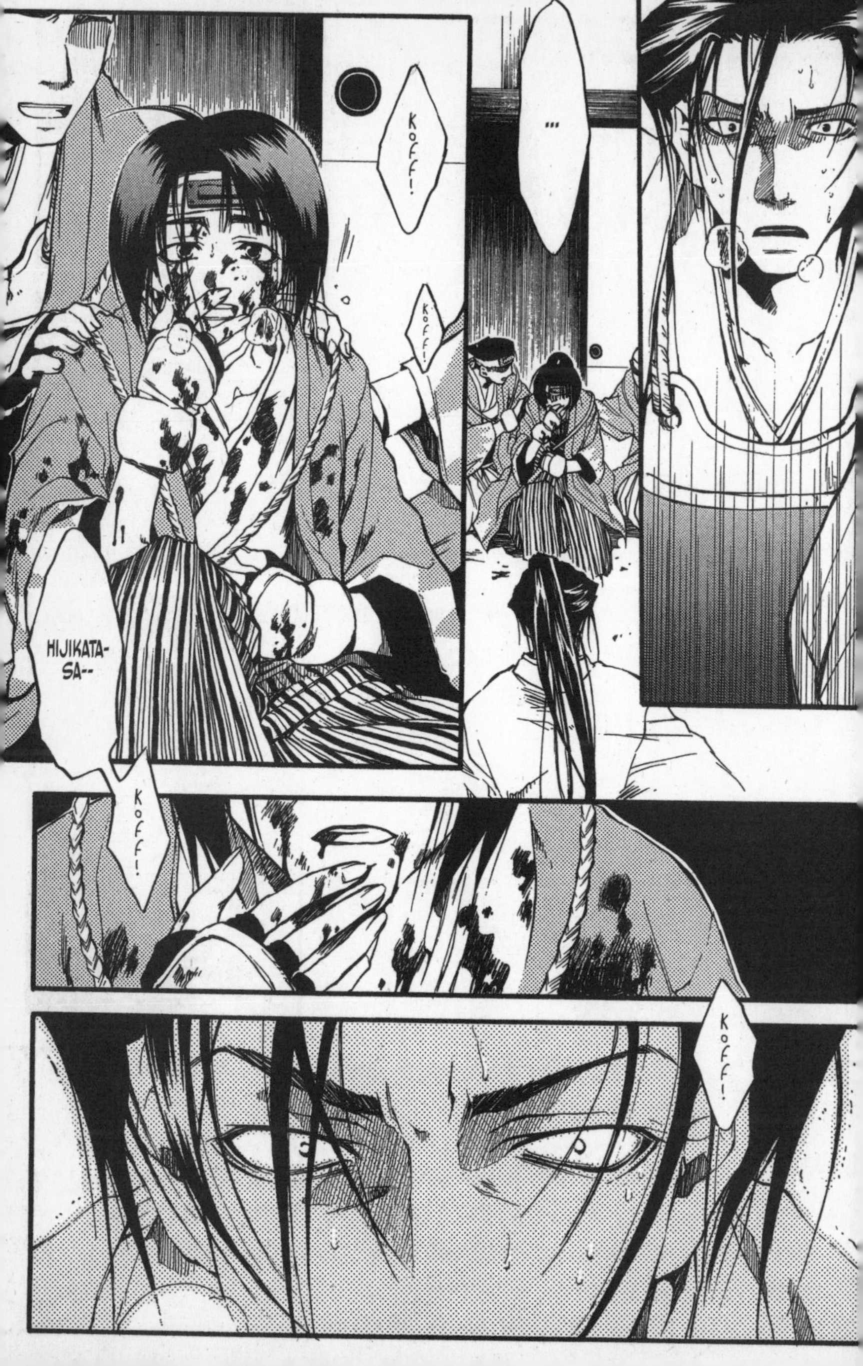
...
Koff!
koff!
HIJIKATA-SA--
Koff!
Koff!

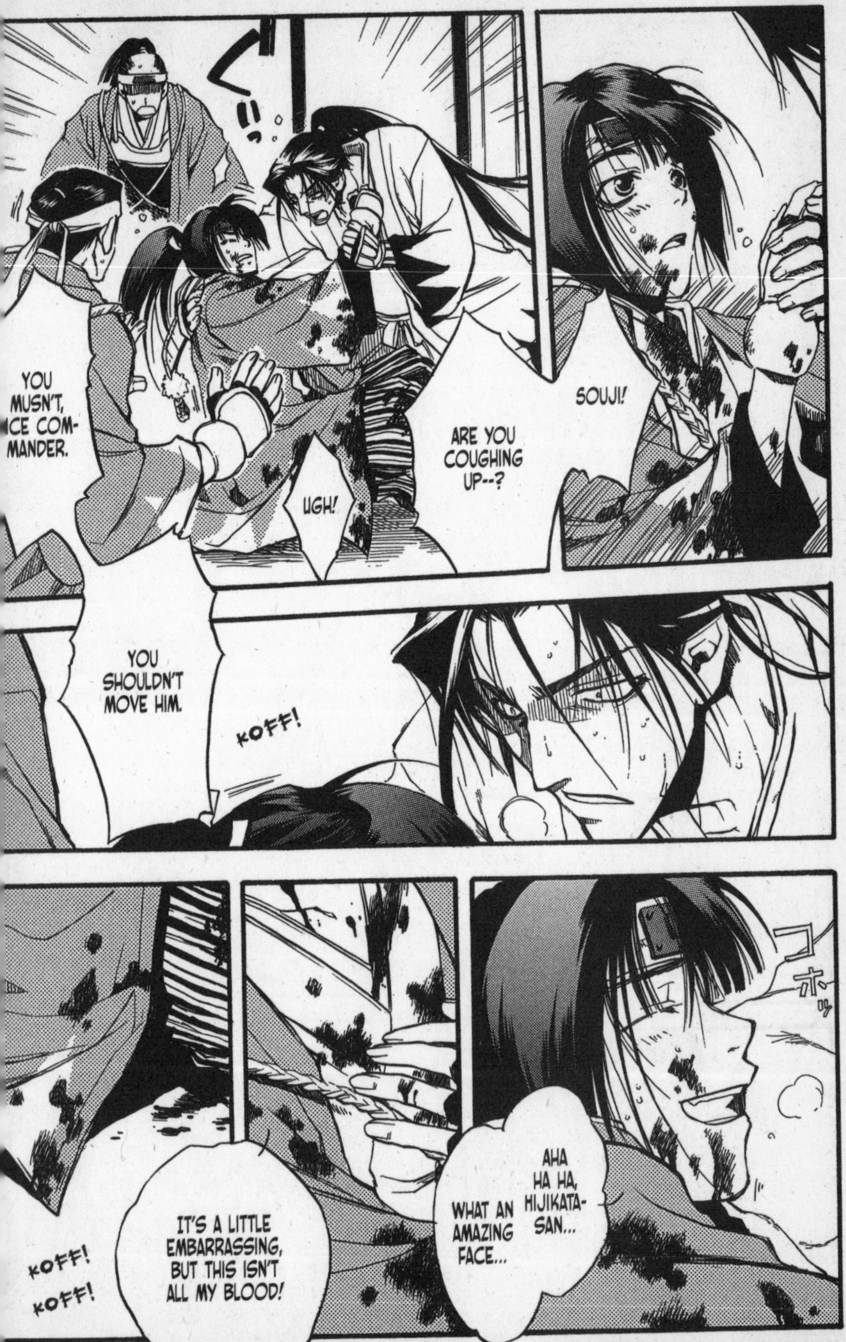
SOUJI!
ぐいっ
ARE YOU COUGHING UP--?
UGH!
YOU MUSN'T, ICE COM- MANDER.
KOFF!
YOU SHOULDN'T MOVE HIM.
コホッ
AHA HA HA, HIJIKATA- SAN...
WHAT AN AMAZING FACE...
IT'S A LITTLE EMBARRASSING, BUT THIS ISN'T ALL MY BLOOD!
KOFF!
KOFF!

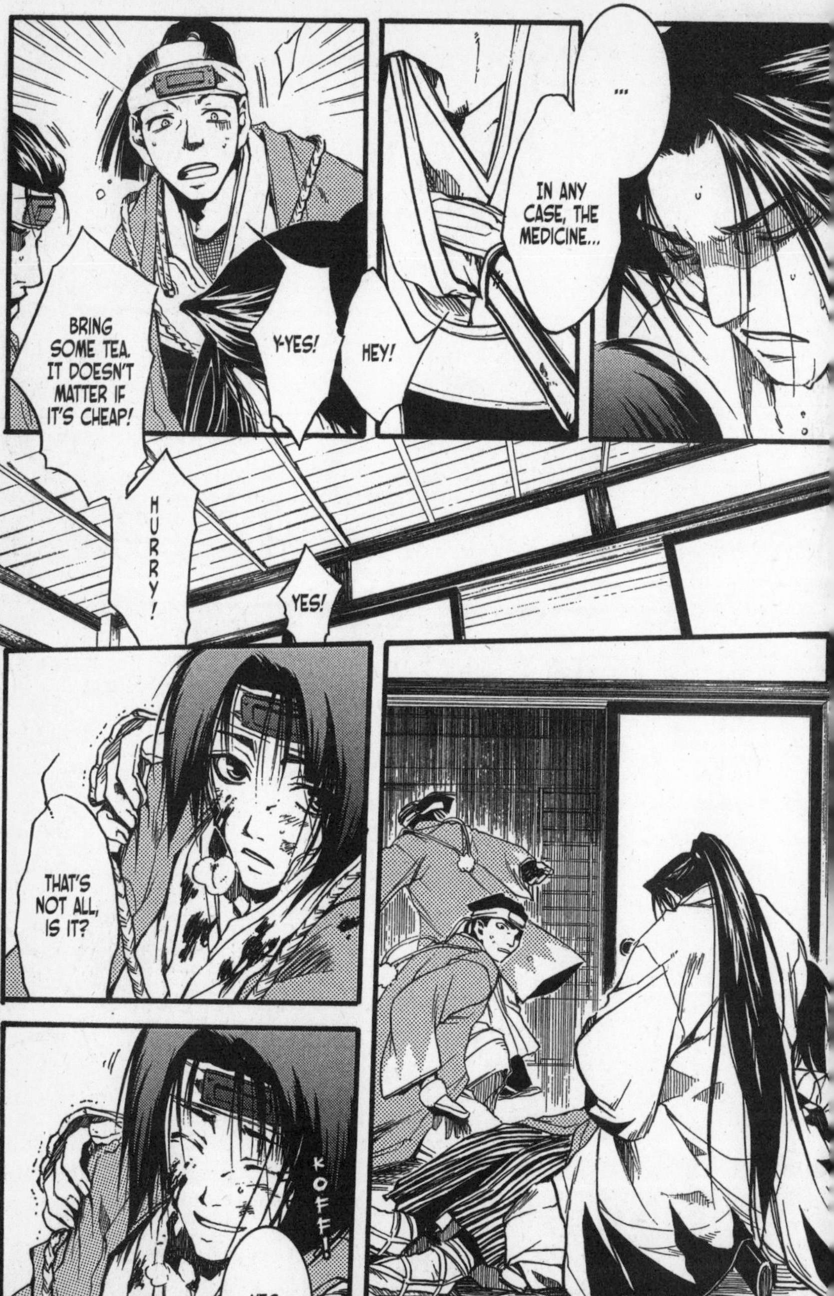
...
IN ANY CASE, THE MEDICINE...
HEY!
BRING SOME TEA. IT DOESN'T MATTER IF IT'S CHEAP!
Y-YES!
HURRY!
YES!
THAT'S NOT ALL, IS IT?
KOFF!
YES.

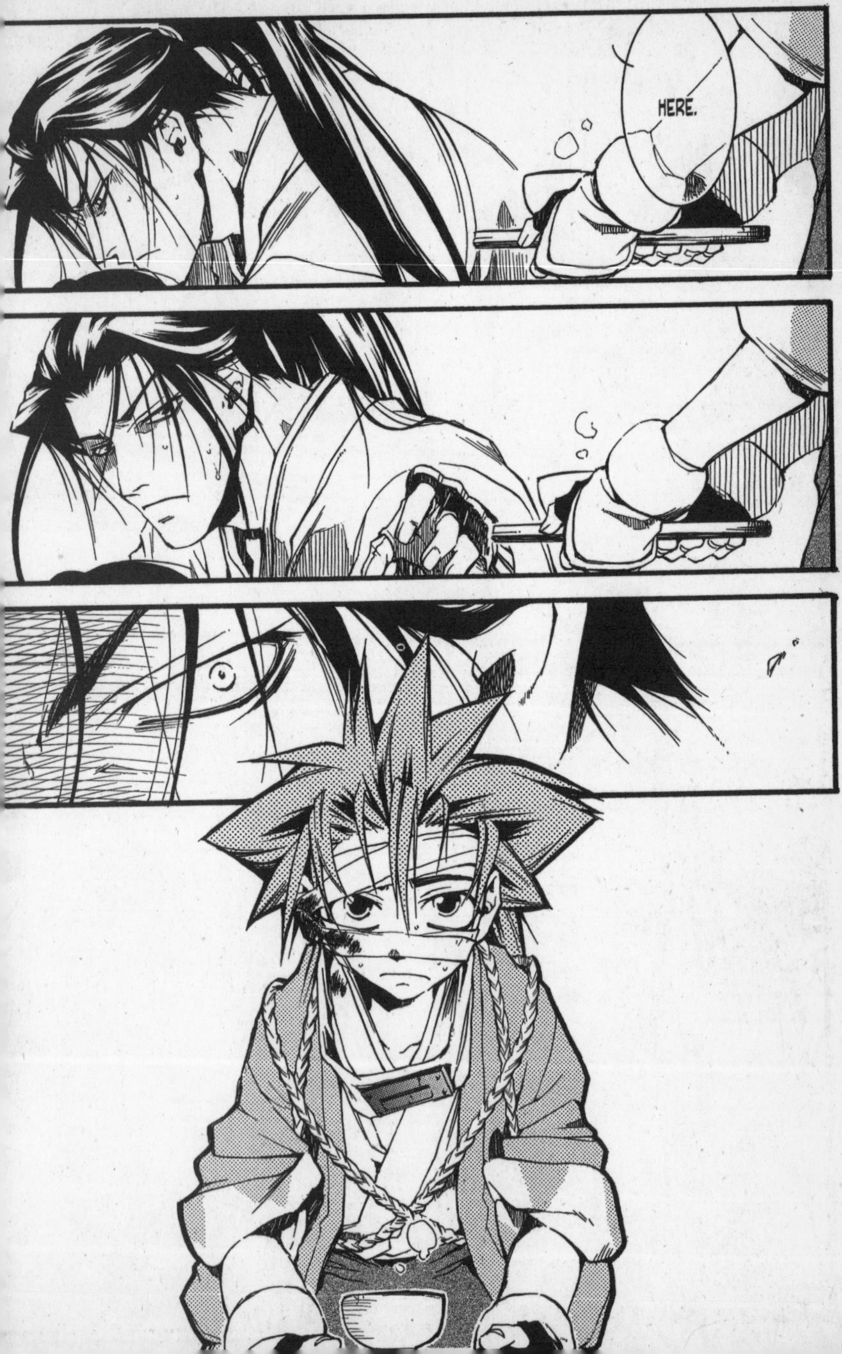
HERE.

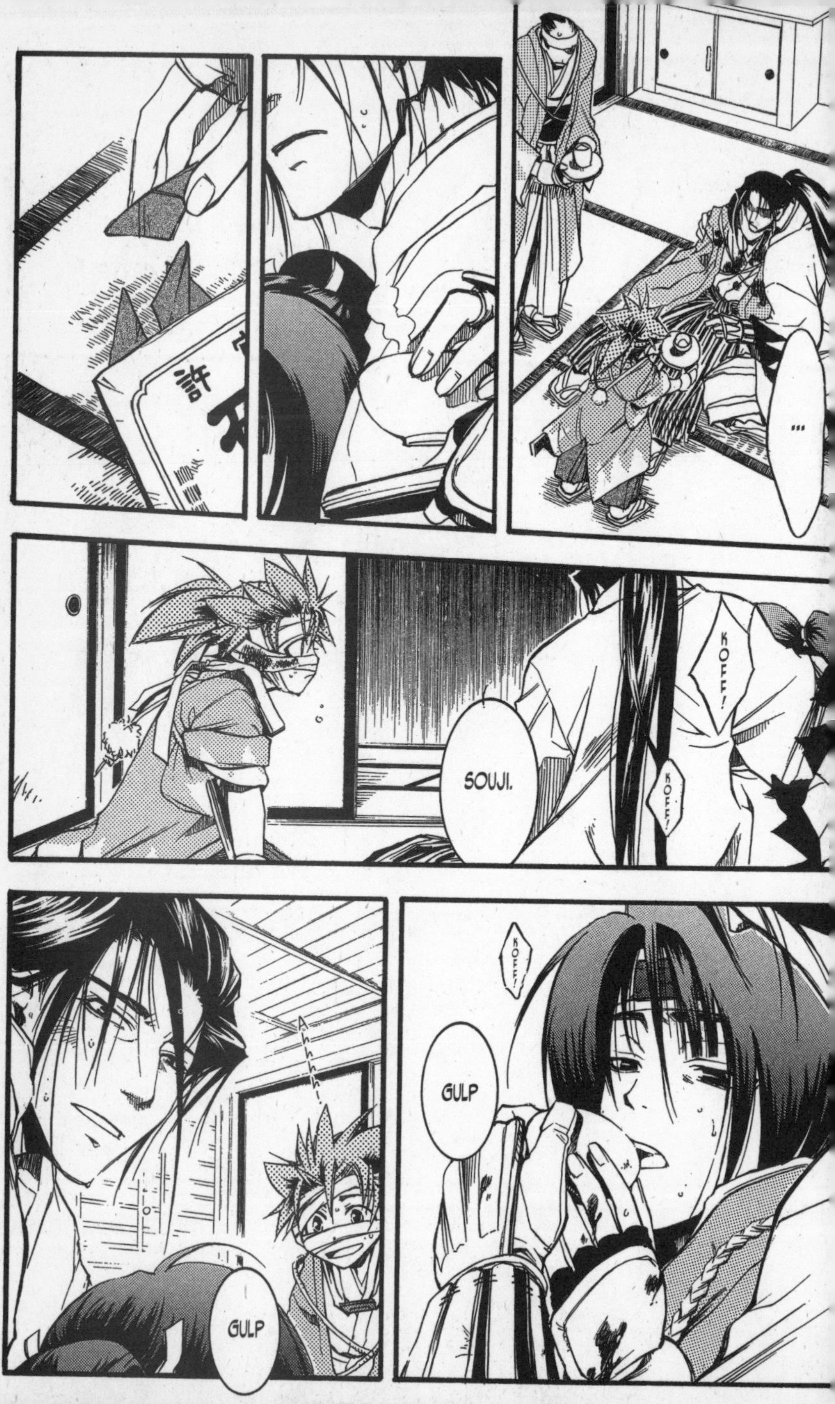
...
許
KOFF!
KOFF!
SOUJI.
KOFF!
GULP
Ahhhh!
GULP

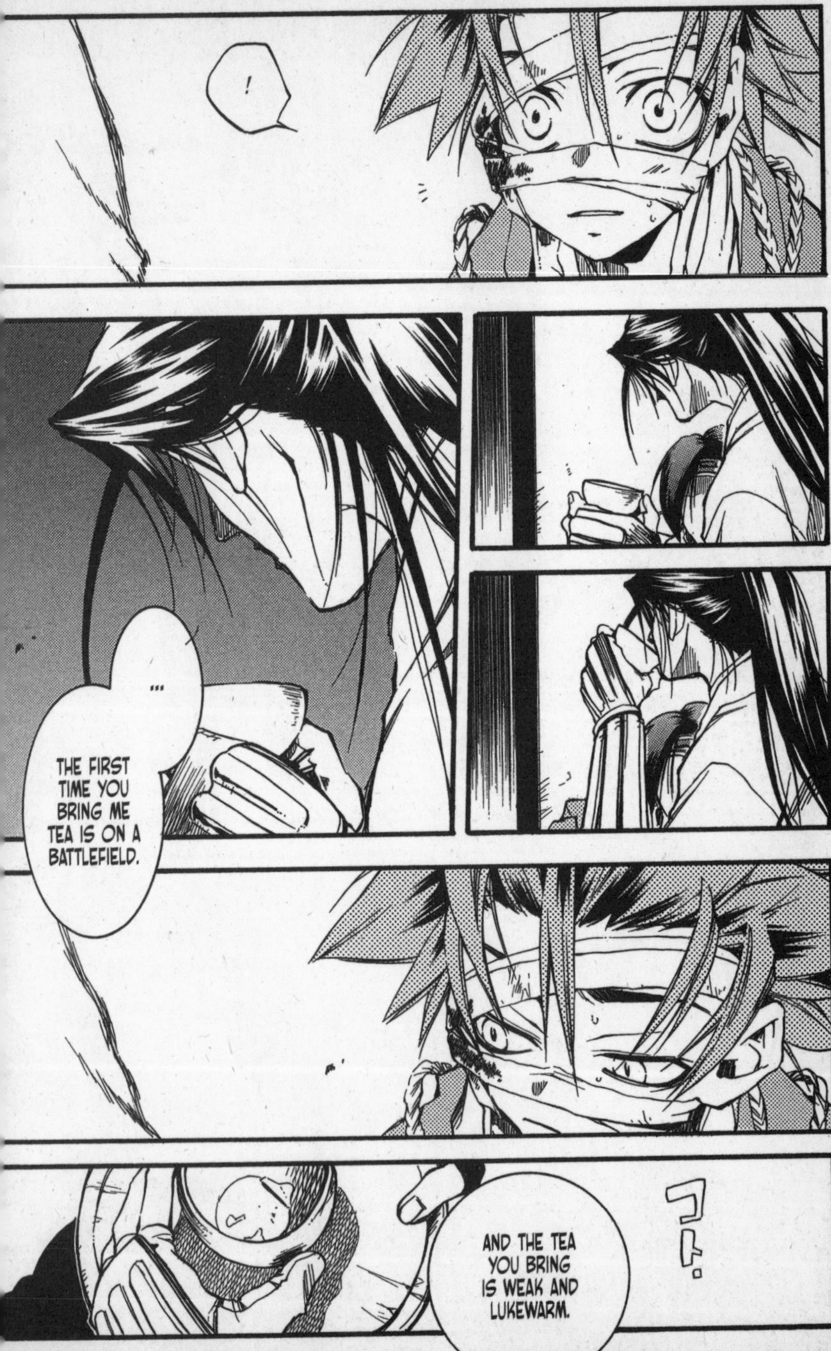
!
...
THE FIRST TIME YOU BRING ME TEA IS ON A BATTLEFIELD.
コト。
AND THE TEA YOU BRING IS WEAK AND LUKEWARM.

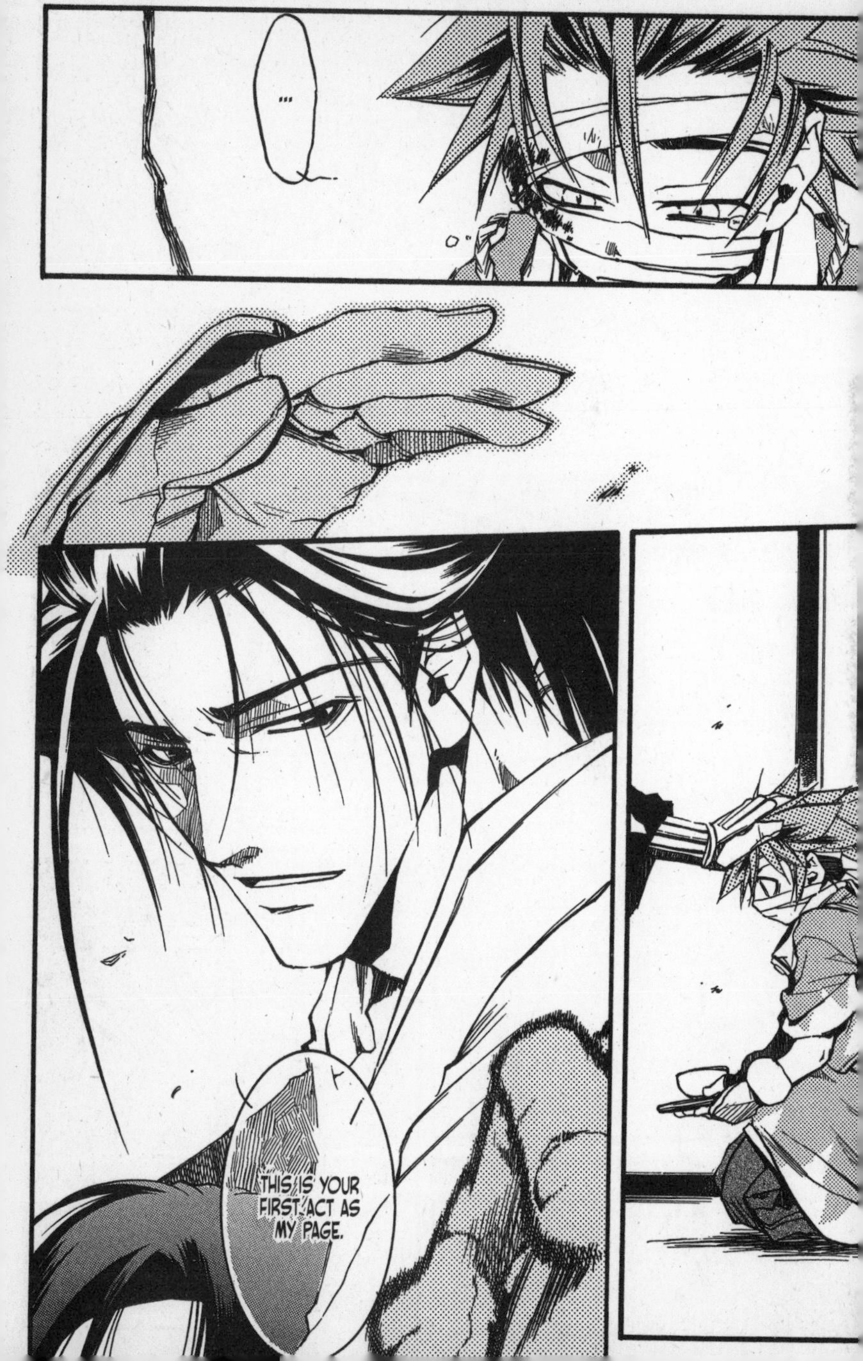
...
THIS IS YOUR FIRST ACT AS MY PAGE.

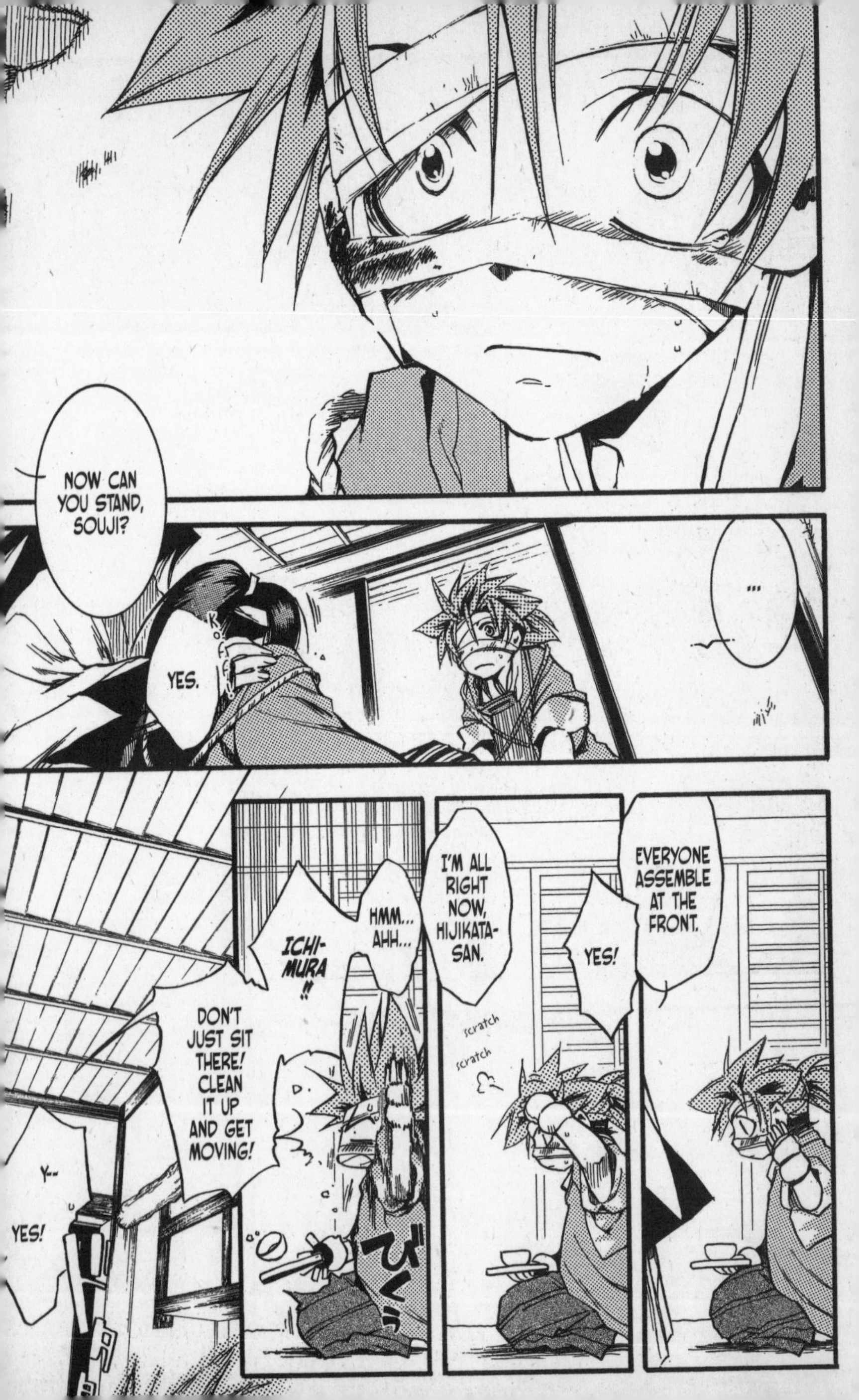
...
NOW CAN YOU STAND, SOUJI?
KOFF
YES.
EVERYONE ASSEMBLE AT THE FRONT.
YES!
I'M ALL RIGHT NOW, HIJIKATA-SAN.
scratch
scratch
HMM... AHH...
ICHIMURA!!
DON'T JUST SIT THERE! CLEAN IT UP AND GET MOVING!
Y--
YES!

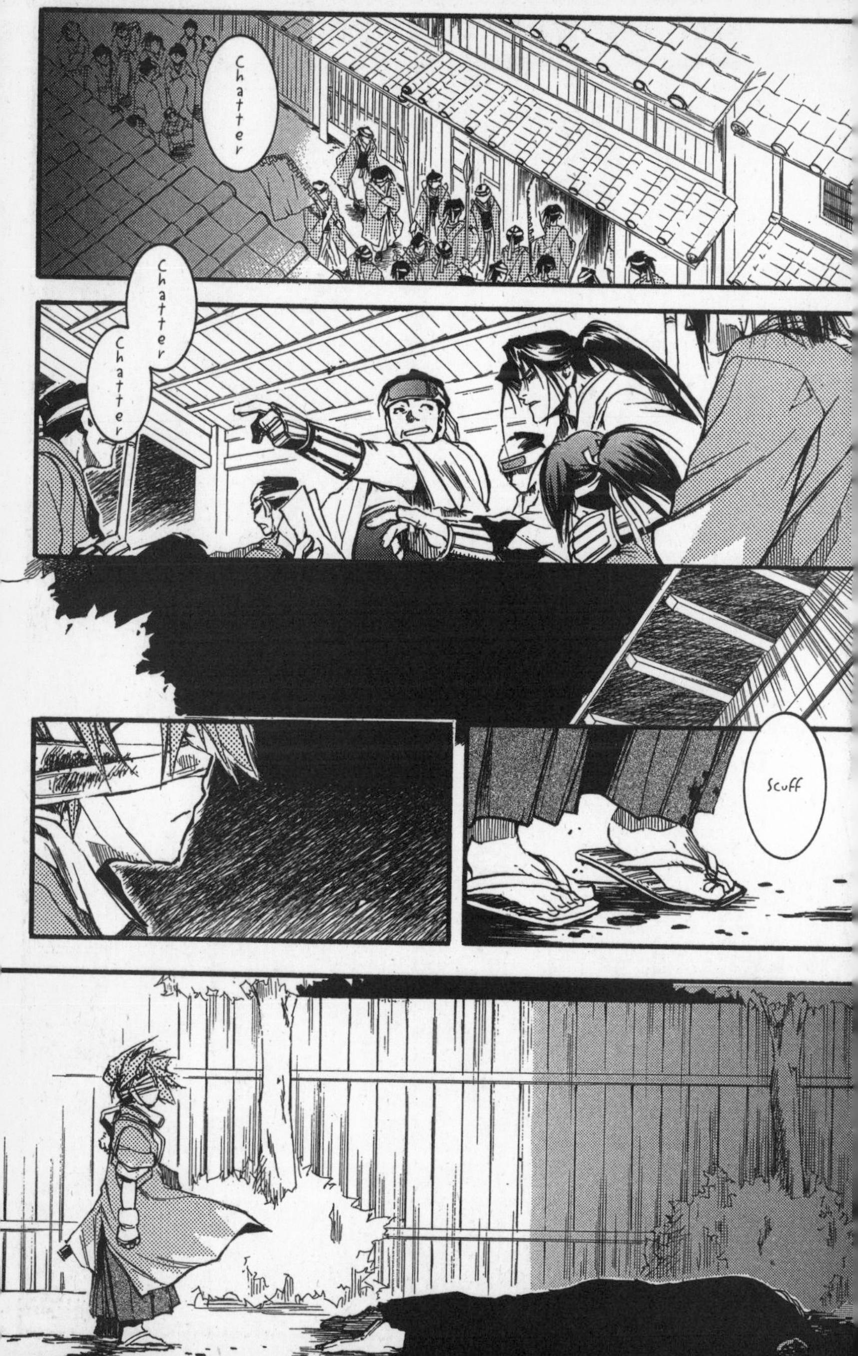
Chatter
Chatter
Chatter
Scuff

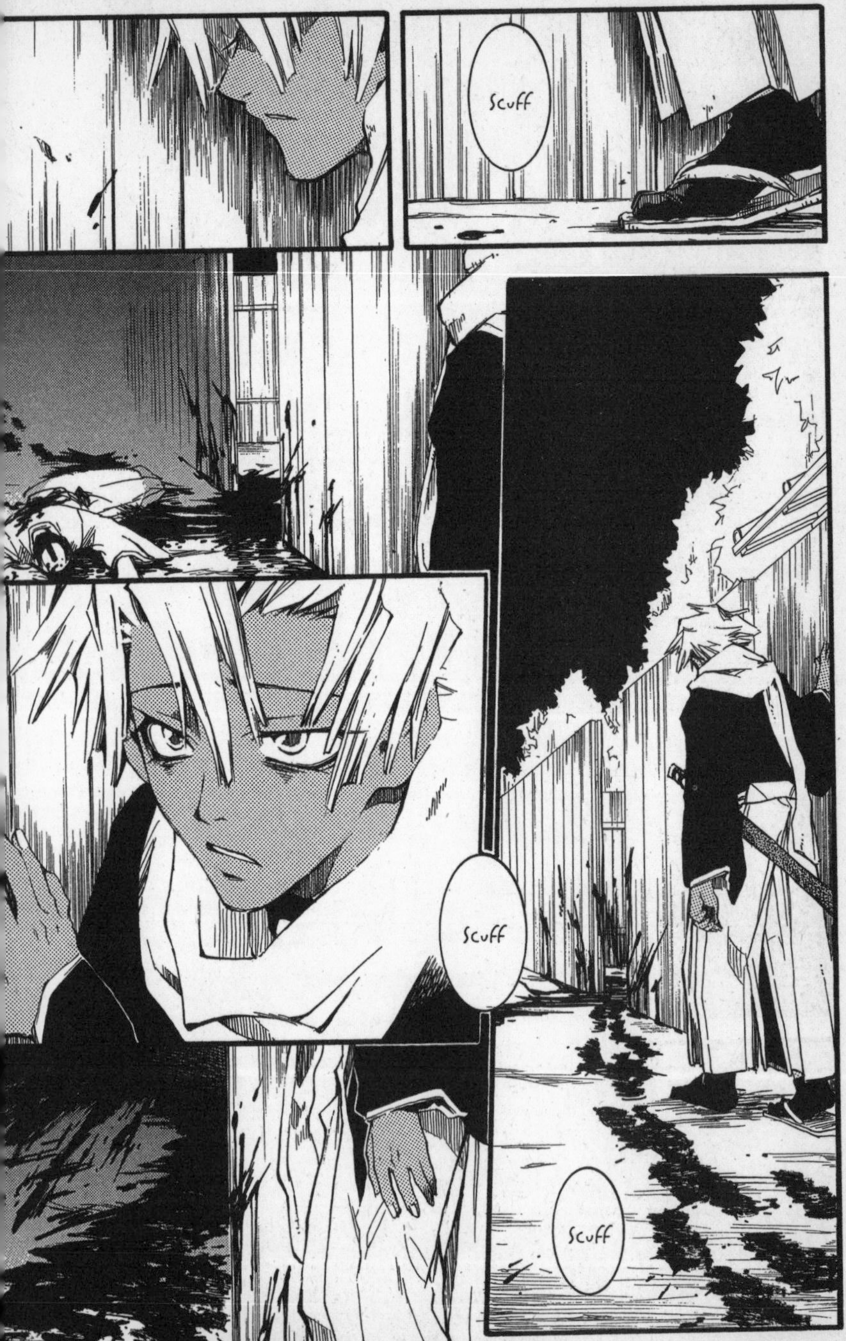
Scuff
Scuff
Scuff

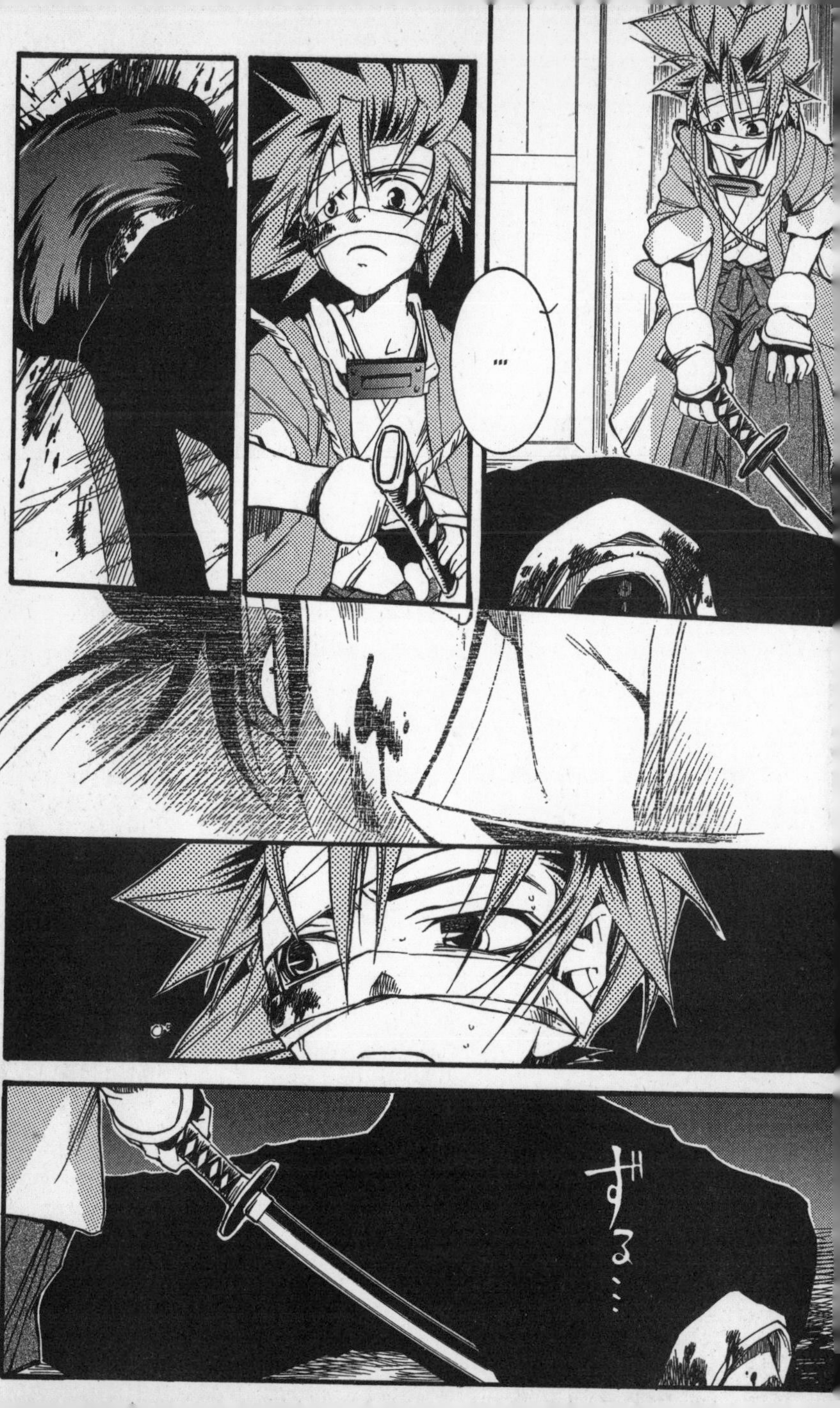
…
ずる…

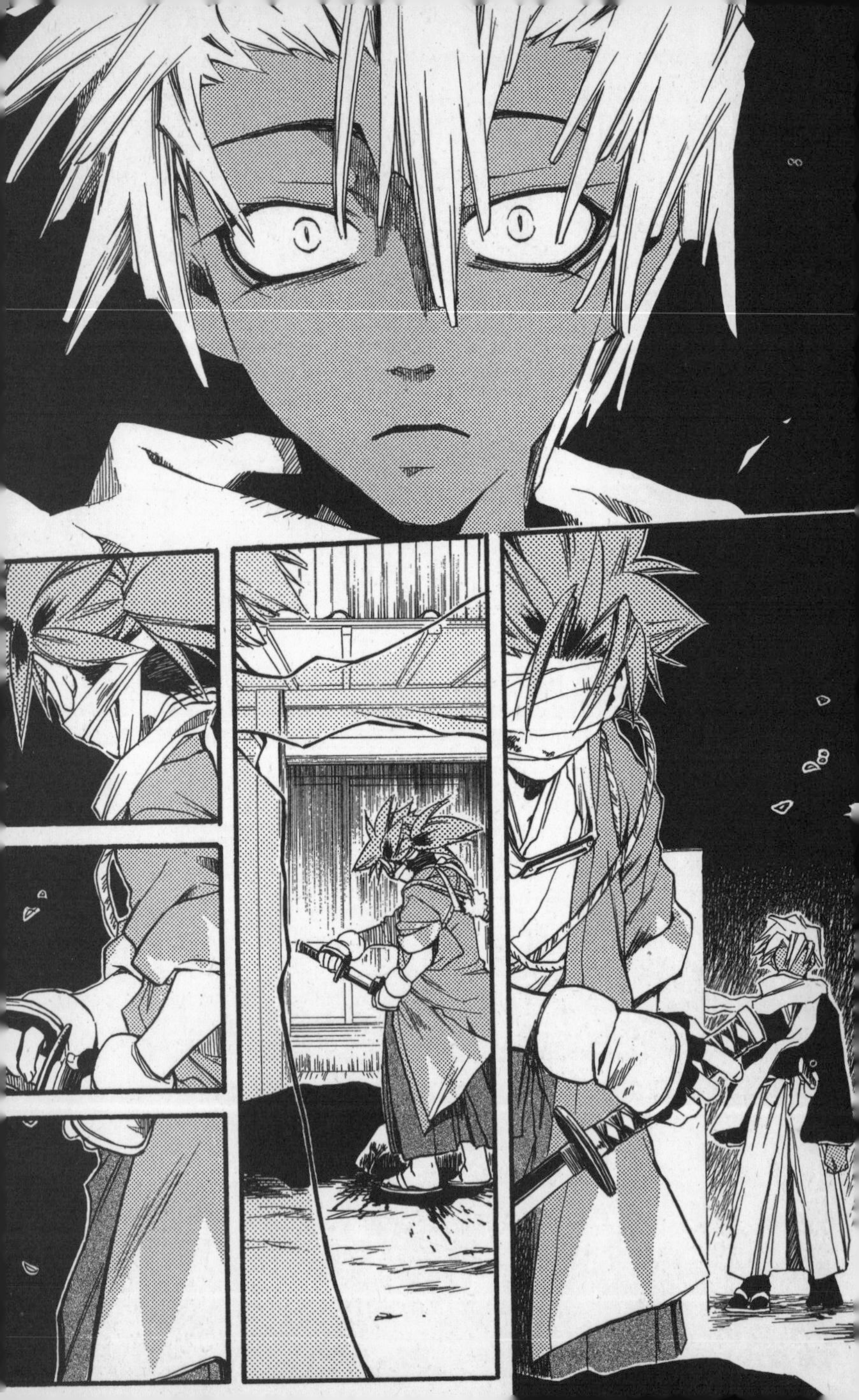

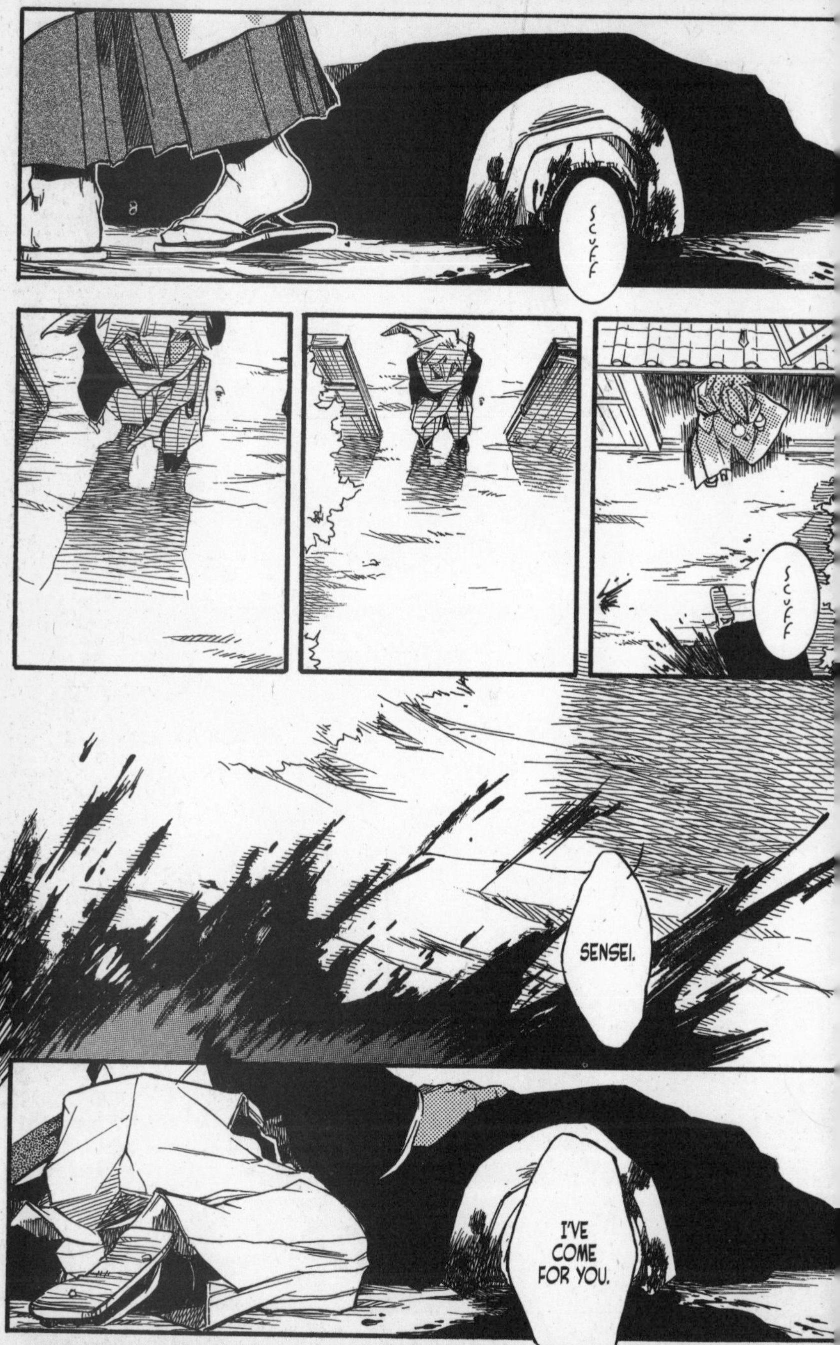
SCUFF
SCUFF
SENSEI.
I'VE COME FOR YOU.

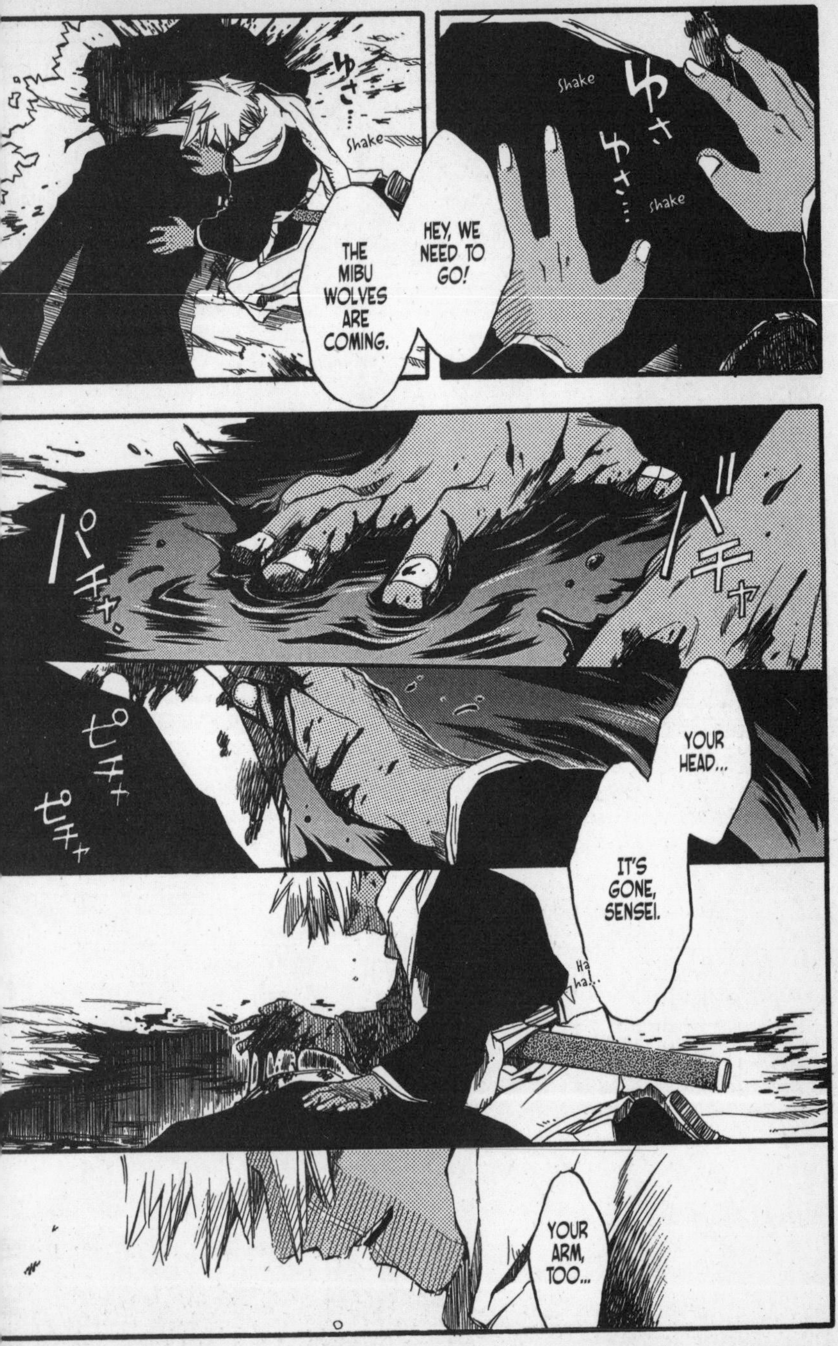

ゆさ
ゆさ…
Shake
shake
HEY, WE NEED TO GO!
THE MIBU WOLVES ARE COMING.
ゆさ…
Shake
パチャ
パチャ。
ピチャ
ピチャ
YOUR HEAD...
IT'S GONE, SENSEI.
Ha ha...
YOUR ARM, TOO...

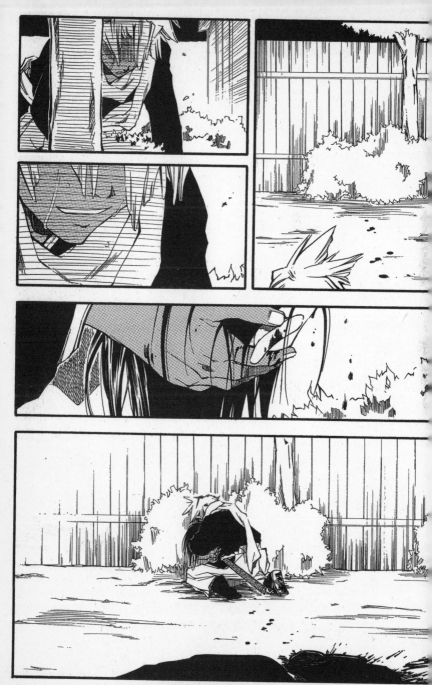

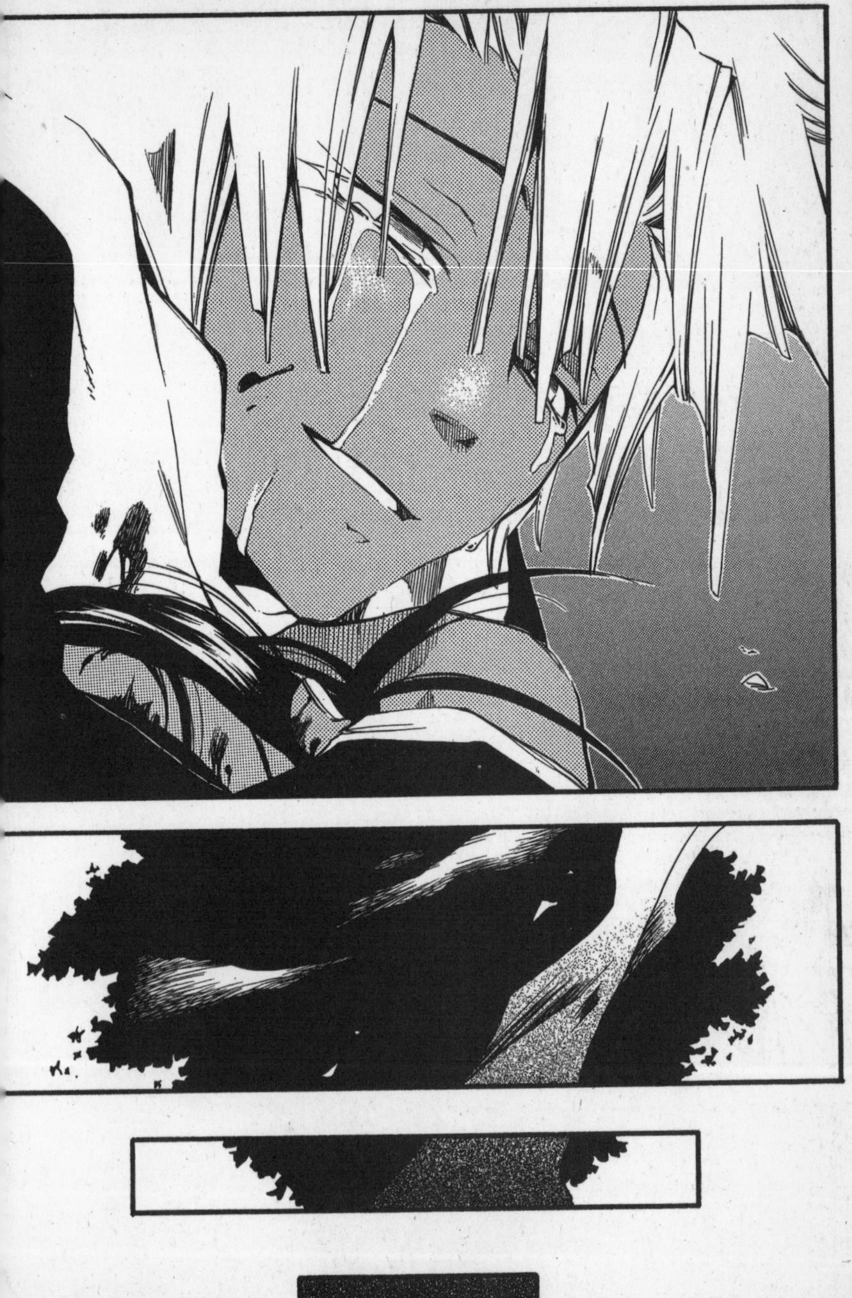

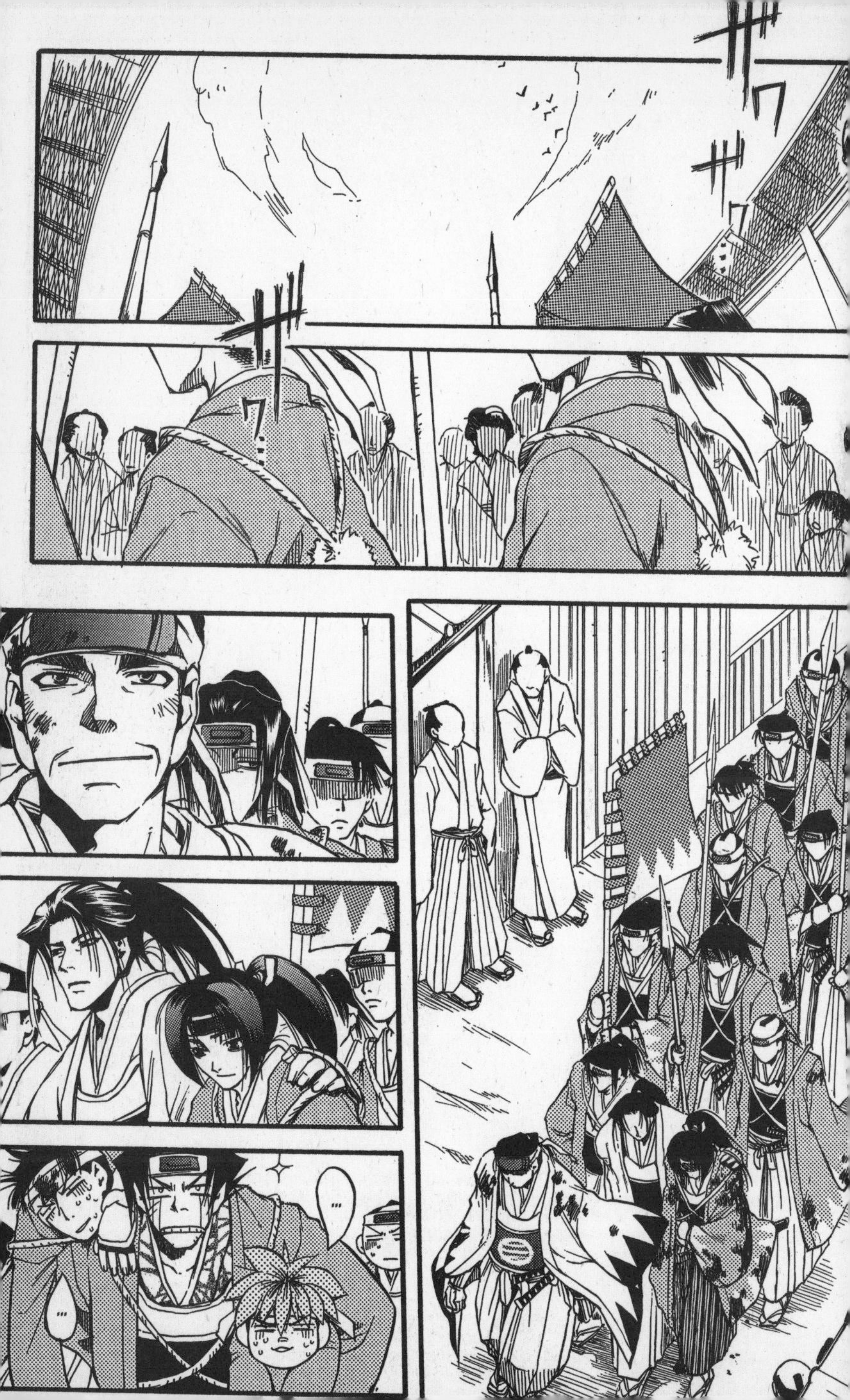
ザワ
ザワ
ザワ
…
…

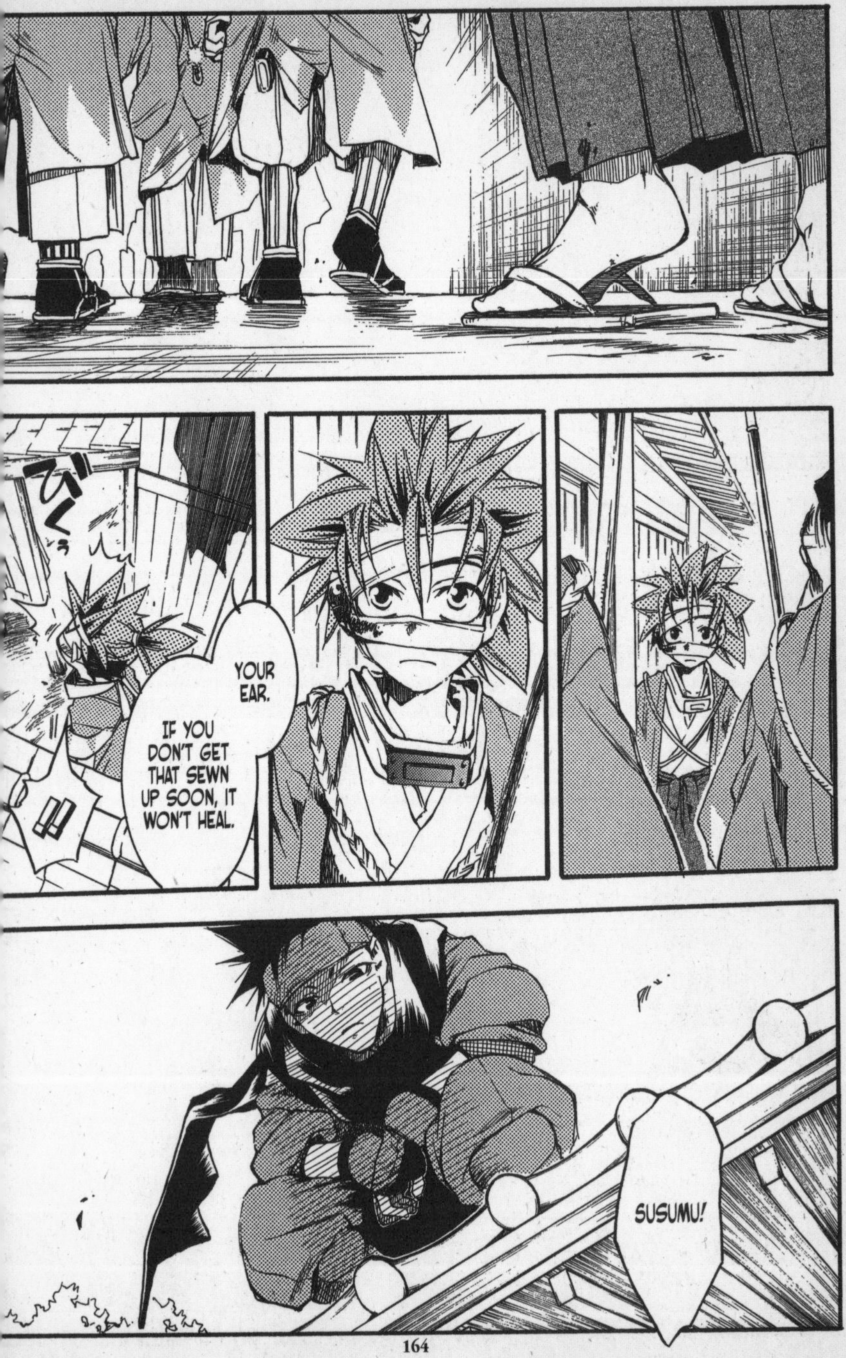
YOUR EAR. IF YOU DON'T GET THAT SEWN UP SOON, IT WON'T HEAL.
びくぅ
SUSUMU!

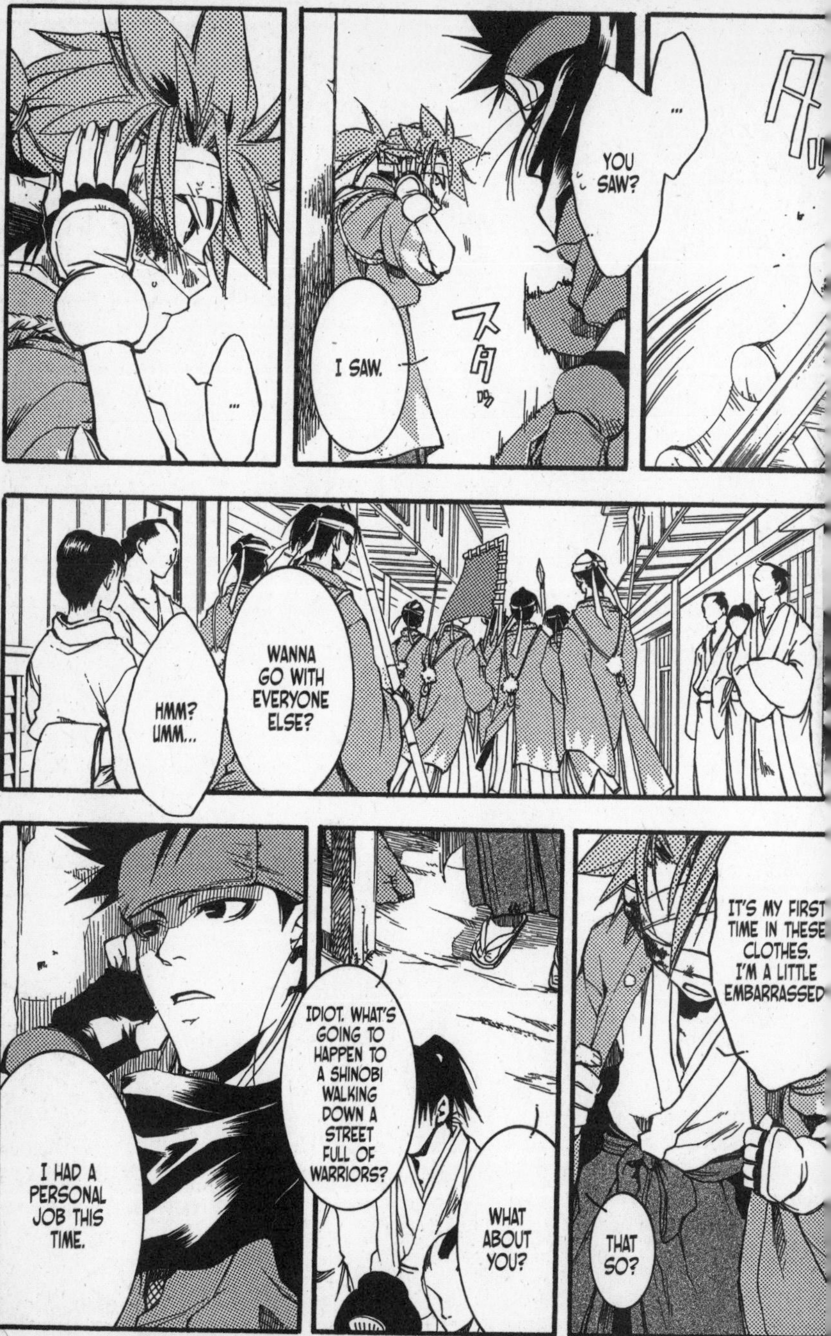

... YOU SAW?
I SAW.
...
WANNA GO WITH EVERYONE ELSE?
HMM? UMM...
IT'S MY FIRST TIME IN THESE CLOTHES. I'M A LITTLE EMBARRASSED
THAT SO?
IDIOT. WHAT'S GOING TO HAPPEN TO A SHINOBI WALKING DOWN A STREET FULL OF WARRIORS?
WHAT ABOUT YOU?
I HAD A PERSONAL JOB THIS TIME.

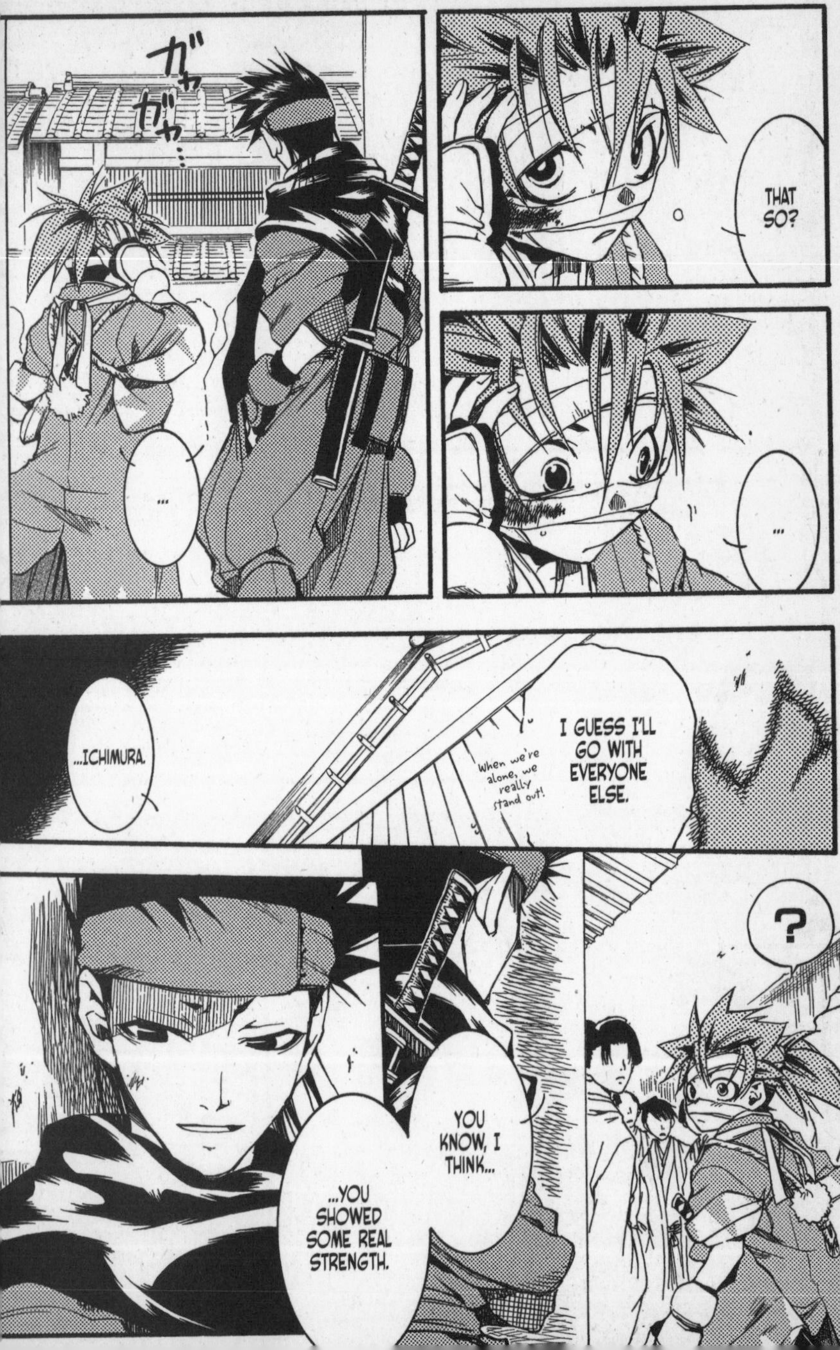
THAT SO?
...
ガヤガヤ...
...
I GUESS I'LL GO WITH EVERYONE ELSE.
When we're alone, we really stand out!
...ICHIMURA.
?
YOU KNOW, I THINK...
...YOU SHOWED SOME REAL STRENGTH.

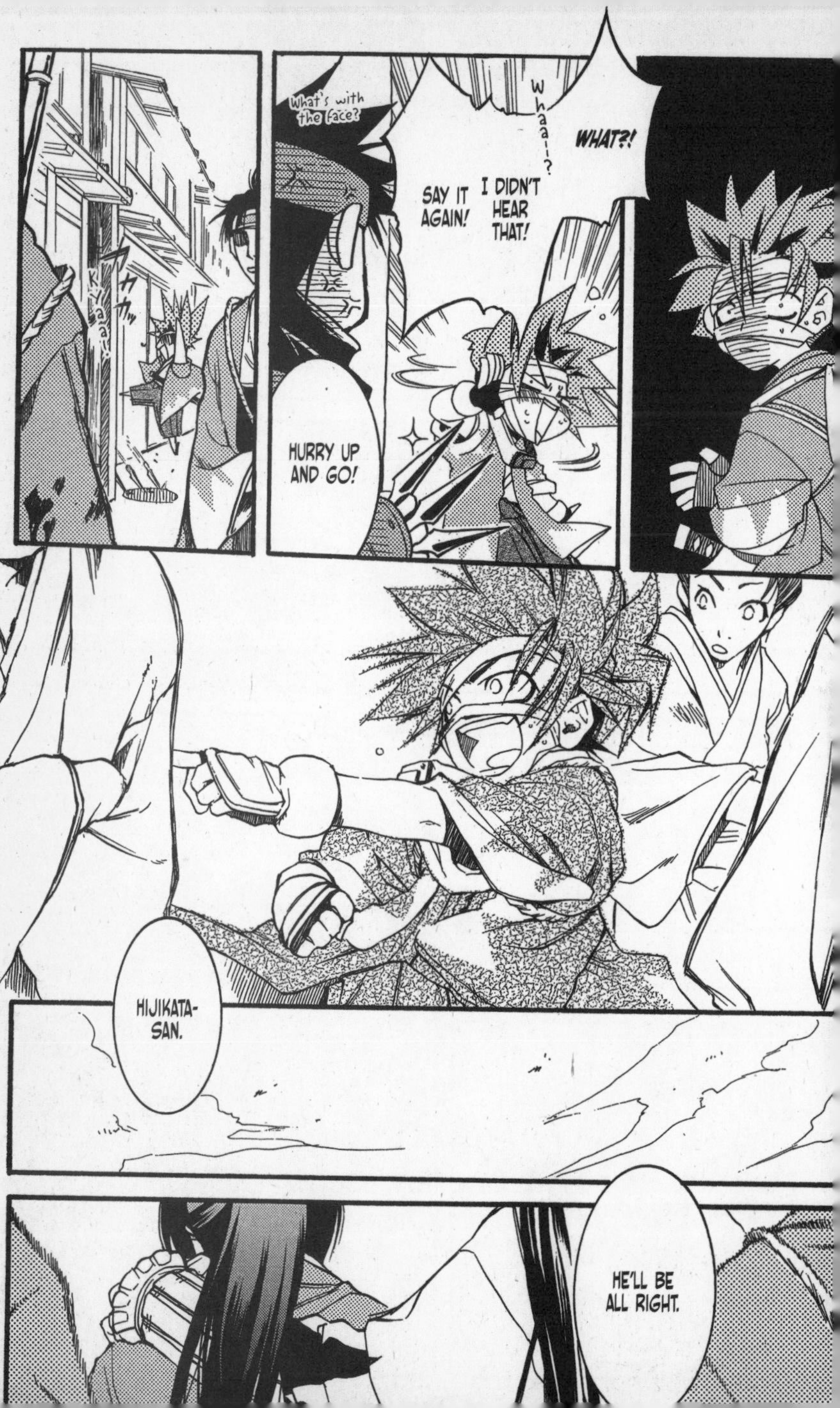

WHAT?!
Whaaa-?
I DIDN'T HEAR THAT!
SAY IT AGAIN!
What's with the face?
HURRY UP AND GO!
HIJIKATA-SAN.
HE'LL BE ALL RIGHT.

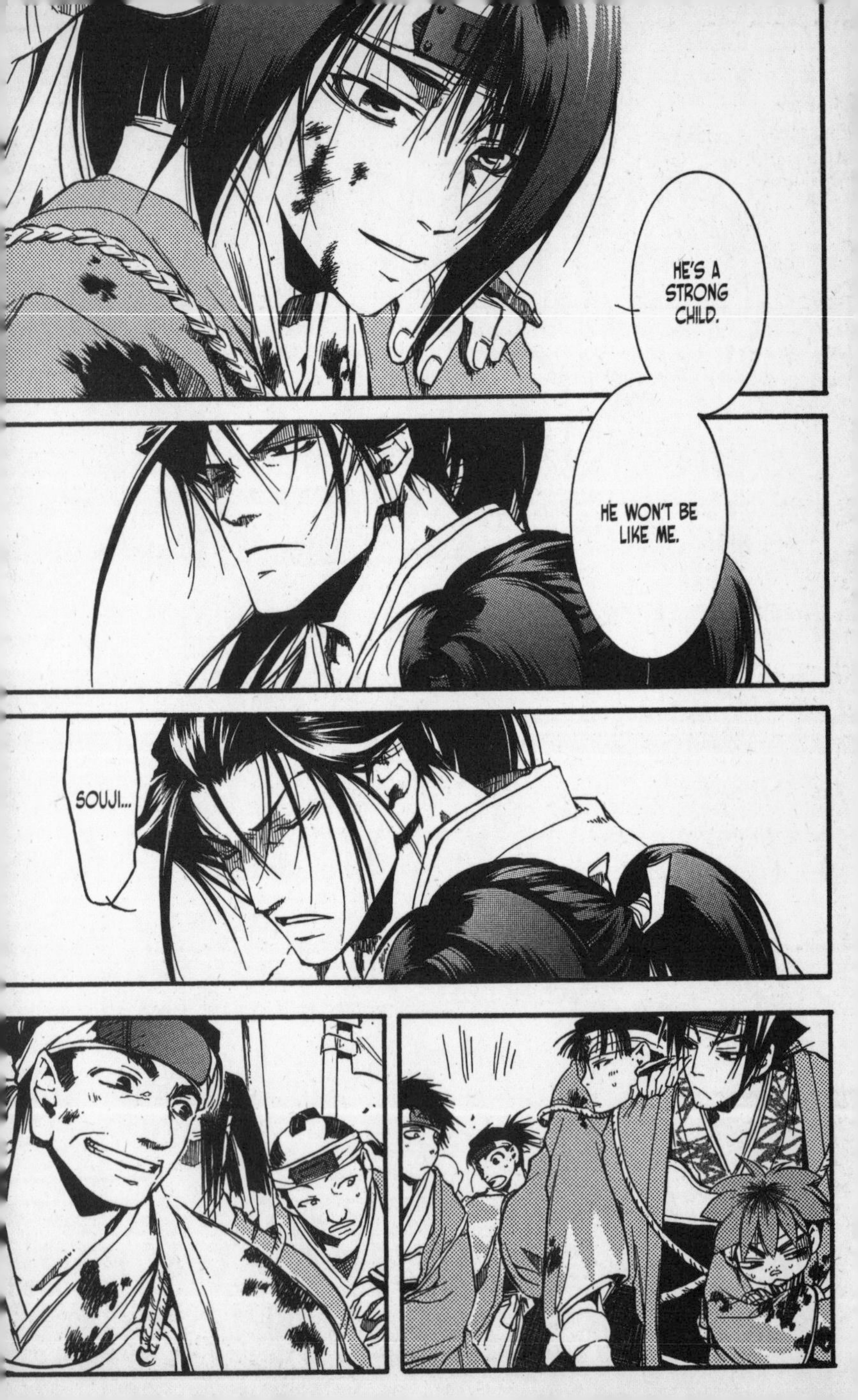
HE'S A STRONG CHILD.
HE WON'T BE LIKE ME.
SOUJI...

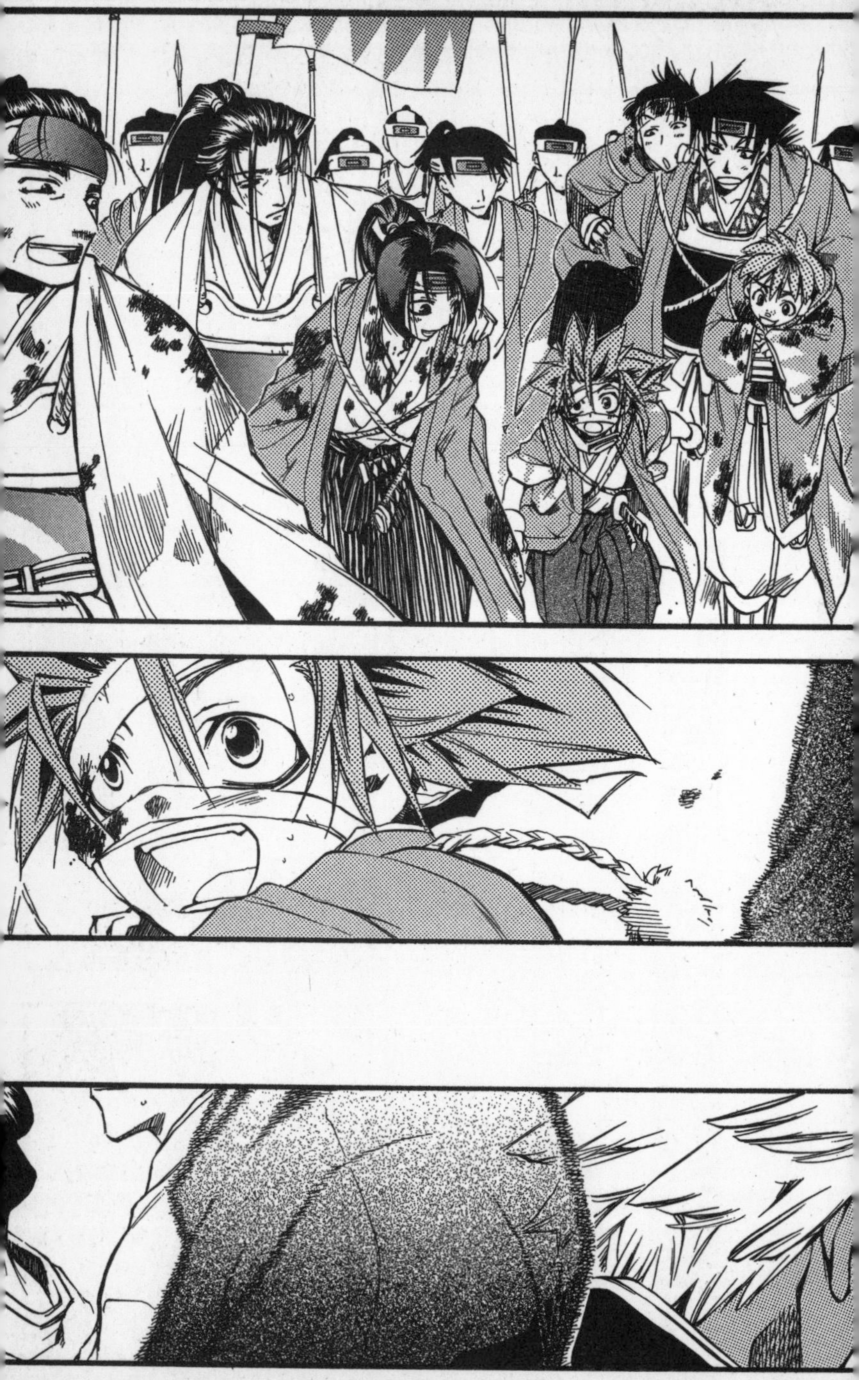

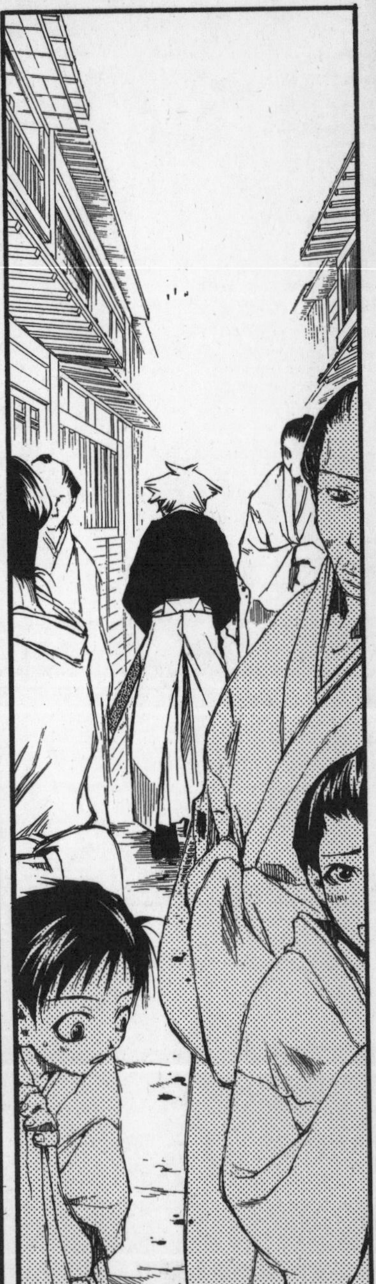

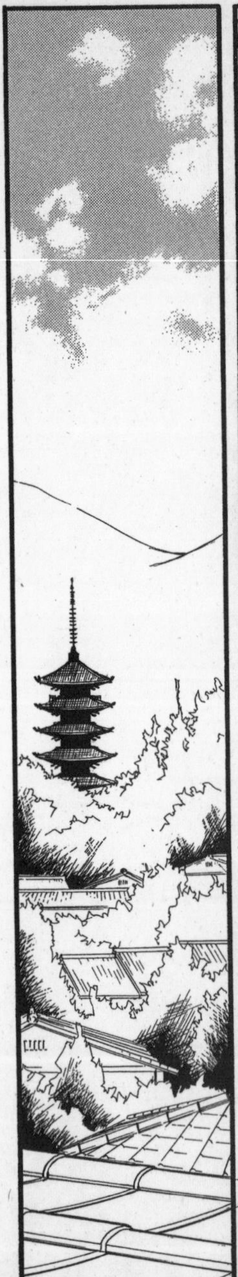

JUNE 5TH, FIRST YEAR OF GENJI. THE IKEDAYA INCIDENT--FIN

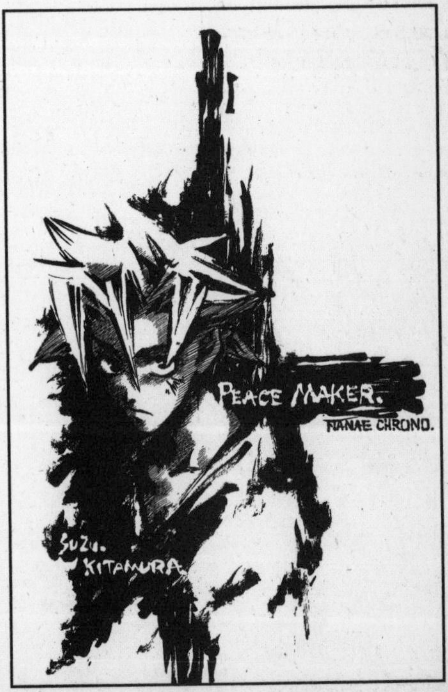
PEACE MAKER.
NANAE CHRONO.
SUZU.
KITAMURA

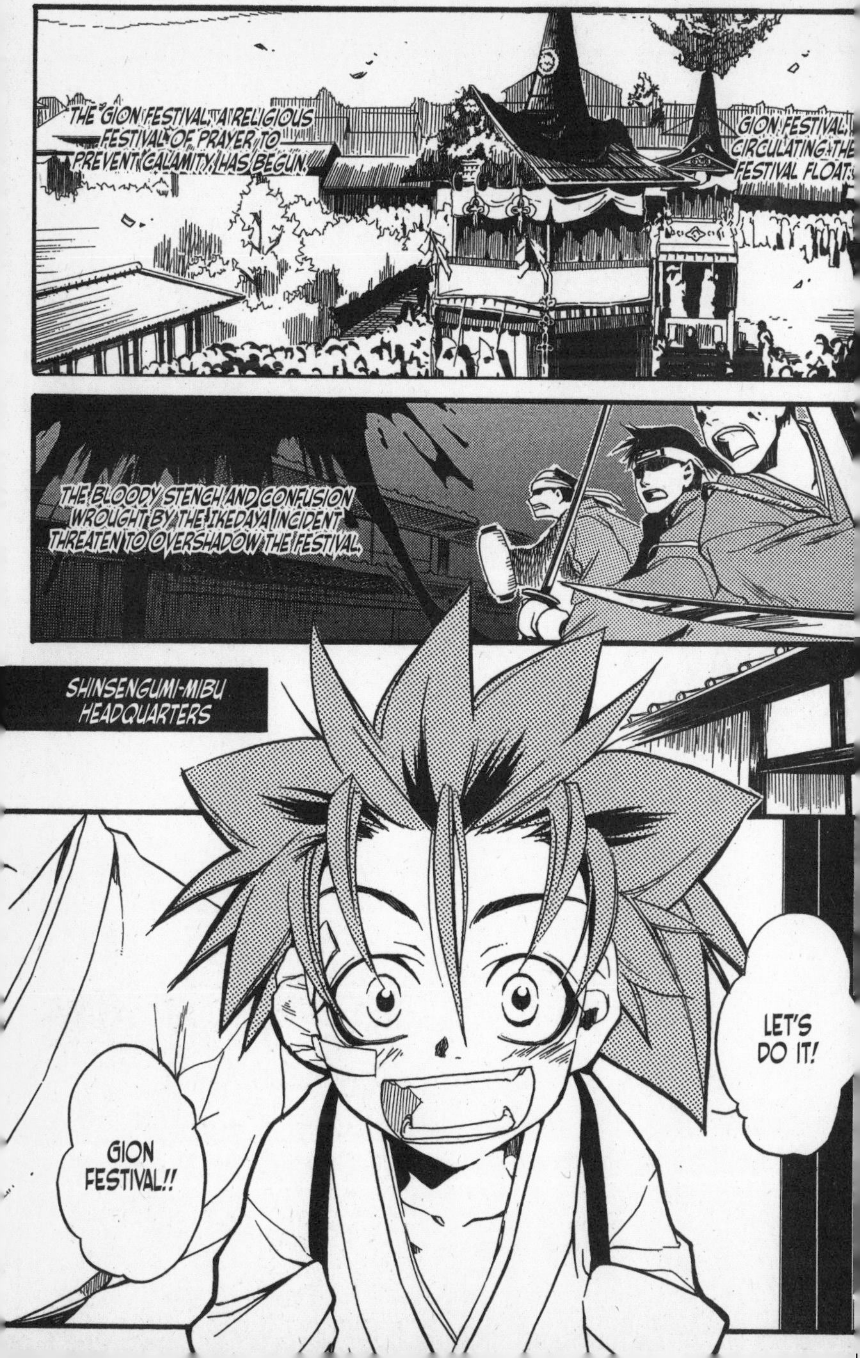
GION FESTIVAL, CIRCULATING THE FESTIVAL FLOAT
THE GION FESTIVAL, A RELIGIOUS FESTIVAL OF PRAYER TO PREVENT CALAMITY, HAS BEGUN.
THE BLOODY STENCH AND CONFUSION WROUGHT BY THE IKEDAYA INCIDENT THREATEN TO OVERSHADOW THE FESTIVAL.
SHINSENGUMI-MIBU HEADQUARTERS
LET'S DO IT!
GION FESTIVAL!!

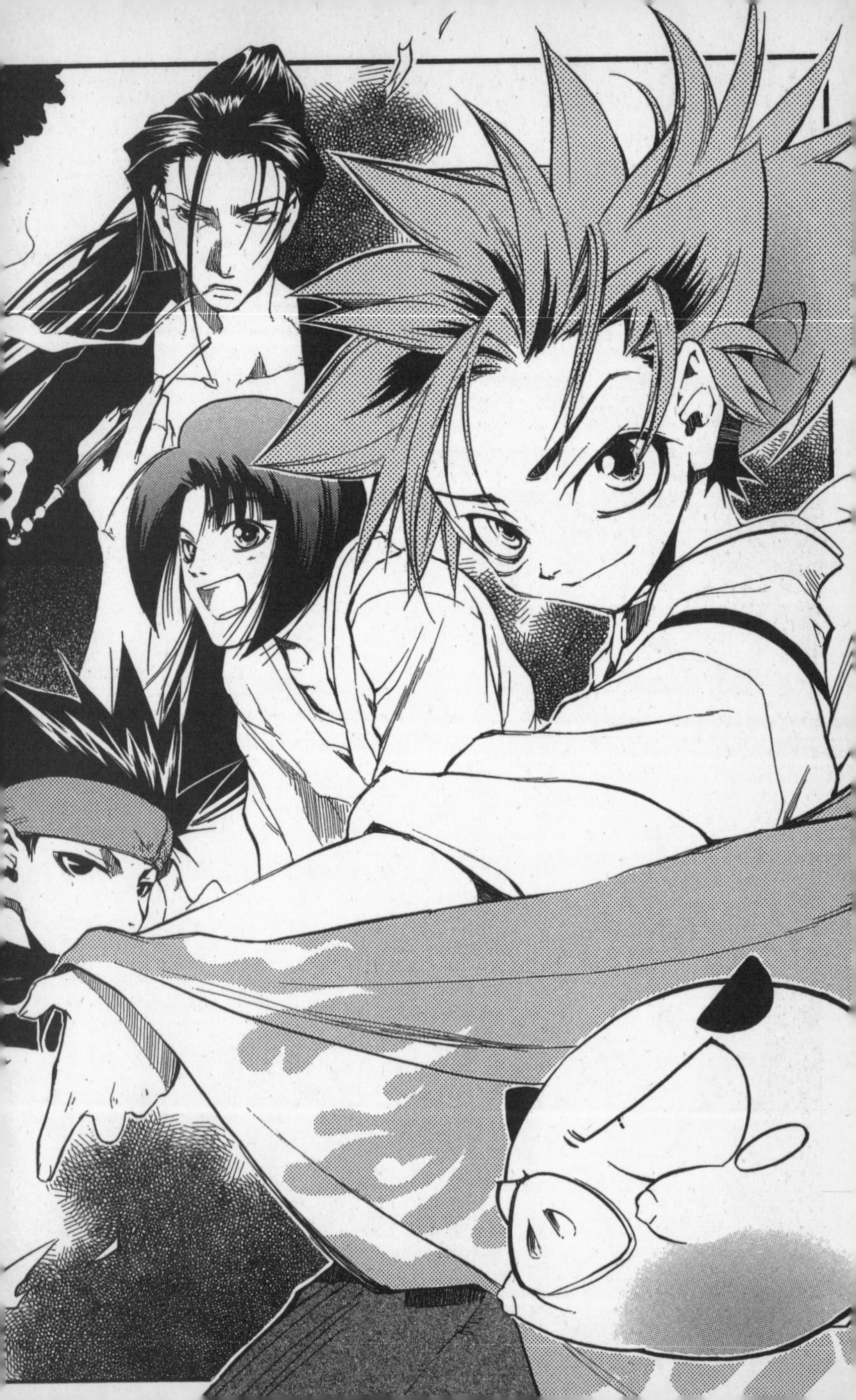

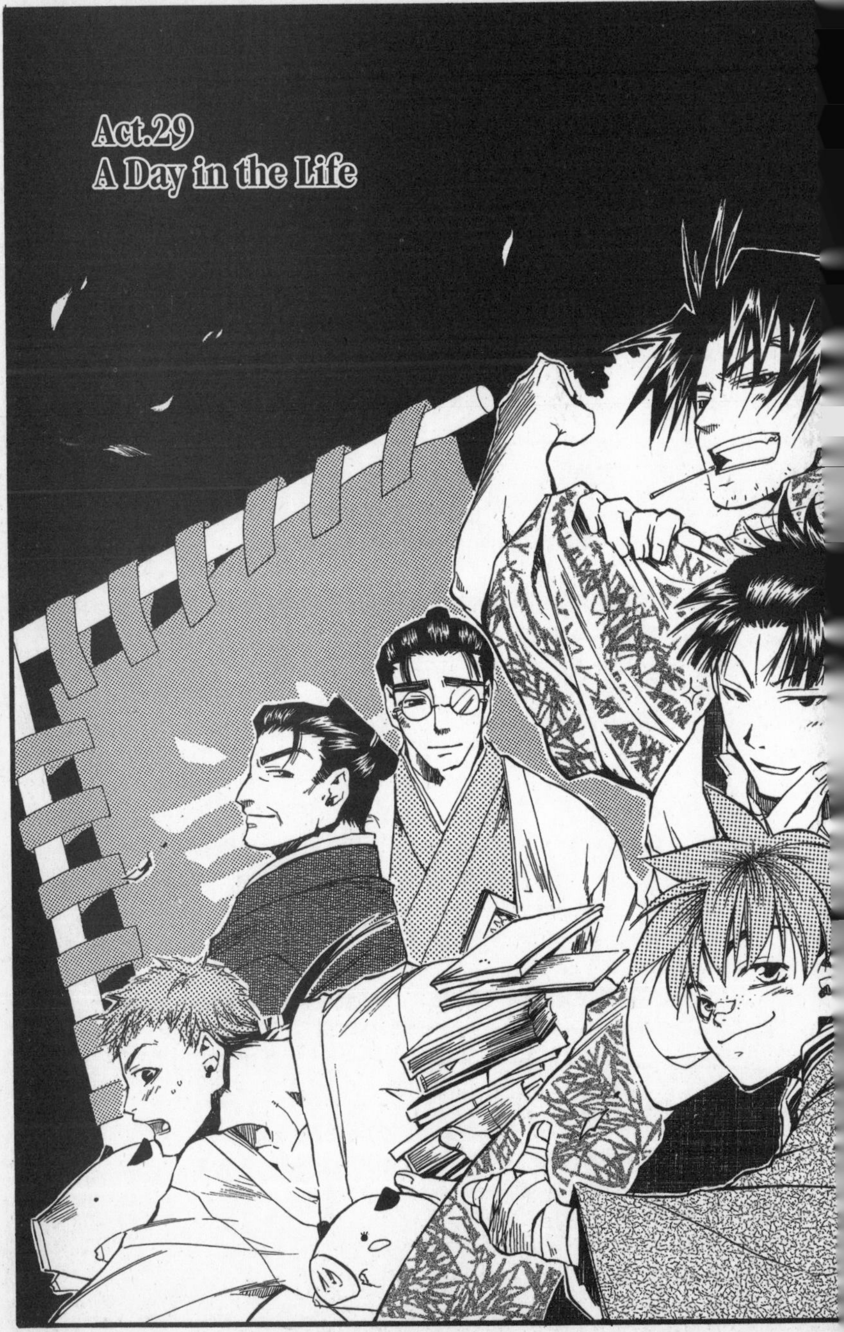
Act.29
A Day in the Life

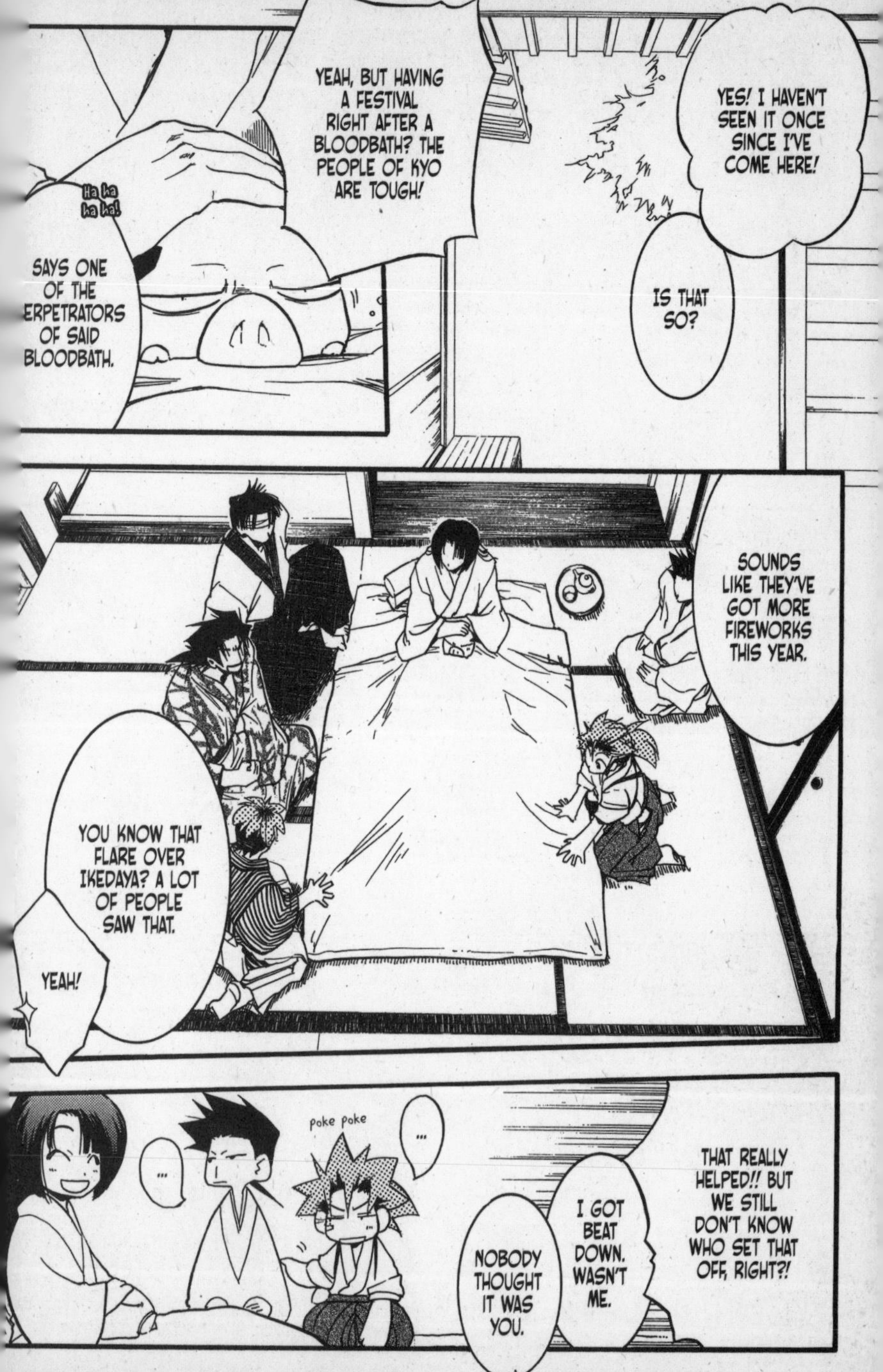
YES! I HAVEN'T SEEN IT ONCE SINCE I'VE COME HERE!
IS THAT SO?
YEAH, BUT HAVING A FESTIVAL RIGHT AFTER A BLOODBATH? THE PEOPLE OF KYO ARE TOUGH!
Ha ha ha ha!
SAYS ONE OF THE ERPETRATORS OF SAID BLOODBATH.
SOUNDS LIKE THEY'VE GOT MORE FIREWORKS THIS YEAR.
YOU KNOW THAT FLARE OVER IKEDAYA? A LOT OF PEOPLE SAW THAT.
YEAH!
THAT REALLY HELPED!! BUT WE STILL DON'T KNOW WHO SET THAT OFF, RIGHT?!
I GOT BEAT DOWN. WASN'T ME.
NOBODY THOUGHT IT WAS YOU.
...
poke poke
...

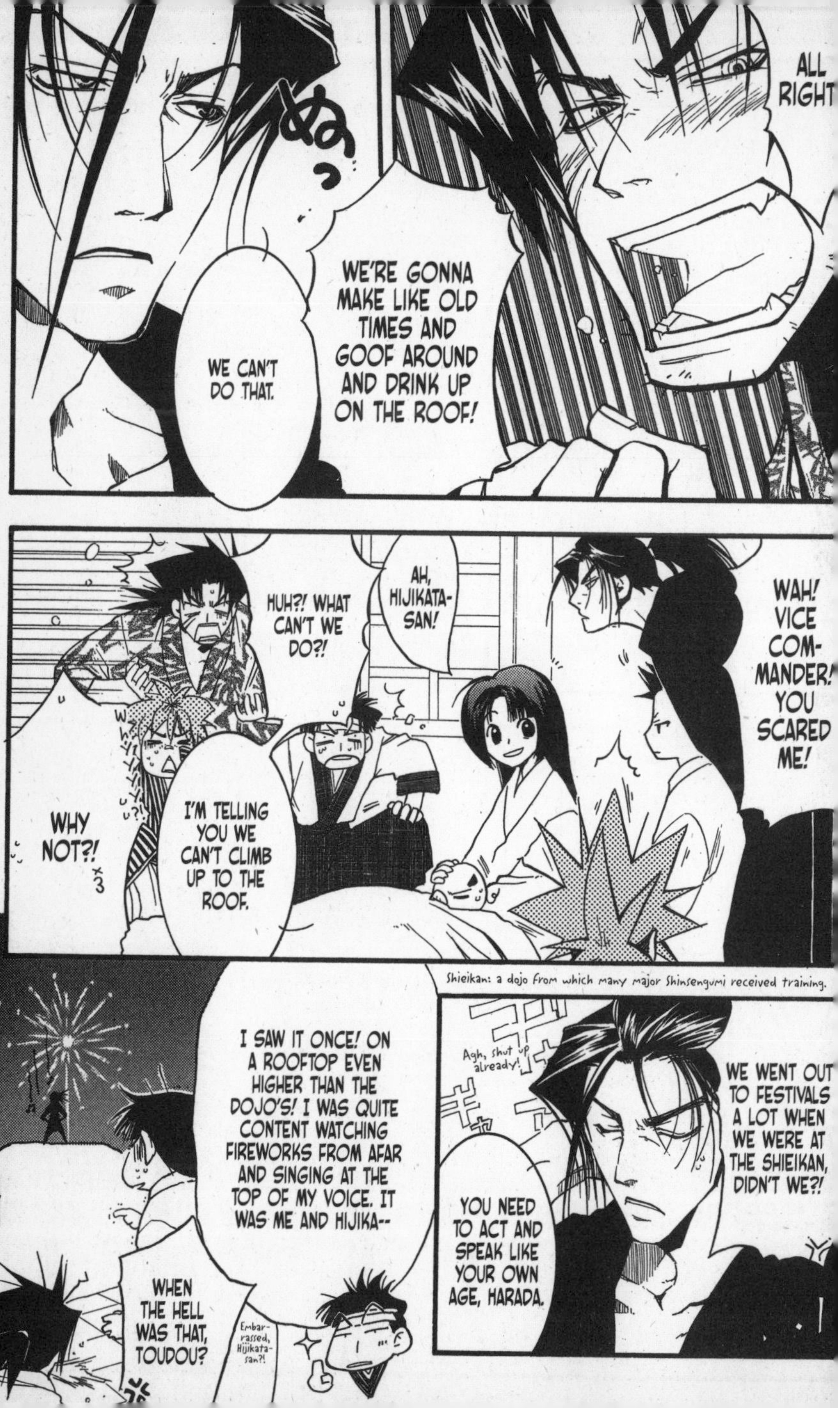
ALL RIGHT
WE'RE GONNA MAKE LIKE OLD TIMES AND GOOF AROUND AND DRINK UP ON THE ROOF!
WE CAN'T DO THAT.
WAH! VICE COM-MANDER! YOU SCARED ME!
AH, HIJIKATA-SAN!
HUH?! WHAT CAN'T WE DO?!
I'M TELLING YOU WE CAN'T CLIMB UP TO THE ROOF.
WHY NOT?!
x3
Shieikan: a dojo from which many major Shinsengumi received training.
WE WENT OUT TO FESTIVALS A LOT WHEN WE WERE AT THE SHIEIKAN, DIDN'T WE?!
Agh, shut up already!
YOU NEED TO ACT AND SPEAK LIKE YOUR OWN AGE, HARADA.
I SAW IT ONCE! ON A ROOFTOP EVEN HIGHER THAN THE DOJO'S! I WAS QUITE CONTENT WATCHING FIREWORKS FROM AFAR AND SINGING AT THE TOP OF MY VOICE. IT WAS ME AND HIJIKA--
Embar-rassed, Hijikata-san?!
WHEN THE HELL WAS THAT, TOUDOU?

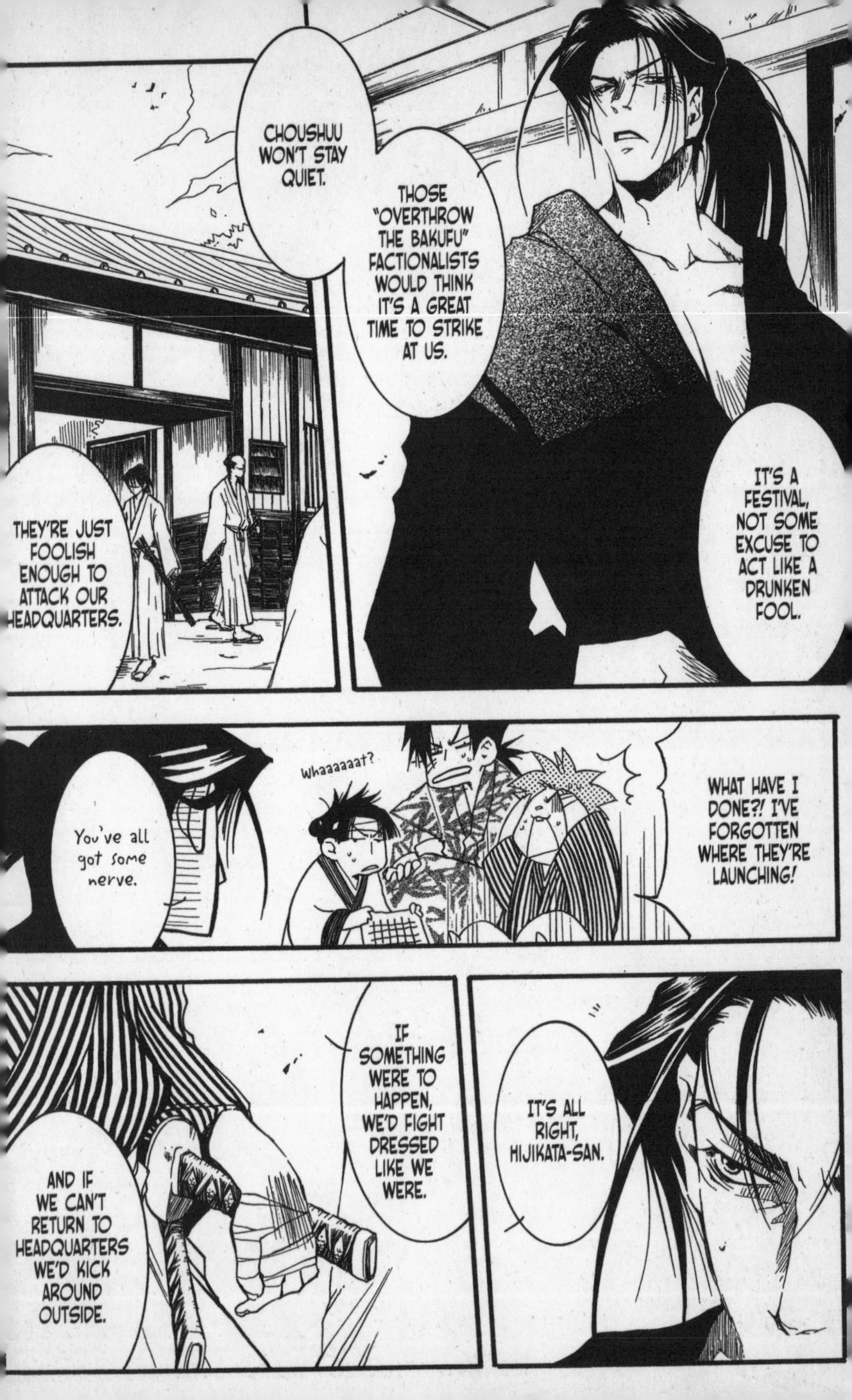
CHOUSHUU WON'T STAY QUIET.
THOSE "OVERTHROW THE BAKUFU" FACTIONALISTS WOULD THINK IT'S A GREAT TIME TO STRIKE AT US.
IT'S A FESTIVAL, NOT SOME EXCUSE TO ACT LIKE A DRUNKEN FOOL.
THEY'RE JUST FOOLISH ENOUGH TO ATTACK OUR HEADQUARTERS.
WHAT HAVE I DONE?! I'VE FORGOTTEN WHERE THEY'RE LAUNCHING!
Whaaaaaat?
You've all got some nerve.
IT'S ALL RIGHT, HIJIKATA-SAN.
IF SOMETHING WERE TO HAPPEN, WE'D FIGHT DRESSED LIKE WE WERE.
AND IF WE CAN'T RETURN TO HEADQUARTERS WE'D KICK AROUND OUTSIDE.

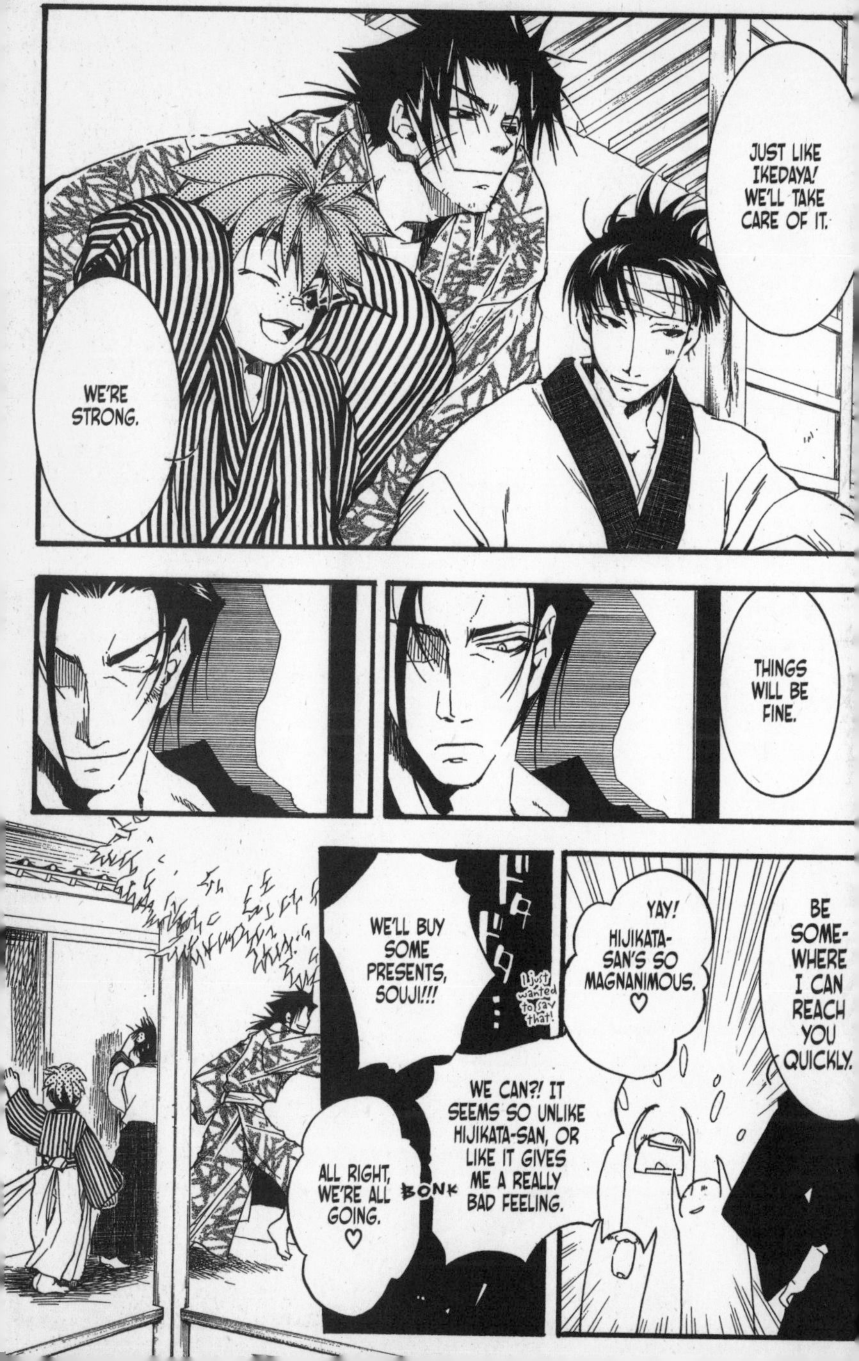
JUST LIKE IKEDAYA! WE'LL TAKE CARE OF IT.
WE'RE STRONG.
THINGS WILL BE FINE.
BE SOME-WHERE I CAN REACH YOU QUICKLY.
YAY! HIJIKATA-SAN'S SO MAGNANIMOUS. ♡
WE'LL BUY SOME PRESENTS, SOUJI!!!
ドタドタ...
I just wanted to say that!
WE CAN?! IT SEEMS SO UNLIKE HIJIKATA-SAN, OR LIKE IT GIVES ME A REALLY BAD FEELING.
BONK
ALL RIGHT, WE'RE ALL GOING. ♡

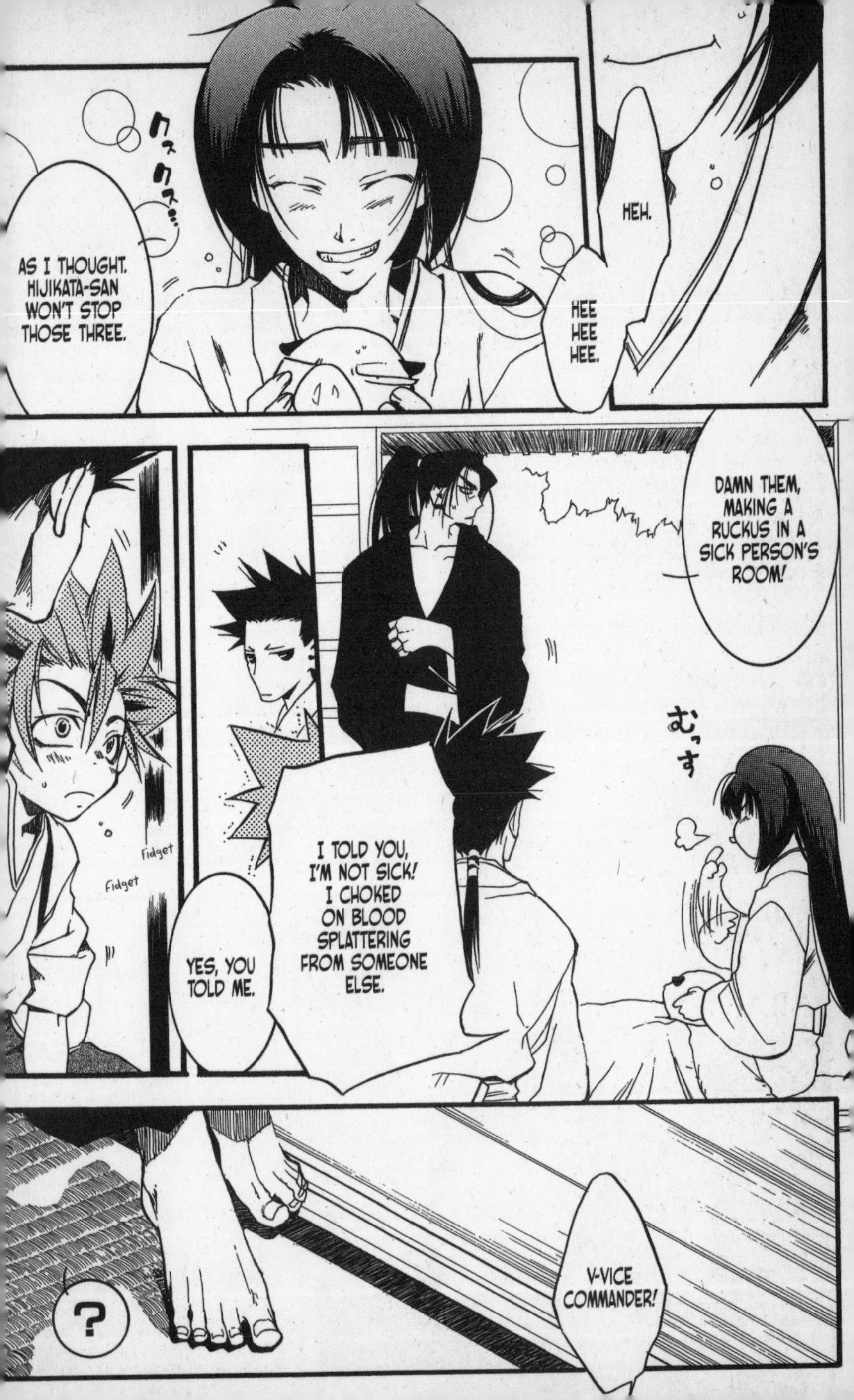
HEH.
HEE HEE HEE.
クスクス…
AS I THOUGHT. HIJIKATA-SAN WON'T STOP THOSE THREE.
DAMN THEM, MAKING A RUCKUS IN A SICK PERSON'S ROOM!
むっす
I TOLD YOU, I'M NOT SICK! I CHOKED ON BLOOD SPLATTERING FROM SOMEONE ELSE.
YES, YOU TOLD ME.
Fidget
Fidget
V-VICE COMMANDER!
?

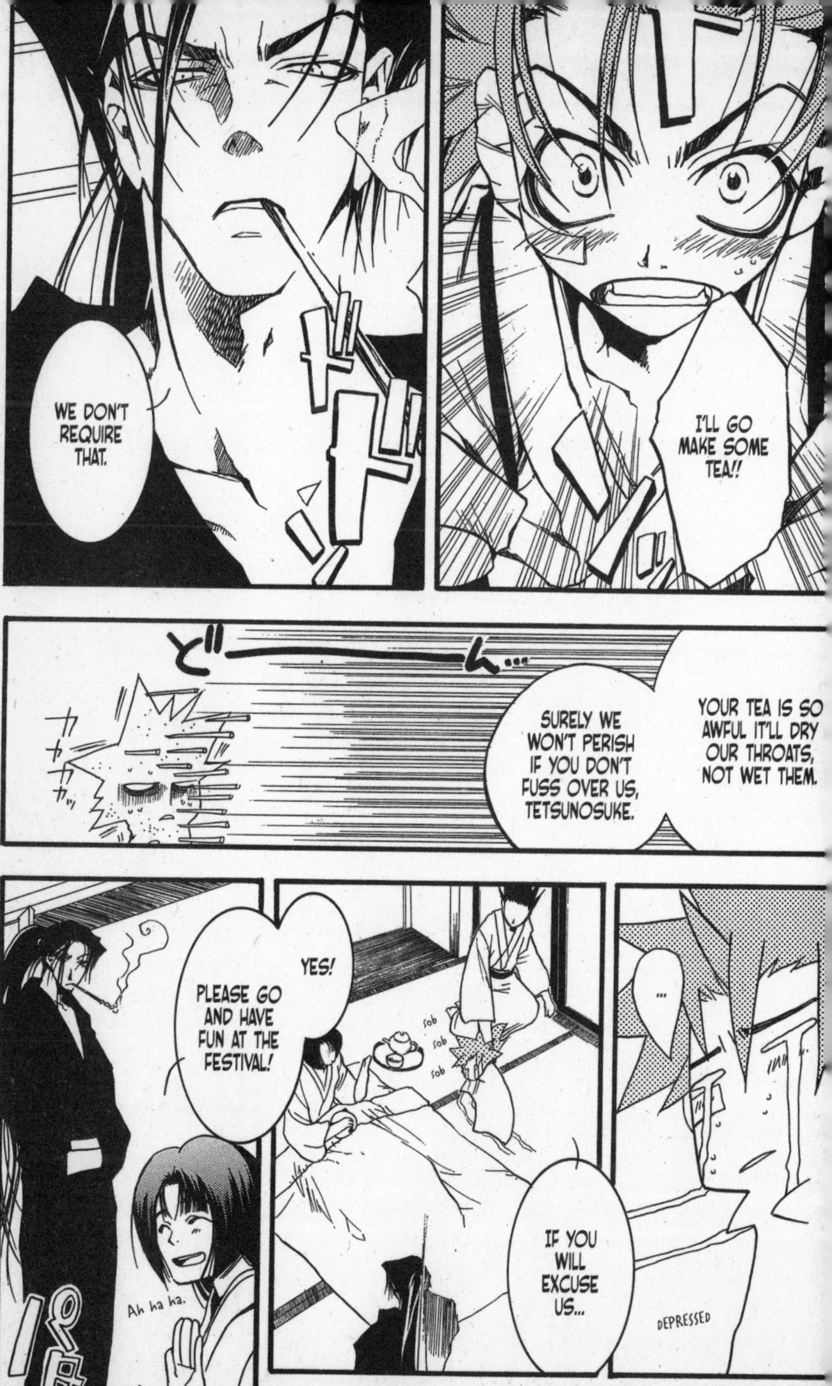
I'LL GO MAKE SOME TEA!!
WE DON'T REQUIRE THAT.
YOUR TEA IS SO AWFUL IT'LL DRY OUR THROATS, NOT WET THEM.
SURELY WE WON'T PERISH IF YOU DON'T FUSS OVER US, TETSUNOSUKE.
どーーーん…
...
DEPRESSED
IF YOU WILL EXCUSE US...
sob sob sob
YES!
PLEASE GO AND HAVE FUN AT THE FESTIVAL!
Ah ha ha.

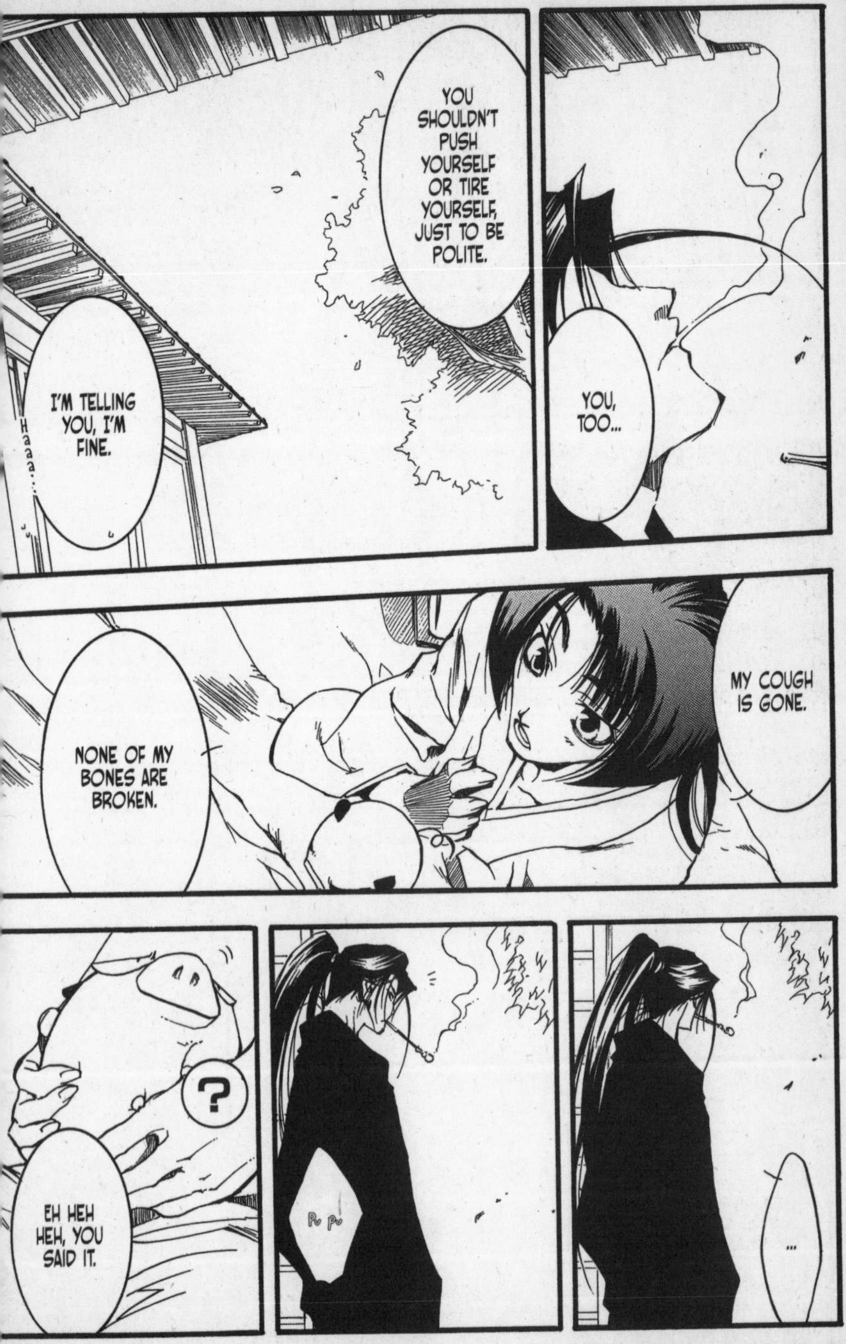
YOU, TOO...
YOU SHOULDN'T PUSH YOURSELF OR TIRE YOURSELF, JUST TO BE POLITE.
I'M TELLING YOU, I'M FINE.
Haaa...
MY COUGH IS GONE.
NONE OF MY BONES ARE BROKEN.
...
Pu pu
?
EH HEH HEH, YOU SAID IT.

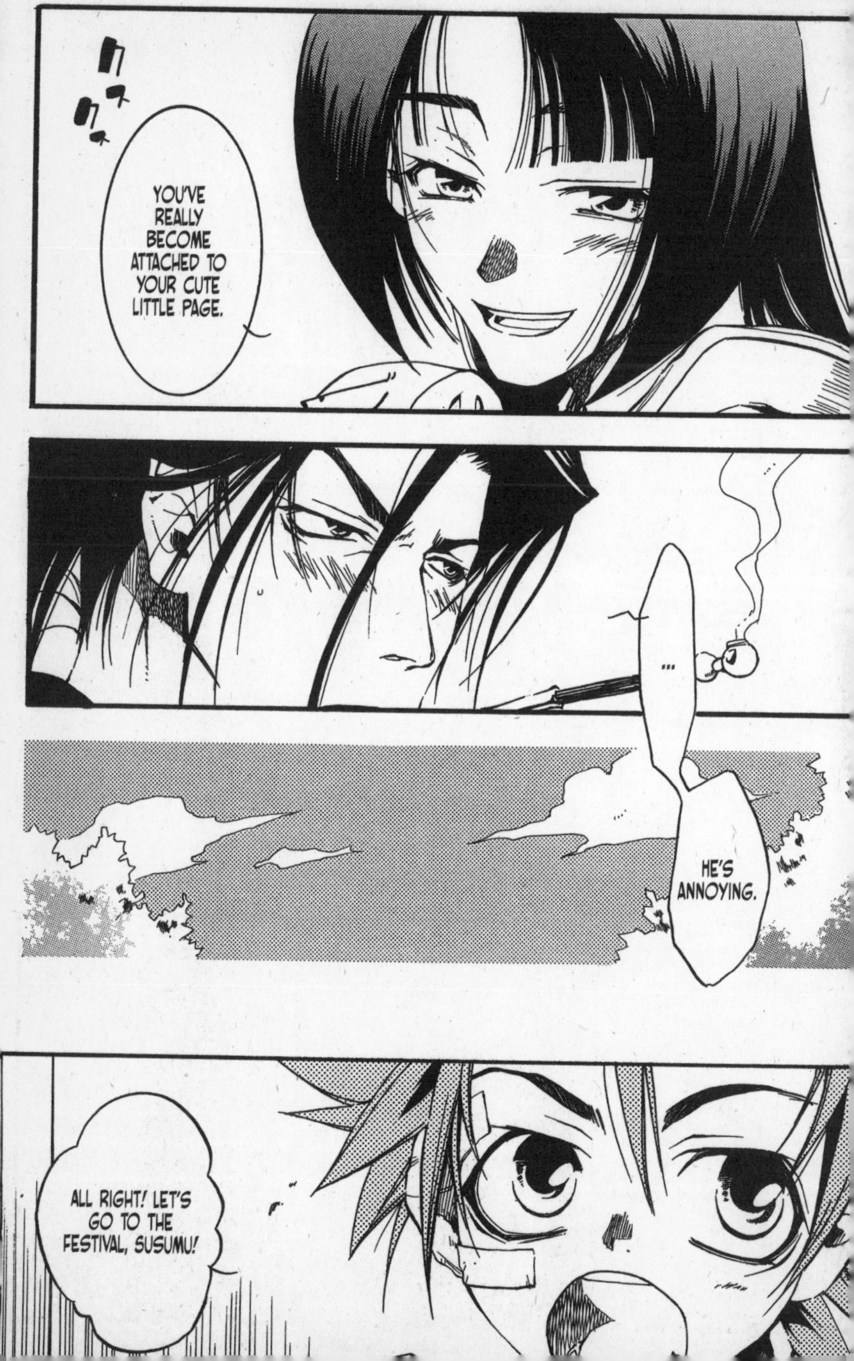
YOU'VE REALLY BECOME ATTACHED TO YOUR CUTE LITTLE PAGE.
...
HE'S ANNOYING.
ALL RIGHT! LET'S GO TO THE FESTIVAL, SUSUMU!

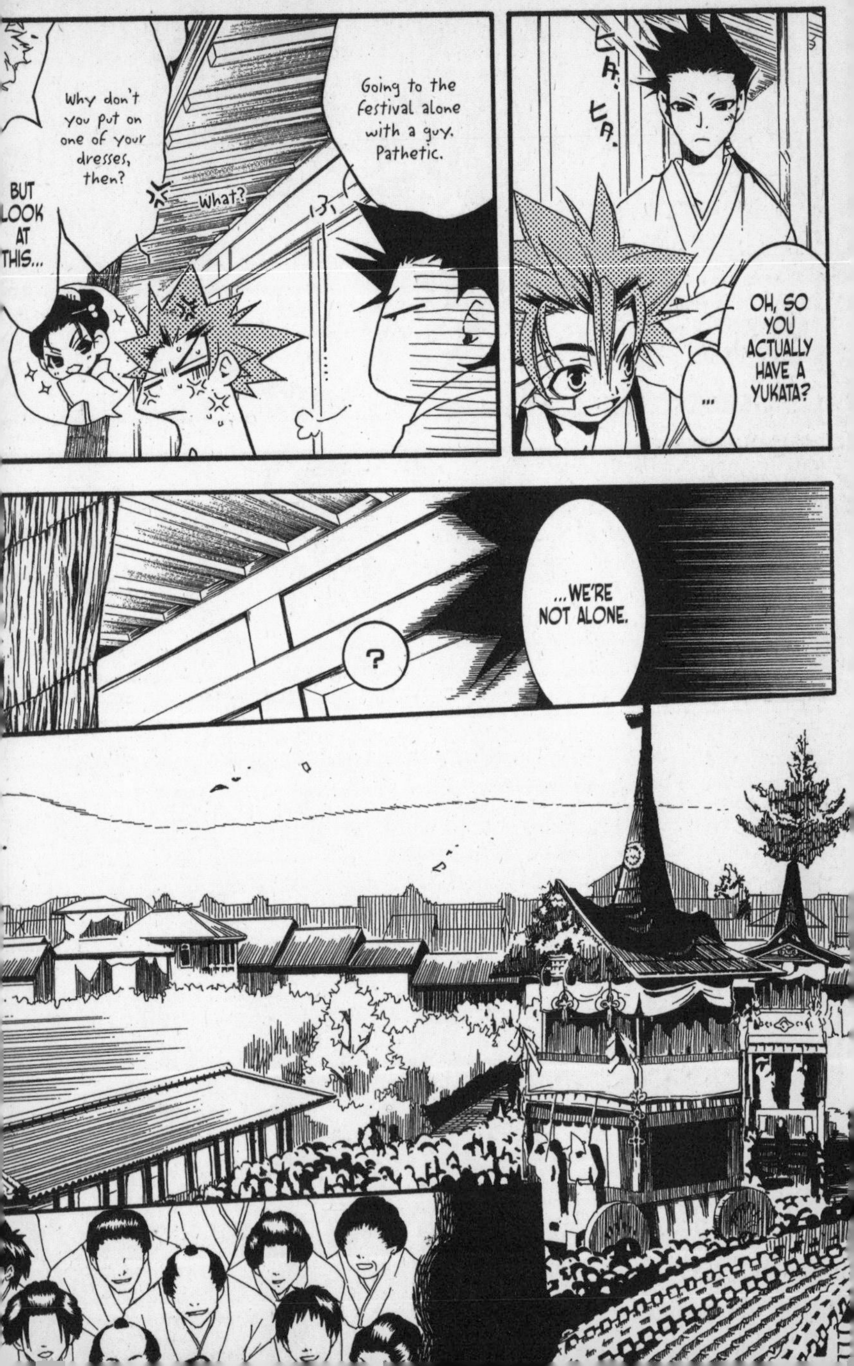
OH, SO YOU ACTUALLY HAVE A YUKATA?
...
Going to the festival alone with a guy. Pathetic.
What?
Why don't you put on one of your dresses, then?
BUT LOOK AT THIS...
...WE'RE NOT ALONE.
?

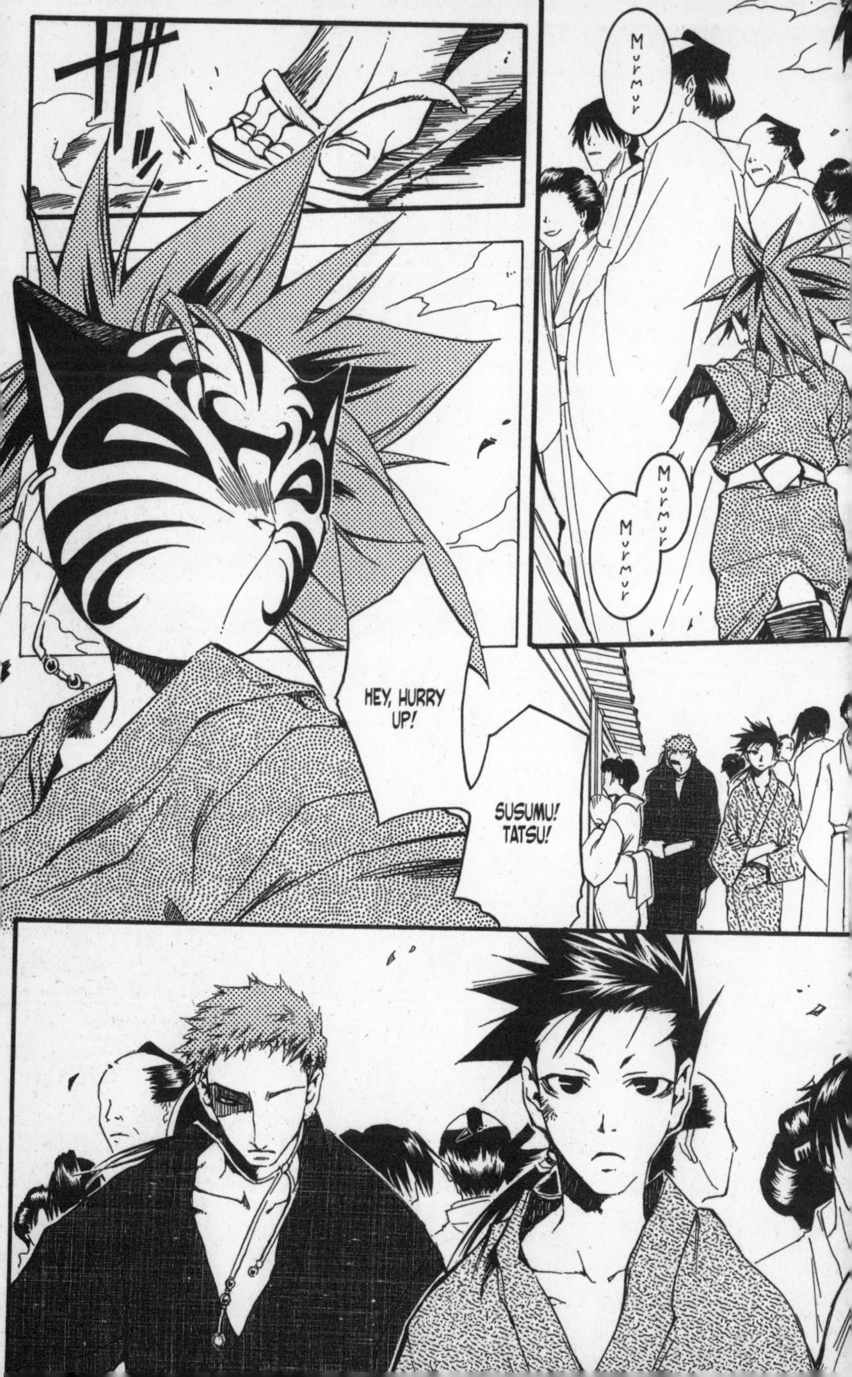
Murmur
Murmur
Murmur
HEY, HURRY UP!
SUSUMU! TATSU!

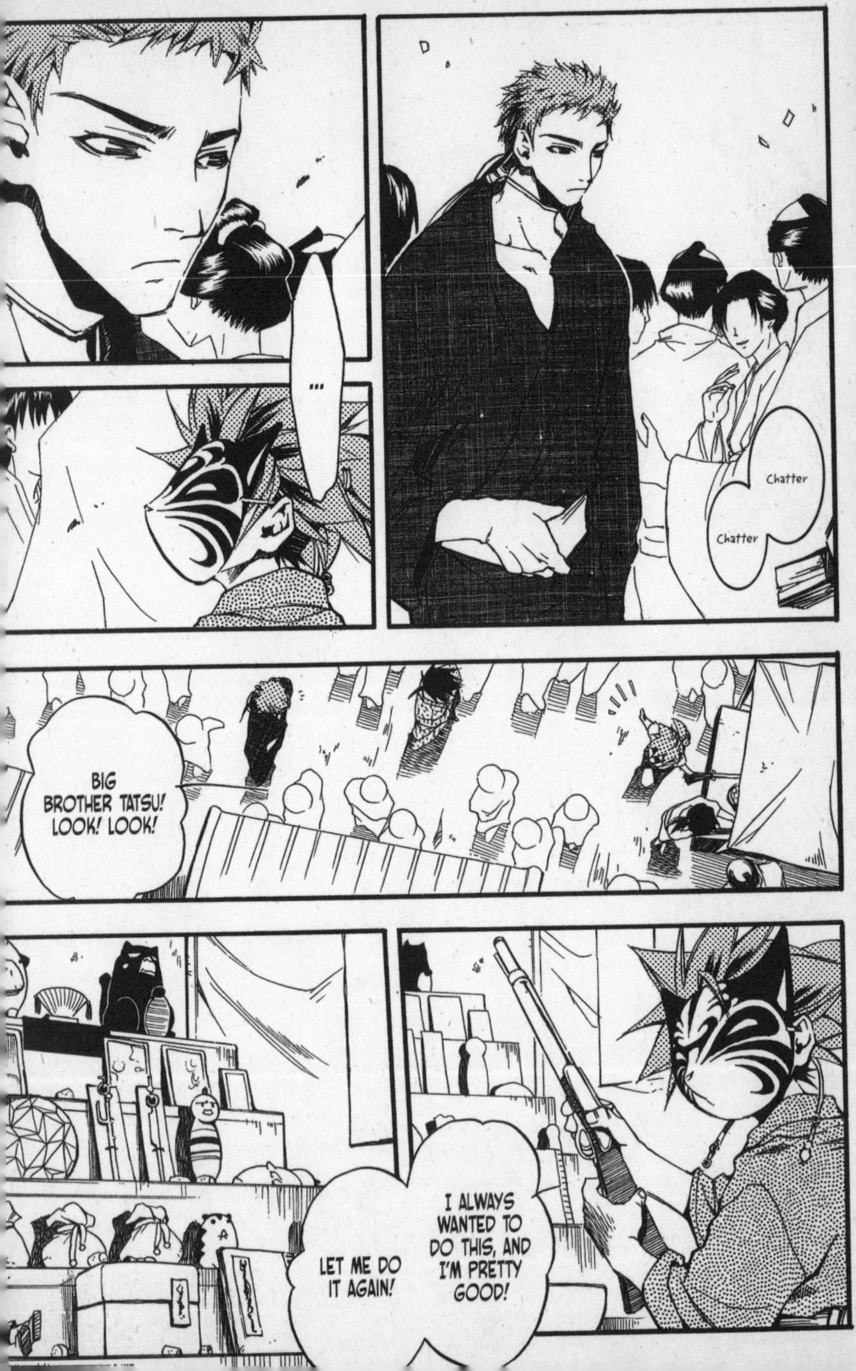
Chatter
Chatter
...
BIG BROTHER TATSU! LOOK! LOOK!
I ALWAYS WANTED TO DO THIS, AND I'M PRETTY GOOD!
LET ME DO IT AGAIN!

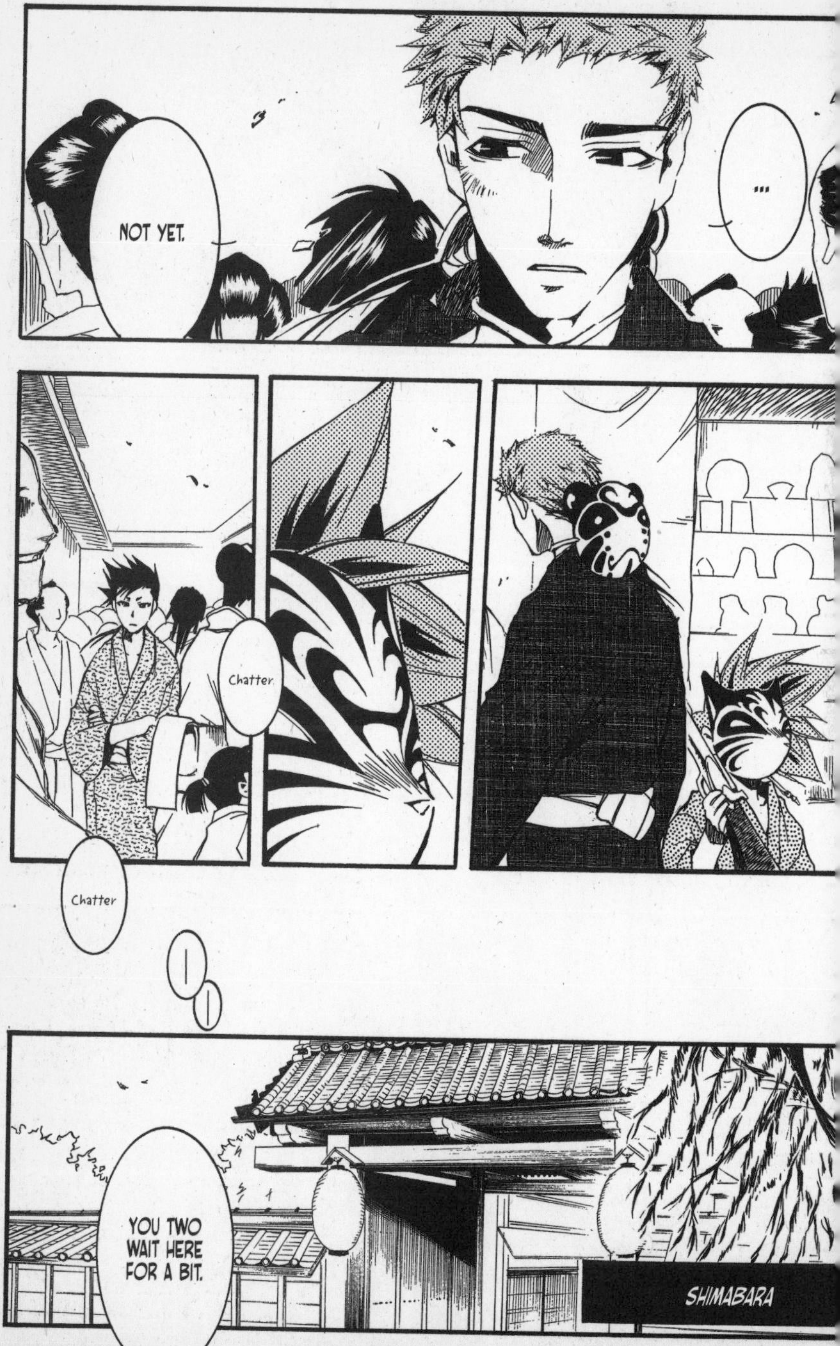
...
NOT YET.
Chatter
Chatter
SHIMABARA
YOU TWO WAIT HERE FOR A BIT.

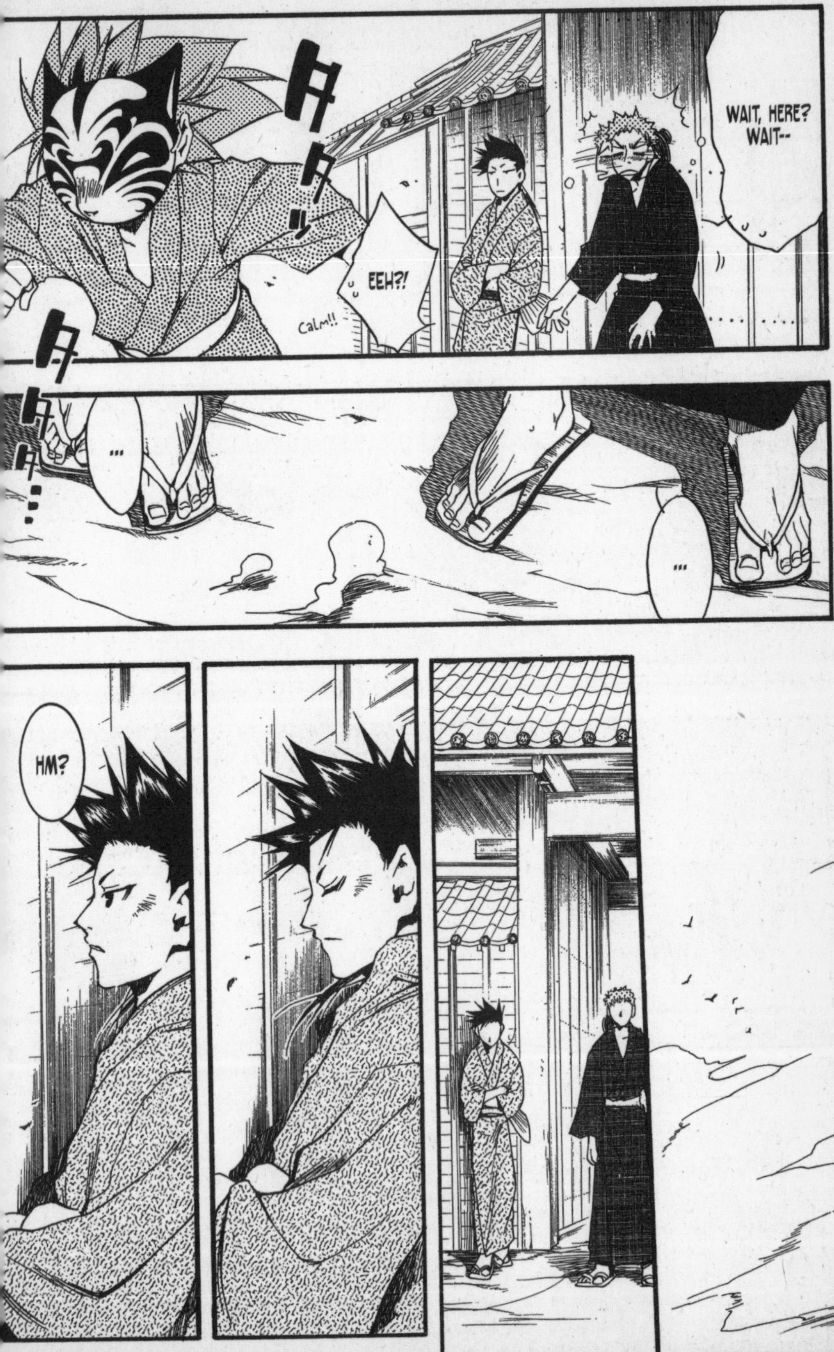
WAIT, HERE? WAIT--
EEH?!
Calm!!
タタッ
タタタ…
...
...
HM?

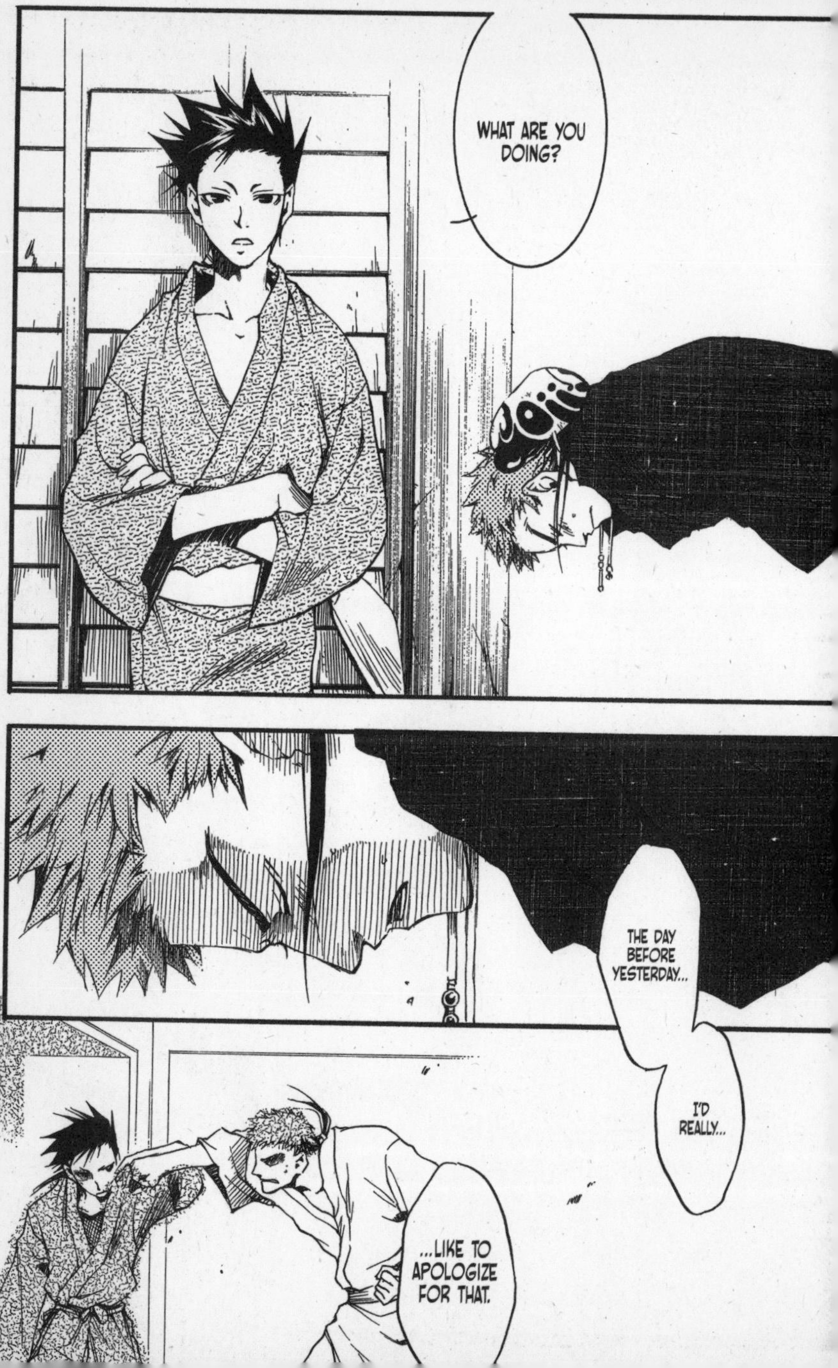
WHAT ARE YOU DOING?
THE DAY BEFORE YESTERDAY...
I'D REALLY...
...LIKE TO APOLOGIZE FOR THAT.

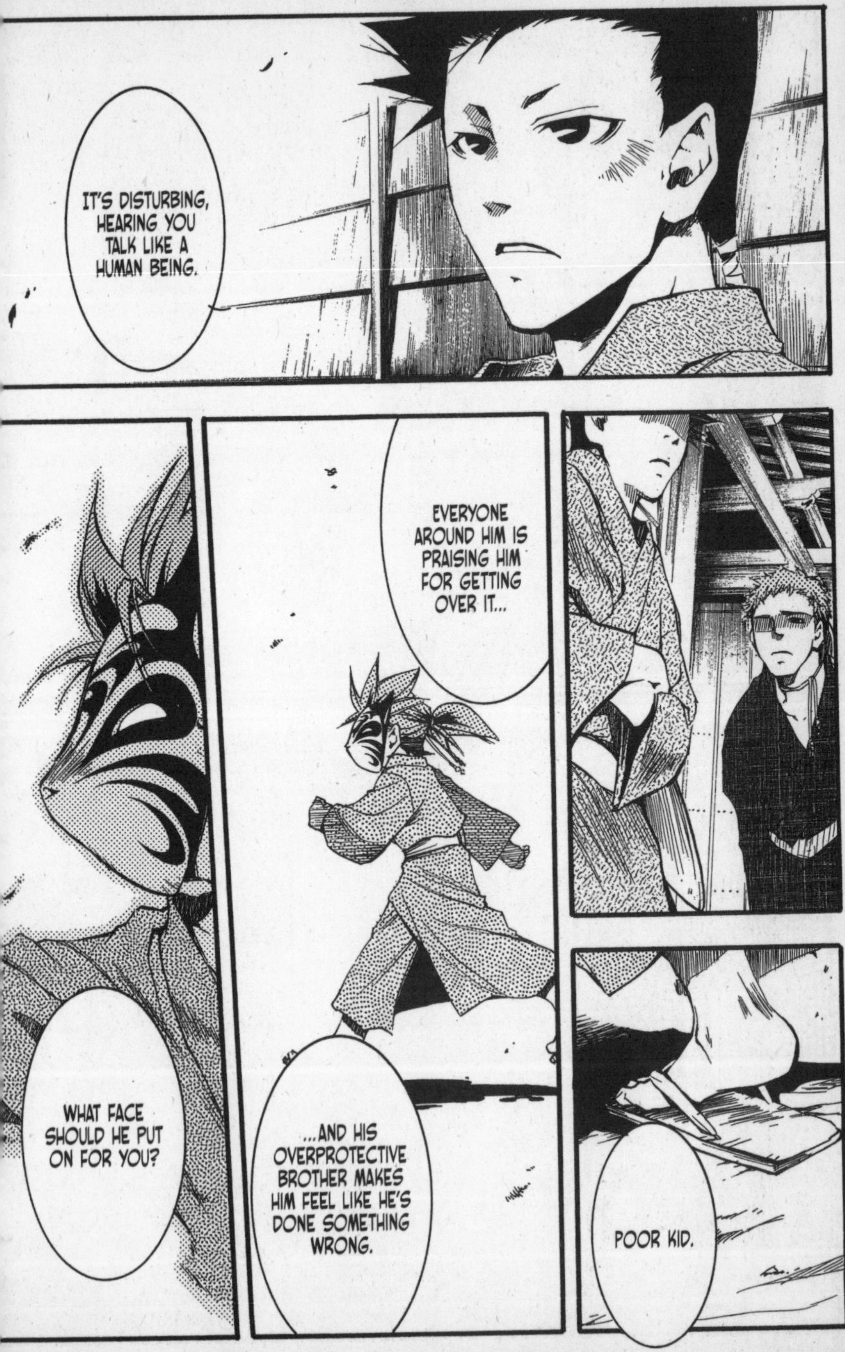
IT'S DISTURBING, HEARING YOU TALK LIKE A HUMAN BEING.
POOR KID.
EVERYONE AROUND HIM IS PRAISING HIM FOR GETTING OVER IT...
...AND HIS OVERPROTECTIVE BROTHER MAKES HIM FEEL LIKE HE'S DONE SOMETHING WRONG.
WHAT FACE SHOULD HE PUT ON FOR YOU?

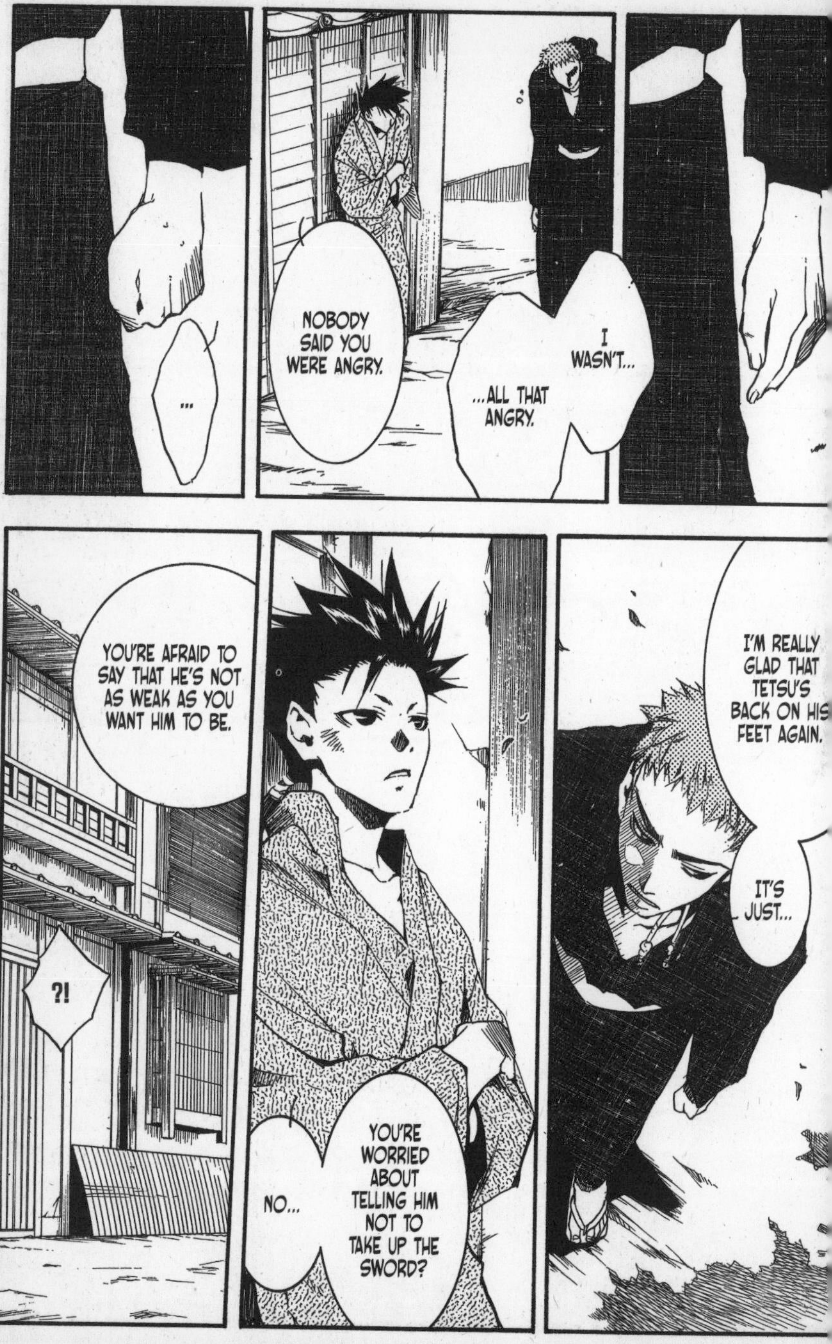
I WASN'T...
...ALL THAT ANGRY.
NOBODY SAID YOU WERE ANGRY.
...
I'M REALLY GLAD THAT TETSU'S BACK ON HIS FEET AGAIN.
IT'S JUST...
YOU'RE WORRIED ABOUT TELLING HIM NOT TO TAKE UP THE SWORD?
NO...
YOU'RE AFRAID TO SAY THAT HE'S NOT AS WEAK AS YOU WANT HIM TO BE.
?!

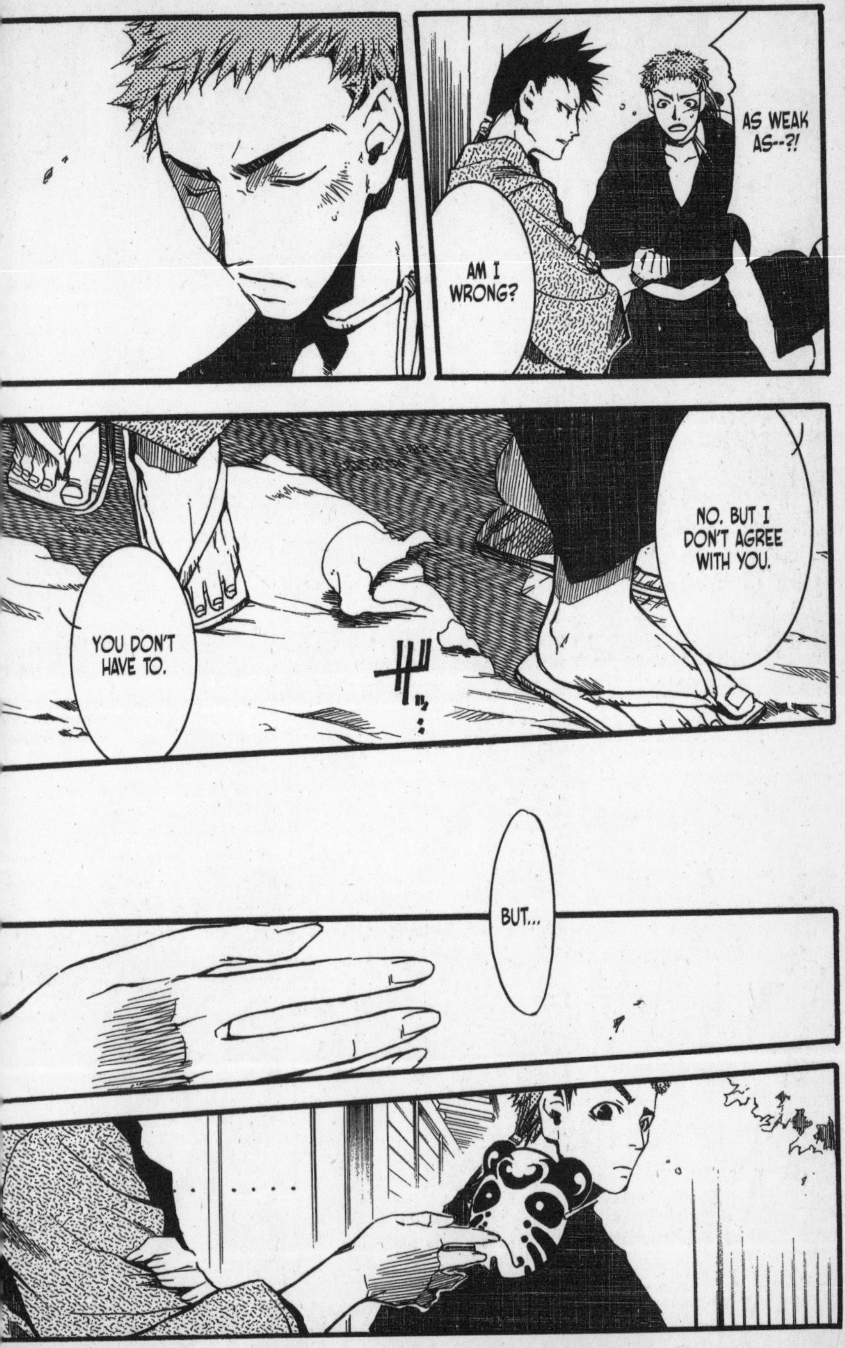
AS WEAK AS--?!
AM I WRONG?
NO. BUT I DON'T AGREE WITH YOU.
YOU DON'T HAVE TO.
BUT...

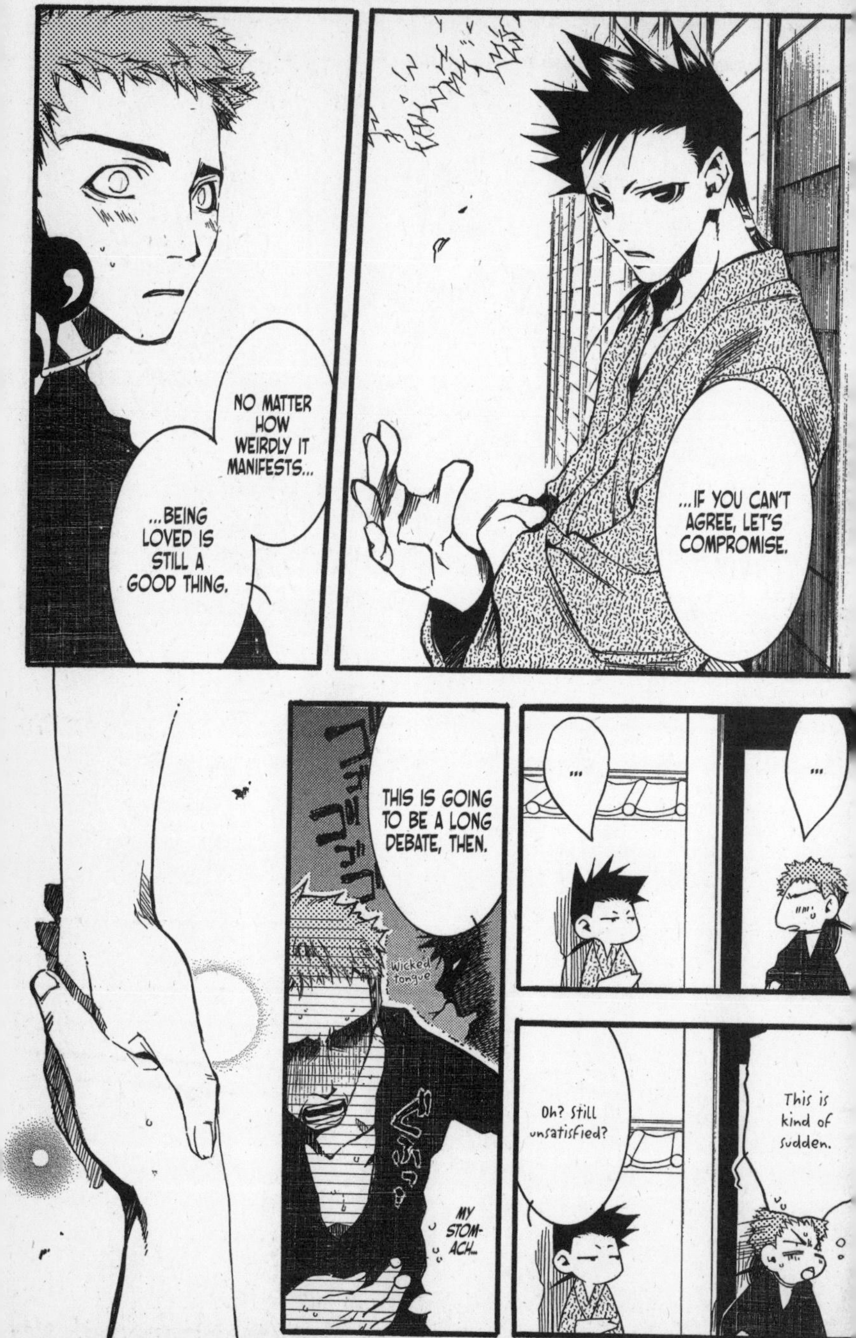
...IF YOU CAN'T AGREE, LET'S COMPROMISE.
NO MATTER HOW WEIRDLY IT MANIFESTS...
...BEING LOVED IS STILL A GOOD THING.
...
...
This is kind of sudden.
Oh? Still unsatisfied?
THIS IS GOING TO BE A LONG DEBATE, THEN.
Wicked tongue
MY STOMACH...

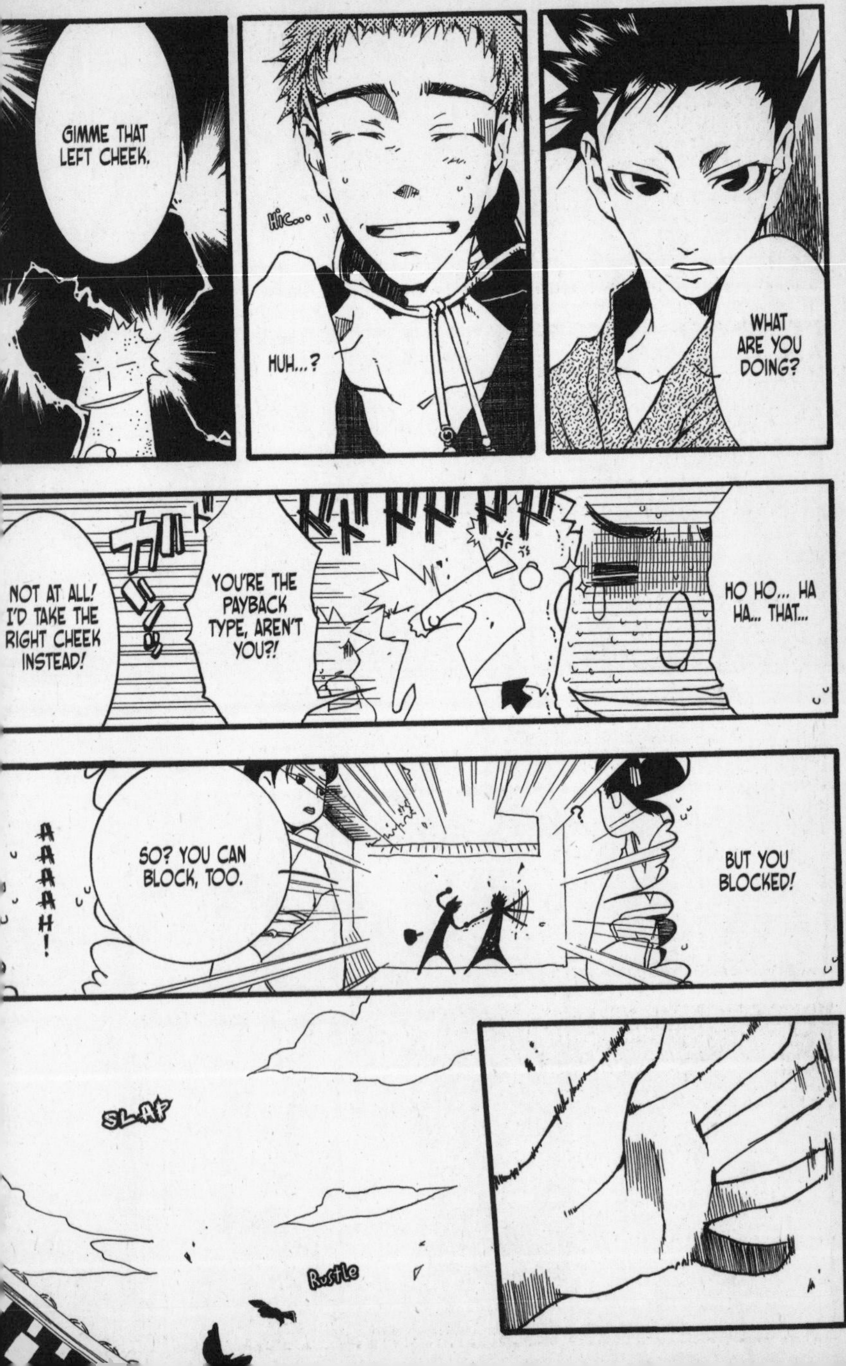
WHAT ARE YOU DOING?
Hic...
HUH...?
GIMME THAT LEFT CHEEK.
HO HO... HA HA... THAT...
YOU'RE THE PAYBACK TYPE, AREN'T YOU?!
NOT AT ALL! I'D TAKE THE RIGHT CHEEK INSTEAD!
BUT YOU BLOCKED!
SO? YOU CAN BLOCK, TOO.
AAAAH!
SLAP
Rustle

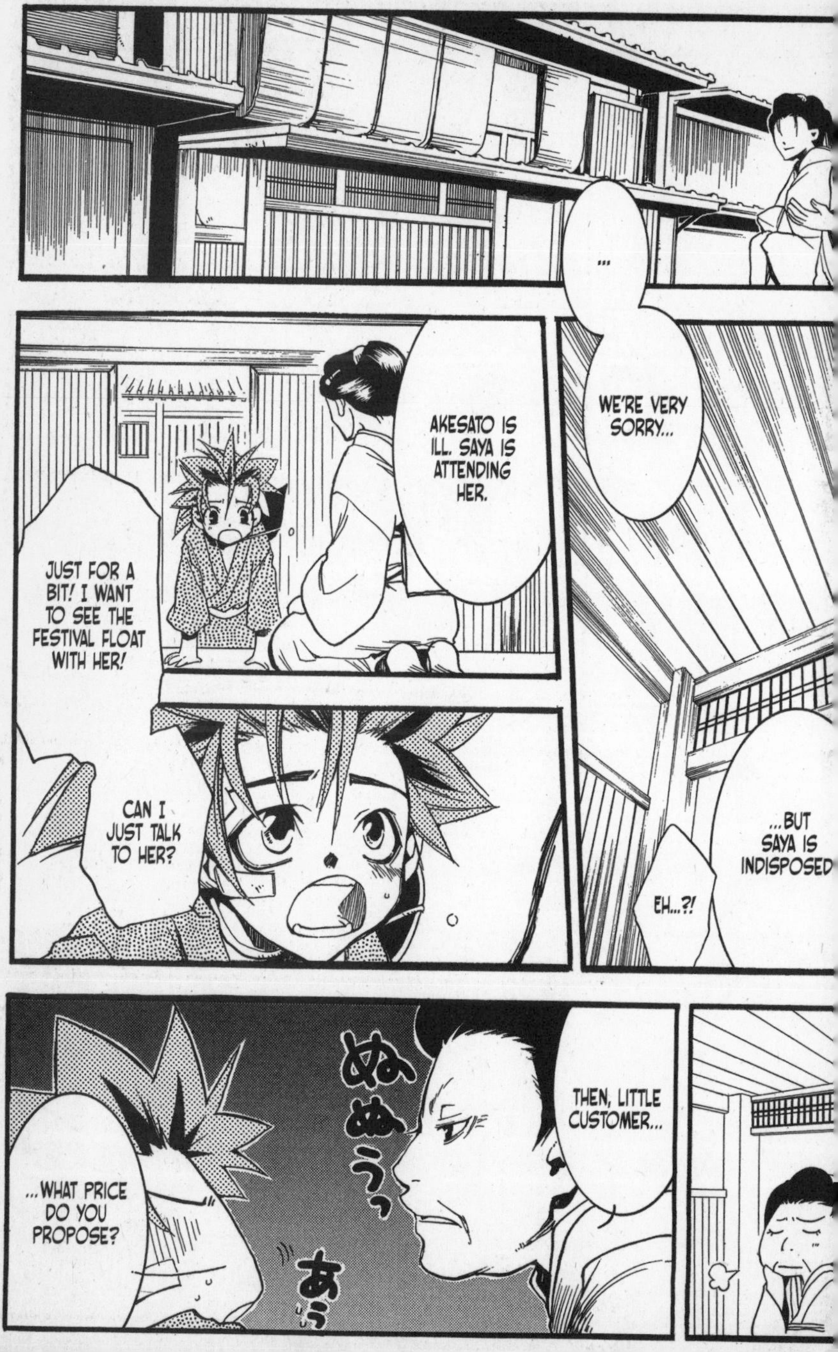
...
WE'RE VERY SORRY...
...BUT SAYA IS INDISPOSED
EH...?!
AKESATO IS ILL. SAYA IS ATTENDING HER.
JUST FOR A BIT! I WANT TO SEE THE FESTIVAL FLOAT WITH HER!
CAN I JUST TALK TO HER?
THEN, LITTLE CUSTOMER...
ぬぬぅっ
...WHAT PRICE DO YOU PROPOSE?
あう

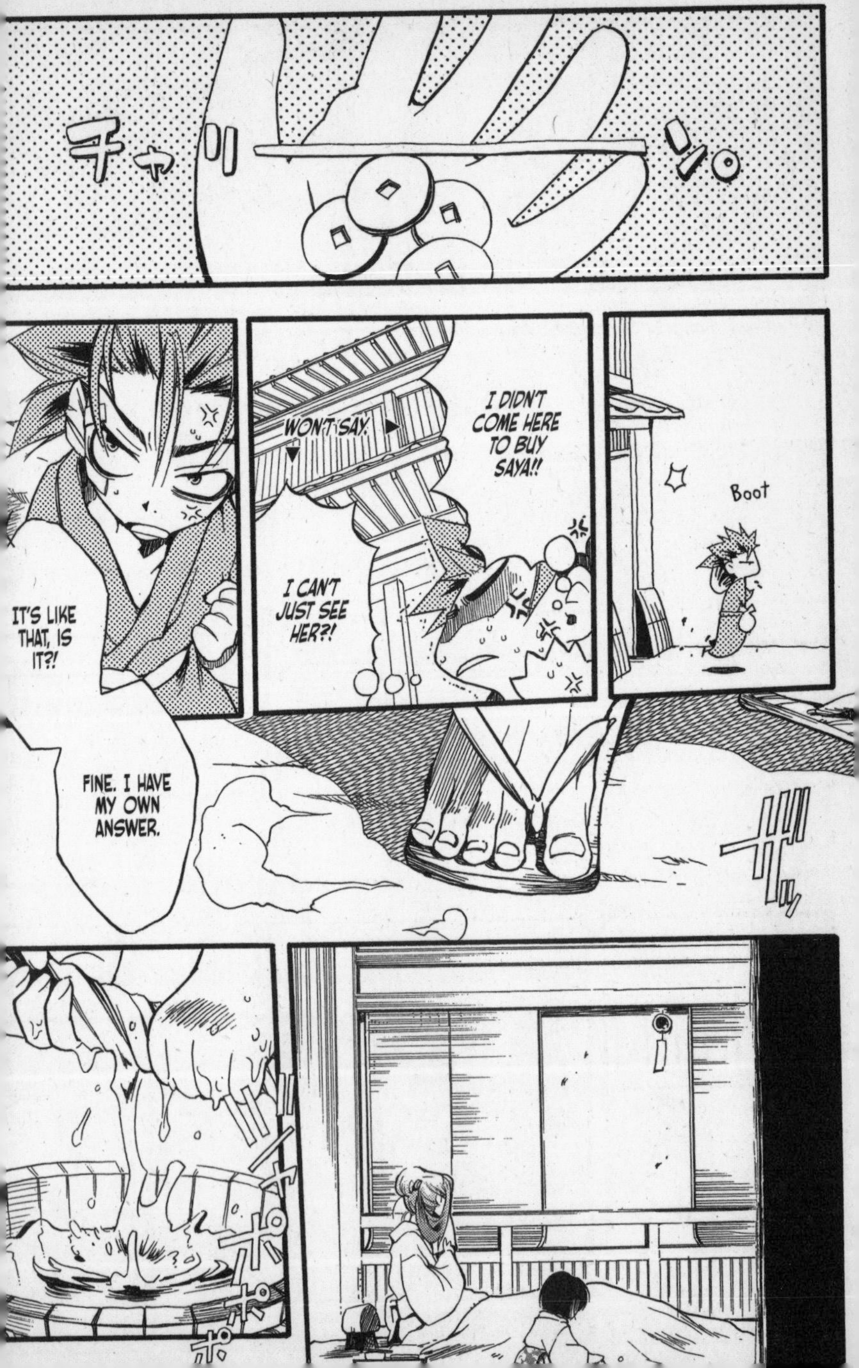
Boot
I DIDN'T COME HERE TO BUY SAYA!!
WON'T SAY.
I CAN'T JUST SEE HER?!
IT'S LIKE THAT, IS IT?!
FINE. I HAVE MY OWN ANSWER.

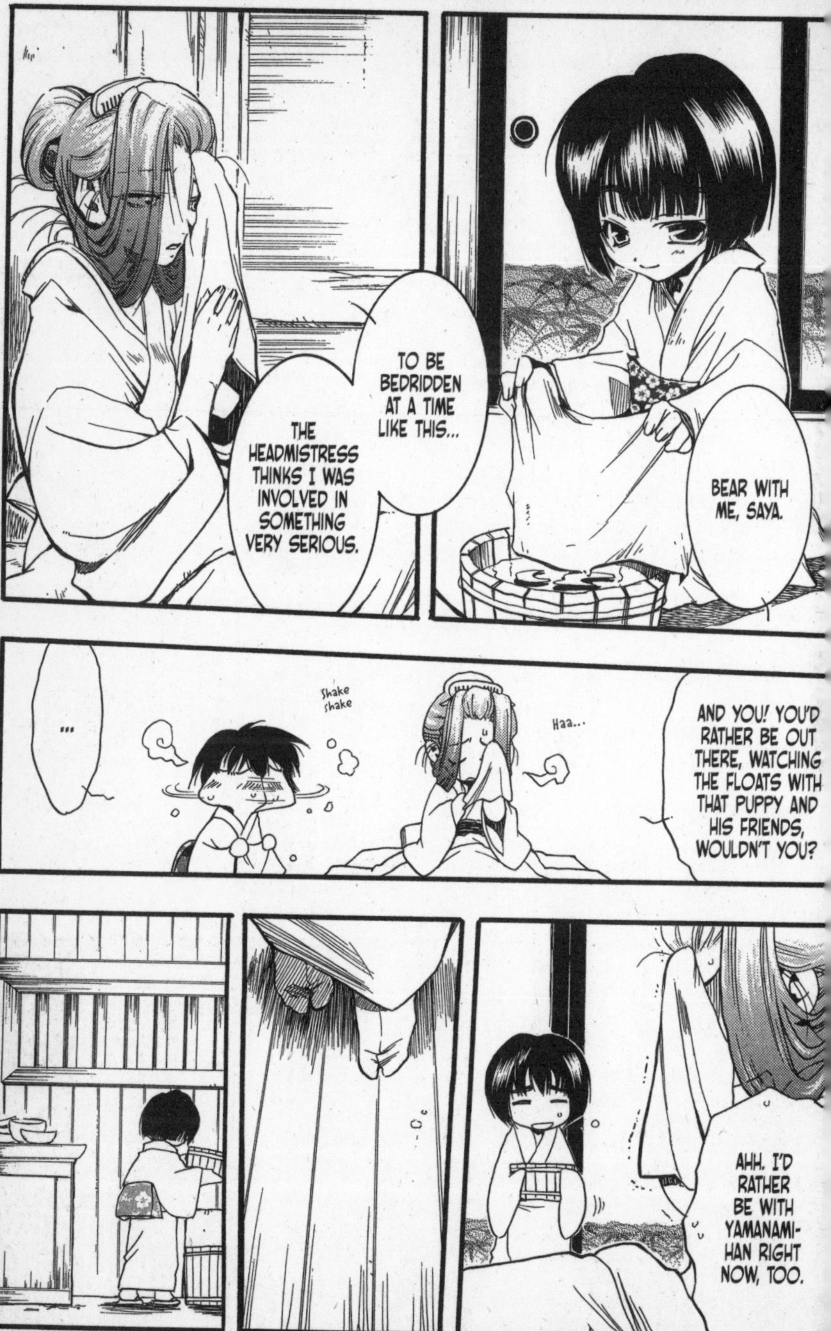
BEAR WITH ME, SAYA.
TO BE BEDRIDDEN AT A TIME LIKE THIS...
THE HEADMISTRESS THINKS I WAS INVOLVED IN SOMETHING VERY SERIOUS.
AND YOU! YOU'D RATHER BE OUT THERE, WATCHING THE FLOATS WITH THAT PUPPY AND HIS FRIENDS, WOULDN'T YOU?
Haa...
Shake shake
...
AHH. I'D RATHER BE WITH YAMANAMI-HAN RIGHT NOW, TOO.

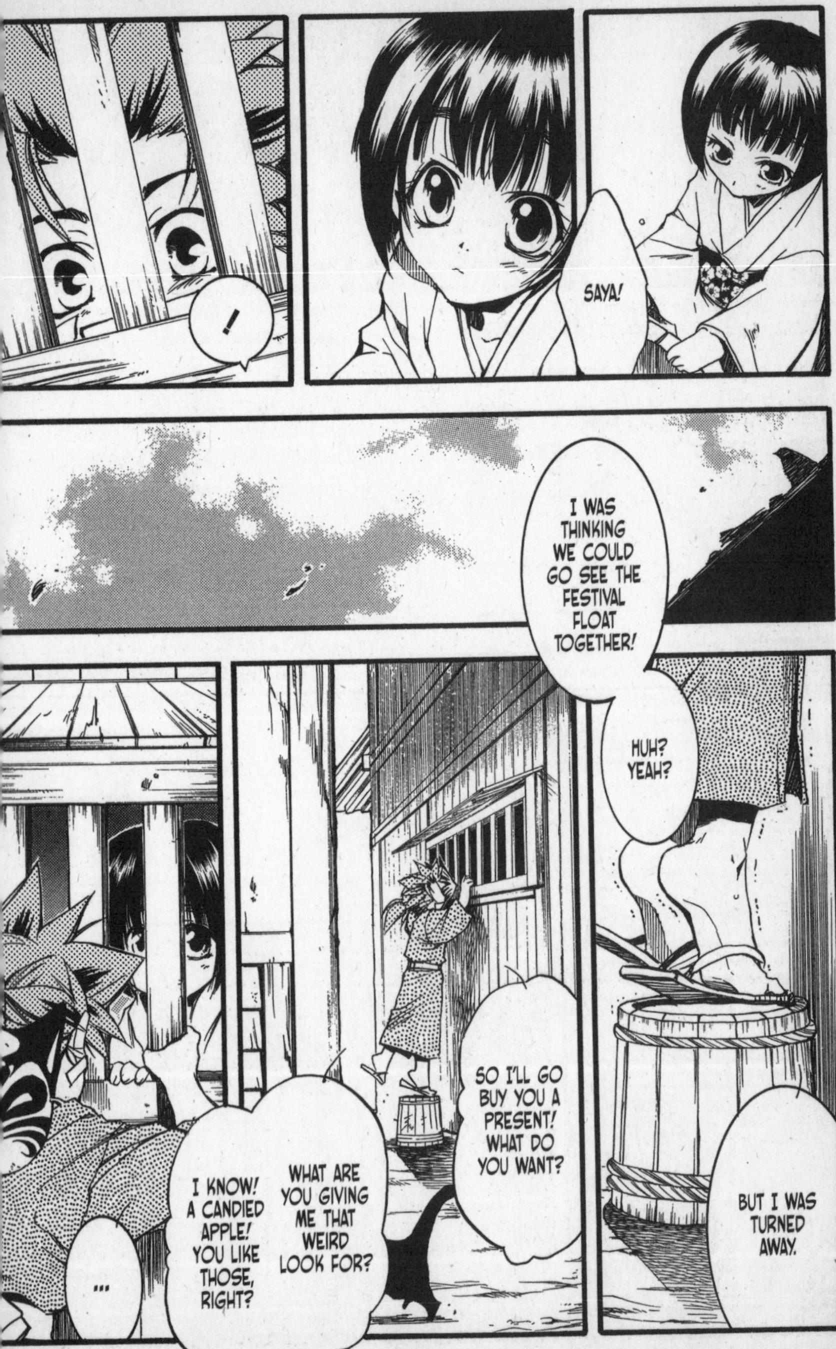
SAYA!
!
I WAS THINKING WE COULD GO SEE THE FESTIVAL FLOAT TOGETHER!
HUH? YEAH?
BUT I WAS TURNED AWAY.
SO I'LL GO BUY YOU A PRESENT! WHAT DO YOU WANT?
WHAT ARE YOU GIVING ME THAT WEIRD LOOK FOR?
I KNOW! A CANDIED APPLE! YOU LIKE THOSE, RIGHT?
...

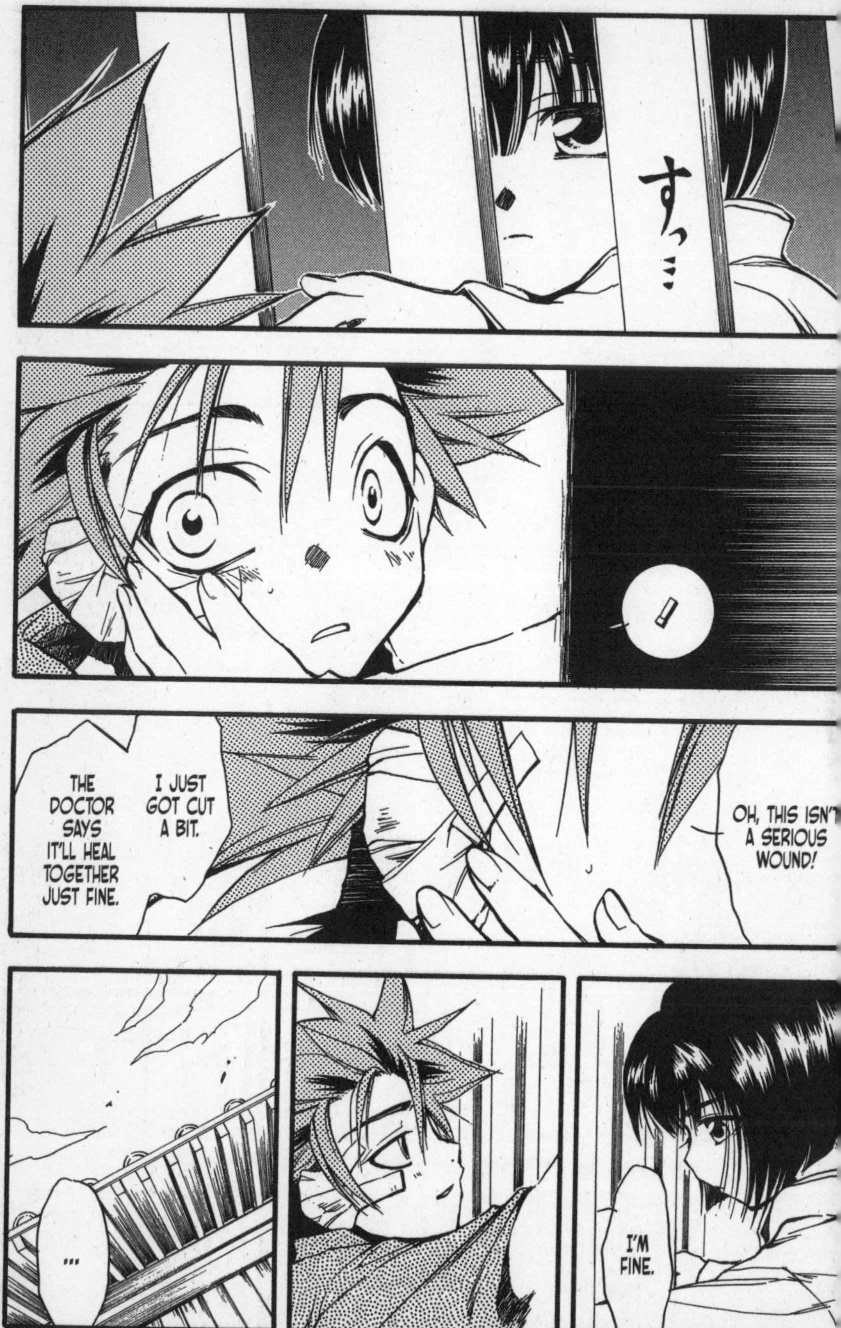
すっ
!
OH, THIS ISN'T A SERIOUS WOUND!
I JUST GOT CUT A BIT.
THE DOCTOR SAYS IT'LL HEAL TOGETHER JUST FINE.
I'M FINE.
...

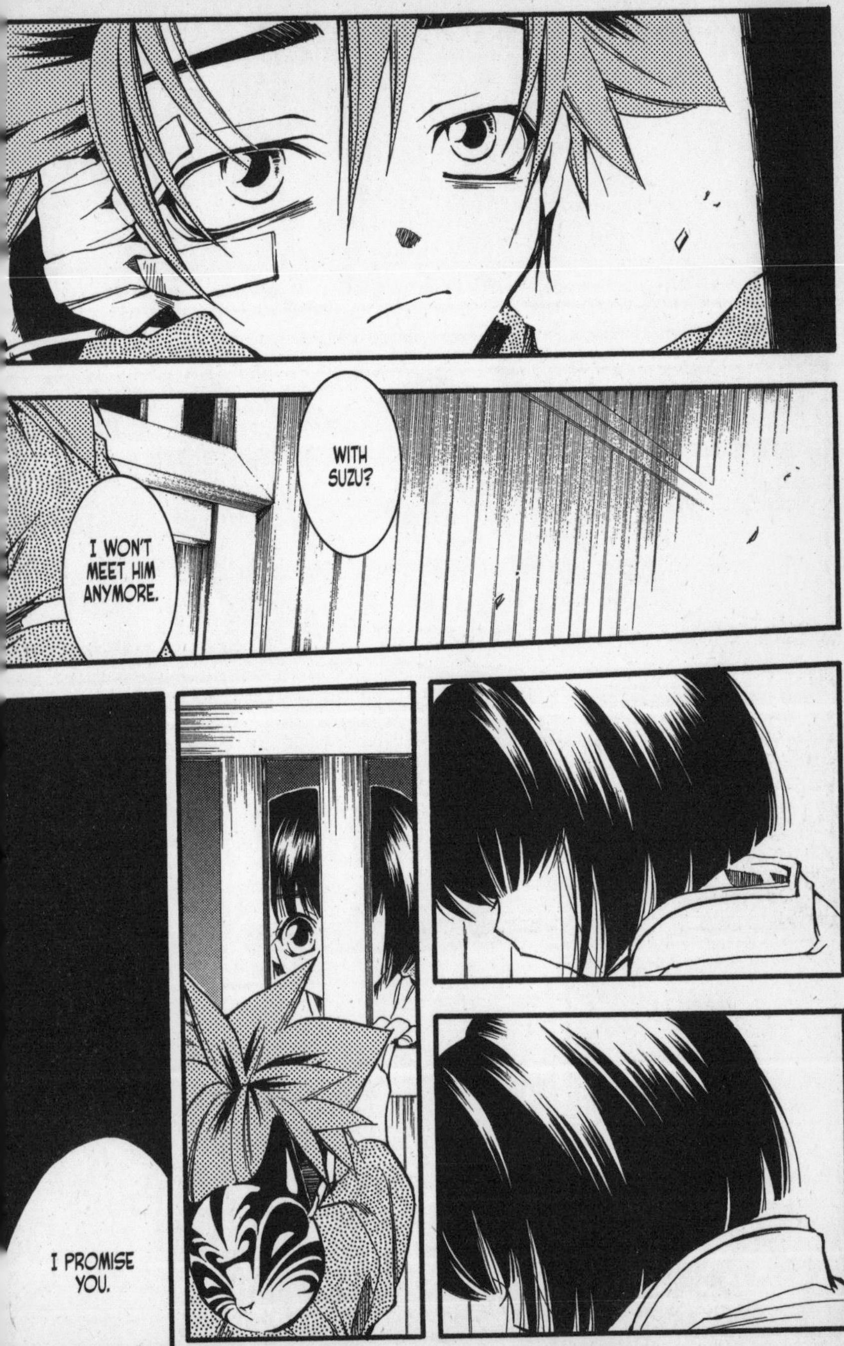
WITH SUZU?
I WON'T MEET HIM ANYMORE.
I PROMISE YOU.

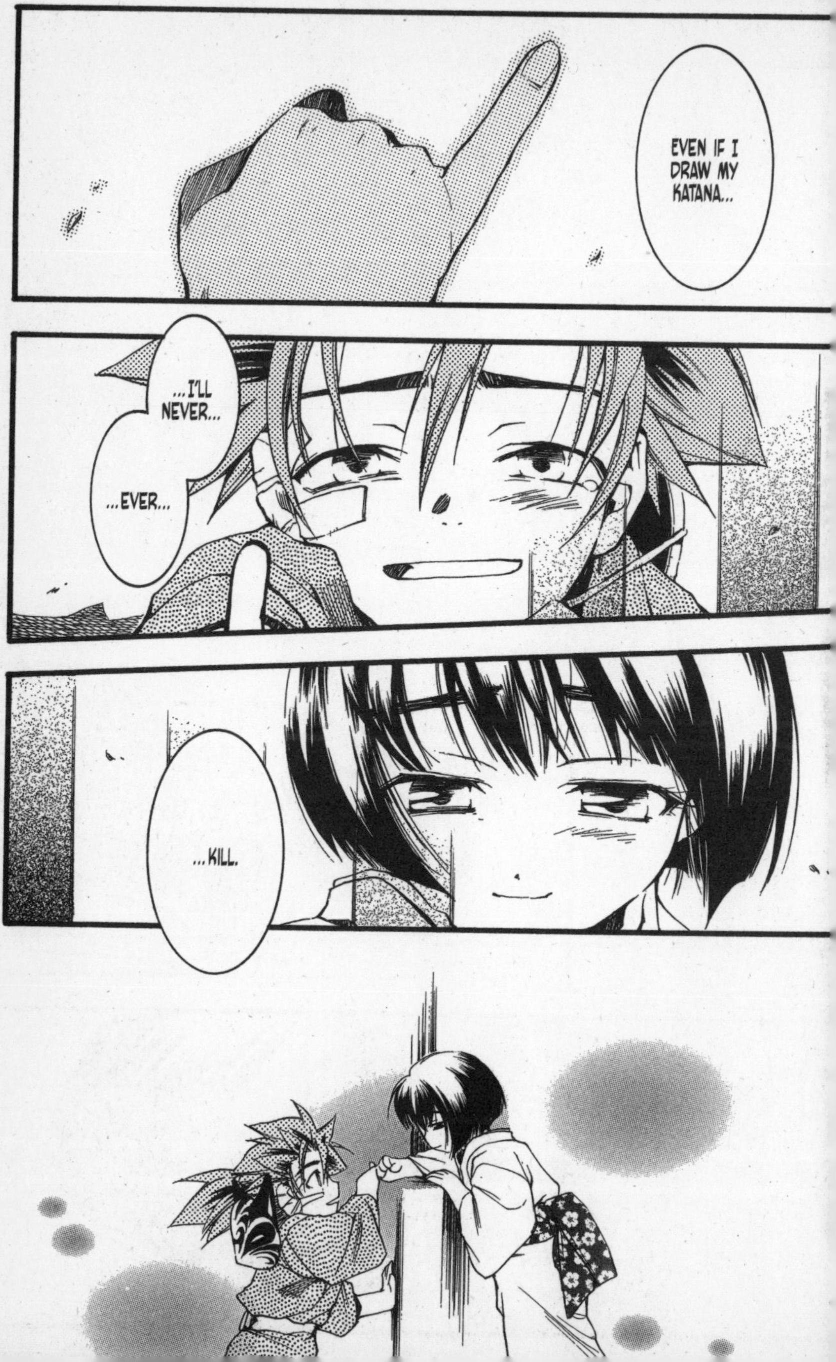
EVEN IF I DRAW MY KATANA...
...I'LL NEVER...
...EVER...
...KILL.

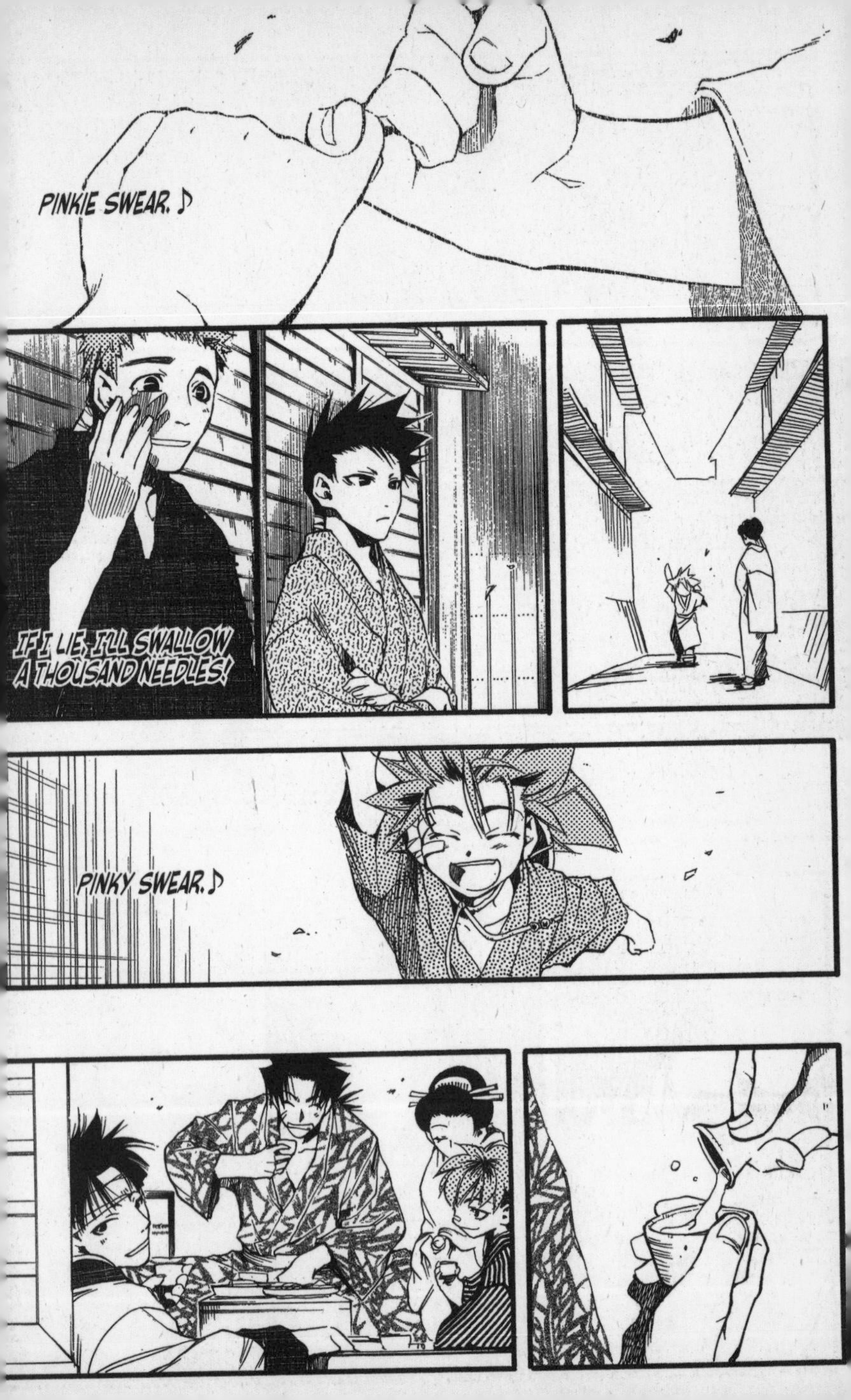
PINKIE SWEAR.♪
IF I LIE, I'LL SWALLOW A THOUSAND NEEDLES!
PINKY SWEAR.♪

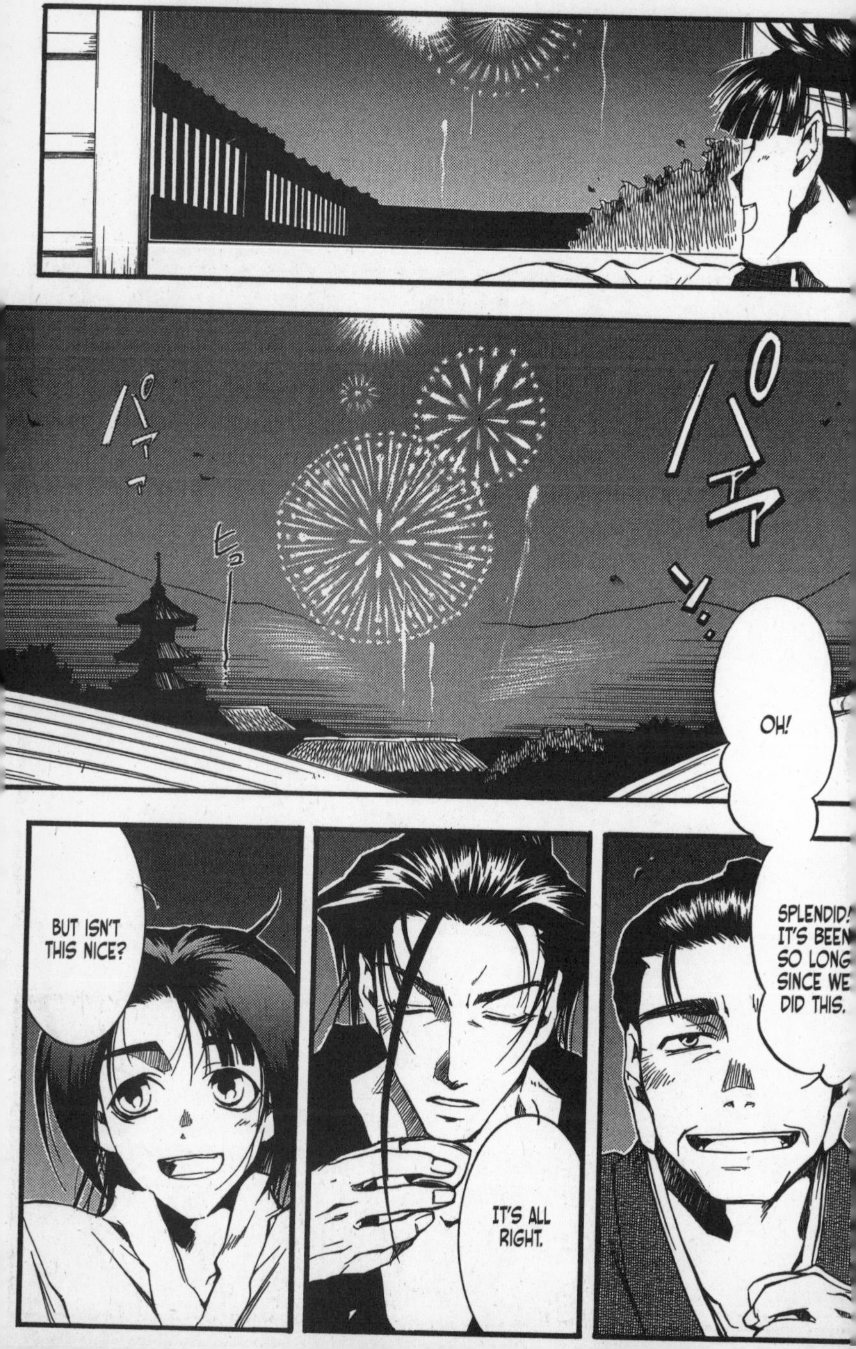
パァァン…
パァァ
ヒュー
OH!
SPLENDID! IT'S BEEN SO LONG SINCE WE DID THIS.
IT'S ALL RIGHT.
BUT ISN'T THIS NICE?

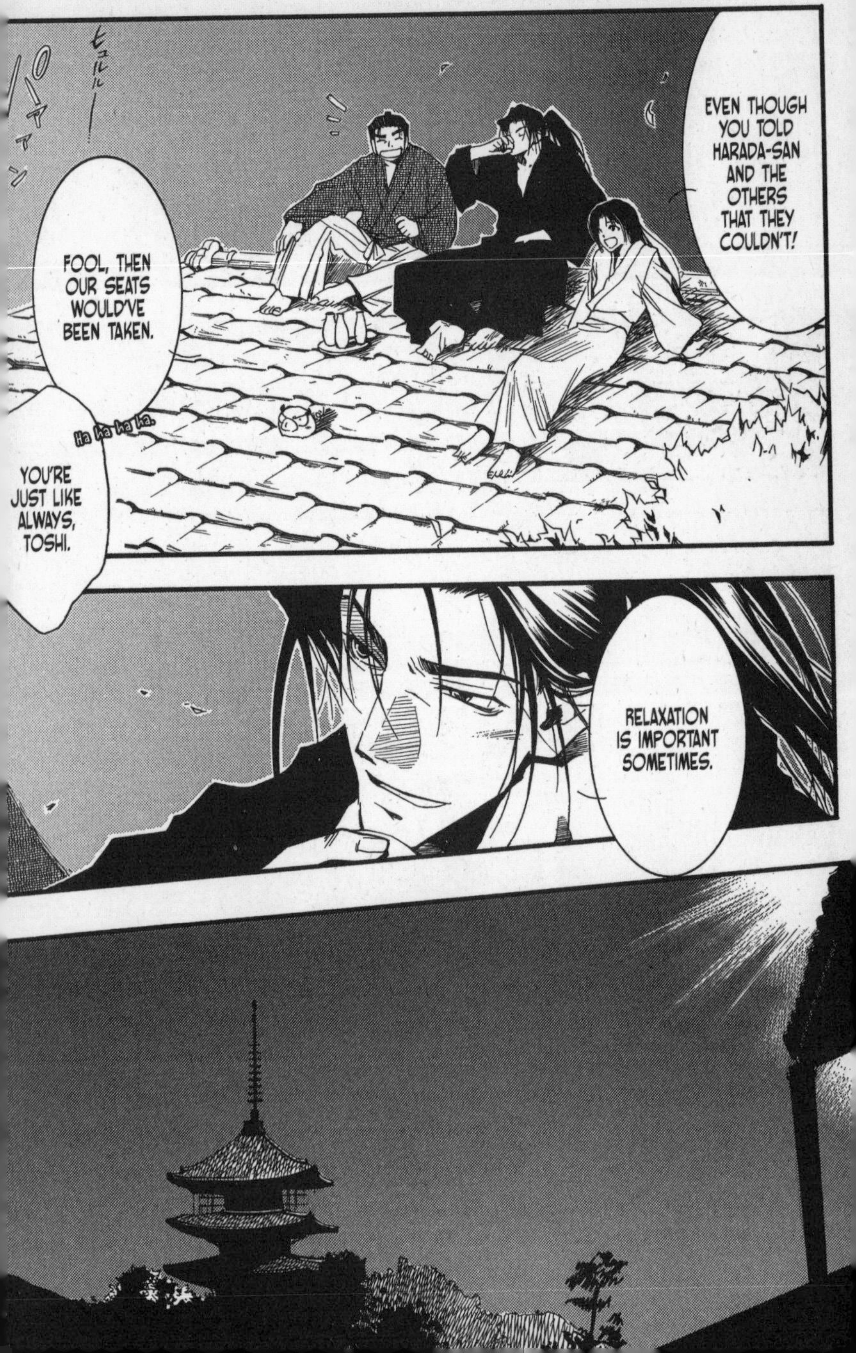
EVEN THOUGH YOU TOLD HARADA-SAN AND THE OTHERS THAT THEY COULDN'T!
FOOL, THEN OUR SEATS WOULD'VE BEEN TAKEN.
Ha ha ha ha.
YOU'RE JUST LIKE ALWAYS, TOSHI.
RELAXATION IS IMPORTANT SOMETIMES.

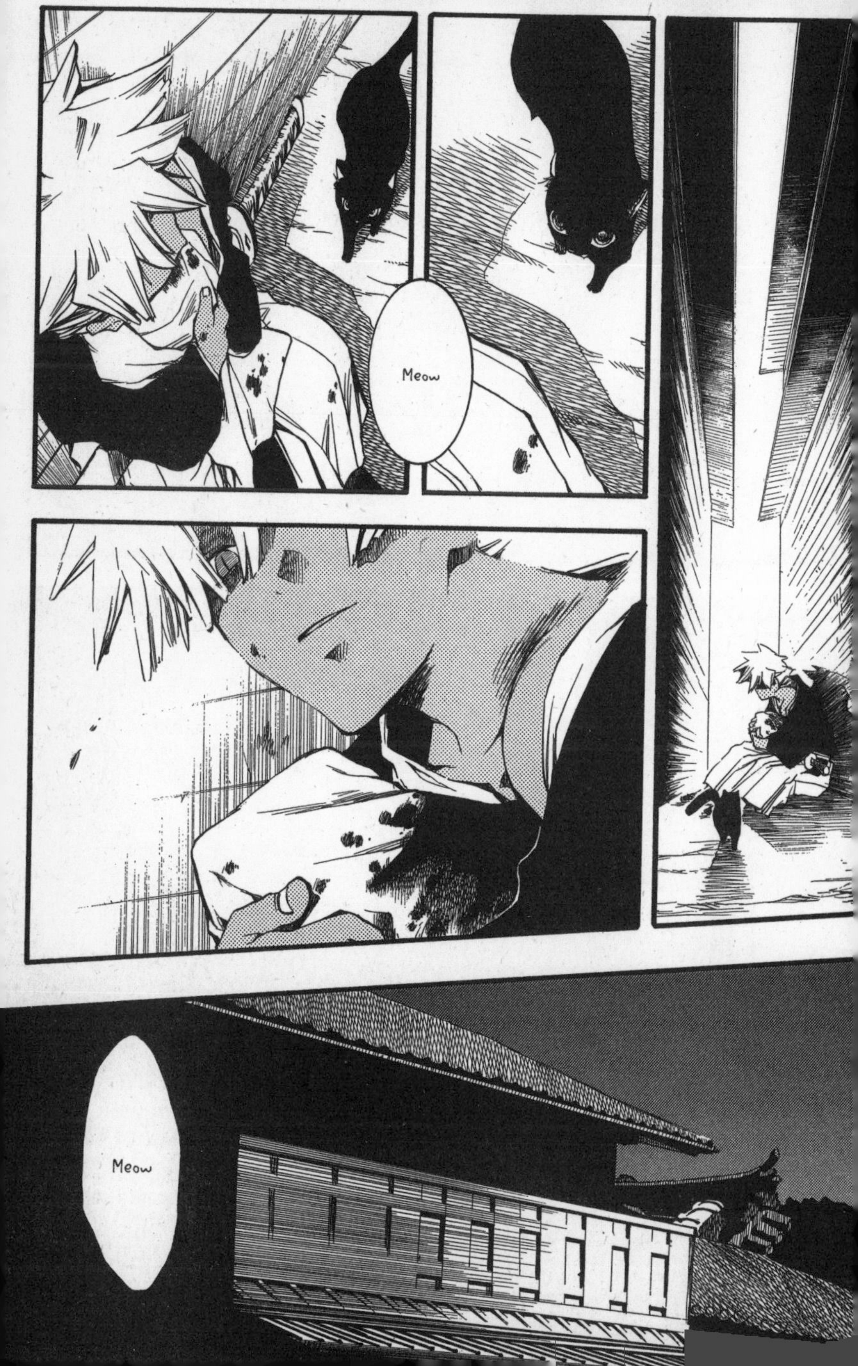
Meow
Meow

End

To be continued in
Peace Maker Kurogane

STOP!

This is the back of the book.
You wouldn't want to spoil a great ending!

This book is printed "manga-style," in the authentic Japanese right-to-left format. Since none of the artwork has been flipped or altered, readers get to experience the story just as the creator intended. You've been asking for it, so TOKYOPOP® delivered: authentic, hot-off-the-press, and far more fun!

DIRECTIONS

1
2
3
4
5
6
7
8
9
10

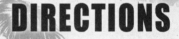

If this is your first time reading manga-style, here's a quick guide to help you understand how it works.

It's easy... just start in the top right panel and follow the numbers. Have fun, and look for more 100% authentic manga from TOKYOPOP®!

THE MANGA REVOLUTION · LEADING THE MANGA REVOLUTION · LEADING
漫画革命

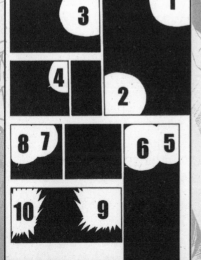

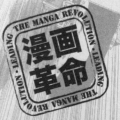

A GUIDE TO THE HISTORICAL ERA OF *PEACE MAKER*

IT IS SAID THAT THE IKEDAYA INCIDENT DELAYED THE MEIJI REVOLUTION BY A FULL YEAR. THE MEIJI REVOLUTION, AN ERA OF EXTREME MODERNIZATION FOLLOWING JAPAN'S NEWLY OPEN FOREIGN POLICY, THREW OFF CENTURIES OF THE SHOGUN'S MILITARY RULE. AS TIMES CHANGED RAPIDLY FROM 1864-70, MANY OF THE KEY MEMBERS OF THE SHINSENGUMI FOUND THEMSELVES ON THE WRONG SIDE OF A LOSING BATTLE.

MUCH OF WHAT WE KNOW OF THE SHINSENGUMI COMES TO US FROM MILITARY RECORDS, LETTERS AND THE MEMOIRS OF NAGAKURA SHINPACHI. AS ONE OF THE FEW FIRST-PERSON ACCOUNT FROM WITHIN THE CORP, SHINPACHI'S MEMOIRS HOLD A SPECIAL VALUE. THE WRITTEN MEMOIRS THEMSELVES DID NOT COME TO LIGHT UNTIL 1998. BEFORE THAT, HISTORIANS RELIED ON A SERIES OF INTERVIEWS DONE IN 1911, FOUR YEARS BEFORE HIS DEATH AND FORTY YEARS AFTER THE INCIDENTS HAD PASSED. THIS MANGA NO DOUBT DRAWS ON ALL THESE RECORDS TO CREATE THE RICH WORLD OF *PEACE MAKER*.

IN THE BRIEF BUT TUMULTUOUS HISTORY OF THE SHINSENGUMI, THE IKEDAYA INCIDENT WAS PINNACLE OF THEIR ACHIEVEMENTS, GAINING THEM INFAMY AND IMMORTALIZING THEIR COURAGE. BUT LIKE HISTORY, THE STORY DOESN'T END THERE! READ THE CONCLUSION OF THE SHINSENGUMI SAGA IN NANAE CHRONO'S *PEACE MAKER KUROGANE*, AVAILABLE FROM TOKYOPOP MARCH 2009!

LEARN MORE ABOUT THE SHINSENGUMI! INVALUABLE BOOKS AND FILMS USED IN THESE ESSAYS:

SHINSENGUMI: THE SHOGUN'S LAST SAMURAI CORPS BY ROMULUS HILLSBOROUGH. TOKYO; RUTLAND, VT: TUTTLE PUB. 2005.
UNSOLVED HISTORY: NINJAS. SILVER SPRING, MD: DISCOVERY COMMUNICATIONS, C2004.
NINJA: THE TRUE STORY OF JAPAN'S SECRET WARRIOR CULT BY STEPHEN TURNBULL. LONDON, CAXTON EDITIONS, 2002.

-HOPE DONOVAN